Forum Italicum
Filibrary Series
No. 22

ItaliAfrica

*Bridging Continents
and Cultures*

Edited by
Sante Matteo

Forum Italicum Publishing, Inc.
Stony Brook, NY

Library of Congress Cataloging-in-Publication Data

Sante Matteo, ItaliAfrica: Bridging Continents and Cultures
1. Italy and Africa-History. 2. Italy and immigration.
3. Italy: Ethnic relations. 4. Italian identity.
5. Literature of immigration.
I. Title   II. Series

ISBN: 1-893127-22-2
ISBN-13: 978-1-893127-22-7

Forum Italicum
Center for Italian Studies
State University of New York at Stony Brook
Stony Brook, NY 11794-3358
U.S.A.
Http://www.italianstudies.org

To Pap Khouma's African Italian son,
and to all Tomorrow's children of all colors

ACKNOWLEDGMENTS

Various offices, departments, and programs at Miami University, Oxford, Ohio contributed generously to make the publication of this volume possible, as well as the symposium on Africa and Italy that spawned these articles, and a companion volume published in Italian (see below): The Irvin Fund of the Department of French and Italian; the College of Arts and Science, the Office for the Advancement of Scholarship and Teaching (OAST), the Office of the Provost, the Graduate School, the Office for Student Affairs; Black World Studies, International Studies; the Departments of Political Science, the Department of Geology, and the Department of Geography.

Africa Italy: An Interdisciplinary International Symposium was held on the Miami campus, November 6–8, 1998, with three dozen speakers from North America, Europe, and Africa meeting to exchange their knowledge and ideas across various disciplines: geography, history, economics, politics, sociology, cultural studies. A volume published in Italy, *Africa Italia: Due continenti si avvicinano* (Santarcangelo di Romagna: Fara Editore, 1999), edited by Sante Matteo and Stefano Bellucci, contains Italian versions of thirteen of the essays published in English in the present volume plus my introduction (see footnote 5, p. 13, for details). I am grateful to Alessandro Ramberti, of Fara, for permission to reprint the articles in English. I also wish to thank Pap Khouma for kindly allowing me to reprint his poem "Figlio" in the Introduction. Teresa Picarazzi's essay, "Italian African *meticciato artistico* in the Teatro delle Albe," appeared under the same title in *Italica* 77.2 (Summer 2000): 224–45. We are grateful to the Editor, Albert Mancini, for permission to reprint it here.

Graphic artist Cheryl Henry and media consultant Karin Hill, of Miami Computing and Information Services (MCIS), designed the cover for the book. Anthony Tamburri helped steer it through the publishing process. Jonathan Strauss, Chair of the Department of French and Italian at Miami University, provided generous monetary support throughout the various phases of the project, as well as moral support, along with all my colleagues in the department, to whom I am grateful. John Hughes,

Associate Dean of the College of Arts and Science, and Bill Rauckhorst, Associate Provost for Scholarship and Teaching, were also instrumental in securing funds. I also wish to express my appreciation to the following individuals: Graziella Parati, who first drew my attention to the existence of immigrant literature in Italy and inspired the idea for a symposium on relations between Italy and Africa; Stefano Bellucci, who organized the symposium with me and co-edited the Italian volume; my colleague Peter Pedroni, for his participation and collaboration in all the endeavors and his constant encouragement; Marcia Simmons, Department Secretary, for her multifarious assistance all along the way; Mario Mignone, Editor of *Forum italicum*, for his responsiveness, encouragement, and patience in bringing the volume to fruition; and Deborah Starewich, the Production Editor, who expertly processed and edited the texts. My greatest debt is to the symposium participants and to the authors of the essays in this volume, for helping to inform and enlighten me and others about this very important topic.

AFRICA ITALY

THE LEGACY OF ITALIAN COLONIALISM

AFRICA AND AFRICANS IN ITALIAN THEATER

AFRICA AND AFRICANS IN ITALIAN CINEMA

AFRICA AND AFRICANS IN ITALIAN LITERATURE

AFRICAN IMMIGRANT LITERATURE IN ITALY

INTRODUCTION
African Italy, Bridging Continents and Cultures

Sante Matteo
Miami University

The *annus mirabilis* 1492 was drawing to a close. For nearly two months after landfall on October 12, Christopher Columbus had sailed from island to island in the archipelago that would come to be known as the West Indies or the Antilles, searching for the "Indian" mainland. On St. Nicholas Day, December 6, he reached a large island with beautiful mountains and plains, which to him seemed "almost like the lands of Castile, only better" (131), and which he accordingly named *La Isla Española* (Hispaniola). The island was inhabited by the Tainos, an apparently healthy, peaceful, and prosperous people who welcomed and assisted the bearded strangers with open arms, prompting Columbus to write in his diary: "I cannot believe that we have found a people with such good hearts, so liberal in giving, and so timid, that they strip themselves of everything to give all that they have to us and, upon arrival, run to bring us everything" (145).

By some estimates there were between three and four million natives who lived on the island. Within a few decades, however, the Tainos had been virtually wiped out, victims of European swords and guns, against which they had little effectual defense, as well as of European germs, against which they had no immunity: "Of all these and of those born subsequently, it is believed that there are not at present, this year of 1548, among adults and children, 500 people who are natives and the offspring and stock of those first dwellers" (Fernández de Oviedo, qtd. in Denevan 51).[1] With the native population thus decimated, not only on Hispaniola,

---

[1] Estimates of the native population in the Caribbean and elsewhere in the Americas at the time of the European arrival vary widely and continue to be widely debated: "For the island of Hispaniola alone, estimates range from 50,000 to 60,000 (Verlinden), 100,000 (Rosenblatt), to a high of 8 million (Cook and Borah), which is not generally accepted" (Lunenfeld 321). The priest Bartolomé de Las Casas, whose father and three uncles ac-

but throughout the newly colonized lands of the "New World," the European colonizers required a new labor force: African slaves. By the end of the seventeenth century French slave traders had established colonies on the western side of Hispaniola, which they called Saint-Domingue, while the Spaniards, who called it Santo Domingo, continued to occupy the eastern end. Today, the island is home to the French-speaking Republic of Haiti, which was the second nation to gain independence in the Americas, in 1804, and the Spanish-speaking Dominican Republic, which became independent in 1844. The inhabitants are mainly black and mestizo descendants of African slaves, European colonialists, and indigenous Americans.

Half a millennium after Columbus's arrival there was a less conspicuous yet very significant journey in the opposite direction, from Hispaniola to Europe. In 1992, Lydia De Jesus Altagracia, along with her two daughters from a previous marriage, Denny, 14, and Eveline, 10, left their native Dominican Republic and crossed the "ocean blue" to move to Italy and start a new life with an Italian husband, Sergio Casabianca. Four years later, in September 1996, another *annus mirabilis*, the elder of the two daughters, Denny Mendez, was crowned "Miss Italy."

The event made news throughout the world, because it was the first time that a "black" woman had received such recognition in Italy. Few people were aware that there were "black" Italians. Ms. Mendez was a very popular choice, chosen overwhelmingly by the judges on the jury, as well as by the vast majority of the millions of viewers watching the

---

companied Columbus on his second voyage, and who himself made his first voyage to the Indies in 1502 (3), writing half a century after the initial encounter on Hispaniola, gives the following account of its consequences: "Yet into this sheepfold, into this land of meek outcasts there came some Spaniards who immediately behaved like ravening wild beasts, wolves, tigers, or lions that had been starved for many days. And Spaniards have behaved in no other way during the past forty years, down to the present time, for they are still acting like ravening beasts, killing, terrorizing, afflicting, torturing, and destroying the native peoples, doing all this with the strangest and most varied new methods of cruelty, never seen or heard of before, and to such a degree that this Island of Hispaniola, once so populous (having a population that I estimated to be more than three millions), has now a population of barely two hundred persons" (29). For detailed discussions of population estimates, region by region, see the articles collected and edited by William N. Denevan, *The Native Population of the Americas in 1492*, and in particular "The Population of Hispaniola at the Time of Columbus," by Ángel Rosenblat.

pageant on television. It was a defining moment for Italian society as it approached the new millennium, shaping a new identity for itself, reflected in a new face, or rather, in many new faces of different hues.

For most of its existence as a unified nation, since 1860, Italy was a poor, economically and industrially backward country with a very high birth rate. It consequently experienced massive waves of emigration at the end of the nineteenth century and through two thirds of the twentieth. Over the last quarter century, however, it has achieved a high standard of living and one of the lowest birth rates in the world, and has thus become the destination of hundreds of thousands of immigrants, many of them from African countries. By some estimates, over the last two decades of the twentieth century, up to a million or more African immigrants entered Italy, whose southern islands are only a few miles from the northern coast of Africa.[2] This influx has given a new face to Italian society and has added intriguing new dimensions to the future of Italian culture. The changes brought about by this extensive multiracial and multicultural encounter are bound to be profound and long lasting. Decades and centuries from now these years spanning the new century and the new millennium will likely be seen as the period when a new Italian nation began to be created. It is significant that this phenomenon of massive immigration has coincided with a period of social and political upheaval in the country, during which new demographics, new social attitudes and expectations, as well as new political parties have been forged and a new Italian constitution has been envisaged. It appears to be an important turning point in Italian history.

Given Italy's geographical proximity to Africa, why should it be surprising to find Africans in Rome and Milan? Should it not be more surprising to find large numbers of Africans in Paris and London, which are farther away from Africa? And yet Africans have been present in France and England much longer and in much larger numbers than in Italy. A glance at a map will show the Italian peninsula as almost a bridge ex-

---

[2]Estimates, official and unofficial, vary widely. It is difficult to get an accurate count because of the large but undetermined number of undocumented, or illegal, immigrants. For a presentation and discussion of the figures compiled by the Catholic organization Caritas, see Stefano Bellucci's article in this volume.

tended across the Mediterranean to connect Africa and Europe, or, to borrow an image suggested by Lycia Santos do Castilla, an umbilical cord between the two continents.[3] The small stretch of sea that separates the two landmasses is not insurmountable, as the constant arrival of African "boat people" now attests. In fact, as geologist Larry Mayer points out in the first article, not too long ago (on a geological scale) the Mediterranean basin was dry, and it would have been possible to walk from Africa to Italy. The wayfarers would have encountered few formidable geological obstacles because it would not have been a journey from one continent to another. In fact, a traveler who walked from what is now Tunisia to what is now Sicily, or to Calabria on the present mainland, would not have left Africa at all, because the geological boundary between Europe and Africa is not the Mediterranean, but the Alps. Geologically Italy is part of the African continent. Why, then, have Italy and Africa been such remote neighbors, or proximate strangers, until now?

Actually they have not always been so. Much of the history and culture of the Italian peninsula — and by extension all of Europe — has been shaped by its contacts with African cultures over the centuries: from the spread of Mesolithic and Neolithic civilization from Northern Africa across the Mediterranean in the Stone Age, after the glacial era; to the protracted and recurring Punic wars between Rome and Carthage in classical times; to the patristic consolidation of Christian hegemony under the tutelage of African writers, such as Athanasius, Origen, and Augustine; to the contacts and trade that resulted from the Crusades, paving the way for the Renaissance; to the colonial wars undertaken in the Horn of Africa by the newly born nation of Italy at the end of the nineteenth century and in Libya at the beginning of the twentieth, and subsequently resumed during the Fascist regime in the 1930s. So, what we have today is not a new, but a renewed contact between Africans and Italians, with the flow of migrants going in a historically new direction. This renewed encounter presents a new set of issues, problems, and opportunities, which have important implications not only for the future of

---

[3]See her note, "L'ombelico di due continenti," which refers specifically to the island of Sardinia and which makes the case that its Nuragic culture had migrated from North Africa in the Mesolithic period.

Italian society but for intercultural and interracial relations throughout the world.

What makes the transracial encounter in Italy unique and worth watching is the fact that most of the African immigrants are going there freely, primarily for economic reasons, without the heavy historical baggage of colonialism and slavery on their shoulders, a historical weight which still affects relations between whites and blacks in other European and in American countries. Racism based on skin color has not been an entrenched, institutionalized aspect of Italian society.

In the Americas, and the United States in particular, slavery effectively obliterated Africans' identities, because family and tribal groups were broken up and dispersed so that practically no one could speak to anyone else in his or her own native African language, but had to use a pidgin version of the masters' language. As a result, after the first generation, memories of their African cultures were erased from personal and collective consciousness: history, religious stories and beliefs, social customs and laws, legends and personal histories, proverbs and traditional wisdom, their very names, and language itself: all displaced by imposed versions of the masters' legal, religious, and social customs. What remained of their Africanness was primarily the dark color of their skin, which became the sign of their status as slaves and which remains a sign targeting them for racist bigotry.

In European countries, such as France and Great Britain, a prior history of extensive colonialism in Africa explains the larger and more long-standing presence of Africans than in Italy. Since many Africans had learned French or English under colonial rule and had become acquainted with many of the customs and practices of the colonizers, it was natural for them to emigrate to those countries with which they had some familiarity. However, precisely because of their colonial past, which created an unequal system of imperialist masters and colonial subjects, it has proved difficult in those societies for Europeans and Africans to meet and interact as equals.

In Italy most of the African immigrants are not from former Italian colonies in Somalia, Ethiopia, Eritrea, and Libya, where in any case colonialization came relatively late and was short-lived. They are not drawn to Italy because of pre-existing linguistic, political, or social ties, but simply because there seem to be economic opportunities there and, especially for many of the illegal immigrants, the *clandestini,* possibly because the peninsula's proximity and long coastline and the state's less stringent immigration control make for a more accessible and more porous border.

Italy's African immigrants maintain ties with their families and their homeland. They have formed supportive communities in Italy and have established ethnic and cultural centers that preserve and promote their language, religion, and cultural practices. Many immigrant groups publish newsletters and newspapers; some have theaters; some have religious missionary activities. Mosques and other centers of worship have been established in major Italian cities. The Africans who have moved to Italy have not abandoned their ethnic and cultural identity, but have retained beliefs and customs, which constitute new mental and social structures to add to those already in place in Italian society.

The status of African immigrants in Italy is more akin to that of Italian immigrants in America at the turn of the last century than to that of previous Africans who left their homes as slaves or ex-colonials. In fact, it is striking how similar the writings of these first African immigrants to Italy are to those of Italian immigrants to the United States and Canada, who tended to be reviled and ostracized as an incorrigibly inferior "dark" race. If, after a few generations, it has been possible, to a substantial extent, for Italian Americans to lose their minority status and the taint of racial inferiority, might it not be equally possible for Africans to attain the same result in Italy? Diversity and equality may be easier to achieve under conditions that are not tainted by a previous history of master/servant relationships.

I do not mean to present too rosy a picture of the situation or to suggest that all Italians have met or will soon accept African immigrants with open arms. Attitudes on both sides, among Italians and immigrants, run the gamut from hostility to benevolence. In some cases, especially for those whose appearance or skin color signals them as "different," the likelihood of being accepted into a new society may seem like an impossible dream, and the hostile environment produces a sense of debasement and hopelessness, as expressed in this poem by the Moroccan poet Bouzidy Aziz:

Nostalgia

Qui sono meno di una bestia
E non merito neanche una grazia,
dicono che capisco solo il linguaggio dei cammelli
e che nel mio cuore ho un gran rancore:
tu lo crederesti madre?
qui cara madre
siamo più o meno tutti uguali,
lo sporco lava-vetri
il delinquente spacciatore
e il "vu cumprà" ignorante
siamo tutti in uno
e non siamo nessuno,
pensieri smarriti
una memoria che ricorda del tempo
la sua amarezza
della patria solo la sua bellezza
e della notte solo la sua oscurità
e la sua lunghezza.
(Ramberti and Sangiorgi, *Voci dell'arcobaleno* 28)

Nostalgia

Here I am less than an animal
and I don't merit even one consideration,
they say that I understand only the language of camels
and that in my heart I harbor great animosity:
would you believe it mother?
here dear mother
we are more or less all equal,
the dirty window-washer
the criminal drug traficker
and the ignorant "vu cumprà" [sidewalk vendor]
we are all in one
and we are nobody,
lost thoughts
a memory which of time remembers

> its bitterness
> of our homeland only its beauty
> and of night only its darkness
> and its duration.[4]

Yet, not all immigrant poems are testimonials of despair; there are also voices of protest: a refusal to accept the injustices of racism and a battle to overcome them: "Non ho scelta devo andare, / andare in tutte le piazze gridando giustizia, / sperando che qualcuno mi ascolti" (I have no choice I must go, / go to all the squares shouting justice, / hoping that someone may listen to me) (from *Non ho scelta*, by the Nigerian poet Samuel Ayotunde Kalejaiye in *Memorie in valigia* 24–25). Beyond feeling victimized and wishing to hide or eradicate their different appearance and foreign customs, some immigrants embrace them as a source of identity and pride:

> *Dove posso fuggire lontano da te*
> Karl Giscard Ines Mampouya (Congo)
>
> Ho cercato di attraversare mari, terre e cieli
> Per nascondermi da te, ma non ci sono riuscito;
> ti vedo sempre nei miei sogni, o tradizione mia!
> Ho cercato di cambiare pelle,
> pensavo mi avresti abbandonato,
> ora ho scoperto che tu sei nera come me,

---

[4]The translations of the poems into English are my own and aim to provide a literal rendering, without attempting to reproduce other poetic elements of the original. All but the last poem cited are found in two of the yearly anthologies devoted to Italian immigrant writing, published by Fara Editore and consisting of literary texts submitted as entries for the yearly Eks&Tra literary prize for immigrant authors. In addition to the volumes cited here, *Le voci dell'arcobaleno*, 1995, and *Memorie in valigia*, 1997, other volumes in the series include *Mosaici d'inchiostro*, 1996, and *Destini sospesi di volti in cammino*, 1998, all edited by Alessandro Ramberti and Roberta Sangiorgi.

An anthology of Italian immigrant writings translated into into English has recently been published, edited and presented by Graziella Parati: *Mediterranean Crossroads: Migration Literature in Italy*. Parati also edited a special issue of *Studi d'italianistica nell'Africa australe/Italian Studies in Southern Africa*, entitled *Margins at the Centre: African Italian Voices* (1995), which contains unpublished Italian texts by and interviews with African writers, as well as critical articles.

tu sei l'espressione della mia Africa
il mio vero essere, o tradizione mia!

Ho guardato nello specchio se eri cambiata un po',
ti vedo sempre la stessa, tu sei come me,
siamo legati da un amore eterno, o tradizione mia!
(Ramberti and Sangiorgi, *Memorie in valigia* 35)

Where Can I Flee Far from You

I tried to cross seas, lands and skies
to hide from you, but I didn't succeed;
I always see you in my dreams, oh my tradition!

I tried to change my skin,
I thought you would have deserted me,
now I've discovered that you are black like me,
you are the expression of my Africa
my true being, oh my tradition!

I looked in the mirror [to see] if you had changed a little,
I see you always the same, you are like me,
we are bound by an eternal love, oh my tradition!

At the other extreme from testimonials of injustice and incomprehension, there are expressions of hope and good will, voices that recognize their diversity not as a fault or a weakness, nor as a cause of exclusion and inferiority, but as a source of strength and worth, a valuable resource that should be cultivated and exalted and not suppressed or overcome: a life-enhancing gift to share with their new neighbors and to offer to their new society:

La ballata di riva
Daghmoumi Abdelkader (Morocco)

Noi siamo i figli della sabbia,
del sole e dei fiori,

siamo i figli del mare.
Siamo venuti dai campi e dalle grandi città.
Noi ragazzi dai mille sogni spezzati,
infranti e traditi,
col cuore tenero e con gli occhi asciutti e bruni;
noi dalla chioma color pece,
siamo venuti a ballare nelle vostre piazze luminose,
nelle vostre case.
Siamo venuti a ballare per i vostri occhi
stanchi e immobili come specchi.
Siamo i bambini nati da gocce d'acqua di fiume in secca
che fino a ieri scorreva lento.
Siamo spighe di grano piene e forti
siamo venuti a cantarvi le nostre canzoni d'amore,
canzoni dolci come mandorle e miele.
Le canteremo ad alta voce
finché toccheremo i vostri cuori
per poi cantarle piano, piano,
assieme, nelle vostre case,
nelle vostre piazze,
nelle vostre città.
(Ramberti and Sangiorgi, *Voci dell'arcobaleno* 23)

The Shore Dance

We are the children of the sand,
of the sun and of the flowers,
we are the children of the sea.
We have come from the field and from the big cities.
We youths of the thousand broken dreams,
shattered and betrayed,
with a tender heart and dry, dark eyes;
we with hair the color of pitch,
have come to dance in your brightly lit squares,
in your homes.
We have come to dance for your eyes
tired and as still as mirrors.
We are children born of drops from a dried river

that until yesterday flowed slowly.
We are stalks of wheat full and strong
we have come to sing to you our songs of love,
songs as sweet as almonds and honey.
We will sing them out loud
until they touch your hearts
to then sing them softly, softly,
together, in your homes,
in your squares,
in your cities.

Such testimonials provide evidence that, despite the many social prejudices and economic deprivations that immigrants currently face, the dream of assimilation is not impossible: they and their descendants will make significant contributions in shaping a new, more diverse Italian culture, just as Italian emigrants and their descendants have done in other societies in many parts of the world.

Italy's newest children are heirs of different cultures. In addition to their Italian relatives, they may have grandparents in Senegal or Togo, aunts and uncles in the Dominican Republic or Brazil, cousins in Morocco or the Philippines. A case in point is the son of Pap Khouma, the Senegalese Italian author of *Io, venditore di elefanti*, who presented the following unpublished poem at the Africa Italy symposium, written for his two-year-old son, the child of an Italian mother and an African father, descendant of diverse cultures and citizen of tomorrow's Italy:

Figlio

È nato mio figlio da te
è nero come l'ebano
è bianco, tutto bianco.

È tuo . . .
È mio . . .

Figlio del caso
o frutto dell'amore
mio figlio è già nato da te,

ma non è nero
e neppure bianco.

Ha il colore indefinibile
di questo tramonto, che fa male
solo agli occhi di un ipocrita.
Mio figlio è qua
ma non è di qui
né di altrove

ha attraversato la frontiera
di tutti i colori
e non ha niente
di strano.

Questo bambino che ci assomiglia
non è tuo
neppure mio
appartiene solo al domani.
Mio figlio è di tutti i colori
e a nessuno assomiglia.

A domani, figlio . . .

Son

My son was born by [or from] you
he is as black as ebony
he is white, all white

He is yours . . .
He is mine . . .

Child of chance
or fruit of love
my son is already born by you,
but he is not black
nor is he white.

He is the indescribable color
of this sunset, which hurts
only the eyes of a hypocrite.

My son is here
but he is not from here
nor from elsewhere
he has crossed the border
of all colors
and is in no way
strange.

This child who resembles us
is not yours
nor mine
he belongs only to tomorrow.
My son is of all colors
and resembles no one.

To [or until] tomorrow, child . . .

To try to understand the nature, the causes, and the possible consequences of this new socio-historical phenomenon in Italy, an international, interdisciplinary symposium was held at Miami University, in
Oxford, Ohio. Over a three-day period, November 6–8, 1998, panelists
from Europe, Africa, and North America explored past, present, and future relations between Italian and African cultures from various discipli-
nary perspectives: geographical, historical, political, economic, sociological, and cultural — literature, theater, and cinema. By considering a
broad historical and multidisciplinary context, the symposium attempted to perceive and elucidate the diverse dimensions, difficulties,
and opportunities inherent in this newest encounter between Africa and
Europe.

This volume contains expanded versions of papers presented at the
symposium.[5] The first section focuses on geographical, archeological,

---

[5]Italian versions of many of the articles in this volume have appeared in Italy in *Africa
Italia: Due continenti si avvicinano*, edited by Sante Matteo and Stefano Bellucci

and historical aspects. Geologist Larry Mayer leads off by demonstrating that the Italian peninsula is African both down deep, i.e. tectonically, and on the surface, since for millennia its topsoil has been deposited by Scirocco winds from the Sahara. Historian Edwin Yamauchi explores Roman incursions into the upper Nile regions of the Meroe cultures from the time of Augustus to the Christian era. Evelyn Edson and John Brackett, also historians, consider later relations between Europe and Africa. Edson looks at cartography to see how Europeans perceived the African continent in the Middle Ages, while Brackett reveals how Italians imagined Africa and Africans in the Renaissance.

The second section deals with economic, sociological, and political issues. Stefano Bellucci, political scientist and co-organizer of the symposium, presents an overview of the number and types of immigrants in Italy and outlines the possible causes and consequences of the phenomenon. Benedetta Rossi explains the economic and social impact of Italian

---

(Santarcangelo di Romagna: Fara Editore, 1999). Parts of this introduction are adapted from my introductory essay in that volume, "Africa e/è Italia. Lettera-introduzione di un figlio lontano." Stefano Bellucci's article in the Italian book, "Immigrazione: teorie di politica economica internazionale," is substantially different from his article in this volume. One article in the Italian book, Anna Maria Medici's "In fuga dal colonialismo. Il viaggio in Italia di un poeta tunisino (XIX secolo)," which was commissioned specifically for that book and was not presented at the Africa-Italy symposium, is not reproduced in this volume. Peter Pedroni's interview with Kossi Komla-Ebri, included in the Italian volume as "Intervista allo scrittore Kossi Komla-Ebri," was conducted in Italian, the year after the symposium, and is here translated into English. The other articles in the Italian book were either translated or rewritten in Italian for that volume and are here presented in their original English version, the language in which the papers were presented at the symposium. Their titles in the Italian volume are: Larry Mayer, "L'Africa incomincia alle Alpi. Terremoti italiani del passato e previsioni per il futuro"; John Brackett, "L'Africa e gli africani nell'immaginario degli italiani del Rinascimento"; Giampaolo Calchi Novati, "L'Italia e il Corno d'Africa: l'insostenibile leggerezza di un colonialismo debole"; Cristina Lombardi-Diop, "Madre della nazione: una donna italiana nell'Eritrea coloniale"; Laura A. Harris, "*L'abbandono*: chi è meticcio, e di chi, nella diaspora eritreo-italiana"; Carla Ghezzi, "La letteratura africana d'immigrazione in lingua italiana: la mia patria è la letteratura"; Gabriella Romani, "Identità italiana e letteratura d'immigrazione"; Peter Pedroni, "Due italiani e due africani: Moravia, Volponi, Komla-Ebri, Wasswa"; Charles Klopp, "Buster Keaton va in Africa: le *Avventure in Africa* di Gianni Celati"; Graziella Parati, "Cinema e immigrazione nell'Italia contemporanea"; Maria Silvia Riccio, "La pelle nera." I am grateful to Alessandro Ramberti of Fara Editore for his kind permision to republish these articles in English.

aid to Niger and how it affects the role of women in land development. Eric Edwin Otenyo and Chrisantus Musambayi Katumanga, political scientists from Kenya, review and critique social and economic relations between Italy and Kenya and anticipate future developments.

The political, social, and cultural legacy of Italian colonialism in Africa is the focus of the third section. Italy's foremost expert on Italian intervention in the Horn of Africa, political scientist Gian Paolo Calchi Novati, examines the current effects of Italy's past "weak colonialism" in the area. Literary scholars Cristina Lombardi-Diop and Laura Harris investigate the colonial legacy through literary texts. Lombardi-Diop looks at the travel narrative of Rosaria Pianavia Vivaldi, who documented the building of the Eritrean colony as well as the Italo-Ethiopian war in the 1890s with photos as well as prose. Harris probes the problem of *metissage* as reflected in Erminia Dell'Oro's novel *L'abbandono*, which relates the story of Fascist colonialism in Eritrea through the eyes of an Eritrean woman and her daughter by an Italian father.

The next section is devoted to the representation of Africans in Italian theater. Italianists Teresa Picarazzi and Wiley Feinstein describe and interpret "An African Harlequin in Milan," a contemporary adaptation by playwright Marco Martinelli of an eighteenth-century comedy by Carlo Goldoni, in the tradition of the *Commedia dell'Arte*, in which the traditional figure of Arlecchino (Harlequin) is played by an African immigrant in Italy. In response, Paul Jackson, chair of the Department of Theatre at Miami University, shows how the racial and cultural images evoked in the play have very different, troubling connotations in an American context.

The representation of Africa and Africans in Italian cinema is the topic of the fifth section. Chandra Harris provides an overview of how blacks have been represented on Italian screens. Graziella Parati, the keynote speaker for the symposium and the Italianist pioneer who has been the most instrumental in introducing African-Italian culture into Italian studies in North America, looks at contemporary cinematic production by and about African immigrants. Silvia Riccio ponders the role of cinema in promoting transcultural understanding by looking at how interactions with Africans are presented in several recent movies, both those which deal specifically with African immigrant issues, such as

Pummarò and *Articolo 2*, as well as those which allude to the African presence only in passing, such as the popular comedy *Tre uomini e una gamba* (Three Men and a Leg).

Section six looks at the depiction of Africa and Africans in Italian literature.[6] Pina Palma studies the perception of the Abyssinian war and how it relates to political consciousness in Carlo Levi's *Christ Stopped at Eboli*. Peter Pedroni shows how Africa is imagined differently in the writings of Italian authors and African authors writing in Italian, focusing on the writings of Alberto Moravia and Paolo Volponi in the first case and Kossi Komla-Ebri, from Togo, and Sinan B. Wasswa, from Uganda, in the latter. Charles Klopp looks into a more recent text by an Italian author, Gianni Celati's *Avventure in Africa*, 1998, where he no longer finds the "horror" of difference of Conrad's *Heart of Darkness*, but an effacement of difference endemic to the human condition in a postmodern perspective.

The last section explores the emerging field of African Italian immigrant literature. Carla Ghezzi, a scholar and administrator at the national Istituto di Studi Italiani per l'Africa e l'Oriente (Institute of Italian Studies on Africa and Asia) in Rome, provides an overview of immigrant writing in Italy and explains how immigrant voices are making themselves heard and, by finding a home in literature, are also making themselves at home in their new country and in their newly acquired Italian language. Literary scholar Gabriella Romani begins by comparing postcolonial issues and their theorization in France and in Italy and proceeds to make a case that Italian immigrant writing, which is essentially ignored by the Italian academy, is an important new cultural force that not only builds bridges between Italian and foreign cultures, but also between Italy's racially homogeneous present and its more diverse, "creolized" future, through a literary strategy which she calls "familiarization" of that which is initially perceived as alien. The last two texts

---

[6]This topic was extensively studied in two special issues of *Studi d'italianistica nell'Africa australe/Italian Studies in Southern Africa*, entitled *Images of African in Italian Literature and Culture*. Part 1, 1992, edited by Piero d'Onofrio, Anna Meda, and Rita Wilson, includes articles spanning Italian literature from Marco Polo, to Goldoni, to D'Annunzio. Part 2 (Twentieth Century), 1993, edited by Meda and Wilson includes articles on Flaiano, Marinetti, Ungaretti, and Moravia.

provide a closer view of immigrant literature by focusing on two prominent African immigrant writers in Italy: Pap Khouma and Kossi Komla-Ebri. Marie Orton, after considering the widespread nature of migration and border crossings in this century, and the cultural implications of the phenomenon, looks closely at the text that launched immigrant literature in Italy, Pap Khouma's best-selling testimonial *Io, venditore di elefanti*, and finds that it is characterized by "hybridity" as a way of resisting oppression and exclusion in the present and prefiguring and promoting inclusion in a redefined future Italian culture based on dialogue.

And it is with a dialogue that the book concludes. Interviewed by Peter Pedroni, the African Italian writer Kossi Komla-Ebri, who emigrated from Togo and is now a physician in Northern Italy, talks about his experiences as an immigrant and about the challenges and opportunities of writing in Italian, his adopted language, and of his dream of creating a *transcultural* or *intercultural* society in which there is interaction, contamination, and assimilation among different ethnic and cultural groups.

❁

Regardless of whether we label this new Italian society as transcultural, intercultural, or multicultural, for Italianists it represents a new field of inquiry. The discipline of Italian Studies will have to change along with Italian society. Just as feminism changed how future cultural production would take shape as well as how the cultural products of the past are reinterpreted, so will this new social development in Italian culture lead us to rethink and retool ourselves, to deal with the current and future aspects of a multiethnic and multiracial Italy, and to reinterpret the culture of the past from the perspective of these new Italians. Already, such books as Pap Khouma's *Io, venditore di elefanti*, written in collaboration with Oreste Pivetta, and Salah Methnani's *Immigrato*, written in collaboration with Mario Fortunato, have led us to perceive Italian institutions and customs through the eyes of "outsiders." Such texts will become a permanent component of Italian literature, and thus of Italian studies.

Still, the novelty is relative: previous encounters with "outsiders" have been common and important in Italian history. For millennia, especially in the centuries when the peninsula was the main crossroads in the *mare nostrum* of the known world, the Mediterranean, Italy has been visited and populated by a great variety of peoples, who have contributed to the extraordinary diversity and richness of Italian regional cultures. Contact with cultural otherness has thus been a constant in Italian history and has consistently fueled Italian cultural development.

In many ways Italy is a paradox, characterized by a pervasive and perennial tension between centripetal and centrifugal impulses. Geographically it is isolated, indeed almost an island, enclosed by Europe's highest mountain chain to the north and by the sea on all other sides; and yet it has always been a point of encounter and transit between Europe, Africa, and Asia, via the Middle East, the most visited and traversed of countries. Historically it has been at the center of great political, religious, and artistic empires; and yet often it has been a fragmented patchwork of independent and disenfranchised societies: ambivalent tendencies that have continued to be manifested in our own time, marked by a persistent regionalism, or *campanilismo,* as well as by the Fascist attempt to reconstitute the Roman Empire. Socially it is a land of people rooted in their communities, generation after generation, for whom banishment is the worst possible punishment, as in the case of such famous exiles as Dante, Foscolo, and Mazzini; but it is also a land of expatriate wanderers, such as quintessential voyagers and explorers Marco Polo, Christopher Columbus, Amerigo Vespucci, and John Cabot (né Giovanni Caboto, of Genoa), for whom travel represents liberation, adventure, or gain. Mythically and archetypically Italy is the locus of the encounter between the Cyclops Polyphemus, representing deep-rooted autochtony and homogeneity, and the ur-traveler Odysseus, who represents ephemeral flux and heterogeneity. Symbolically it is a culture planted and harvested both from its own deep roots, profoundly immersed in the local humus, and from fertile foreign spores spread by cultural winds from other shores.

Within this radical ambivalence, marked by the impulse to barricade and the countervailing impulse to flee, resulting from continuous contacts with "outsiders," at times conflictual, as in imperial conquests and invasions, at other times consensual, as in tourism and migration, negotiating otherness has long been an essential component of the Italian imaginary. The advantage derived from contact with otherness is that it provides binocular or stereoscopic vision, an Odyssean second eye or lens with which to perceive the world in perspective, as opposed to the limited monocular vision of the Cyclops. Historically Italian literature has been an Odyssean venture because, for most Italians, learning to read and write has usually meant leaving behind their maternal language, or dialect, in order to acquire the transregional language of literacy, standard or literary Italian (and before that, literary Latin). In translating, or traveling linguistically and conceptually, from their local, spoken language to a "national," written language, Italian authors have perpetually reenacted the Odyssean journey beyond the boundaries of their existential and psychic homeland to other linguistic and cultural shores, thus acquiring a kind of cognitive stereoscopic vision, through an obligatory encounter with otherness: their own. In the polarity between Italy's multilinguistic oral reality and its mostly monolinguistic written tradition, the perpetual dialogue with "otherness" has served as the motor driving cultural production. The texts of Italy's new immigrants are thus merely new voices introduced into an old, ongoing dialogue.

But perhaps we are all Odysseus' children, all of us who live in industrialized or post-industrial societies and are uprooted and exiled from our place of birth, from our extended families and our home communities, ending up in far-flung, unfamiliar places in search of an education, or work, or adventure. We can never go home again because both "we" and "home" have changed too much in the meantime to remain familiar to each other. It is for this reason that the plight and the stories of immigrants are interesting and enlightening for all of us, not because they are unique or different from our own, but, quite the contrary, because they document and reveal, perhaps more directly and more dramatically, our common experiences and concerns in trying to make a life in today's rapidly changing world.

And it is also for this reason that the changes taking place in Italy are of interest and might be instructive to the rest of the world. If, as Larry Mayer claims, the Italian peninsula is the leading wedge of a geological process which will eventually unite Europe and Africa into one continent, then perhaps demographically it can serve a similar function: as the point of encounter where different races and ethnic cultures can meet and flourish, where their differences will neither be stifled nor targeted for exclusion or hostility, but, as Kossi Komla-Ebri envisions, will instead be celebrated and shared for the common enrichment of all. It is a new Italy already under construction.

Works Cited

Columbus, Christopher. *The Log of Christopher Columbus*. Trans. Robert H. Fuson. Camden, ME: International Marine Publishing, 1987.

De Las Casas, Bartolomé. *The Devastation of the Indies: A Brief Account*. Trans. Herma Briffault. Introd. Bill M. Donovan. Baltimore: Johns Hopkins UP, 1992.

Denevan, William M., ed. *The Native Population of the Americas in 1492*. Madison: U of Wisconsin P, 1992.

D'Onofrio, Piero, Anna Meda, and Rita Wilson, eds. *Images of Africa in Italian Literature and Culture, Part 1*. Special issue of *Studi d'italianistica nell'Africa australe/Italian Studies in Southern Africa* 5.2 (1992).

Fortunato, Mario, and Salah Methnani. *Immigrato*. Rome: Theoria, 1990.

Khouma, Pap. *Io, venditore di elefanti: una vita per forza fra Dakar, Parigi e Milano*. Ed. Oreste Pivetta. Milan: Garzanti, 1990.

Lunenfeld, Marvin, ed. *1492: Discovery, Invasion, Encounter: Sources and Interpretations*. Lexington, MA: Heath, 1991.

Matteo, Sante, and Stefano Bellucci, eds. *Africa Italia: due continenti si avvicinano*. Santarcangelo di Romagna: Fara, 1999.

Meda, Anna, and Rita Wilson, eds. *Images of Africa in Italian Literature and Culture, Part 2 (Twentieth Century)*. Special issue of *Studi d'italianistica nell'Africa australe/Italian Studies in Southern Africa* 6.1 (1993).

Parati, Graziella, special ed. *Margins at the Centre: African Italian Voices*. Special issue of *Studi d'italianistica nell'Africa australe/ Italian Studies in Southern Africa*. Ed. Anna Meda and Rita Wilson. 8.2 (1995).

___, ed. *Mediterranean Crossroads: Migration Literature in Italy*. Madison, NJ: Fairleigh Dickinson UP, 1999.

Ramberti, Alessandro, and Roberta Sangiorgi, eds. *Memorie in valigia*. Santarcangelo di Romagna: Fara, 1997.

___, eds. *Le voci dell'arcobaleno*. Santarcangelo di Romagna: Fara, 1995.

Santos do Castilla, Lycia. "L'ombelico di due continenti." D'Onofrio, Meda, and Wilson 93–98.

GEOGRAPHY AND HISTORY

ITALIAN EARTHQUAKES
A Legacy of the Past and a Preview of the Future

Larry Mayer
Miami University

Abstract

Earthquakes occur along the length of the Apennines in Italy and in the orogenic belts of northern Africa. They represent elastic energy released from rocks when they fracture. Historical records, paleoseismology, and geological data indicate that Mediterranean earthquakes have occurred for millions of years and define the edges of tectonic plates that are colliding with one another. The African plate has been converging with Europe since the Atlantic Ocean began to open, about 190 million years ago. The relationship between the motions of Africa with respect to Europe is currently defined by modern earthquakes and suggests that Italy and Africa have much in common during the history of this convergence.

Earthquakes

From space, Africa, Italy, and the entire the Mediterranean region appear silent. Despite the silence, the view from space clearly shows us distance. Today, the tip of Tunisia near Carthage is only about 150 km away from Sicily's Marsala: they are closer than Cincinnati, Ohio, is from Columbus, Ohio. The familiar geography from space testifies to the precision with which modern geographers have described the coastal boundaries of the continents. The view from space reveals much about the natural architecture of the Earth's surface and the integration of landscape elements such as mountains and rivers. From space, we can see the green of vegetation and the brown of deserts and occasionally we will see massive dust storms blowing out of the Sahara.

However, from space we cannot appreciate that the planet itself is in fact not silent at all. Under the ground surface, there are audible and nearly continuous rumblings taking place which reveal that, despite their peaceful, almost serene appearance from space, Africa and Italy are players in Earth's most dramatic story. The story is about how even global scale features can be transitory and how ephemeral geography can be. The modern regional topography of Africa, Arabia, and Eurasia (Figure 1) represents the current chapter of this story. The topographic features of the region, including the Himalayas, Indian Ocean, and the Alps, all reveal part of the story.

The goal of this paper is to illustrate the relation of Italian earthquakes to the development of the physiographic boundaries between Italy and Africa. Geologists find that these modern boundaries are as ephemeral as post-WWII Italian governments. This paper begins with an earthquake.

Colfiorito Seismic Zone

On September 26, 1997, at 00:33 GMT and at 09:40 GMT, two moderate sized earthquakes of (moment) magnitude 5.7 and 6.0, struck the Umbria-Marche region of central Italy. The earthquakes began with the breaking or rupture of rocks at a depth of about 10 km, at the hypocenter, underneath the Colfiorito basin (Cello et al, 1998a). Shortly afterward, the resulting shock waves reached the surface in Colfiorito basin, the epicentral location. The basin is a Quaternary depression filled with river and lake deposits. From the epicenter, the shock waves traveled outward and were widely felt across central Italy. These moderate earthquakes caused the death of 12 people, injured 140, and, due to structural damage to buildings, left about 80,000 homeless (Cello et al, 1998b). Although these were not exceptionally strong earthquakes, they did significant damage to many small historical towns because of the shallow hypocentral depth. Only 20 km away from the epicenter, Assisi's Holy Monastery and Upper Basilica were heavily damaged by the second earthquake (Marsan and Gorelli, 1997). In this local part of central Italy, no one remembered a damaging earthquake, but many had occurred in the past. Historical data suggest that the strongest previous earthquake, near the Colfiorito basin epicenters, occurred in 1279, or 718 years earlier.

If you asked someone living near Colfiorito, Italy, about earthquakes before the 1997 Colfiorito earthquake, you might have heard that there are no earthquakes in "this" part of Italy. After all, the year 1279 was a long time ago and many of us cannot even remember where we put our house key in the morning. Perhaps you might have been told about recent strong earthquakes in "other" parts of Italy, such as Potenza (1857, 1991), and Irpinia (1980) and perhaps Fucino (1915) which killed 33,000 people. Giotto, the painter of the Assisi frescos was born in 1277, only two years before the last strong earthquake. A view of instrumentally recorded earthquakes (Figure 2) reveals, that Italy has serious seismic hazards and that these earthquakes may be part of a more regional pattern.

Reality viewed through a geological filter suggests that all of these modern Italian earthquakes are related to larger scale forces that have been tearing Italy apart for a few million years. These forces define a dynamic geological relation between Africa and Italy that also existed in the historical past and recent geological record. This long-term record can be easily demonstrated.

Information Content and Earthquakes

Unlike human history, which is relatively short, sometimes feels excruciatingly long, and largely operates at short time scales, geological history is very long and often leaves its records behind. Through an incredible clockwork, geological processes integrate the past into the present, and thus weave an intricate tapestry of interlocking cycles each with their own time duration. Some geological processes take millions of years to run their course and others take only seconds. The erosion of mountains is an example of the former, and an earthquake is an example of the latter. Each process can leave its legacy in the geological record. Italian earthquakes, and earthquakes throughout the Mediterranean region, brief but deep statements from the Earth, relate Africa to Italy in a fundamental way.

Earthquakes are the sudden release of elastic strain, stored in rocks, upon breakage or faulting. A small volume of rock can only store very little elastic strain, and when this small volume of rock breaks, it generates a very small earthquake. However when the large amounts of elastic energy stored in tremendous volumes of rock are suddenly released, great earthquakes result. Large earthquakes often break rocks all the way up to the surface, resulting in a visible scar on the landscape called a fault scarp. Given enough of these earthquakes, these two-meter high fault scarps can add up to become mountains.

Earthquakes, though most only last several tens of seconds, while a long earthquake may last for a minute or so, take global scale forces to organize. Such global scale forces take millions of years to evolve and their evolution affects everything on planet Earth: mineral resources, topography, geography, climate, and even the course of human events. In certain locations on our planet, near the boundaries of tectonic plates, earthquakes are as inevitable in the geologic environment as death is for humans. To most people, earthquakes are no more than random geologic events that only last several seconds. To geologists, earthquakes are more like the pulse of the planet's crust, telling us something about how the huge tectonic plates are moving and leading us to question how the geography of the planet itself was organized. Because forces that generate earthquakes are related to motion of the Earth's tectonic plates, earthquake studies reveal fundamental characteristics of where those plate boundaries are. The locations of what people commonly use to define boundaries, such as mountain chains, rivers, oceans, etc., are commonly related to the same processes that generate earthquakes.

Previous Records of Earthquakes

Geological historians and archeologists have sifted through several millennia of data from the Mediterranean region to reconstruct a history of earthquakes. These data come from earthquake damaged buildings, accounts from Greek and Roman historiographers, Muslim annalists, reports written to government officials, and travel narratives. Useful earthquake catalogs of North Africa and Arabia from 184 CE (Ambraseys et al, 1994) and Italy from 461 CE (Boschi et al, 1997) exist. Along the Dead Sea Fault, the geological boundary between Africa and Arabia, the earthquake record is over 4000 years long, dating back to the Hittites.

These catalogs demonstrate that earthquakes have been occurring throughout the region's history.

Geologists have sought to extend the earthquake record through the application of isotopic dating technology, especially carbon-14. In many applications, isotopic dating allows geologists to extend the earthquake record back to about 25,000 years before the present. The study of earthquakes derived using these methods, or paleoseismology, indicates that earthquakes which happened in the historical period were actually preceded by older pre-historical earthquakes. In areas were there is no historical record of earthquakes, paleoseismology is a critical method of establishing the existence of an earthquake hazard. Earthquake records also establish the existence of zones of high crustal strain caused by the motions of tectonic plates. Italian earthquakes indicate that Italy itself sits astride such a boundary. Modern earthquakes in Africa are concentrated into three major zones: the Atlas mountain trend in Morocco and Tunisia, the East African rift zone, and along the boundary between Africa and Arabia. Of these three seismic zones in Africa, the northern one (Figure 2) is of direct relevance to this paper.

Relationship to Geologic History

Italian peninsular earthquakes occur within an orogenic belt called the Apennines (Figure 3). The Apennine belt consists mostly of rocks that formed below sea-level and were subsequently crunched into a mountain belt by the motion of Italy relative to its neighbors on the other side of the Adriatic sea. Earthquakes in northern Africa occur within an orogenic belt called the Atlas belt. The Atlas mountain belt formed as the African and European plates collided. Reconstruction of the positions of tectonic plates through the past can allow us to document and better visualize the relation Italy and Africa have in this dynamic interaction.

Plate Tectonics

The current positions of continental land masses is only a snapshot in time of an ongoing process that moves the Earth's plates from one place to another. As material in the upper mantle moves in complex rolls, between depths of 200 and 700 km, it carries with it the outermost shell of the planet, the lithosphere. About 195 million years ago, during the Early Jurassic, North America, Africa-Arabia, South America, Europe, India and Australia, all fit together into one large supercontinent called Pangea (Figure 6). Two great Oceans existed at this time, the Pacific Ocean and the Tethys Ocean (see Figure 4). Shortly, the continent would begin to break apart and the new Atlantic Ocean would form at the expense of the Tethys Ocean, which would be consumed by subduction.

About 100 million years ago, during the Late Cretaceous, the growth of the Atlantic ocean had split apart South America from Africa, Europe from North America, and North America from Africa (Figure 5). India and Australia began to drift to the northwest. The opening the Atlantic Ocean signaled the end of the Tethys Ocean, which would be consumed as Africa-Arabia, India, and Australia moved towards Eurasia.

India began "knocking on Eurasia's door" by about 50 million years ago, during the Eocene, and parts of the Tethys Ocean were being squeezed up into suture zones between the colliding continental blocks (Figure 6C). The collisional zone between India and Eurasia actually extended to the west where it defined the boundaries between Arabia-Africa and Eurasia. Arabia and Africa continued to move as a single plate during this time. By 15 million years ago, during the Middle Miocene, most of the great Tethys Ocean was gone (Figure 6D). Some of Tethys was caught in between the colliding continents and uplifted into the actively forming orogenic belts as ophiolites. The Mediterranean came into existence as a complex patchwork of ocean basins and Africa and Arabia began to move differently, separated by the Dead Sea Fault (Figure 1).

The topography of the area clearly shows the effects of these collisions (see Figure 3A). The collisional zone formed a continuous orogenic belt (Figure 1). In the Mediterranean region, the plate interactions were a little more complex, resulting in at least seven orogenic belts (Figure 3B): Atlas-Rif, Apennines, Alps, Dinarides, Hellenides, Carpathians, and Taurides. The floor of the Mediterranean consists of at least seven basins (Figure 3C): Alboran, Balearic, Ligurian, Tyrrhenian, Adriatic, Ionian, Aegean, and Levant.

About this time, water from the Atlantic into the Mediterranean was blocked by Gibraltar. Also, uplift of the Carpathian mountain belt blocked water flow from the Lac Mer, the ancestral Black Sea, into the Mediterranean and soon the Mediterranean dried up leaving only a few isolated saline lakes. The evaporation events, well known as the Messinian Salinity Crisis (Hsü, 1972), left thousands of meters of salt behind. Water levels were so low that the Nile Delta prograded many kilometers to the north, leaving a bulge in Egypt's shoreline which is still clearly visible. During the Messinian, it was possible to travel a short distance directly from Tunisia to Italy, completely on dry land. Around 5 million years ago, water from the Atlantic rapidly flooded the Mediterranean basins through spectacular waterfalls that breached the dam at Gibraltar (Hsü, 1972) and the Sahara became a desert.

The collisions that signaled the end to Tethys are continuing today, as Arabia crushes into Anatolia, squeezing it out of its way and toward Greece. In the processes of these collisions, some of the world's greatest oil reservoirs formed and Italy is a major producer of natural gas. If we examine the relation between recent seismicity and these Mediterranean orogenic belts, we discover that these orogenic belts also define zones of earthquakes (Figure 3D). The earthquake zones delineate the modern boundaries between the Africa and Eurasia tectonic plates. Finally we discover that Italy, despite its political association with Europe, is essentially part of the African plate. Italy represents a promontory which indented Europe at the location of the Alps. Because the motions of Africa and Europe are relative, it is not possible to say whether Italy led the African assault on Europe, or if Europe impaled itself on Italy.

Climate and Soils

The climates of southern Italy, including Sicily, and those of northern coastal Africa from Gibraltar to Tunisia are very similar because they are all true Mediterranean climates. Due to the geological affinity between Italy and northern Africa and their similar climates, soils in these regions also share similar characteristics and classification. They are broadly classified as brown or red Fersiallitic soils (Duchaufour, 1982).

The soils of southern Italy have another connection to Africa. The Sahara desert currently supplies about 100 million tons of dust northward to Italy and Europe, and eastward to Israel, Lebanon and Turkey each year (Yaalon, 1997). Geochemical fingerprinting, using stable isotopes, shows that fine silt and clay in Italian, as well as Greek, carbonate soils are derived from eolian dust from the Sahara. Presumably this dust has been blowing across the Mediterranean and blanketing southern Europe for the past 5 million years. Vegetables grown in southern Italy may actually be growing in African soil.

If the tectonics, rocks, climate, and soils of a region somehow define it, then Italy and Africa are truly from the same family.

Postscript

The current positions of continental land masses represent only a snapshot in time of an ongoing process that moves the Earth's plates from one place to another. As material in the upper mantle moves in complex rolls, between depths of 200 and 700 km, it carries with it the outermost shell of the planet, the lithosphere. As Galileo had remarked, it still moves. Italian earthquakes are both a legacy from the past and a preview of the future. Within the next 50 million years, the Mediterranean will close completely and the suturing of Africa to Europe will be complete (Figure 6). Italy, Africa, and Europe will be part of a single super-continent, united, albeit in geological terms. The sociological development of the region is, broadly speaking (or more narrowly, depending on your viewpoint), the result of timing. The intersection of human and planetary evolution of the region occurred when African and Italian geographic boundaries existed as physiographic features. If humans in the region had first developed 50 million years into the future, perhaps we would be holding a conference on Africeurasia – Australia, mate.

References

Ambraseys, N. N., C. P. Melville, and R. D. Adams. 1994. *The Seismicity of Egypt, Arabia, and the Red Sea.* Cambridge University Press.

Boschi, E., E. Guidoboni, G. Ferrari, G. Valensise, and P. Gasperini. 1997. *Catalogo dei Forti Terremoti in Italia dal a.C. 461 al 1990.* Istituto Nazionale di Gefisica, Rome.

Cello, G. et al. 1998a. "Evidence for Surface Faulting during the September 26, 1997, Colfiorito (Central Italy) Earthquakes." *Journal of Earthquake Engineering* 2: 1–22.

Cello, G. et al. 1998b. "The Resolution of Geological Analysis and Models for Earthquake Faulting Studies." *International Workshop Field Trip Guidebook.* Camerino, Italy.

Duchaufour, P. 1982. *Pedology.* Trans. T. R. Patton. London: Allen and Unwin.

Hsü, K. J. 1972. "When the Mediterranean Dried up." *Scientific American* 227.6: 26–36.

Marsan, P., and V. Gorelli. 1997. "Rapporto preliminare sui danni al sacro convento di Assisi a seuito della sequenza sismica del settembre-Ottobre 1997." *Ingegnaria sismica* 3: 57–69.

Scotese, C. R. 1997. *Paleogeographic Atlas.* PALEOMAP Progress Report 90–0497. Department of Geology, University of Texas at Arlington, Arlington Texas.

Yaalon, D. H.,1997. "Soils in the Mediterranean Region: What Makes Them Different?" *Catena* 28: 157–69.

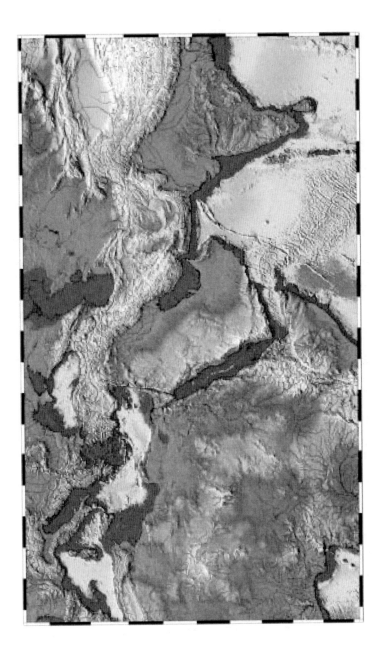

Figure 1. Shaded relief representation of the topography of North Africa, Southern Europe, Arabia, and Southern Asia. The elevations of the sea floors is also shown. The most spectacular feature is a nearly continuous belt of mountains from the Himalayas to the Alps. Data from NOAA.

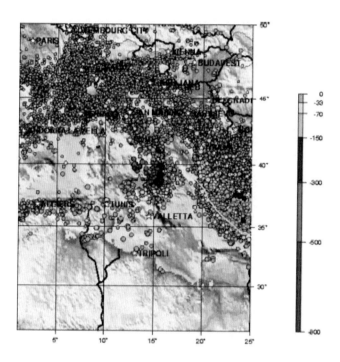

Figure 2. Earthquakes of northern Africa and Italy. Image from the US Geological Survey NEIC.

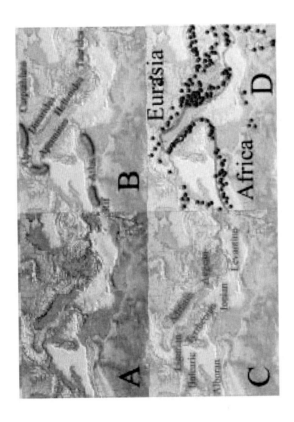

Figure 3. Tectonic features of the Mediterranean region. A. Shaded relief. B. Orogenic belts. C. Mediterranean basins. D. Schematic earthquake distribution and plate boundary interpretation.

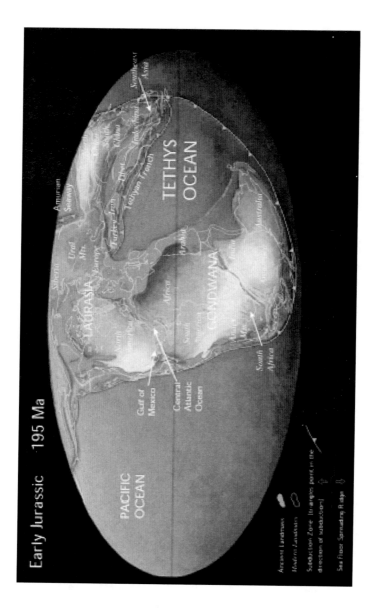

Figure 4. Plate tectonic evolution of the Mediterranean (from Scotese, 1997): Early Jurassic.

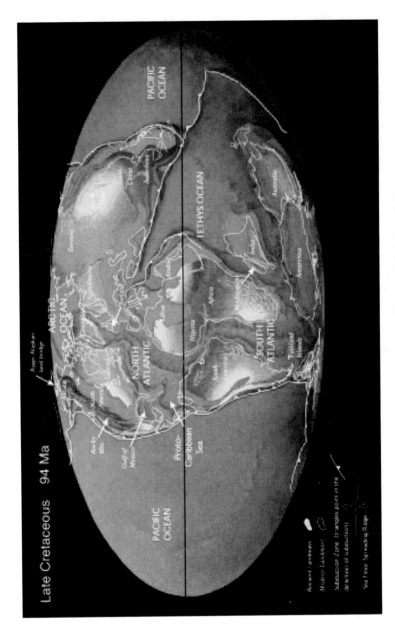

Figure 5. Plate tectonic evolution of the Mediterranean (from Scotese, 1997): Late Cretaceous.

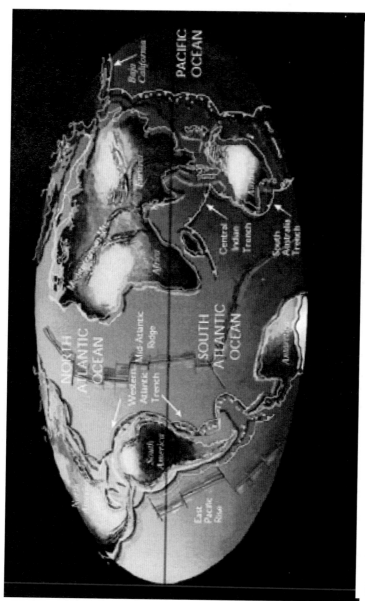

Figure 6. Projected plate positions 50 million years into the future (from Scotese, 1997).

THE ROMANS AND MEROE IN NUBIA

Edwin M. Yamauchi
Miami University

Introduction

In earlier times the area between the First and Second Cataracts of Egypt was called *Wawat*. Upper Nubia between the Second and Fifth Cataracts was called *Cush* (*Kush*) from the XIIth Dynasty (early 2nd millennium B.C.E.) (Gardiner 597; Faulkner 284). It is a word that was transliterated in the Hebrew Scriptures, for example, in the proverbial statement of Jeremiah 13:23: "Can the Ethiopian (Heb. *Kushi*) change his skin?" (Holladay 154). Miriam and Aaron objected when Moses married a Cushite woman (Num. 12:1). An independent confirmation of the Nubian element among the descendants of the family of Moses is the name Phinehas (1 Sam. 1:3), which is derived from the Egyptian *pi-Nehesyu* "the Nubian."[1]

The name *Ethiopia* is derived from the Greek *Aithiops* "Burnt Face" and was the general Greek word for Africa, especially for Nubia.[2] It was not used in the ancient period for the modern country called Ethiopia (known as Abyssinia until 1901), which is to the east of the Sudan on the coast of Africa.

In the Roman era the area was known as *Nubia* after the Noba tribe who occupied the region. Scholars sometimes distinguish *Lower Nubia*, the region between the First and Second Cataracts in the modern country

---

[1]From the Middle Kingdom on, there were Nubians who became prisoners, served as soldiers or courtiers, and on occasion as part of the royal family. But contrary to the Afrocentric views of Anta Cheikh Diop and his American disciples, the Egyptians did not depict themselves as black. See Yurco, "Were the Ancient Egyptians Black or White?" For a critique of Afro-centrism, see Lefkowitz.

[2]*Aithiops* is derived from *aithô* "to burn" + *ops* "face." See, *A Lexicon Abridged from Liddell and Scott's Greek-English Lexicon* (19). See also Snowden, *Blacks in Antiquity*; idem, *Before Color Prejudice*; and idem, "Attitudes towards Blacks in the Greek and Roman World: Misinterpretations of the Evidence."

of Egypt, from *Upper Nubia,* the land between the Second and the Sixth Cataracts.

The modern name of the country, the *Sudan,* is derived from the Arabic phrase *Bilad al-Sudan,* "Land of the Blacks" (Wehr 440).

Meroe

Meroe, the capital of a Nubian kingdom, which flourished for a millennium from c. 650 B.C.E. to 350 C.E., was situated about 960 miles south of the Mediterranean and was located 600 miles from Aswan.[3] It was located on the east bank of the Nile, between the Fifth and the Sixth Cataracts, 145 miles north of Khartoum, the capital of Sudan. Herodotus (2.28–31) was the first classical writer to refer to Meroe.

After the Meroitic civilization had declined in the 4th century C.E., Herodotus's account of Meroe was dismissed as legendary until the site was rediscovered by James Bruce in 1772. Excavations were conducted at the site from 1909 until 1914 by E. A. W. Budge and John Garstang. These excavations were poorly conducted and but partially published. Garstang uncovered a great temple of Amun, which is some 150 m. in length. There is a small kiosk, where the sacred boat of Amun was placed. He also identified a temple on the outskirts with the "Table of the Sun" described by Herodotus (3.17). However, the Sun Temple discovered by Garstang dates to the first century C.E., and should not be equated with the Sun Temple described by Herodotus (Burstein, "Herodotus and the Emergence of Meroe" 3).

Important archaeological work was accomplished in Nubia by George A. Reisner from 1916–25 in the excavations of the royal cemeteries at Napata and Meroe, from which the basic chronology of Nubian history was established.[4] Some of Reisner's interpretations, however, were vitiated by his bias that viewed Napata and Meroe as simply offshoots of Egyptian civilizations rather than as a legitimate indigenous culture.

---

[3] For general accounts see: Shinnie; Millet; Kendall and Doll; Edwards; and Burstein, "The Kingdom of Meroe."

[4] Reisner's assistant, Dows Dunham, published the results in five volumes, *The Royal Cemeteries of Kush.*

W. B. Emery then worked at Ballana and Qustul in the 1930s. But it was the threatened inundation of Nubia by the building of the High Dam at Aswan that stimulated a flurry of excavation and survey work from 1961–1975. Work began on the dam in 1960. Its completion ten years later created Lake Nasser, which stretched some 300 miles south into the Sudan. Some 40 expeditions were undertaken to accomplish as much as possible.[5] In return for US participation in the UNESCO efforts, a temple from Dendra, which Augustus had built, was sent to the Metropolitan Museum of New York, where it is housed in a special wing.[6] The most spectacular achievements were the raising of the colossal statues of Ramesses II at Abu Simbel and later the temples of the island of Philae to new sites above the level of the water. Both Nubians, Egyptians, and Roman Emperors erected structures on Philae, called "The Pearl of Egypt" by Pierre Loti. It remained the last outpost of paganism until the sixth century C.E.

Excavations have been conducted at Meroe by P. L. Shinnie and A. Hakem for the University of Khartoum. A French excavation at Wadi ben Naqa on the Nile south of Meroe uncovered a first-century C.E. royal palace (see Vercoutter). In 196970, the major temple of Musawarat es-Sufra was excavated by F. Hintze for Humboldt University (see Hintze and Hintze). This impressive site includes three major temples, stone ramps, and an elephant statue. A large enclosure has been interpreted as a training center for the training of elephants.

Work has continued at Qasr Ibrim, which is the only site of Egyptian Nubia that has not been inundated. Once on a high bluff, it is now an island. The site that was originally a Ptolemaic fortress was occupied by the Romans in 30 B.C.E., and then by the Meroites.

The numerous pyramids in the region of Napata and at Meroe are smaller and steeper than the Egyptian pyramids. The burial chambers were below the surface of the earth. There is striking evidence that as in

---

[5]See Keating, and Säve-Söderbergh. The discoveries have been summarized in a magisterial fashion by Adams.

[6]SeeAldred. Augustus is depicted as a pharaoh before various Egyptian gods. Coptic graffiti dated to 577 come from a time when the temple was transformed into a church; Bernardo Drovetti (1776–1852), who collected antiquities for the Turin Museum, also incised his name on the wall of this temple.

early Egyptian history and also at Kerma in the 17th century B.C.E. servants were killed to accompany their masters and mistresses to the afterlife.

Prior History of the Area

The Egyptians established contact with the southern regions as early as the Old Kingdom. During the Middle Kingdom, the Egyptians advanced their southern frontier to the Second Cataract, building numerous forts to regulate the immigration of the Cushites northward. When Hyksos invaders occupied Lower Egypt, they established friendly contact with the Cushites. But when the Hyksos were expelled from Egypt c. 1570, the Egyptians reestablished their dominance over the south.[7]

For a brief period, the Cushites established their dominance over Egypt itself during the XXVth Dynasty in the 7th century B.C.E.[8] One of their pharaohs, Taharqa (Tirhakah), is mentioned in Isaiah (37:9) as engaging the Assyrian army when Sennacherib invaded Palestine in 701 B.C.E. The Assyrians later pursued the Cushites far to the south of Egypt, destroying Thebes in the process. After the Assyrians left, Psammetichos II (XXVIth Dynasty) attacked Napata in 593 with the help of Greek and Carian mercenaries, who left their graffiti on the colossal statues of Ramesses at Abu Simbel (Yamauchi, *Greece and Babylon* 64–66).

When the Persian king Cambyses invaded Egypt in 525, he sent an expedition against the Nubians (Yamauchi, *Persia and the Bible* ch 3). Later Darius and Xerxes counted Cush (*Kusa*) as part of the Persian Empire. Cushite troops, wearing leopard and lion skins, served in Xerxes' army (Her. 7.69). Darius used ivory from Cush for his palace of Susa. Biennial gifts of gold, ebony, and ivory were sent to the Persians. On the Apadana stairway at Persepolis, the Cushite delegation leads a long-necked animal, which looks like an okapi but which may have been intended to represent a giraffe — the tallest animal in the world and therefore a spectacular trophy.

---

[7]See Trigger; Hochfield and Riefstahl; Davies; O'Connor; Yurco, "Egypt and Nubia."
[8]See Kitchen 362–98; and Russmann.

Meroitic Civilization

After withdrawing permanently from Egypt about 590 B.C.E., the Cushites still maintained a remarkable kingdom for about a thousand years until about 350 C.E. The first king of this era of the Kingdom of Cush was Aspelta (592–568). About 250 B.C.E. the royal cemetery was transferred from Napata to Meroe. In the Hellenistic and Roman periods a distinctive phase of Nubian civilization, known as Meroitic, flourished for six centuries from c. 250 B.C.E. to 350 C.E.

Contacts with Ptolemaic Egypt were frequent in the third century B.C.E., which has been called the period of the "early Meroitic miracle." It was during this era that the famous Lion Temple was built at Musawarat el Sufra. The temple was dedicated to the chief god of the Meroites, Apedemak. During this period Arakakamani (Ergamenes II, 218–200 B.C.E.) built temples at Philae. According to Diodorus, Ergamenes, who had a Greek education and had studied philosophy, defied the heretofore powerful priests.

The *Meroitic script* may have been developed in the second century B.C.E. The script consists of 23 alphabetic letters derived from Egyptian signs. Thanks to a bilingual in Meroitic and Egyptian from the reign of Natakamani (12 B.C.E.–12 C.E.), F. L. Griffith was able to decipher the phonetic values of the script in 1910. Unfortunately the language still remains largely incomprehensible. The corpus consists of about 300 texts from about the 2nd century B.C.E. to the 3rd/4th century C.E.

The Roman Intervention into Meroe

After his decisive victory at Actium in 31 B.C.E. over the naval forces of Antony and Cleopatra, Octavian pursued the couple to Egypt. When they committed suicide, Octavian (later to be renamed Augustus in 27 B.C.E.) made Egypt his personal province.

He installed as governor Cornelius Gallus, a poet who was a friend of Virgil's. Recent excavations at Qasr Ibrim have recovered a papyrus copy of a poem composed by Gallus. In 29, he pushed south past Philae, to gain control of the section of the Nile called the Triakontaschoinos, probably to secure access to the gold mines in the region. At Philae he set up a trilingual (hieroglyphic, Latin, Greek) inscription. The kingdom of

Meroe was declared a Roman protectorate and, thus, was under an obligation to pay an annual tribute. A governor (tyrannus) was appointed over the Triakontaschoinos, the stretch of the Nile Valley, 30 schoinoi (320 km.) in length.[9]

Upon recalling Cornelius, Augustus replaced him with Aelius Gallus. Aelius was sent by the emperor to conquer Meroe, a commision that he did not accomplish, despite Augustus's boast in his *Res Gestae*:

> At my command and under my auspices two armies were led almost at the same time into Ethiopia and Arabia Felix; vast enemy forces of both peoples were cut down in battle and many towns captured. Ethiopia was penetrated as far as the town of Nabata, which adjoins Meroë. (Brunt and Moore 33)

In 25 B.C.E. taking advantage of the fact that soldiers were withdrawn to provide troops for Aelius Gallus's campaign in Arabia, under the leadership of the queen Amanirenas the Meroites launched an attack upon Syene (Aswan) and on the islands of Philae and of Elephantine by the First Cataract (Jameson 71–84). It was no doubt on this occasion that they carried off a magnificent bronze head of Augustus, which the excavators later found buried under the threshold of a temple at Meroe, so that all who entered would tread over the enemy's head. Some remarkable frescoes have been recovered from this temple. One figure represents a light-skinned Roman, a second figure a black Negro, and the third figure a brown-skinned prisoner.

In 24 B.C.E. Augustus's new commander, C. Petronius, launched a punitive expedition, which reached as far south as Napata. He pursued the treacherous Akinidad, who had been appointed by the Romans as tyrannus, and the Candace, whom he described as "a masculine sort of woman, and blind in one eye. . . ." A later Meroite attack upon the Roman garrison at the fortress of Primis (Qasr Ibrim) was unsuccessfull. Petronius returned to Primis and left 400 men there with two years' supplies.

---

[9]See Kirwan; Desanges; and Török.

Through diplomacy, peaceful relations between the Romans and the Meroites were established. The Meroites obtained very favorable terms on a treaty signed at Samos in 20 B.C.E. The Romans withdrew from Qasr Ibrim, and the Meroites were not required to pay tribute. The frontier was established at Hiera Sycaminos.

According to Seneca *Nat. Ques.* VI.8.3, and Tacitus *Annales* XV. 36, Nero sent a party of praetorians to Meroe to scout the area, possibly in preparation for an invasion, which was never carried out as Nero committed suicide in the summer of 68.

The peaceful relations established between the Romans and the Meroites were maintained for three centuries, with only a garrison of three cohorts (about 1500 soldiers) stationed at Syene, until Diocletian in 297 withdrew the garrison and entrusted the defence of the area against the marauding Blemmyes to the allied Nobades tribe (Speidel 768–75).

The Ethiopian Eunuch

According to Luke's *Acts of the Apostles* (8:26–40), the deacon Philip was called from his ministry in Samaria to the side of the so-called Ethiopian eunuch from Meroe.[10] It is not likely that the man was a Jew.[11] Jewish traditions (Deut. 23:1) would have prevented a eunuch from becoming a proselyte.[12] He was most probably sent on a diplomatic or trade mission.

The conversion of an Ethiopian may be seen as of great significance. As Cain Hope Felder notes:

> Today there are those who tend to exclude black people from any role in the Christian origins, and they need to be reminded that quite possibly a Nubian was the first Gentile convert. (141)[13]

---

[10]Josephus connected the kingdom of Meroe with such figures as Moses's Cushite wife (*Antiquities* 2.252–53) and the Queen of Sheba (*Antiquities* 8. 165, 175). Ethiopians conflated Candace with the Queen of Sheba. See Ullendorf.

[11]See Yamauchi, "Was Nehemiah the Cupbearer a Eunuch?"

[12]The newly published text from Qumran, *Miqsat Ma'aseh ha-Torah*, also refers to this impediment. See Martínez 79–85.

[13]This was the view of Eusebius (H.E. 2.1.13), who saw in his conversion the fulfilment of Ps. 68. See also: Squillaci; and Meester.

References

Adams, William Y. *Nubia Corridor to Africa*. Princeton: Princeton UP, 1984.

Aldred, Cyril. *The Temple of Dendur*. New York: Metropolitan Museum of Art, 1978.

Brunt, P. A., and J. M. Moore, eds. *Res Gestae Divi Augusti*. London: Oxford UP, 1967.

Burstein, Stanley M. "Herodotus and the Emergence of Meroe." *Journal of the Society for the Study of Egyptian Antiquities* 11 (1981): 1–5.

___. "The Kingdom of Meroe." Yamauchi, *Africa and Africans* ch. 4.

Davies, W. V., ed., *Egypt and Africa: Nubia from Prehistory to Islam*. London: British Museum P, 1991.

Desanges, J. "Les relations de l'Empire romain avec l'Afrique nilotique et érythréenne, d'Auguste à Probus." *Aufstieg und Niedergang der römischen Welt* II.10.1 (1988): 3–12

Dunham, Dows. *The Royal Cemeteries of Kush*. Cambridge: Harvard UP, 1950–63.

Edwards, David N. *The Archaeology of the Meroitic State*. Oxford: Tempus Reparatum, 1996.

Faulkner, Raymond O. *A Concise Dictionary of Middle Egyptian*. Oxford: Oxford UP, 1962.

Felder, Cain Hope, ed. *Stony the Road We Trod: African American Biblical Interpretation*. Minneapolis: Fortress, 1991.

Gardiner, Alan. *Egyptian Grammar*. 3rd ed. London: Oxford UP, 1957.

Hintze, Fritz, and Ursula Hintze. *Civilizations of the Old Sudan: Kerma, Kush, Christian Nubia*. Leipzig: Verlag für Kunst und Wissenschaft, 1968.

Hochfield, S., and E. Riefstahl, eds. *Africa in Antiquity I. The Arts of Ancient Nubia and the Sudan*. Brooklyn: Brooklyn Museum, 1978.

Holladay, W. L., ed. *A Concise Hebrew and Aramaic Lexicon of the Old Testament*. Grand Rapids: Eerdmans, 1971.

Jameson, Shelagh. "Chronology of the Campaigns of Aelius Gallus and C. Petronius." *Journal of Roman Studies* 58 (1986): 71–84.

Keating, Rex. *Nubian Rescue*. New York: Hawthorn Books, 1980.

Kendall, Timothy, and Susan K. Doll. *Kush: Lost Kingdom of the Nile*. Brockton: Brockton Art Museum, 1982.

Kirwan, L. P. *Rome beyond the Southern Egyptian Frontier*. London: The British Academy, 1978.

Kitchen, K. A. *The Third Intermediate Period in Egypt*. Warminster: Aris & Phillips, 1973.

Lefkowitz, Mary. *Not Out of Africa*. New York: Basic, 1996.

A Lexicon Abridged from Liddell and Scott's Greek-English Lexicon. Oxford: Clarendon, 1958.

Martínez, Florentino G. *The Dead Sea Scrolls Translated*. Leiden: Brill, 1994.

Meester, P. "Le pelerin d'Ethiope." *Telema* 18 (1979): 5–18.

Millet, Nicholas B. *Meroitic Nubia*. Ann Arbor: University Microfilms, 1969.

O'Connor, David. *Ancient Nubia: Egypt's Rival in Africa.* Philadelphia: University Museum, 1993.

Russmann, Edna R. "Egypt and the Kushites: Dynasty XXV." Yamauchi, *Africa and Africans* 3.

Säve-Söderbergh, T., ed. *Temples and Tombs of Ancient Nubia.* New York: Thames and Hudson, 1987.

Shinnie, P. L. *Meroe.* London: Thames and Hudson, 1967.

Snowden, Frank J., Jr. "Attitudes towards Blacks in the Greek and Roman World: Misinterpretations of the Evidence." Yamauchi, *Africa and Africans* ch. 8.

___. *Before Color Prejudice.* Cambridge: Harvard UP, 1983.

___. *Blacks in Antiquity.* Cambridge: Harvard UP, 1970.

Speidel, Michael P. "Nubia's Roman Garrison." *Aufstieg und Niedergang der römischen Welt.* II.10.1 (1988): 768–75.

Squillaci, Domenico. "La conversione dell'Etiope." *Palestra del Clero* 39.22 (15 Nov. 1960): 1197–1201.

Török, L. "Geschichte Meroes." *Aufstieg und Niedergang der römischen Welt* II.10.1 (1988): 275–77.

Trigger, Bruce. *Nubia under the Pharaohs.* Boulder: Westview, 1976.

Ullendorf, E. "Candace (Acts VIII.27) and the Queen of Sheba." *New Testament Studies* 2 (1955–56): 53–56.

Vercoutter, J. "Un palais des 'Candace' contemporain d'Auguste." *Syria* 39 (1962): 263–99.

Wehr, Hans. *A Dictionary of Modern Written Arabic.* Ithaca: Cornell UP, 1961.

Yamauchi, Edwin, ed. *Africa and Africans in Antiquity.* E. Lansing: Michigan State UP, forthcoming.

___. *Greece and Babylon.* Grand Rapids: Baker Book House, 1967.

___. *Persia and the Bible.* Grand Rapids: Baker Book House, 1990.

___."Was Nehemiah the Cupbearer a Eunuch?" *Zeitschrift für die alttestamentliche Wissenschaft* 92 (1980): 132–42.

Yurco, Frank J. "Egypt and Nubia: Old, Middle and New Kingdom Eras." Yamauchi ch. 2.

___. "Were the Ancient Egyptians Black or White?" *Biblical Archaeology Review* 15.5 (1989): 24–31.

DEFINING AFRICA
European Views of the Continent in the Middle Ages

Evelyn Edson
Piedmont Virginia Community College

L ibya to the Greeks, Africa to the Romans — it was the third part of the ecumene, or inhabited, known world. It was both familiar and foreign to Europeans of the Middle Ages. The Mediterranean coast was their neighbor, while deep in the south was a land of unknown extent, cut off from them by deserts and a torrid climate. "Africa" meant everything from St. Augustine and urban civilization to Troglodytes, cannibals and empty spaces. From the early Middle Ages up to the 14th century, the geographical authorities on Africa were primarily classical: Pliny's *Natural History*, Solinus's *Collections of Marvels*, Seneca's *Natural Questions*, Sallust's *Jugurthine War*. After 1300 European voyages on the Atlantic and eastern coasts, as well as expeditions into the interior, began to modify the traditional picture, both as it was presented in writing and on maps.[1]

The origin of the name, Africa, is, like those of the other continents, lost in the past. Isidore of Seville, who wrote a popular encyclopedia in the 7th century C.E., suggested several possible meanings for the name. It was derived from "aprica," sunny, or it was named for an obscure grandson of Abraham, Afer or Epher, who was thought to have led an army into Africa.[2] A modern work lists ten possibilities, including a Phoenician derivation from their word for "colony." In Roman times Africa was the province in the area around ancient Carthage, which lends support to this idea (Miller 10–12). The Greek name, Libya, was attributed to a granddaughter of Zeus, who in turn produced a granddaughter named Europa, thus implying that Africa was named before its northern neighbor.

---

[1] The most complete account of medieval travelers in Africa is by Charles de la Roncière.
[2] Isidore, *Etymologies* XIV.5 and IX.2. A modern edition is edited by W. M. Lindsay (Oxford: Clarendon, 1911). Afer is mentioned in Genesis 25:4.

The Middle Ages had inherited two schematic diagrams of the known world from Greek geographers, via Roman popular science writers. One was a simple T-O diagram (Figure 1), which as early as the 6th century B.C.E. made visible the separation of the world's three "parts," not yet called continents.[3] The T-O diagram was usually oriented to the east, as the verb implies. Asia was the largest of the three continents, with Europe and Africa dividing the other half of the circle between them. The divisions between the continents were traditionally the Mediterranean, the River Nile, and the River Don/Black Sea complex. While the T-O diagram shows the division of the continents, the world is perceived as a circle, a figure of unity, which transcends the separation. The continental division is unique to European geography. Arab geographers, though they inherited the same Greek tradition, used a model in which the inhabited world was divided into seven climates, and these in turn into ten longitudinal sections.[4]

Although the T-O seems rigidly divided, the boundaries between the continents were far from fixed. Since the Nile split Egypt down the middle, the border between Africa and Asia was commonly moved to the west of the Delta, or even to Catabathmon, placing Egypt in Asia (Sallust XVII.2). Herodotus had proposed that Egypt might be thought of as a fourth part of the world, belonging neither to Asia or Libya, but only to itself, due to its unique character as the creation of the river, as well as the unusual qualities of its civilization (Herodotus II.16). In the first century C.E., Ptolemy protested, "Let us not divide Egypt in making a division of the continents by the Nile, because continents are divided more properly, where it is possible, by seas than by rivers." An Egyptian himself, Ptolemy, alone of ancient writers, placed Egypt in Africa, with the boundary as the isthmus of Suez (Ptolemy II: prologue).

The other model commonly found in medieval European maps is a zonal diagram (Figure 2), according to which the world was divided into five zones: two frigid zones at the poles, a torrid zone at the equator, and temperate zones in between. In this model, North Africa formed part of

---

[3]For a discussion of the idea of the continent and its various permutations, see Lewis and Wigen.

[4]This is the model used by al-Idrisi, a 12th-century geographer at the court of Palermo. It was derived from Ptolemy. See Ahmad 158.

the habitable northern temperate zone, while its southern reaches might extend into the torrid zone, unfriendly to human habitation. Described by such influential classical authors as Virgil, in the *Georgics*, and Macrobius, in his commentary on Scipio's dream, zonal diagrams continued to be drawn alongside the T-O with no sense of contradiction. These two models, T-O and zonal, had influence on more complex geographical representations, the detailed world maps displaying cities, rivers, mountains, and peoples.[5] For the Middle Ages the chief concern was not to alter the traditional forms, but to remember them and fill them with meaning.

Going further south into the torrid zone, Europeans became more vague about what might be found. The names of Ethiopia and India were often interchangeable — we hear of the two or even three Indias and the two Ethiopias — and Asia and Africa were thought to be joined by land. Homer refers to the Ethiopians being divided into two groups, those who live where the sun rises and those who live where the sun goes down (*Odyssey* I.23f). In the *Metamorphoses* of Ovid, the young Phaethon walks from Ethiopia to India, seeking his father, the Sun (I: 777–79). Medieval geographers were equally uncertain.[6] The 11th-century, Anglo-Saxon world map has five references to Ethiopia on it, all strung along the southern edge.[7]

Adding to the confusion was the idea of the four rivers flowing from Paradise. If one of these could be identified with the Nile, as it usually was, and Paradise was in the Far East, then the source of the Nile might be found in Asia (Chatillon 9: 213, 220). Alexander, busy conquering India, thought he had found the source of the Nile in a tributary of the Indus, since it abounded in crocodiles, and had Egyptian beans growing beside it. He was about to equip a fleet to sail to Egypt by means of this

---

[5]Examples of more complex maps being structured according to a zonal model are those of Lambert of St.-Omer (13th century) and the Ripoll map (1055–56). Both are discussed and reproduced in my book, *Mapping Time and Space: How Medieval Mapmakers Viewed Their World* (105–11 and 80–86).

[6]For example Honorius Augustodunensis wrote in his *Imago Mundi* in the 12th century that there was one Ethiopia in the east and one in the west with Garamantes and Troglodytes between. Corpus Christi College, Cambridge, MS 66, p. 15. Text reprinted in Kamal #785.

[7]British Library, Cotton Ms. Tiberius B.V.1, f.56v.

river passage, when he was discouraged to hear that "vast rivers, fearful waters, and first the ocean" intervened (Strabo, *Geography* XV.1.25).

Ptolemy thought that the link between Asia and Africa, which made an enclosed sea of the Indian Ocean, occurred far to the south of the equator, and this configuration was shown on the earliest restored maps accompanying the *Geography* (Ptolemy VII.5; 159). Arab mapmakers, more familiar with the southern seas, did not connect the two continents but extended Africa far to the east, showing the Indian Ocean as a gulf.[8] The land link between Asia and Africa disappeared from European maps only with the Portuguese circumnavigation of Africa in the 15th century. In the Middle Ages the history of the peripatetic Prester John, the mysterious Christian king who would rise to fight the infidels, shows the blurring of the continents as he migrated from Asia to Africa, being identified first with one, then with another, without any real change of character.[9]

The relative size of the continents was also a matter for dispute. Herodotus thought Europe was the largest of the three (IV.42) following Hecateus (500 B.C.) who had divided the world into two parts only: Europe on the one hand, and Asia and Africa on the other (Thrower 19). In the lst century C.E., the Greek geographer Strabo complained that "a threefold division denotes a division into three equal parts," and asserted that Africa was much smaller than the other two (XVII: 275). Pliny thought Europe to be the biggest — and best — of the three, mostly because it contained Rome, the conqueror of the rest (III: 1.2). The classical view was summed up by Strabo, who maintained that Africa was not only inferior in size but also in resources and population. It was hot, mainly desert away from the coast, and the population was scattered and nomadic. Furthermore the whole country was a "nursery for wild beasts" (XVII.3; 275). The Romans of his day possessed all parts of the world worth having, including the Mediterranean coast of Africa. "The

---

[8]For examples on maps, see Harley & Woodward vol. II, book 1, fig. 7. 21, plates 8, 11.
[9]He is identified with Ye-lü Dashi, who defeated the forces of the Seljuk Sultan Sanjar in 1141 by Gumilev (6 and *passim*). Gumilev's theory is based on the account of the 12th-century German historian Otto von Freising. By the 15th century, Portuguese explorers were in Africa looking for the apparently long-lived monarch. For an account of his history and a translation of his supposed letter, see Ross.

rest of the country is uninhabited," he declared, "or the inhabitants lead a miserable and nomadic life" (Strabo XVII.23; 295).[10]

Augustine said that Asia was fully one-half the world, while Europe and Africa divided the other half (Augustine XXVI.17.2), and most medieval Christian authors respectfully followed him. In the 7th century, Isidore of Seville described Asia as stretching "across the east from north to south" (Isidore XIV.2). Placing Egypt in Asia, he divided Africa from it by its western border (Isidore XIV.5). In manuscripts of his work, Isidore's statement is often graphically presented in the form of the T-O diagrams, with which we are already familiar.

Once continents were divided from one another, the next question was what they should contain. A popular medieval geographical illustration was the list map, which showed the contents of the continents: lists of place names, probably an aid to memorization (Figure 3). Here the T-O is a way to sort out categories rather than a literal representation of the world's geography. Another diagram, frequently found in the last chapter of Isidore's *De natura rerum,* organizes a descriptive text into a T-O graph.

For Christians, the tripartite world they had inherited was a felicitous parallel to the division of the earth among the three sons of Noah, progenitors of all the nations of the world. In chapters 9 and 10 of Genesis, where the partition of the world after the Flood and the "confusion of languages" at Babel is described, the text is geographically vague. The discussion is in terms of genealogy or tribes, and the words "Asia, Africa, and Europe" nowhere appear. Where places can be identified, it is obvious that the three sons' inheritances overlap the usual borders of the continents. This picture was simplified in the Middle Ages, with Shem, the eldest son, being usually assigned to Asia, while Ham received Africa and Japhet, Europe.

The earliest Christian source to make the tripartite division is Epiphanius, a bishop of Salamis in Cyprus in the fourth century.[11] He deals with some of the Biblical details by explaining that Ham's son Ca-

---

[10]Most scholarly work on European perceptions of Africa concerns the imperial era. See Schwartz, who includes a section on the late medieval period.

[11]There is some confusion and overlapping between Asia and Africa (see *The Panarion of St. Epiphanius* 241–42).

naan, being discontented with the torrid land in Africa that fell to his lot, invaded Palestine and took it wrongfully from his cousins. He proceeded to beget a number of bad guys, such as the Philistines and the Amorites. In the time of Joshua, the descendants of Shem rightfully reclaimed their own, the walls of Jericho falling by the will of God. By the 9th century, Alcuin had reduced the division to a soundbite. In his "Questions and Answers on Genesis," he writes, "Question. How was the world divided by the sons and grandsons of Noah? Answer. Shem, as it is reckoned, received Asia as his share, Cham Africa, and Japhet Europe" (100, col. 532).

A T-O map, showing the division of the earth among the sons, appears in many manuscripts of Isidore's *Etymologies,* though Isidore himself does not describe this division. It became a standard of medieval cartography, often structuring larger, more complex maps and entering into common discourse. We see Noah's sons posed around the world map of the *Nuremberg Chronicle* (Figure 4), published in 1492, on the eve of Columbus's discovery of new lands that would not fit into the neat three-part division.

Variant traditions, however, continued to survive throughout the Middle Ages. Shem and Cham were sometimes interchanged, possibly due to the similarity of their names; Cham was also occasionally conflated with Cain, as the two bad boys of Genesis. One of the most well-known proponents of an alternate tradition was John de Mandeville, whose *Travels* were a best-seller of the 14th century. In one version of his book we learn, to our surprise, that Shem received Africa as his inheritance, while Ham (Cham) got Asia. The great Khan of the Mongols, Mandeville says, was called "the Grand Cham," because of his ancestor (138).

The continents were also defined by their climates. Traditionally Asia was temperate, Africa torrid, and Europe frigid, corresponding to the conventions of the zonal division of the earth. This was an oversimplification, of course, but so was the T-O diagram. These climates were not neutral: Shem's inheritance was thought to be superior to the extreme climates inhabited by his brothers' descendants. Paradise was also found in the east, in the portion allotted to Shem. The theory that climate was a determinant of character — i.e., that those living in tropical climates were indolent, while denizens of the north were energetic — was not a commonplace of the Middle Ages. We find the idea in the late 14th century *Muqaddimah* of Ibn Khaldun, who equates temperance of climate with temperance of character. The Africans of the equatorial zone, as well as the Slavic peoples of the north, he says, are equally removed from the temperate zones, which "produces in them a disposition and character similar to those of the dumb animals, and they become correspondingly remote from humanity" (Ibn Khaldun i: 168–69). In Europe the thesis achieves its fullest development in Montesquieu's *Spirit of the Laws*, where it passed for scientific thought and exercised great influence as an explanation of Europeans' self-perceived cultural superiority (IXV.2).

The continents were not distinguished by race in the Middle Ages (Braude 116). The Africans with which Europeans were most familiar were those of the coast, who looked much like their Mediterranean brothers and sisters. It is noteworthy that many of the early geographical authorities were in fact African: St. Augustine, Macrobius, Ptolemy. The dark skins of those living in the torrid zone — the Ethiopians, or sunburnt ones — were remarked upon, and various theories developed to account for the phenomenon, but "Ethiopians" could be found in Asia as well as Africa. In the *Marvels of the East,* an early medieval text that circulated in illustrated form, one of the marvels of "Asia" was the black-skinned Ethiopians.[12] Only after the European exploration of the West African coast began in the 14th century were the people of Africa categorized as black. The three-sons-of-Noah theory of the origins of the human race implied that everyone was at least related, and physical differences were no more than the accidental variants between members of one family.

In addition, the migration of people from continent to continent blurred any divisions that might have been proposed. In mythological times (the days of Hercules), Medes, Persians and Armenians had settled in Africa, where they became the Moors and the Numidians, according to the Roman historian Sallust. In historical times the Phoenicians came from Asia to conquer the north African coast and establish the city of

---

[12]British Library, Cotton MS Tiberius B.V., Part I, f. 86.

Carthage. They also landed in Spain and Sicily, while Greeks sent colonies to Egypt and Libya. The great Arab empires stretched from Asia through Africa to western Europe, and during the Middle Ages several major assaults on Spain originated in Africa, each one leaving people behind.

As trade revived in European cities, the Genoese, Pisans, and Catalans set up trading stations in Africa, while the Aragonese had designs on an African coastal empire. The islands of the Mediterranean were ruled first by Romans, then the Byzantines, the Arabs, the Normans, and the Spanish. This complex political and economic history meant that the two continents were in constant communication, if often in the form of altercation, especially over the narrow straits at Gibraltar and Sicily.[13] Here languages, cultures, and races mixed and could not be separated into handy compartments.

North Africa was depicted on medieval maps as similar to the rest of the Mediterranean area, as we see on the Hereford Cathedral map of 1285. But, around the fringes of the world — to the north, south, and east, especially in extreme climates — Europeans believed, or hoped, that people very different from themselves dwelt. From Herodotus onward there was a tradition of savage tribes with shocking customs — cannibalism, nudity, and free love — or alternatively races of philosophers and those who lived in unnatural harmony. Homer had distinguished the Ethiopians, both by their remoteness and their unusually law-abiding nature. Pliny's catalog of exotic races in Africa included the Atlas tribe who had no names and never dreamed, the Troglodytes who lived in caves, dined on snakes, and had no voices but made squeaking noises. Even stranger were those of variant physical form: the Blemmyae who had no heads and whose eyes and mouths were in their chests; and the Strapfoots who had feet like leather thongs and crawled instead of walking. Tales of these folk continued to be salaciously relayed in geographies and travel accounts for centuries, and their interesting images appeared on maps as a sort of geo-porn (see Friedman). Some, such as the pygmies, were found to have been based in reality. The same is true of the Ascii, who spookily cast no shadows. Roger Bacon explained that

---

[13]An excellent account of these political vicissitudes can be found in Phillips 143–63.

this was because they lived on the equator with the sun directly overhead (i: 305–06).[14]

Such marvels were not confined to Africa, but appeared around all the world's edges. Alexander's travels had made the Western world aware of the wonders to be found in India. Isidore describes as denizens of India the Cynocephali, or dog heads, and the Cyclops with their single eye (XI.3). He assigned the headless Blemmyae to Africa, while in the far east dwelt noseless people, those with an upper lip so large as to cover their faces, and those who had such small mouths that they had to receive nourishment through straws. In the north, particularly around Scythia, the adventurous traveler might find Hippopodes, who had horses' hooves for feet, and the Panotii who could wrap their enormous ears around their bodies. But it was also the land of the Hyperboreans, who lived lives of great happiness and in such good health that they did not die until they felt they had lived long enough. At this point it was their custom to dive off a high cliff into the sea. Isidore observes sagely that some monsters are only inventions (unlike the real monsters just described). These include the three-headed Geryon encountered by Hercules in Spain, and the harpies who were part woman and part bird (XI.28–30). He thought they were still useful for allegorical purposes; the three heads of Cerberus, for example, represented infancy, youth, and old age (XI.33).

Rare and interesting animals could also be found far from home. Elephants, camels, and ostriches mix comfortably on the Hereford Cathedral map with manticores, unicorns, griffons, and two-headed goats. Precious stones, aromatic incense, ferocious beasts, and poisonous serpents lurked in out-of-the-way places. Sub-Saharan Africa, the supplier of wild beasts for the Roman games, became the theoretical home to still more bizarre varieties from the animal kingdom.[15] Gold and ivory were also drawn from this region by lengthy and torturous trade routes, inspiring 14th-century merchant adventurers to undertake ambitious voyages.

---

[14]Bacon's work is from the 13th century.

[15]The bestiaries included a number of animals from "Ethiopia," such as the dog-heads (perhaps a type of monkey), the dragon or serpent, and the yale or eale with its long flexible horns. See *The Bestiary* (*passim*).

On a very large and detailed map like the one from Hereford Cathedral of 1285 the full riches of the world of monsters and marvels can be seen. They showed little attachment to a single region, but cropped up here and there. The Sciopods, for example, noted for their great single foot, which shaded them from the sun, are placed on the fourth, southern continent in one famous medieval map,[16] but on the Hereford map, they appear in northeast Asia. Islands off remote coasts were another good location for monstrosities, which helped explain why they were so seldom seen by reliable sources. In our own day, they have moved to planets of our own and other solar systems, where their existence is occasionally reported in the tabloid press. Human delight in these monsters, mixed with an agreeable frisson of horror, endures.

In the early modern period, medieval polyphony[17] on the subject of Africa was to come to an end. Printing established canonical texts, while 15th-century voyages brought back contemporary eye-witness accounts to replace the two-thousand-year-old tales of Alexander. Clearer, or harsher, categories decreed that a person must be one race or another, that continents and countries must have defined borders, that something cannot be both A and not-A at the same time. Monsters retreated to increasingly remote regions — the Abominable Snowman of the Himalayas — and sections of the map filled up with physically verifiable features, replacing mythical towns and kingdoms.

It was the end of certain pleasing fantasies. In the 12th century, a letter circulated through Western Europe, purported to emanate from the "Emperor of Ethiopia," Prester John. Almost certainly a European forgery, it describes his kingdom as a dream-world of not-Europe, richer, more wonderful:

> Honey flows in our land, and milk everywhere abounds. In one region there are no poisonous beasts and no noisy frog croaks, no scorpions are there, and no serpents creeping in the grass. . . . Flattery finds no place; there is no division among us; our people have abundance of wealth. . . . The chamber in which our sublimity reposes is marvellously decorated

---

[16]This is the map accompanying St. Beatus's *Commentary on the Apocalypse*, now at the Cathedral of Burgo de Osma in Spain.
[17]The felicitous phrase is Braude's.

with gold and precious stones of every kind. . . . The [dinner] table made of the most precious emeralds is supported by four amethyst pillars; by virtue of which stone, no person sitting at the table can become inebriated. . . . If indeed you can number the stars of heaven and the sands of the sea, then you may calculate the extent of our dominion and power. (Ross 174–78)

References

Ahmad, S. Maqbul. "Cartography of al-Sharif al-Idrisi." *Cartography Is the Traditional Islamic and South Asian Societies, History of Cartography.* Vol. 2, Book 1. Ed. J. B. Harley and David Woodward. Chicago: U of Chicago P, 1992. 156–74.

Alcuin. "Interrogationes et Responsiones in Genesin." *Patrologia Latina.* Vol. 100. Ed. J. R. Migne. Paris, 1844–99.

Augustine. *City of God.* Ed. and trans. R. W. Dyson. Cambridge: Cambridge UP, 1998.

Bacon, Roger. *Opus Majus.* Ed. John Henry Bridges. Frankfurt-am-Main: Minerva, 1964.

The Bestiary. Trans. T. H. White. New York: Putnam, 1954.

Braude, Benjamin. "The Sons of Noah and the Construction of Ethnic and Geographical Identities in the Medieval and Early Modern Periods." *William and Mary Quarterly* 3d ser. 54.1 (Jan. 1997): 103–42.

Chatillon, Gautier de. *Alexandreis.* Trans. R. Relfryn Pritchard. Toronto: Pontifical Institute of Medieval Studies, 1986.

Edson, Evelyn. *Mapping Time and Space: How Medieval Mapmakers Viewed Their World.* London: British Library, 1997.

Friedman, John B. *The Monstrous Races in Medieval Art and Thought.* Cambridge, MA: Harvard UP, 1981.

Gumilev, L. N. *Searches for an Imaginary Kingdom: The Legend of the Kingdom of Prester John.* Cambridge: Cambridge UP, 1987.

Harley, J. Brian, and David Woodward, eds. *History of Cartography.* Chicago: U of Chicago P, 1987 et seq.

Herodotus. *The Histories.* Trans. Aubrey de Selincourt. London: Penguin, 1972.

Ibn Khaldun. *The Muqaddimah: An Introduction to History.* Trans. Franz Rosenthal. New York: Pantheon, 1958.

Isidore. *Etymologies.* Trans. W. M. Lindsay. Oxford: Claredon P, 1911. 2 vols.

Kamal, Prince Youssouf. *Monumenta cartographica Africae et Aegypti.* Cairo, 1926–51.

Lewis, Martin W., and Kären E. Wigen. *The Myth of Continents: A Critique of Metageography.* Berkeley: U of California P, 1997.

Mandeville, Sir John. *Voyages and Travels.* Ed. Arthur Layard. New York: Appleton, 1899.

Miller, Christopher. *Blank Darkness: Africanist Discourse in French*. Chicago: U of Chicago P, 1985.

Montesquieu, Charles Secondat, Baron de. *Spirit of the Laws*. Trans. Thomas Nugent. New York: Hafner, 1949.

Ovid. *Metamorphoses*. Loeb Classical Library, vols. 42–43. erd ed. Cambridge, MA: Harvard UP, 1977.

The Panarion of St. Epiphanius. Trans. Philip R. Amidon. Oxford: Oxford UP, 1990.

Phillips, J. R. S. *The Medieval Expansion of Europe*. Oxford: Oxford UP, 1988.

Pliny. *Natural History*. Trans. H. Rackham. Cambridge: Harvard UP, 1949. 10 vols.

Ptolemy, Claudius. *The Geography*. Trans. and ed. Edward L. Stevenson. 1932. New York: Dover Books, 1991.

Roncière, Chalres de la. *La Découverte d'Afrique au moyen âge: Cartographes et explorateurs*. Cairo: Société Royale de Géographie d'Égypte, 1925. 2 vols.

Ross, E. Denison. "Prester John and the Empire of Ethiopia." *Travel and Travellers of the Middle Ages*. Ed. A. P. Newton. New York: Barnes & Noble, 1968. 174–94.

Sallust. *Jugurthine War/The Conspiracy of Catiline*. Trans. S. A. Handford. London: Penguin, 1980.

Schwartz, Stuart B., ed., *Implicit Understandings: Observing, Reporting, and Reflecting on the Encounters between Europeans and Other Peoples in the Early Modern Era*. Cambridge: Cambridge UP, 1994.

Strabo. *Geography*. Trans. H. L. Jones. Cambridge: MA: Harvard UP, 1983–1989. 8 vols.

Thrower, Norman J. W. *Maps and Civilization*. Rev. ed. Chicago: U of Chicago P, 1996.

Figure 1. The T-O diagram was a schematic representation of the inhabited earth known to medieval Europeans. Reduced to its simplest form, it showed only the three continents, divided by bodies of water and surrounded by the Ocean. 11th century. Bodleian Library, MS Auct.F.2.20, f. 16 (Isidore, *De natura rerum*). By permission of the Bodleian Library.

Figure 2. The zone diagram showed half the globe of the earth, including the southern hemisphere, divided into five climatic zones. This illustration, from Macrobius's *Commentary on Scipio's Dream,* shows the northern hemisphere divided from the southern by an equatorial ocean. The inscription around the rim refers to the tides. 11th century. 120 mm. in diameter. Bodleian Library, MS D'Orville 77, f.100r. By permission of the Bodleian Library.

Figure 3. The list map is an elaboration of the simple T-O. Here the three continents are filled with the names of peoples and places. English, c. 1265, 90 mm. in diameter. "Psalter map," British Library, Add MS 28,241, f. 9v. By permission of the British Library.

Figure 4. World map with the sons of Noah, from the Nuremberg Chronicle. This map shows the enclosed Indian Ocean and the southern link between Africa and Asia common to Ptolemy maps of the 15th century. German, 1493. 44 x 31 cm. Second Age of the World, Nuremberg Chronicle. From the collection of Eric W. Wolf.

AFRICA AND AFRICANS IN THE
IMAGINATION OF RENAISSANCE ITALIANS

John Brackett
University of Cincinnati

Several years ago, during one of my Summer stays in Florence, I happened to be watching a television commercial for some food product that utilized a cartoon-style setting of Africa and Africans which so caricatured the physical and geographical differences between Africa and black Africans on one hand, and Italy and Italians on the other, that I remember thinking, "This is little black Sambo all over again; they couldn't get away with this today in the United States!" There was the little black African figure of my youth — complete with his very black skin, curly hair, and super thick lips — running around in his little village, set in an African landscape, denoted by a couple of palm trees and a grass hut. What was so offensive about the Sambo image was the primitiveness connoted by his very black skin, the exaggerated physical features, and the poor quality of the imagined material civilization of Africa itself.[1] Later on I was set to thinking about other African presences that I had encountered since first coming to Italy in 1982 for dissertation research: I recalled the tall African women I had seen in the streets of Florence at times, obviously models, beautiful but different; I recalled the West African men of Florence, the famous "vu cumpra," whose importunity plagues tourist and native alike, regardless of color. It occurred to me, despite the stark physical differences between Italians and black Africans (one might also include Somalis and Ethiopians but they, as brown-skinned people, seem somehow more acculturable), and the primitive exoticism exemplified in the cartoon commercial (and by the

---

[1] Roberts 2–3. Although the main black representation dealt with by Roberts is female, the issue of representations of the black body as "grotesque" in the Bahktinian sense, holds true for representations of the black male body as well. "Sambo" is noted as an example by the author. At issue is the depiction of Africans as "other," as degraded, i.e., in this case, under-sized, protuberant and incomplete; missing are intelligence and civilization.

models), that this was all innocent somehow, devoid of actual degradation or hatred in the Italian context, when compared with the United States or certain other countries of Europe.

The origins of this article are in reflections on personal experience, but these recollections become historical in seeking some roots of modern Italian images of Africa and Africans in the Renaissance, as very distinct from Europeans, as exotic and even in some cases devoid of material civilization, but not on the whole denigrated and marginalized, stripped of basic humanity. Without question, much of this difference is tied to the existence of slavery in the United States, and the colonial presence in Africa of other European countries. In Italy, little black Sambo is not quite the trenchant image it is in the United States, with its different racial history.[2]

Time-traveling back to the fifteenth and sixteenth centuries means that we must leave behind much contemporary mental baggage. The Renaissance is perhaps best defined as a grouping of transitional moments leading to the formation of the modern, distinct from the medieval: for example, between the emergence of nascent national identities — of "peoples" defined through sharing the same historical experiences, the same language, the same political space, the same skin color — as opposed to a primary group definition by religion and local culture. Except in a cultural sense, there were no Italian *people* then but many Italian *peoples*, or "razze." The Florentines were different and better than the Pistoians, the Pisans, and the Sienese. They spoke different languages and lived according to local traditions — they shared the peninsula and

---

[2]George's concern in "The Civilized West Looks at Primitive Africa, 1400–1800" is to use the African example to explain the operation of *ethnocentrism* in Europe over time. For the fifteenth century, she avails herself of the same sources that I will use, the recollections of Cadamosto and the Malfante letter, both discussed further ahead. These are the only Italian sources for this period. My intention is to test for a localized Italian outlook that is combined with the more generally discernible European features of an outlook based on the Classics and Christianity. In any case, I have always found the concept of ethnocentrism to be a rather blunt instrument for getting at ways of viewing the "Other" from any societal perspective. George's use of evidence is highly selective, and, as we will see below, leaves out a number of observations that, when taken into consideration, provide a more nuanced understanding of the reactions of these two Italians to Africa and Africans than does the clumsy concept of ethnocentrism.

the Christian religion; apart from the Venetians, they were known to each other primarily by narrow groupings of negative characteristics. On the other hand, Renaissance humanism was opening the door to a special sense of group derived from an historical connection to classical Rome. Likewise, there was no single Africa and no African identity. In focussing on Africa and Africans in the imagination of Renaissance Italians we must recognize that geographically there were a number of Africas, peopled with many types of African peoples colored from brown, or white, to black; and that to a great extent the sources of knowledge drawn upon by Italians to understand these lands and their peoples were a combination of learned books of great authority (Classical and Christian), medieval travel literature, maps of various types, and personal experience, real or claimed, all shared with some other literate and well traveled Europeans. Often the personal experiences of Italians were had in the service of non Italians, the Spanish and Portuguese, principally, and those who decided to share this knowledge intended to share it with interested readers of any "nationality." There existed a common European *canon*, then, limited to a literate "international" elite, which was accompanied by the experiences of increasingly large numbers of adventurous sailors and merchants.

For my purposes I will focus on two Italian merchant-adventurers of the fifteenth century, the well known Alvise da Ca' da Mosto, or Cadamosto, a Venetian, and Antonio Malfante, about whom, deplorably, we know nothing. Cadamosto's account of his two voyages along the coast of West Africa, made in 1454, were first published in 1507 in Vicenza in the collection, *Paesi novamente retrovati*. Malfante's brief letter of a trip to West Africa, dated 1447, written to a Genoese, Giovanni Moriano, was brought to light by M. Charles De La Ronciere in 1919 (see Crone). Cadamosto's voyage was by sea in the service of the Portuguese, while Malfante journeyed by land across the Sahara and back, apparently on his own commission. Both visited Africa primarily as traders, though we will see that Cadamosto also saw himself as an explorer. These were not the only Renaissance Italians to travel to Africa: Both mention encounters with others who preceded them or came after, nor are they the best known chroniclers of things African to write primarily for Italians. The Christianized Moor, Leo Africanus, is probably the best known and most celebrated author, but all three were Renaissance men, literate and learned in classical geography, and concerned with fame — combining erudition and experience to reach their conclusions.[3]

How did they organize their impressions, according to what principles? Stephen Greenblatt in his, *Marvelous Possessions The Wonder of the New World*, sets out to examine what he calls the "representational technology" of Europeans in the Renaissance, also in his words, a "lumbering jerry-built" mimetic machinery, rather than a smooth functioning tool (23). Greenblatt's purpose is not to distinguish truth from fiction in the narratives of Columbus, primarily, since he argues that Europeans learned nothing about the Amerindians, but to elucidate the mental structure that the explorers used to organize their perceptions of the Americas and its peoples. The elements of this technology were: Christianity and classical learning, both powerfully linked to the imagination through a particular sense of wonder. Wonder at the unknown, for Aristotle and Albertus Magnus, preceded knowledge. Greenblatt was smart enough not to attempt a definition of imagination, and I don't know that it can be defined except by association, through what it allows consciousness to do in organizing perceptions of the world for us in a dreaming or waking state. Imagination is likely the fundamental creative property of consciousness that makes arrangements of systems of knowledge, and the development of emotions possible in great variety.[4]

---

[3]Greenblatt and Todorov both discuss the learned classical and medieval sources for what was known of the world's geography and its peoples (and other beings), mythical and real. This knowledge was common to many travelers; it was part of Cadamosto's education, and was likely familiar to Malfante as well.

[4]Any attempt to define imagination and its workings means attempting to grapple with the more fundamental question of how the mind works. Very simply, *Webster's New Encyclopedic Dictionary* defines "imagination" primarily as, "the act or power of forming a mental image of something not present to the senses or never before wholly perceived in reality." This exactly conforms to what *The Oxford Companion to the Mind* categorizes as "imaging." Further, in the section entitled "Artificial Intelligence" (dedicated to the use of computers to better understand how the mind works), the *OCM* defines "*representation*" as its main theoretical concept, i.e., ". . . how a (programmed) system constructs, adapts, and uses its inner representations in interpreting — and changing — its world. In focussing on geographic images and images of the races of man, the focus is on the origins and stocking of material that is acquired through experience and, up to the Renaissance, reading, along with perhaps viewing some art.

At least, this is what I take from the opening lines of the "Preface" of Foucault's, *The Order of Things,* where he briefly discusses a passage from Borges regarding the arrangement of knowledge in a "certain" Chinese encyclopedia which seems to make no sense to Europeans (xv). My interest is epistemological: What can we know about the representational technology of Renaissance Italians as they applied it to Africa and Africans? If wonder seems much less apparent in Cadamosto and Malfante than Greenblatt argues was the case with Columbus and others in their encounters with the Americas, perhaps that is because *something* was "known" about Africa and Africans to Italians, and this knowledge had been long-standing. Before Columbus, nothing was known to Europeans of the Americas or of their inhabitants.

In the fifteenth century, the geographical *Africa* that Europeans knew from ancient authorities like Ptolemy, and recent experience, was limited to the continent's north coast, and was often alternatively called Libya. Libya extended indeterminately southwards, disappearing into the Sahara, west to the Straits of Gibraltar, and east to Egypt (Thrower 23–24).[5] Below Egypt was Abyssinia (Ethiopia, alternatively), the land of the blacks according to ancient sources like Herodotus, Pliny, and Ptolemy. It is pictured in a 1486 version of Ptolemy's world map printed in Ulm, extending below "Affrica" to meet the Atlantic (Thrower 61). J. H. Plumb wrote that:

> in 1698 William III decided that it was time to have geography taught to William, Duke of Gloucester — the only surviving son of Princess Anne — and a series of maps of simplicity and clarity were especially drawn for the purpose. One was devoted to Africa. The Niger, rising in a great lake close to the Nile, runs in a thick bold line, straight to the Atlantic; two great inland oceans, near the Zambesi, provide the headwaters of the Nile: Congoland is there, but no Congo. The center of Africa is empty; its emptiness distinguished with three names largely and beautifully printed — Negroland, Nubia, Abisinia: the space between them is dotted with little brown, fluffy mountains. . . . In essence, the map is the

---

[5]Claudius Ptolemy was the second century librarian at Alexandria. Though it is not known whether he made maps himself, he was the ultimate cartographic authority right up to the Renaissance.

same map that Leo Africanus described for Pope Leo X in the early 16th century. (Howard 1)

By 1507, in a world map produced by Martin Waldseemuller, we can see the benefits of the Portuguese circumnavigation of the African continent in that the coast, at least, is pictured in substantial detail (Thrower 72–73). Little would be known about the interior before the nineteenth century because of the prevalence of disease, and the defense made by Africans against European penetration. Cadamosto mentions being forced out of the Gambia River because some of his sailors had sickened with fever (Crone 73). In another instance, his caravel was forced out of the Gambia River after a battle with armed blacks determined not to let them pass (Crone 58–59). The heat was another barrier to exploration. Cadamosto wrote of Mali that it was too hot for horses, and the pasturage very unsuitable for four-footed animals in general. He said that of the majority of animals coming to Mali by caravan no more than 25 out of 100 returned. Human beings suffered as well: the Arabs and the Tuaregs also died of the great heat which caused the blood to putrefy. Salt was the only remedy for people, hence its great value as a trade item for gold with the blacks from further south (Crone 21).

The voyages along the West African coast settled a longstanding climatological dispute between the likes of Aristotle and St. Augustine, and Avicenna, among others, as to whether the extreme heat of the equatorial zone would allow life forms to spread to inhabit the southern zones of the world: Aristotle said no, Avicenna yes. Knowledge gained from the experiences of explorers proved the latter correct. Aristotle had advanced the idea of a spherical earth with frozen northern and southern caps, with temperate zones extending towards a centerline, the equator, with the heat increasing steadily as one approached the earth's dividing line. That zone he argued was too hot for life to survive in it, thus it was reasonable to argue that life forms migrating north to south would not have been able to traverse the equatorial zone to establish themselves in the south. Cadamosto and his compatriots established that the equatorial zones were temperate, not so hot as to be hostile to life.[6]

---

[6]Grafton, Shelford, and Siraisi 1. Here, Grafton cites the recollection of the Jesuit Jose de

During the Renaissance actual knowledge of the continent began to replace the many errors of ancient erudition, though, as is characteristic of that period, the old continued to overlap the new. In the early sixteenth century, Leo Africanus published the record of his travels in Africa, presenting better knowledge of the interior of West Africa, its kingdoms and its peoples, than Europeans had previously possessed. Better knowledge of Africa's interior would only really begin to advance significantly beyond that point in the years immediately following the end of the Second World War. As Grafton says, tradition continued to hold the center of European systems of knowledge. But what about the human inhabitants of Africa? How were they alike or different from the Italians, in terms of their appearance, behavior, and level of civilization?

From antiquity through the middle ages, the Earth was believed to be populated by "monstrous," unusual races of men (Friedman 1). Some took their names from their manner of life, such as the Apple-Smellers (who had no mouths to eat with), or the Troglodytes, who lived in caves somewhere in the interior of Africa; some were physically unusual such as Pygmies (who also were believed indigenous to interior Africa) and Giants (some examples of whom inhabited Africa), or completely fabulous, such as the Blemmyae or men with faces on their chests — also native to Africa. These beings were always far away, in Ethiopia (confused by Pliny with India), for example, and in Africa.

Clearly, while all African peoples were not monstrous, as the Romans had known, and as Italians knew from their business dealings with the North of Africa, Africa was still held to be home to certain of these beings. In Africa the learned and travelers found a mixture in uncertain proportions of the familiar, the fantastic, the misunderstood, and the unknown.[7] What was the family of human beings, though? Seemingly,

---

Acosta: "I will describe what happened to me when I passed to the Indies. Having read what poets and philosophers write of the Torrid Zone, I persuaded myself that when I came to the Equator, I would not be able to endure the violent heat, but it turned out otherwise. For when I passed [the Equator], which was when the sun was at its zenith there, having entered the zodiacal sign of Aries, in March, I felt so cold that I was forced to go into the sun to warm myself. What could I do but laugh at Aristotle's *Meteorology* and his philosophy? For in that place and that season, where everything, by his rules, should have been scorched by the heat, I and my companions were cold."

[7]Friedman writes that much of what Pliny The Elder (d.79 AD) wrote in his *Natural*

mankind was composed of beings arrayed along a spectrum from normal to monstrous, with an unclear line between the human and the animal. This is the origin of the action of a party of British hunters in Namibia in the nineteenth century, famously reported by Stephen J. Gould, who shot, cooked and ate a Hottentot. One criterion of judgment was diet: in the works of some Greek and Roman travel-writers, peoples are named by a particular item of food, e.g., the Apple-smellers, the Dog-milkers (in Ethiopia), the Fish-eaters of the coast of Ethiopia (Friedman 27–29). Other criteria were related to the presumed lack of speech, or the difficulty for Greeks and Romans of hearing and pronouncing foreign speech. Other marks were an existence outside of a city setting, the use of inferior military technology exemplified by carrying a club as a sole weapon, and cannibalism.

In the fifteenth century, climate was still believed to have been primarily responsible for causing the differences between human beings, who had all been created by God, after all. Differences in skin color, especially, were attributable to adaptations to greater or lesser intensities of heat. The skin of blacks was that color because it was burned that color by the heat; the name *Ethiopia* means "burned faces" in ancient Greek. If blacks were transferred from Africa to Europe, for example, within a couple of generations they would be indistinguishable from whites. But as long as they lived in the extremes of climate these extremes — of heat, for example — would lead to behavior that was brutish or uncivilized in various ways.

It was also common in the Christian tradition to connect the benighted races with the biblical Cain, as their first parent (Friedman 31). For Africans this meant that their black skins were a sign of their descent from Cain, and thus of their inferior inherited moral status. When encountered, therefore, the European could expect the black African to behave in an uncivilized fashion, with an appearance that reflected their depraved inner condition (54).

To this point we have been examining the universe of the learned man familiar with the written sources of erudition, but this is only half of

---

Histories about Africa was fairly accurate, since he had access to the *formulae provinciarum* or Senate documents relating to various countries (7).

the knowledge carried to Africa by merchant-adventurers like Cadamosto and Malfante. They also possessed the empirical knowledge of the mariners and merchants who preceded them in Africa. Malfante especially would have been familiar with records of routes and maps of North Africa, which discussed places and peoples. He might have known, for example, *The Sphere*, a treatise that circulated widely in the fifteenth century, written by the Florentine businessman Gregorio Dati, the fourth section of which lays out travel routes in North Africa (Grafton, Shelford, and Siraisi 66). Cadamosto sailed in modern ships equipped with the inventions which had revolutionized maritime travel in that period. In making their judgments about Africans, then, they were not bound by a representational apparatus linked only to Classical and Christian erudition but their minds were also opened by virtue of practical experience.

Let us now take a closer look at the experiences of these two fifteenth century Italians, coming by very different routes to Africa. Italy from the high middle ages on was a leader in navigation, map-making and trade in Europe. Italians were among the first southern Europeans to engage North African Arabs and Berbers in trade. Alvise da Ca' Da Mosto, at age twenty-two, claimed to have been the first Venetian to have sailed beyond the Straits of Gibraltar, and down the coast of West Africa. His family, though originally from Lodi, obtained sufficient standing for admission to Venice's most representative republican institution, the *Consiglio Maggiore*. Alvise had extensive service aboard ships, sailing in the Mediterranean, and out to Flanders and back. Family troubles in Venice forced him to leave the city with his brother, and seek a career in Portugal, in the service of Prince Henry the Navigator (1394–1460) (Crone xxx–xxxi). Later in life, after his period of travel to Africa had ended, Alvise held a number of minor offices in Venice; he was Governor of the fortress at Corone in Morea, and died on an embassy to Rovigo in 1483. Though we have no direct evidence of his education, his writings and his service, as well as the status of his family, attest to a very high level of education. His travels would have been prepared with a reading of the classical travel writers. Cadamosto's accounts are controversial in that there is some doubt that he actually made the second of his two claimed voyages; he may have simply added his name to the record of a Portuguese explorer known to have been in the same areas at about the same time. We cannot resolve that issue here but it can be said that there seems to be as much evidence to support the authenticity of his accounts as to doubt them (xlii).

In general, Cadamosto commented on his observations of the land and its products, the climate, as well as the people and their customs, as he observed them. His commentary begins with a description of the Canary Islands, from which he wrote that he set sail "... from this island making due south towards Ethiopia ..." (Crone 14). Arriving at Capo Bianco, 570 miles away, Cadamosto notes that this region was not:

> inhabited by these Barbari except as far as the Cape Cantin. . . . From this cape along the coast to Capo Bianco commences the sandy country which is the desert that ranges on its northern confines with the mountains, which cut off our Barbary from Tunis . . . on the south it marches with the Blacks of lower Ethiopia. (15)

For Cadamosto, Ethiopia extended below Africa to the west coast. Ethiopia had been known from ancient times as a juxtaposition of contradictory images: as a sunburnt land whose inhabitants were so vexed by the heat that they cursed the sun when it arose each day; as home to several varieties of the monstrous races of men; as home to a branch of Christianity whose adherents maintained official relations with the Vatican; as the likely kingdom of the mysterious Prester John. Some of the first people encountered were the desert dwelling Tuaregs, brown, not black, in skin color, however, who were Muslims. If this was a shock, Cadamosto does not register it but he was not a believer in Prester John that I can tell, though he does express the hope for the conversion of these Muslims to Christianity. He observed that the inhabitants drank camel milk, and the milk of other animals because they had no wine but this does not seem to have triggered in him any repulsion whatsoever, which could have been linked to the food taboos mentioned above (16). Cadamosto may have been more adventurous than most in this respect, since he reports having eaten and liked Ostrich eggs! He notes the progress of the rapidly developing slave trade, the shades of brown of the people, and that he has yet to reach the "First Kingdom of the Blacks"

(18). As a parting judgment he notes that they have no political order, and that:

> They are very poor people, liars, the biggest thieves in the world, and exceedingly treacherous. They are men of average height, and spare. They wear their hair in locks down to their shoulders, almost in the German fashion — but their hair is black, and anointed every day with fish oil, so that it smells strongly, the which they consider a great refinement. (19)

On this occasion, Cadamosto adhered to the established practice of linking physical appearance and perhaps poverty with bad character.

Cadamosto next encountered certain people of Mali (southern Mauritania), blacks who were engaged in the salt-gold trade with mysterious and fantastic blacks still further to the south, likely the Lobi people. He recounts an incident from the past when the Emperor of Mali put into action a plan to learn more about the silent people with whom he engaged in the gold trade. He set some of his warriors to go early to the place of exchange, hide until these men arrived with their gold, then capture one and interrogate him about his people. The trap successfully produced one captive, who, after refusing to eat or to speak with his captives, died within four days, leaving the emperor in his previous ignorance. These people were reportedly well made but possessed a facial disfigurement — an enlarged lower lip that Cadamosto wrote hung down to their breasts, exposing their gums and teeth. It was three years before the trade resumed with these southern blacks, during which time the people relating this story to Alvise had to live without their gold. Likewise, the gold traders suffered sickness and death from the putrification of the enlarged lower lip for the same three years, before being forced to renew the trade to obtain salt. Upon hearing this story related to him, Cadamosto states, "This is what I understood from this incident, and since it is related by so many we can accept it. Because I have seen and understood such things in the world, I am one of those who are willing to believe this and other matters to be possible" (25). Alvise felt the need to justify his acceptance of the truth of this story because he was making his own contribution to the travel literature category of the strange and fabulous. These gold-bearing blacks, with the enlarged lower lip, the exposed blood red gums and teeth, their refusal or inability to speak, their general timidity, even the fact that they died from lack of salt, fit the mold of the other monstrous races of Africa. Though he had not seen them himself, he continues the medieval tradition of being willing to sustain the accuracy of hearsay evidence by citing the number of people who had heard the same story. He buttresses the call for the belief of his readers based on his own experience of the world, that he has seen for himself strange, perhaps wondrous, things in his travels. This raises the question of identity at the extremes of distance from home; Alvise does not fall back on his education, his class, or his Venetian citizenship but on his individual experience of the world, experience that he shared with men of even low birth and station, which trumps other forms of authority, as it establishes him as a *man of the world* whose sense of self, like that of Leo Africanus, comes to transcend narrow cultural definitions.[8] The man who encounters the Other far from home is transformed by the experience, lifted up from the level of a mere provincial entity to a broader plane of existence.

Cadamosto's ships then pass down the coast to the Senegal River, which he believes to be a branch of the Nile flowing through all of Ethiopia, and which commences the land of the blacks. He marvels that south of the Senegal the men are all very black, with well formed bodies, living in a fertile green land with trees, while those to the north are small, brown, and live in desert conditions. Alvise encounters the Wolof people of Senegal, about whom he records a number of observations. Theirs was a true kingdom, even though its kingship did not descend by inheritance, with lords below the king. However, the king ruled over a "... very poor people, and has no city in his country, but villages with huts of straw only" (Crone 29). His assessment of the economy is accu-

---

[8]Maalouf 1. This version of Leo's personal accounts opens with these words: "I, Hasan the son of Muhammad the weight-master, I, Jean-Leon de Medici, circumcised at the hand of a barber and baptized at the hand of a pope, I am now called the African, but I am not from Africa, nor from Europe, nor from Arabia. I am also called the Granadan, the Fassi, the Zayyati, but I come from no country, from no city, no tribe. I am the son of the road, my country is the caravan, my life the most unexpected of voyages." Cadamosto does not make a bald statement such as this but he and many others were kindred spirits with Leo Africanus.

rate, that is, the king took tribute in horses, while both he and his people otherwise survived by raiding their neighbors. The common people have little clothing, going naked except for a form of pants made from goat-skin; the king and the lords wear cotton garments, grown from their own cotton with cloth made by their women. As with women in Mediterranean culture, spinning was their definitive form of work; yet, in Senegal, men shared in this activity, Cadamosto noted. When it came to war, these were no club-bearing "wild men" but their weaponry was less varied and potent than that of the Europeans (Alvise's men carried crossbows, for example, and some cannon on board their ships), and most significantly, black warriors had no armor.

Sailing fifty miles further down the coast, Cadamosto encountered more Wolofs at Cayor. Hearing that the ruler of this land, the Damel of Cayor whom Alvise called Budomel, was interested in trade, Cadamosto arranged to meet with him to trade horses and silk. The Damel promised in return to provide 100 slaves, and he invited the Venetian home with him. Here Cadamosto wrote that his real motive for accepting this invitation was to see the sights and report information, unusual in that he did not put trade above his sight-seeing.[9] Their habitations and customs were the same as those of his previous hosts but he does write here that the blacks were "exceedingly lascivious" (38). The Damel asked Cadamosto if he had any means whereby he could satisfy many women, since he had many wives, also sleeping with their female attendants when he wished. Excessive sexuality was another trait of the less civilized or uncivilized. But these people were to be counted as humans to Cadamosto, they simply had no knowledge of certain refinements of civilization through lack of materials or lack of instruction. For example, they had cotton cloth but lacked the knowledge of carding it to make cloth of a larger size. They had markets but not much of interest because the land was poor. On the other hand, Alvise took some villagers to his ship to show them, among other things, a country pipe (a sort of bagpipe) that amazed the Wolofs, who initially thought that it was a living animal that sang sweetly different sounds. Cadamosto explained that it was not a

---

[9]Crone notes the exceptionality of Cadamosto's motivation when compared to other merchant/adventurers (37).

living being but an instrument made by hand. Most interesting of all is that he demonstrated to them how to make candles from the honeycombs of bees. They were accustomed to eating the honey and discarding the wax as of no use. Through a simple lesson he was able to show them how to remove the remaining honey and make candles from the residual wax (50–51). He describes the women as light-hearted, always ready to sing and dance, especially the girls. In short, his view of their material deficiencies is not that these were innate but that they were due to the vagaries of location. Unlike the Lobi, whom he had not seen but only heard about, the Wolofs did not fit into the category of the bizarre.

Inexplicable cruelty, on the other hand, could be encountered at any moment. Sailing still a bit further south, Alvise's caravel meets two other ships sailing with the Portuguese. The captains decide to throw in together arriving at the estuary of the Solum and Jumba rivers, where they encounter a less than friendly group of blacks living in a beautiful country. A decision was reached to send ashore one of their black interpreters (Christianized and taught Spanish and Portuguese in Iberia) to negotiate with these men. For unknown reasons, the natives killed the black interpreter, an event which "stupefied" the Europeans; Cadamosto remarked that "they must be very cruel men to do such a thing to a Negro of their own race. . ." (56). Here, race refers to the "race" of blacks. Cadamosto seldom refers to Europeans as "whites," but as Christians, when he speaks of Europeans in Africa as a group. Quickly the Portuguese ships weighed anchor and sailed south to the mouth of the Gambia river where they hoped to be able to trade for gold.

Once, sailing up this wide and deep river, the caravels found themselves followed by the war canoes of a local people. A fight erupted between the Africans and the Europeans, crossbow and mortar against bow and poisoned arrow. The Portuguese ships were able to force the canoes to withdraw, after which Cadamosto and his compatriots began an attempt at negotiation with the blacks. The Europeans wanted to trade for gold or other valuable items, but the Africans would have none of it, having been forewarned of the arrival of the white men. The European sailors found themselves charged with cannibalism, the result of taking blacks away as slaves: these natives believed that the Europeans took Africans to eat their flesh, and stated their resolve to have nothing to do with them on any terms. Cadamosto and his compatriots then decided to turn back to the coast and return to Spain.

Cadamosto begins the story of his second and last voyage as though it were a continuation of the narrative of the first, quickly coming to his caravel's reentry into the mouth of the Gambia River. This time, the natives approach more circumspectly in their canoes. Ultimately one boards the ship, and, after some conversation, the caravels are led up the river to meet with a local Mandingo ruler. The Mandingo were now open to trading with the Europeans, and to generally more hospitable behavior. Some of the native men hunted and killed an elephant for Alvise, which he ate "to be able to say that I had eaten of the flesh of an animal which had never been previously eaten by any of my countrymen" (72). Another observation on food recounts that the Mandingo ate dog flesh, knowledge of which was a first for Alvise. Here again Alvise demonstrates a desire to expand his own stock of unique personal experience, which he accomplishes in this case by jettisoning the food taboos common in other travel literature. At last, encountering Negroes whose language their interpreters could not speak or understand, the Europeans decided that it would be fruitless to continue further south unable to communicate with new peoples, deciding to return once again by ship to Spain.

Antonio Malfante, in contrast to Cadamosto, encountered little in the way of water, traveling overland from the Barbary coast. We know really nothing about his background, not even where he was from in Italy. The fact that his letter was written in Latin indicates a high level of education, and familiarity with classical sources.[10] Journeying on horseback for twelve days in the featureless desert, Malfante noted that they guided themselves by the Sun and stars, as though they were aboard a ship, reaching at last the oasis of Tuat.[11] The inhabitants were Muslims who, Malfante stated, had never seen a Christian before, though there were many Jews there. At this juncture, the primary cultural distinction is religion rather than skin color in the country of the Moors. His next observation, made in commenting on the extreme heat of the place, was that

---

[10]Crone, "Introduction" xliv. His letter was composed in Latin.
[11]Crone, "The Letter of Antoine Malfante" 85.

the people were "the great majority are Blacks, but there are a small number of whites [i.e. tawny Moors]" (86). A brief itinerary of the major cities to the south, in the land of the Blacks based on the knowledge of "those known to men here" follows (87). Malfante's patron gives him even more information about the blacks further to the south; much of it has the flavor of the stories of fantastic peoples from medieval and classical travel writers.

Antonio is told that further to the south are innumerable great cities and territories with black inhabitants whose religion is idolatry. These people were continuously at war with one another in defense of their law and faith of their idols: "Some worship the sun, others the moon, the seven planets, fire, water; others a mirror which reflects their faces, which they take to be images of gods; others groves of trees . . ." (88). Malfante's "patron" claimed to have lived fourteen years in the land of the blacks, and Malfante finds him worthy of credence, apparently because of his wealth.[12] He tells Malfante that the people all go naked, except for a loincloth; that their land is watered by a river that flows through Egypt (like Cadamosto, misapprehending the Niger for the Nile). Most familiar as a charge of being uncivilized is the statement that:

> These peoples, who cover the land in multitudes, are in carnal acts like beasts; the father has knowledge of his daughter, the son of his sister. They breed greatly, for a woman bears up to five at birth. Nor can it be doubted that they are eaters of human flesh, for many people have gone hence into their country. Neither there nor here are there ever epidemics. (89)

As we have seen, a people's status as civilized human beings could not be more challenged than to say that they engaged in totally unfettered and fecund sexuality, and that they were cannibals on top of that. Even further, the blacks were apparently immune to outbreaks of disease; why, we cannot precisely say, unless their robust health was linked to their protean sexuality. More charges include that they were unlettered and without books, obviously untrue, as a man who actually had visited

---

[12]The man was worth 100,000 *doubles* (42).

Timbuctu, for example, the most important seat for the spread of Islam in West Africa in this period, home to many Muslim scholars and Koranic schools producing many manuscripts, would have known. Malfante's informant turns to knowledge relating to trade, noting that India bordered these lands and that Indian merchants who were Christians came to trade. In reality, here he was referencing Abyssinia believed to have been one of the Three Indias, and home of Prester John, the mysterious Christian potentate. The merchants were Ethiopians, Coptic Christians.

My sense is that Malfante invented his informant, alleged to be brother of "the most important merchant in Thambet" or Timbuctu (87, 88). As I mentioned above, anyone who had actually been to Timbuctu in this time period would have seen the large mosque built in 1325 by Mansa Musa, and noted the flourishing community of Muslim scholars (dispersed briefly 1468–1493@), and thus would not have charged that the blacks of that city, at least, were unlettered and without books. Likewise, it is difficult to believe that this merchant would have known and incorporated the stereotypes of the European travel literature of the middle ages and Classical period, to have made the stock kinds of charges of uncivilized behavior that Malfante would have known so well himself. For example, the charge that the blacks of the south lived without marriage arrangements is straight out of Pliny's descriptions of the Ethiopians and the "Garamantes." Remember, Malfante knew Latin. Malfante's letter can best be taken as a contribution to the tradition of that fantastic literature, although there is some useful information on trade. Malfante was not nearly as knowledgeable as Cadamosto.

But how knowledgeable were other Europeans, on the other hand? What did they know of Africa? Eldred Jones writes of England that *Mandeville's Travels* remained influential there as late as 1611, despite English voyages beginning in the mid-sixteenth century.[13] 1555 was a crucial turning point with the publication by Richard Eden of the first two accounts of English voyages to Africa. These were of Thomas Windham's voyage to Guinea in 1553, and John Lok's trip to Mina in 1554–55.

---

[13]Jones, *Othello's Countrymen: The African in English Renaissance Drama* 8. See also his later volume, *The Elizabethan Image of Africa*.

Their accounts contained actual real-life observations along with fantastic stories from the usual sources. English elites relied upon the same mix of Classical and medieval sources as did the Italians. But, they were about 100 years behind them in having their own observations to integrate in with fantasy, and it was still another sixty years before these had an impact. The Dutch case provides another example. Only created as a state near the end of the sixteenth century in rebellion against the Spanish, by this period its only contact with Africa of any kind was through Spain's African relations. This contact provided the opportunity for some mythology to develop but no more before the period of Dutch colonial expansion in the seventeenth century (see Blakely). The Portuguese preceded the Italians in their direct experience of West Africa by perhaps as much as 100 years, as far as we know, but shared in their knowledge of the ancient and medieval sources. I can agree with George in her assessment of Portuguese reporting as being negative in the vein of Classical judgement. Perhaps this is because they were involved in a national enterprise to wrest away from the Moslems control of the trade in gold and slaves. The Portuguese accounts reflect a remarkable lack of interest in anything having to do with the culture of Africans, noting only a few details of dress or ornamentation of the body.[14] Their concerns were overwhelmingly economic; for the rest, they seemed content to rely on tradition.

Cadamosto's accounts contain little if any fantasy, from the past or from his own imagination, though his report on stories told to him about the Lobi seem fantastic but true, while Malfante's letter, though mostly fantasy, contains real knowledge — especially striking is his ability to name important cities to the south, names which would only enter general circulation with Leo Africanus' accounts of travel in Africa in the early sixteenth century. But Cadamosto's accounts reflect something more about his own personality, and possibly that of many of his countrymen. The most notable aspect of his reportage was his willingness to withhold value judgments in practically every instance. The one exception is that he labels the Tuaregs as being the most treacherous and

---

[14]Crone, "The Voyage of De Sintra" 78–84; "The Voyages of Diogo Gomes" 91–102; "Extracts from the 'Decades da India' of Joao de Barros" 103–47.

thieving of men. George, in her article exploring the operation of ethnocentrism, cites this one example as though it were a typical continuation of the assessments of Classical authors, a conclusion that is not borne out by the evidence. She wrote of the Greeks:

> But more than a mere scantiness of data limits these accounts of the African primitive; they are characterized, too, by a selection of data on the basis of an attitude of superiority and disapproval, and by the reporter's increasing propensity, as he moves farther from the sections of the continent relatively familiar to him at first or second hand, to substitute antagonistic fantasy for fact. (63)

This structure of negative evaluation continued, with some modification based on observation, into the fifteenth century, but ethnocentrism still fashioned misunderstanding on the whole. While both of these statements are largely true of Antonio Malfante, they do not fit Cadamosto. Instead, there are many other instances when Alvise might well have been expected to register his disgust at certain practices; when he notes, for example, that some Mandingos eat dog flesh. But he reports this fact without comment as simply being something new to him. We have seen still other examples of his reporting sufficient to refute George. What was really remarkable was Cadamosto's willingness to grow beyond the provincialism of his own largely Venetian culture, casting aside the Plinian lenses of his education to become a citizen of the world, ready to meet and experience new peoples and places on a foundation constructed by his own imagination. While I would not extrapolate this openness to the majority of Italians, I would argue that it was made possible, as a choice, by the culture of the Italian cities during the Renaissance, where empirical observation, will, and learning from experience had transformed many men of no distinction by birth into wealthy and famous figures.

Works Cited
Blakely, Allison. *Blacks in the Dutch World.* Bloomington: Indiana UP, 1993.
Crone, G. R., ed. and trans. *The Voyages of Cadamosto and Other Documents on Western Africa in the Second Half of the Fifteenth Century.* London: The Hakluyt Society, 1937.

Foucault, Michel. *The Order of Things: An Archeology of the Human Sciences.* New York: Vintage Books, 1994.

Friedman, John Block. *The Monstrous Races in Medieval Art and Thought.* Cambridge, MA: Harvard UP, 1981.

George, Katherine. "The Civilized West Looks at Primitive Africa, 1400–1800." *Isis* 49 (March 1958): 62–72.

Grafton, Anthony, April Shelford, and Nancy Siraisi. *New Worlds, Ancient Texts: The Power of Tradition and the Shock of Discovery.* Cambridge, MA: Harvard UP, 1992.

Greeblatt, Stephen. *Marvelous Possessions: The Wonder of the New World.* Chicago: U of Chicago P, 1991.

Howard, C., ed. *West African Explorers.* Forward J. H. Plumb. London: Oxford UP, 1951.

Jones, Eldred. *The Elizabethan Image of Africa.* The Folger Shakespeare Library: U of Virginia P, 1971.

___. *Othello's Countrymen: The African in English Renaissance Drama.* London: Oxford UP, 1965.

Maalouf, Amin. *Leo Africanus.* Trans. Peter Sluglett. New York: Norton, 1989.

The Oxford Companion to the Mind. Ed. Richard L. Gregory and O. L. Zangwill. Oxford: Oxford UP, 1987.

Roberts, Diane. *The Myth of Aunt Jemima: Representations of Race and Region.* London: Routledge, 1994.

Thrower, Norman J. W. *Maps & Civilization: Cartography in Culture and Society.* Chicago: U of Chicago P, 1972.

Todorov, Tzevtan. *The Conquest of America: The Question of the Other.* Trans. Richard Howard. New York: Harper & Row, 1984.

Webster's New Encyclopedic Dictionary. New York: Brill, 1993.

POLITICS, ECONOMICS, AND SOCIOLOGY

THE INTERNATIONAL POLITICAL ECONOMY OF IMMIGRATION
The Changing Face of Italy

Stefano Bellucci
University of Pavia (Italy)

Introduction

Italians are facing one of the biggest changes in their society in centuries: significant immigration from Third World countries. Italy has never before experienced such an influx of relatively poor people although for the best part of the twentieth century many Italians themselves followed the immigration trail. In 1999, Italy was the fourth country in Western Europe in terms of number of immigrants, with a total of around 1.5 million immigrants — some 250,000 people more than in 1998.[1] As dependents are not counted within the Italian system of registration — they come within the authorization given to the wage-earner in the family — the 1.5 million figure is arrived at by increasing the number of valid permit holders (1.252 million) by 19 percent to take into account this factor. This figure also includes EU citizens. However, in terms of ratio of the population, Italy ranks below the majority of the other EU partners. The data collected by the Italian Ministry of the Interior is not a comprehensive list of foreign immigrants in Italy because it obviously does not include irregular or illegal immigrants — whose number is currently estimated at between 200,000 to 800,000, almost all from poor countries. Therefore, allowances should be made for this hidden immigration in reaching a genuine total figure.

The phenomenon has started a big debate at various levels in Italian society — from journalists, academics, and politicians to the man in the street. This paper, however, will limit itself to a discussion of the international political economy of labor immigration in Italy. In other words, it aims to assess the situation in Italy within a wider international context.

---

[1]The country with the highest number of immigrants is Germany, followed by France and Great Britain, respectively. Caritas di Roma, *L'immigrazione nell'Italia del 2000: anticipazioni del "Dossier statistico immigrazione 2000,* based on data from the Italian Ministry of the Interior, due to be published in October 2000.

Before addressing the central question as set out above, it is useful to say a few general words about Italy. Italy remains one of the most permissive countries in terms of immigration laws in Europe. This is due to a number of reasons that are not going to be discussed in any detail in this paper but which can be explained in simple terms by the fact that Italy has not been prepared for this influx of people. Therefore, more than being "generous" in spirit, Italy has simply been caught unprepared in the face of this level of immigration and consequently lacking the necessary organizational network to deal with it. Historically, Italy has not had a colonialist tradition such as France or Britain, and until the 1970s it was a relatively poor country within Western Europe. In addition to those events that have had a global impact on immigration — e.g., the end of the Cold War, the increasing international demographic trends, the desperate situation in which many countries find themselves in other parts of the world — Italy's unique geographical position also plays its part in the increase of immigrants in Italy. Italy's location in the middle of the Mediterranean means that it is close to poor countries both to the east and to the south.

The resulting increase in immigration in Italy has rarely been discussed in a public forum without the topic being sensationalized or distorted for political gain. A vicious circle is created whereby a general lack of perspective about the bigger picture is present in the treatment of the subject by the mass media, who then influence public opinion that in turn influences politicians who in turn influence the mass media, etc. The result is policymakers who react to alarmism rather than informing the public in a sensible way. The reaction to this alarmism by the recent centre-left governments was to regularize illegal immigrants on a massive scale. These extemporaneous and tactical actions, while generous in spirit, have not been backed up by a long-term policy of immigrant integration. In fact immigrants in Italy are no better off today than twenty years ago. They are not adequately represented and they cannot vote in local elections even after twenty years of holding a regular residence and work permit and paying Italian taxes.[2]

---

[2]See, in this regard the study by the Fivol Association "Associazioni e Rappresentanza" in Caritas di Roma, *Dossier Statistico Immigrazione 1999* (Roma: Anterem, 1999) 209.

Fig. 1, Increasing number of immigrants in Italy

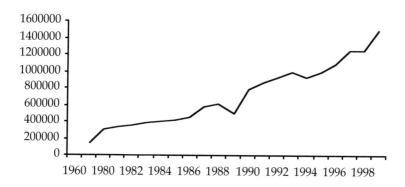

Source: Caritas di Roma/Italian Ministry of the Interior

The Economics of Labor Migration

At the core of any study on immigration is the definition of the term: "... the phenomenon of migration, in particular labor migration ... can only be fully understood in the tension between population and natural environment" (Van der Broeck 1–2). The Italian situation shows that many foreign workers come to Italy in order to escape very difficult economic circumstances, which impact negatively on their environmental and social life at home, more than to improve their skills or wages as is the case for many European migrants. This is, therefore, an example of "survival" labor migration.

Historically, since the early years of industrialization in the Western world, mass migration — including from the Third World — has traditionally been the result of shortages in the labor force. A review of the patterns in European labor migration after World War II, reveals that the benefits of guest-workers were far smaller for migrants and sending countries than commonly believed (see Castles and Miller; Van der Broeck). In fact, migration usually benefits receiving states more than sending states, although political elites in sending countries see emigration as a way of avoiding internal problems. Economically-motivated migrants respond to wage differences between regions — the so-called development gap theory of migration.

A) The Situation in Italy

The data set out below help to place Italy's immigration patterns within a wider context. According to this information, the majority of immigrants in Italy hail from North Africa and Eastern Europe (see tables 1 and 2). This confirms, if confirmation were needed, that the immigration phenomenon in Italy and other economically advanced countries is closely linked to the problem of under-development generally. From an economics point of view, immigration conditions development in developed countries, whether in a negative or positive manner. Immigration policies of receiving states therefore inevitably have deep repercussions on Third World countries.

Table 1: Places of origin of immigrants

	Absolute Value 1998	% 1998	Absolute Value 1999	% 1999	Estimation (+19%) 1999	> % 1998 /99
EUROPE	481,061	38.5	499,061	39.9	593,883	23.5
European Union	171,061	13.7	145,787	11.6	173,487	1.4
Eastern Europe	281,077	22.5	329,404	26.3	391,991	30.5
AFRICA	360,050	28.8	356,804	28.5	424,597	17.8
North Africa	233,771	18.7	231,908	18.5	275,970	18.5
AMERICA	164,040	13.1	153,025	12.2	183,100	11.0
Latin America	105,098	8.4	102,950	8.2	122,511	16.6
ASIA	241,232	19.3	239,774	19.1	285,331	18.3
Far East Asia	123,870	9.9	123,453	9.9	146,906	8.6
AUSTRALIA	2,823	0.2	2,481	0.2	2,952	4.6
Non-classified	1,009	0.1	849	0.1	1,137	12.7
TOTAL	1,250,214	100	1,251,994	100	1,490,000	19.2

Source: Caritas di Roma/Italian Ministry of the Interior (2000).
NB: As explained in the Introduction, in order to reach a total estimate of foreign nationals who live in Italy with valid permits, the figure for these people (1,251,994) needs to be increased by about 19 percent to allow for dependents who would not otherwise appear in any official records.

Table 2: Top 10 countries of origin of immigrants

	Partial 1999	% 1999	Total estimation 1999	> % 1999/98
1. Morocco	146,491	11.7	174,324	19.0
2. Albania	115,755	9.2	137,748	50.5
3. Philippines	61,004	4.9	72,595	7.4
4. Yugoslavia	54,698	4.4	65,091	59.3
5. Romania	51,620	4.1	61,428	65.5
6. USA	47,568	3.8	56,606	1.4
7. China	47,108	3.8	56,059	47.4
8. Tunisia	44,044	3.5	52,412	10.9
9. Senegal	37,143	3.0	44,200	23.1
10. Germany	35,372	2.8	42,093	3.3

Source: Caritas di Roma/Italian Ministry of the Interior (2000)

This intrinsic connection between immigration and under-development is the starting point for this paper, which aims to analyze the correlation between immigration and the economic development of periphery countries. In this context it is useful to refer to the data set out in Table 3 regarding reasons for staying.

Table 3: Reasons for staying

	1999 without additional increase of 19%	%
Employee	632,907	57.2
Self-employed	58,292	5.3
Family	278,163	25.1
Asylum	5,349	0.5
Study	22,097	2.0
Tourism	9,244	0.8
Religious reasons	40,584	3.7
Residence "elettive"	16,672	1.5

Source: Caritas di Roma / Italian Ministry of the Interior (2000)

Unsurprisingly, the table shows that in 1999, the vast majority of permits were given for work reasons and indeed the other data vary little from those collected since the 1970s. It follows that the largest number of immigrants are found in the North of Italy, which is the most productive and populated area of the country. The table also shows that 90 percent of the work permits issued relate to employees. With regards to employee work, the national average for immigrants is about 73 percent of work-permit holding workers. With regards to self-employed immigrant workers, about 98 percent of work-permit holders are in gainful employment. The difference between these two figures is significant, as it demonstrates that although immigrants are integrated to a certain extent within the Italian labor market, they still have a way to go before establishing equal opportunities with their Italian counterparts. Their immigrant status places them in a weaker position with the employment structure.

This "weak" position is partly due to the Italian Government's policy of issuing more work permits to immigrants from countries dubbed "high immigration," which generally represent the poorest ones. The objective behind this policy is to improve the conditions of these target countries, by undertaking to absorb a part of the work force that is not employed there and who would probably enter Italy illegally otherwise. At the top of this category are countries from Africa and Eastern Europe, and more in particular, Morocco, Albania and ex-Yugoslavia, etc. It goes without saying that most of the workers from these countries have very limited options if they lose their jobs and this restricted bargaining power places them at a disadvantage compared to Italians — and in more general terms compared to workers from the EU.

Foreign workers are more vulnerable if they lose their jobs because this can result in their official documents not being renewed by the Italian government. The "fear" of going home or of not succeeding in Italy means that "survival" immigrant workers will accept lower wages and less benefits to retain jobs.[3]

---

[3]This also places survival immigrants in a different position to that of Italians who went in search of their future abroad after the Second World War. Italians in Germany or Switzerland in the 1950s and 1960s, for example, had much greater bargaining power compared to immigrants from the Philippines or Morocco today in Italy. This is because

From the perspective of labor economics, immigration for work reasons has repercussions on the low wage market and on the economic system of the receiving country. On this point, Briggs, an expert in mechanisms aimed at regulating the low wage market, has noted that many economists who follow the free market are not in favor of opening frontiers and allowing the free circulation of workers. Similarly in Italy, those political parties who claim to be great believers in the free market, have the most restrictive policies when it comes to immigration. Simons, a laissez-faire advocate from the Chicago School, states that open access for immigrants is to be neither encouraged nor accepted. Simons dismisses as "dishonest or stupid" the argument that the logical extension of the free trade program is for there to be free circulation of workers. The free market has the potential to raise the standard of life everywhere, whereas open immigration would even out the standard of life, though in order to do so, the European level would drop rather than rise.

Since the 1990s, after a decade of relative openness, the EU has, generally speaking, started to restrict immigration. Although initially the effects of labor immigration on the efficiency of the economic system, the fairness of the labor market, and the social security policies of various European countries were not seen in a negative light, this perception has been gradually worsening. Today, for example, some commentators claim that immigration offers no benefits to receiving countries at all and others go so far as to question the benefits of it to the sending countries.

This last assertion does not withstand close analysis, especially in view of research in the fields of economic and social sciences. In fact, studies on the effects of immigration in Europe demonstrate quite the opposite. Within western Europe, the flow of poor European migrant workers has practically stopped with the increase in inter-EU commerce, which has developed during the process of western European integration. The subsequent increase in unemployment in Europe has meant that there are now fewer opportunities for European migrant workers. In part, this is because: "economics assumes that migration is self-stopping,

---

the Italy of that era was not in the same situation as Albania, Morocco, the Philippines, etc. Italians tended to go abroad mainly because working conditions and wages were better than in Italy and they therefore came more within the "economic" immigrant category.

since it sets in motion price/wage adjustments that reduce incentives to migrate."[4] However, in some cases, immigration can also be self-feeding, and in these circumstances changes in the market do not affect immigration trends. The economic and political differences that existed between European countries forty years ago are arguably greater than the differences that now exist between developed countries of the centre and under-developed countries of the periphery, from where most of the immigrants within the EU come.

In any event, far from diminishing immigration is a phenomenon on the increase. Even if countries try to block legal mechanisms for entry, it is naïve to think that this would stop immigration. Briggs claims for example that "informal" means of entry would proliferate despite attempts to block access by receiving countries, thus demonstrating in practical terms that to deal with immigration effectively requires an understanding of the state of affairs in the sending countries.[5]

Finally, Bonifazi (in Caritas di Roma 49–62) comments on another central aspect of the issue, namely that in the face of an aging European population — with a birth rate below the death rate — immigration will be necessary in order for Europe to remain economically viable.[6] It is an obvious point, but, nevertheless, worth making: as more Europeans become pensioners, a young work force will be needed to keep the economic system afloat. This assertion has been criticized by those who

---

[4]Werner provides many useful tables, including data on foreign nationals in the EC between 1975 and 1992 and data on the development of inter-EC trade and commerce. This has increased from 45 to 60 percent between the countries making up the European Community at the time, between the 60s and the 80s, similarly, GDP per capita within the EC increased to the same extent. If the average GDP per capita in the EC is 100 the standard deviation between the 11 countries of the European Community has fallen from 37 in 1960 to 24 in 1993. Given that the economy and the labor market react positively to European integration, Werner believes that "an EU-wide immigration policy should be developed" (Van der Broeck 162–68).

[5]Even this argument, which follows the direction of the structuralist school of thought, is confirmed by the data on immigration, according to which, in the face of the progressive shutting down of European frontiers in EU countries, there is a concomitant increase in the number of illegal immigrants in the respective country. See Caritas di Roma 90.

[6]According to *The Economist*, "the European Union would need to import 1.6m migrants a year simply to keep its working-age population stable between now and 2050" (6 May 2000).

claim that it has been economically proven that production levels can increase without there being an increase in the work force and that European businesses, for cost reasons, are increasingly keen to decentralize and make use of those periphery areas that are most cost-effective. It is also argued that the decrease in the number of the population of working age is a good way of lowering the unemployment rate — which stands at nearly eighteen million in the EU and around four million in Italy — and including within the work-force sections of society who have been traditionally excluded — young people, women, and old people.

It is important, however, to remember that the labor market is very fragmented at a regional and sectorial level, both in the EU and in Italy. As well as areas of near full employment, for example in Trentino Alto Adige in Italy, with about 3 percent unemployment, there are regions with very high levels of unemployment, such as Calabria, with over 25 percent. Therefore, according to a "functionalist" sort of assessment, it is only in certain specific regions and sectors of employment that foreign workers are required, especially given their flexibility — which arises out of their lack of contractual bargaining power. In these areas according to this approach, they can create their own niche in the labor market, whereby their presence is complementary and not in direct competition with the local work force. Given these circumstances, the immigrant worker becomes an agent for change.

B) Functionalism vs. Structuralism

Up to now, the approach used to analyze the problem of immigration has been a functional one. The functional perspective concentrates, above all, on macro-economic processes, particularly on the decision-making behavior of individuals, who naturally and rightly seek to better their living conditions and find success. Migrant workers, in their quest for a better life, respond to a real or perceived vision that their home country is economically inferior and that better opportunities are available in other countries. The functional theory assumes that the aggregate effect of the migration of all of these individuals will be an eventual geographical reduction in the inequality between different countries and the gradual decline in the impulse to migrate — this has already been the case in EU countries.

Immigrant workers in Italy generally come from countries where agriculture is the dominant sector, and thus the emigration of workers, according to the functional viewpoint, represents a transfer of surplus workers from the agricultural sector to the industrial sector (in the form of the Italian economy in the case under review) (see Lewis). It is therefore assumed that the social procedures are merely made up of the aggregate activities of individuals. According to this theory, competition in the work place within countries with advanced economies, together with the remittances sent back by migrant workers to their countries of origin, helps to reduce the economic differences between varying geographic areas and types of economies. On the one hand, salaries in capital rich countries would be brought down, and on the other, the remittances sent back to poorer countries would create investment and savings, leading to growth.

Regarding these remittances, a distinction must be made between "survival" and "economic" immigrants. In order to do this, one must look at the circumstances in which immigrants are taken on, the field of work in which they are employed, and how much they earn. It is only by answering these questions that one can see that sending back money alone, while helpful, does not mean that the country in question becomes developed or modernized — as the functionalists argue. The remittances can normally be divided into three categories, which are discussed below. From a temporal point of view, there are also three stages: the first being the initial economic precariousness of the new arrival (no savings possible), the second being the intermediary phase when the immigrant worker has entered the labor market in the receiving country (savings can be sent back to home country), and, thirdly, when the immigrant worker is fully settled and can afford for his family to come and join him and can aspire to a better standard of life. This last phase often means that larger sums of money cease to be sent back to the immigrant's home country.

In Italy, it is probably safe to say that immigrants are still at the first phase, even though, from the 90s onwards, some immigrants are also reaching the second phase. From a purely human point of view, the third phase is clearly the most desirable for individual immigrants even though ironically it is less economically beneficial to their home country. In 1998, for the first time, the immigrant remittances going out of Italy were greater than the remittances coming into Italy, sent by Italian immigrants abroad (Caritas di Roma 279–86). This, of course, does not mean that living conditions in Morocco or Albania, for example, have improved.

With regards to the type of remittances sent back home by immigrants, there are, as mentioned above, three main categories. Ghosh has noted that not all of the $70 billion worth of remittances in the world go to under-developed countries. In 1995, France received $6.5 billion in remittances from workers, compensation of employees, and migrant transfers. This sum was more than the total returns sent to the Philippines, Mexico, or Turkey. It has also been observed that in today's world migrant workers from developed countries follow quite a different pattern. Above all, they tend not to settle forever abroad, which creates a continuous flow of remittances as they do not enter into the third temporal phase, and, furthermore, they are often employed in well paid jobs, which means their money transfers are more significant.

Having reappraised to a certain extent the importance to be given to remittances in the economic development of developing countries, one can conclude that money transfers are important, but only insofar as the sending country has in place an economic and social structure and the necessary economic policies so that the remittances can be put to the best economic effect and used in the overall development of the country. The functionalist theory is therefore hampered in the real world by political problems. Many of the countries that export immigrant labor counted on the functionalist theory of immigration, but the economic development that was expected failed to materialize due to poor government.

Finally, it should also be noted that not all migrant workers find employment and success in their adopted countries. The functionalist viewpoint mistakenly took this for granted. Furthermore, this approach failed to discuss the inflation-creating mechanisms that the money transfers create in the economies of the countries of origin of the immigrants. Immigration patterns often include (skilled) employees who already had employment in the economy of their home country, while lesser skilled workers who were unemployed remain so. Immigration therefore does not always reduce the level of unemployment in the countries of origin of the immigrant workers.

A completely different outlook from functionalism is offered by the structuralist approach. This approach focuses attention on the macro-economic processes that produce socio-spatial inequality between the centre and the periphery, and is heavily critical of the poor living conditions of individuals belonging to certain social classes and living in certain geographic areas — which are commonly defined as peripheral areas. According to this outlook, labor migration made up of these people is no longer seen as a result of a rational decision taken by the individual, but rather as a result of the socio-spatial inequality that systematically exists in both the global and national economic systems. International labor migration does not only reflect the geographical-spatial inequalities, it also brings with it a certain leveling effect — as has been seen in Europe — between developed and developing countries. However, as a result of the fact that often it is the more qualified workers that become immigrants, this leads to further inequality between periphery countries and the centre.

According to the macro-social framework of the structuralists, it is not demography or the socio-economic characteristics of the migrant worker that can explain international migration, but instead the politico-economic relationship of an "exploitative" nature that exists between receiving states and sending states. It is not the number of individuals that create the labor migration phenomenon, but rather the special circumstances, or indeed the worldwide economic structure. Within the structuralist school of thought, three different theories co-exist: the neo-Marxist dependency theory, the world-system theory, and the modes of production theory. It is interesting to look at the situation in Italy in the context of these various theories to assess whether and to what extent they are applicable.

It is unlikely that the dependency theory applies to Italy, as the immigration of workers in Italy does not come in any real number from ex-Italian colonies (Eritrea, Libya, Somalia and part of Ethiopia) — see, table 2. According to the dependency theory, the relationship between the centre and the periphery is born of the relationship between *métropole* and colony, and economically this pattern is reproduced in current times in the form of neo-colonialism.

However the dependency theory becomes more viable if Italy is considered as part of a broader centre, which includes all the developed capitalist economies — other EU countries, the Western world, generally, and Japan, etc. In this case the centre-periphery paradigm works in the sense that the centre represents the former colonizers in general, which today results in the presence of neo-colonialist mechanisms that benefit the centre more than the periphery. Neo-colonialism results in a centre-periphery relationship which perpetuates underdevelopment through the international markets of primary goods. In fact, the dependency theory sees the centre-periphery relationship as a "capitalist exchange" that offers advantages to the centre but disadvantages to the periphery, thus the theory is intrinsically anti-capitalist.

Regarding the discussion on remittances, this has also been analyzed from the point of view of the dependency theory, according to which the selection of the migrant workers which occurs in the international labor market penalises periphery countries. In fact, the centre chooses the best workers, who then contribute substantially to the developed countries' economy. Therefore, developing countries lose their most skilled workers and the remittances that are sent back to the home country do not compensate for the brain drain on the local economy. The Third World periphery therefore becomes complementary to the capitalist system in the centre, as the latter can make use of the low-cost work force and balance any fall in profits due to salary increases and the expensive working conditions of its employees in the centre, as a result of the struggle of the metropolitan working class (see Amin). Although this is difficult to measure in the case of Italy because the relevant data are not available, the low level of associationism, discussed below, could be seen as evidence of the lesser bargaining power of foreign workers, together with the fact that immigrant workers take up jobs that Italians do not want to do, either because the pay is too low or because the working conditions are not acceptable. In brief, as far as Italy is concerned, the dependency theory places too much emphasis on historical aspects (colonialism) and fails to take into account the social relations in existence in the sending countries by only attributing the exploitation of immigrant workers on the wage differential between them and the workers of the centre.

The less radical "world system theory" seeks to explain the internal mechanisms of periphery countries and to assess how these react to the global market economy. This theory is also not particularly applicable to Italy although it is relevant to the countries of origin of the immigrants in Italy. The global economy establishes capital flows and flows of goods and creates the ideological conditions that allow for potential immigration (see Portes and Walton). It is the penetration within the internal markets of the periphery and the total "commodification" of everyday life that produces migration. Therefore, there are relationships that go beyond capitalist speculation. What this theory fails to consider is to what extent the different non-capitalist social interaction in the periphery can condition the transfer of value incorporated in the work carried out by the migrant worker.

The third structuralist theory is known as the "modes of production theory." According to this theory, in the periphery, types of production that existed prior to the advent of colonialism co-exist with capitalism in the traditional social make-up of the periphery. As these different forms of production are distributed spatially in an uneven manner, the uneven distribution promotes labor migration. The value is transferred through the "super-exploitation" of workers — i.e., workers contribute to the production system in the most capitalist sectors of the economy, but their work is reproduced in the less capitalist sectors.

The workers from the traditional low capital sectors, as for example the agricultural sector, who come into contact with more advanced systems of production, can only offer their labor. They, therefore, migrate to the higher capital production districts. The increasing demographic trend in traditional rural areas accentuates this pattern (see Kearney).

The great migration of workers from Western Africa or from Eastern Europe to Italy, for example, can be attributed to the emergence of what has been defined as the "new international division of labor" (NIDL) (Gibson and Graham). In Italy with expansion of the tertiary sector there has been a similar increase in the number of jobs for less skilled workers that need to be filled, such as work in the tanning, foundry, construction, carpentry, and mining industries and menial work in hotels and restaurants, etc. (Caritas di Roma 233). The multinational capital centre can choose to transfer part of the production abroad with direct investments, and this is what often occurs with Italian businesses that move their premises and factories to lower capital places such as Albania, Western Africa, Slovenia, and other Eastern European countries. This has not had the effect of stemming the migratory flow from these countries toward Italy (although this is debatable in the case of Slovenia) and what is more, in some economic sectors, it is in fact impossible for capital to be transferred and reallocated, as for example with the construction industry, the specialized agricultural industry, or retail and social services. The migration of periphery economies has resulted in the need for workers at "fixed locations" in Italy.

There are advantages to be gained by local businesses who take on immigrant workers. First of all, employers in the receiving state only give work contracts if the immigrant worker's job is directly and immediately productive; therefore employers do not pay the "statutory taxes and benefits." Furthermore, immigrant workers are only used when the host employer requires their labor, and the employer, therefore, has no responsibility to pay social security contributions for unemployed immigrant workers.[7] Secondly, the very nature of intensive work means that the work contracts are of a short/limited nature.[8] Furthermore, this reduces labor power as workers tend to find employment when they are at the peak of their physical strength, thus in Italy the great majority of immigrant workers are between the ages of 20 and 35. Thirdly, the legal and political status of immigrant workers is lesser than their Italian counter-parts including the fact that immigrants do not benefit from the same social protection that Italian workers have and this limits their capacity to effectively organize and protect their own interests.

It is in the interest of employers in capitalist areas to separate immigrant workers from the social networks of their home communities, as

---

[7]Only a small percentage of immigrant workers (about 20-25 percent) are within the INPS (The Italian social security system) (Caritas di Roma 266–78).

[8]Construction workers are only employed during the building process, nursemaids only while the children in their care are of a certain age, technicians only for the period of time necessary for a group of national technicians to be formed, agricultural workers are mainly seasonal, etc.

this could reinforce their associational power and increase their demand for better work conditions and higher wages. However, it is interesting to note that in Italy little interest has been shown for the associational behavior of immigrant workers. Both the public sector as well as the employer associations do not deal in any real way with this issue. Strangely enough, however, even though immigrants in Italy do stick together to find mutual support, this has not produced the level of "class consciousness" that would give them more bargaining power in the Italian work market.

Conclusion: Italy as a "Half-Way House"

Neither the functionalist nor the structuralist approach is perfect in explaining the way that events are playing out in Italy. As for their theoretical validity, clearly there are arguments for and against in both cases.

This almost ideological opposition between the various types of approach regarding the phenomenon of labor immigration has been considered by various academics as having a negative impact on the study of the economic problems that relate to immigration (Gross and Lindquist) — especially in the quest to find a real solution to the problem of marginalization that immigration brings with it. There have been attempts to reconcile the two types of approaches to the question of international labor migration, and to find a middle course between the two frameworks, although these commendable attempts have not been rewarded with much success. This is not surprising given that the economic and ideological bases for these two theories are in many ways irreconcilable, including the respective solutions proffered by their proponents.

On the one hand, the functionalist theories have resulted from economic studies based on neoclassical theories that favor free market modernization, whereas, on the other hand, the structuralist approach has developed from radical theories that favor the dependency theory, according to which there is always a poorer periphery and a wealthy centre, and where the distance between the two is forever increasing. With regards to the Italian situation discussed in this article, it would seem that labor migration between countries is a unified social process, which by extension indicates that decisions and individual acts are conditioned by "contextual (structural) forces" that operate at various levels in the migratory process — from the reasons for emigrating to the different phases of adjustment in the host country.[9]

After having analyzed the theory behind the Italian phenomenon, it is also important to consider a few simple but significant facts that remain outside of the labyrinth of macroeconomic equations to understand that it is time to implement a cohesive immigration policy. It is not only the future of Third World populations that depends on it but the future of richer countries as well. In the last 25 years, consumption per capita has increased at a regular pace in industrialized countries, by about 2.3 percent per year generally, and by 6 percent in the Tiger economies of eastern Asia. At the other end of the scale, in western Asia consumption per capita has remained level, whereas in Africa there has been a dramatic decrease in individual family consumption, by 20 percent compared to 25 years ago. The living and environmental conditions of two thirds of the population of the planet are terrible, and their political regimes are little better. It is clear from this brief analysis — and quite apart from any idealistic visions of the world as a place where all individuals should be free to circulate — that immigration from underdeveloped countries is here to stay and Italy and other rich countries need to accept this and find a practical and political working mechanism to deal with it.

Those political forces in Italy and other countries in Western Europe that blindly oppose immigration will make the situation worse rather than better, as their tactics will force "survival immigrants" to enter and remain in their host country illegally. On the other hand, the more moderate political forces that are in favor of a more relaxed approach to the question are wrong to implement short-term, extemporaneous attempts to regularize immigrants without instituting long-term integration programs and, above all, guarantees for immigrant workers. As we have seen from the brief summary on the research undertaken on the subject of labor migration, the problem does not lie with those individual workers who seek to improve their earning potential — i.e., the "economic immigrants" — nor does it lie with the fact that remittances may or may

---

[9]It is, in some ways, the same conclusion reached by Fawcet and Arnold.

not be useful in creating further development in the economies of sending countries.

From all points of view, labor immigration from Third World countries results directly from the fact that these countries are underdeveloped. A radical solution is therefore almost obligatory. The problems relating to underdevelopment are so vast that, in order to genuinely change matters, the whole world system as we know it today would have to be reorganized. International immigration is only one aspect of a much wider problem. To truly understand the problem, politicians and people generally need to take a more holistic approach when dealing with labor immigration. This would allow for 1) a clearer understanding of the reasons why certain workers, for example from Africa, emigrate to Italy; 2) an acceptance of the inevitability of the phenomenon as long as present circumstances prevail in poor countries; and 3) a realization that immigrant workers need to be better integrated in the work force, and generally, immigrants should not be feared. Indeed fear and resistance will do nothing to alter the situation and will only prevent a sensible working solution to the issue.

The risk is that, in seeking to curry political favor, European governments/political parties might use repression as a tool to deal with immigration. Overuse of emotive jargon, such as expressions like "bogus asylum seekers," and the implementation of emergency legislation and draconian measures increase alarmism and inflame public opinion. This type of reaction makes sensible debate impossible and confirms the worst fears of a significant segment of the local population, not to mention the fact that it plays into the hands of racists.

References

For an accessible review of immigration data regarding Italy, the *Dossier statistico sull'immigrazione,* edited by Caritas di Roma, is recommended. It is published every year around October. The author is grateful to the research and documentation department of Caritas Diocesana di Roma for its prompt and efficient assistance with data.

In addition, there are two main centres for data on the foreign population of Italy. The first is the *Archivio dei permessi di soggiorno* run by the Italian Ministry for the Interior in conjunction with the *uffici stranieri* of local police headquarters. The second is the *Archivio delle iscrizioni anagrafiche della popolazione residente nei comuni* which is run by the Italian Statistics Institute (ISTAT) in conjunction with the General Register Offices of local Town Councils.

Works Cited

Amin, S. "Introduction." *Modern Migrations in Western Africa.* Ed. S. Amin. London: Oxford UP for International African Institute, 1974. 65–124.

Briggs, V. M. "Mass Immigration, Free Trade, and the Forgotten American Worker." *Challenge* 38 (1995): 37–44.

Castles, S., and M. J. Miller. *The Age of Migration: International Population Movements in the Modern World.* New York: Guilford, 1993.

Fawcet J., and J. Arnold. "Explaining Diversity: Asian and Pacific Immigration Systems." *Pacific Bridges: The New Immigration from Asia and the Pacific Islands.* Ed. J. Fawcett and B. Carino. New York: Center for Migration Studies, 1987. 453–73.

Ghosh, B. *Gains from Global Linkages: Trade in Services and Movements of Persons.* Basingstoke: Macmillan, 1996.

Gibson, K., and J. Graham. "Situating Migrants in Theory: The Case of Filipino Migrant Construction Workers." *Capital and Class* 3 (1986): 131–49.

Goss, B., and J. Lindquist, "Conceptualizing International Labor Migration: A Structuration Perspective." *The International Migration Review* 29.2 (1995) 317–42.

Kearney, M. "From the Invisible Hand to Visible Feet: Anthropological Studies of Migration and Development." *Annual Review of Anthropology* 15 (1986): 331–61.

Lewis, W. A. "Economic Development with Unlimited Supplies of Labor." *The Manchester School of Economic and Social Studies* 22 (1954): 131–91.

Portes, A., and J. Walton. *Labor, Class, and the International System.* New York: Academic P, 1981.

Simons, H. C. *Economic Policy for a Free Society.* Chicago: U of Chicago P, 1948.

Van der Broeck, J., ed. *The Economics of Labor Migration.* Lyme, NH: Elgar, 1996.

LIBERE, INSIEME?
Gender, Ethnicity and Coalition Politics in Italy

Jacqueline Andall
University of Bath

A frican and Asian women in Italy are concentrated in the domestic work sector, with Italian women employing them as their domestic employees. The relationship between Italian and migrant women is, therefore, interdependent but hierarchical. In this chapter, I shall explore the extent to which this structural positioning is compatible with a politics of coalition between women. This will be examined through an evaluation of a political initiative promoted by Italian women active within the *Partito Democratico della Sinistra* (Pds). In 1991, they established a progressive association for migrant and Italian women called *Libere, Insieme.*

Coalition Building Between Women

The initial tendency among Western European feminists to universalize their experience as representative of all women has been well documented and feminist accounts of women's situation have since attempted to be more inclusive. In addition, the potential and desirability for a politics of coalition between different women has been concurrently promoted and problematized by a number of scholars. Reflecting on the theme of international feminism, Rosi Braidotti posed the following pertinent questions:

> How aware are European feminists of the realities of migrations in our own countries? Is it not the case that many feminists share with the dominant culture a basic resistance to the simple idea that internationalization begins at home? How sensitive are feminists in the host countries to those migrant women whose rights of citizenship are vastly inferior and whose intellectual potential is so often ignored? Why are there not close communication networks between migrant women and the rest of the women's movement? (Braidotti 8–9)

Yuval-Davis has suggested that the ambivalent nature of women's citizenship, where they are included in the wider national or ethnic grouping but simultaneously governed by separate gender regulations, contributes to their ambivalence both toward their own ethnic group and to women from other ethnic groups. A critical factor for successful coalition building is seen to relate to the balance that can be achieved between the diverse cultural and historical specificities of individual women and the effect these have on the common goals to be pursued. Tension is exacerbated where explicit or implicit hierarchies are inscribed into the relationship. Dorothy Rosenberg observed precisely this phenomenon in relation to attempts at coalition building between East and West German feminists after the fall of Communism. Citing a discussion regarding some East German feminists' view of separatism as an impediment to coalition building she observed how they were told by West German feminists that "that discussion is over." In other words, "The West German model and its representatives required acceptance and implementation, not modification" (147).

Strategies have nevertheless been proposed to form workable coalitions between different women with common goals and objectives. For example, June Jordan[1] has drawn attention to the potential for an international coalition among women by identifying a universal currency of women's problems. Her perspective involved a distinction between the universalization of women's experiences and the acknowledgement of instances of shared experiences. Brah (93) has argued that "coalitions are possible through a politics of identification, as opposed to a 'politics of identity.'" Her model allows women to identify with the experiences and struggles of other groups but this identification must be rooted in an understanding of the "interconnectedness as well as the specificity of each oppression" and the ability to see the "particular" within the "universal," and the "universal" within the "particular." Yuval-Davis (192–93) has proposed "dialogue, rather than fixity of location" and has promoted the adoption of transversalist principles whereby each participant is rooted "in her own membership and identity but at the same time tries to shift in order to put herself in a situation of exchange with women

---

[1]See her interview in Parmar.

who have different membership and identity." Ravi Thiara has recommended a degree of caution in relation to this latter model by suggesting that while coalitions can be constructed more easily across seemingly acceptable differences, there is a need to recognize that some differences may be irreconcilable. These concepts have yet to be comprehensively applied to the Italian situation, nonetheless, a brief examination of African and Asian women's experiences within Italian society indicates possible constraints to the project of coalition building.

The majority of African and Asian women in Italy are employed as domestic workers. The link between migrant women and Italian women is thus inextricably bound up in the domestic work relationship, which, as several studies have shown, tends to be constructed as a relationship between women (Rollins; Gregson and Lowe). The resurgence of paid domestic work throughout Europe has undoubtedly led to a new international division of labor between women (Friese) and traditional forms of domestic service have been perpetuated in Southern Europe (Anthias and Lazaridis). When the first flows of female migrants arrived in Italy in the late 1960s and early 1970s, they were employed exclusively as live-in workers.[2] Female single-sex flows and therefore independent female migration characterized the early migration to Italy. In 1996, women represented 85.2% of the Cape Verdean community, 81.6% of the Eritrean community, 71.5% of the Ehiopian community and 66.3% of the Somali community (King and Andall). Migrant women from these communities have frequently retained responsibility for their households across international borders. Within Italy, there have been many cases where the difficult transition from live-in domestic work to hourly paid work has forced mainly African women to place their children in residential homes to accommodate the rigid organization of live-in work.[3]

The different regional economies within Italy are also likely to condition the nature of women's coalition politics. The Lazio region, where the

---

[2]One of the first groups of labor migrants to Italy were Cape Verdean women. See Andall, *Gender, Migration and Domestic Service.*

[3]This was particularly problematic for those Eritrean and Ethiopian women present in Italy as refugees. They did not have the option, as did some other ethnic groups, of sending children back to the country of origin to be cared for by the extended family. See Andall, *Gender, Migration and Domestic Service.*

Libere, Insieme association took shape, employed almost triple the number of labor migrants in the domestic services sector as it did in the industrial sector (ISMU) employing, in 1992, 32% of all legally resident domestic workers in the country. The attempt at coalition building by Pds women activists in Rome, in the early 1990s, was therefore rooted in an economic and social climate where domestic work assumed some prominence.

The Libere, Insieme Association

During the 1970s and 1980s, despite the increasingly visible presence of migrant women, progressive Italian women activists failed to acknowledge them. As the Italian feminist historian Rossi Doria stated in the early 1990s:

> There is no other European country where there is . . . a comparable demand for live-in domestic workers. This is a sign of Italian women's high level of emancipation (which is riven with contradiction and which perhaps partly explains our current silence regarding female migrants). (80)

The political feminism that developed in Italy during the 1980s was centred within political parties and trade unions (Beccalli). In the 1980s, a younger generation of feminists aimed to integrate feminist perspectives into party politics and the then Italian Communist Party (Pci) was seen as the most accessible party (Guadagnini). By the mid 1980s, Pci women pursuing a gendered political agenda had come to privilege relationships between women as a principal reference point. Their adoption of a Women's Charter in 1986 (*Carta delle donne*) confirmed their desire to adopt a feminist political practice as the foundation for their political presence as women within the party (Boccia). In the introductory premise to the Charter, the women with whom Communist women desired dialogue were clearly identifed:

> We intend to meet women in parties, women in feminist movements, women in associations, in trade unions, intellectual women and individual women. But above all we intend to consult and involve "ordi-

nary women," those whom we meet in our everyday lives, . . . those who are weaker, more alone, more exposed. (Sezione femminile della direzione del Pci 4)

Communist women would no doubt have positioned migrant women within the category of "ordinary women." However, at this stage of their theory and practice, migrant women were still an invisible social category, receiving no explicit mention in the Charter. This is not at all to argue that Communist women were politically insular. The contents of the Charter indicated that Communist women did seek female alliances beyond a national constituency of women. However, this related to a European female constituency and to women in the developing world. Braidotti's observation that internationalization needs to begin at home was clearly pertinent here.

The political programme for the *Libere, Insieme* association was produced in the Spring of 1991. The association was temporarily based at *Botteghe Oscure*, the headquarters of the Pds, indicating the primary involvement of Pds women. However, it defined itself as an autonomous association and was composed of women from the Pds, the non-governmental organizations, the trade union movement, and the Left generally. In April 1993, Teresa Savini, a principal activist, stated that there were approximately 100 members, over half of whom were ethnic minority women. These were mainly African, Filipina, and South American.[4]

The founding political document of *Libere, Insieme* clearly asserted areas of difference and areas of commonality between women: "We are women who have *different* languages, countries, personal histories and life conditions but have *equal* rights, needs, desire for liberty and affirmation" (Libere, Insieme 1). The organization was clearly conceived not simply as a broad cultural grouping but rather as integral to the development of progressive female political practice in Italy. Indeed, Pds women activists had clearly begun to see ethnic minority women's exclusion from their gendered political activity as a failing:

---

[4]See interview with Savini in *Il Manifesto* 15 April 1993

> *We Italian women* on the Left, from the PDS, from the non-governmental
> organizations, from the trade union movement, are aware that it is no
> longer possible to establish a political project of female strength and of
> social transformation without taking on board the great subjective
> strength which has pushed so many women from Africa, Latin Amer-
> ica, Asia, the Middle East and the East, to leave their own countries and
> their own certainties to face a new country with different customs, a dif-
> ferent culture and language; to live in our cities, to work, almost always
> without rights, in our homes.
>
> This presence questions the quality of our project, the possibility that
> it can really become a useful instrument of change in the lives of so
> many women. (Libere, Insieme 1)

Thus, establishing and pursuing the objectives of *Libere, Insieme* was intended to contribute to the validation of a broader political project. This
was not to be a prescriptive venture. Rather, a common elaboration of
how this new relationship between Italian women and ethnic minority
women would evolve was envisaged. Furthermore, it was not assumed
that defining such a relationship would be straightforward. In fact, the
document referred to the need to create a new language: ". . . it is necessary to work out a common language to explore the multiple worlds of
women and the different paths to emancipation and liberation" (Libere,
Insieme 1). Combating social inequality between women and providing
support for those women who experienced hardship was seen as a pre-
requisite for liberating all women.

While the Italian women involved in the association were engaged in
an expansion of their broader political project, the priorities of ethnic
minority women were somewhat different: "*We women from different
countries* want to live as protagonists" (Libere, Insieme 2). The question
of culture had not been highlighted by the Italian women, however it
predictably assumed some importance for ethnic minority women who
articulated the desire to retain their respective cultures and language.

Sections four and five of the document outlined the different priorities of Italian and ethnic minority women respectively and the final section focused on a set of common objectives. The *Libere, Insieme* association did not preclude a relationship with those ethnic minority women
who had opted to organize also on the basis of ethnicity. It was envis-

aged that it would be possible for women within the association to "relate to everything that women were doing in other associations, organizations and political groups" (Libere, Insieme 2). This approach was undoubtedly reflective of the ideological evolution of Pds women activists who had begun to place great value on the importance of establising autonomous relationships with diverse constituencies of women.

The links between bondage and liberation were encapsulated in the final statement of the political document: "We are convinced that it will not be possible to construct a really humane and just world, a world for women and men, if each of us does not have the opportunity to become the 'mistress' (*padrona*) of her own life" (Libere, Insieme 2).

The reference to a world for women and men mirrored the political vocabulary of Pds women and reflected their adherence to the concept of sexual difference.[5] Nonetheless, the significance of this final assertion lay in the association's desire for all women in the Italian context to establish full control over their own lives. As research has shown (Andall, *Gender, Migration and Domestic Service*), the power of the Italian employer, particularly within the live-in domestic work relationship, was likely to ensure that the concept of "mistress" for ethnic minority women would signify power of and exploitation by other women rather than any expression of their own female autonomy. It was of some importance that the political document did not attempt to disregard this issue as a source of potential conflict between Italian and migrant women. Under the section delineating the objectives of the Italian women within the association it was stated:

> This presence of [female migrants] calls into question a big contradiction for us: in order "to exist" and affirm ourselves in society we delegate to them the family and care work that we cannot or do not want to do. Often our choice for maternity means that it is impossible for them to have or keep a child with them. (Libere, Insieme 2)

It was not clear how this contradiction would be addressed, but its very articulation suggested a realistic approach to constructing a useful

---

[5]See Caverero for a discussion of this concept.

dialogue between different constituencies of women. Indeed, the very structure of the political document reflected a recognition of the different perspectives that women involved in the organization would have. The first three sections were all expressed in the first-person plural: "We are women, We want to construct a relationship, We feel we have a common destiny." The fourth and fifth sections presented the respective priorities of Italian women and ethnic minority women with the final section outlining a series of common objectives.

Two major political initiatives were organized by the association in 1992 and 1993. These consisted of a week-long program of political and cultural events held at the *Palazzo delle Esposizioni* in Rome. *Libere, Insieme* attained some public prominence through this mobilization and there was widespread coverage in the press. For the purposes of this chapter, I will focus on the political aspect of these initiatives, although it does not appear that there was any decision to privilege either the cultural or the political activities of the association. The political events consisted of five round-table debates, with both Italian and ethnic minority women acting as round-table discussants.

The association's mobilization did not promote a single unified view of the way forward. Rather, it provided a platform for interested parties to present analyses and to suggest strategies for the future. This facilitates a critique of the respective perspectives of individual contributors but makes the task of evaluating the association itself more problematic. What I would want to argue, however, is that rather than adopting a perspective that acknowledged the interconnectedness of factors such as class, ethnicity, and gender, the Italian participants tended to privilege gender as the central analytical framework with which to understand migrant women's experiences. This primacy of gender reflected Pds women's own theoretical attachment to the importance of a gender-determined viewpoint and presence in politics. Their use of the slogan "women's power from women" promoted female solidarity as the source for women's political power (Guadagnini). A less favorable view would submit that privileging migrant women's gender over ethnicity or class constructs was not incidental, rather it served to obscure what were clearly unpalatable truths regarding both the reality of the relationship between Italian and migrant women within Italian homes and the direction of Italian women's emancipation.

The general theme for the 1992 mobilization was "Women between Modernity and Tradition" and two round-table discussions were held. The first focused on the cultural identity of migrant women and the second on their conditions and rights. In her introduction to the first discussion, Rossi Doria set the tone:

> . . . There are many identities, even for us. . . . Identity is not a total belonging, but a plurality of belongings, whereby all of us, I repeat both foreign women and Italian women, are firstly single women, with an individual history and who, alongside and within this individual history, have a series of collective belongings, including that of ethnicity. (ALI[6] 1992a:2)

This first round-table discussion was clealy conceptualized as a means of providing greater knowledge about migrant women. Notably, it was principally the ethnic minority participants who fostered an alternative approach to the issue of cultural identity by challenging assumptions regarding migrant women. As has occurred in other European countries, so called "traditional" migrant women have been expected to embrace "modernity" as an emancipatory strategy (Morokvasic). But as one Eritrean discussant confirmed: "Our desire for emancipation as women . . . ends the moment that we end up in the houses of Italian families" (Maricos in ALI, *Le identità culturali* 36).

In the second round table, representatives from migrant women's associations outlined the principal problems facing their members. These predictably included their undocumented status, lack of housing, long working hours, and problems relating to maternity. The audience attending the debate was exposed to a range of perspectives and could participate after the official speakers. The audience's contributions largely confirmed the different priorities of Italian and migrant women. The interventions by Italian women tended to indicate their interest in the different cultural practices of ethnic minority communities. For ex-

---

[6]Abbreviation for Associazione Libere, Insieme.

ample, one woman called for more discussion on the question of infibulation and Somali women. Contributions from migrant women, on the other hand, highlighted specific aspects of their working and general conditions within Italy. Salua Dridi for example, a Tunisian migrant, raised an issue that had not received adequate attention from the principal round-table discussants:

> I would like to speak about a very delicate subject, that is of migrant women who work as live-in domestic workers. They really are victims . . . because of their employment conditions in the country of immigration, inside a house working 24 hours like a slave. This is quite ridiculous because you cannot take a woman, make her work such hours and only let her out on Thursdays and Sundays. . . . That woman has the right to go out, to talk, to meet other people, otherwise psychologically and morally she will break down. . . . (Dridi in ALI, *Donne migranti* 38)

The response from an Italian woman who defined herself as an original Italian feminist was revealing:

> Salua Dridi's protest should be extended to the lives of all women because a 24 hour day is a normal day for all women and all housewives. So, we can say that what is being reproposed for domestic workers is relevant for all women. (Panotti in ALI, *Donne migranti* 39)

This collapsing of the "specific" features of migrant domestic workers' twenty-four-hour servility into the "universal" features of the female condition marginalizes class and ethnicity as integral and connected factors which contribute to migrant women's social marginality. Although there is a connection to be made regarding paid domestic work and Italian women's unpaid domestic work within the home, some recognition of the weaker and more disadvantaged position of the live-in worker is warranted.

It was only in the final stages of this discussion, inspired by Salua Dridi's comments, that some attempt was made by one of the Italian discussants to confront this issue. Rossi Doria unequivocally emphasized the personal responsibility of Italian women with regard to this contradiction:

> . . . neither good intentions nor a trade union perspective will be enough [to solve this issue]. It requires the commitment of all of us women to find a way of coming together, . . . to face this issue as a real internal contradiction. It is a contradiction for us western women, and we cannot off-load responsibility onto the government, nor onto the State. . . . (Rossi Doria in ALI, *Donne migranti* 43–44)

To a large extent, this first initiative of the association displayed that Italian and migrant women had different priorities. Both the official speeches and the informal contributions of migrant women were focused on their material conditions within Italy. While the Italian contributions were attentive to the material conditions of migrant women, their content revealed a more focused interest in the value of a mixed women's association and their desire to learn about other cultures. A racialized dichotomy of goals could thus be identified. Moreover, during this first major mobilization, a critical issue — the contradiction of migrant women's work liberating some Italian women — was not afforded proper attention.

In 1993, a round-table discussion was organized around the theme of domestic work. Chaired by the president of the Cape Verdean women's association, it had among its discussants a representative from the national domestic workers' organization, the ACLI-COLF.[7] By the mid 1980s, this organization's perspective reflected a view of domestic workers and Italian employers as common victims. As its representative stated:

> . . . it is no longer so much bourgeois families, or even families from more diversified social classes who request live-in domestic workers, but it is women who need other women, it is they who find themselves crushed between the labor market, their family of origin, their current family, their children and their elderly parents. I believe that this is a different stage with respect to previous years from which a different level of solidarity may emerge — a greater solidarity given that both

---

[7]Associazioni Cattoliche Lavoratori Italiani. COLF is an abbreviated form of *collaboratrice familiare*. For more on this organization, see Andall.

domestic workers and women face the same problems. (Alemani in ALI, *Colf* 8–9)

This was a further example of the primacy of gender masking the relevance of class and ethnicity. Bocca Rossa, an Italian woman attending the debate rejected this proposition out of hand. She was unequivocally critical of the apparent amnesia of some feminists regarding feminist political mobilization in the 1970s, and specifically the manner in which it had rigorously challenged the division between productive and reproductive labor and between male and female tasks:

> Italian women can now afford a domestic worker instead of fighting for social services: they have resolved their problems on the backs of domestic workers. . . . I know that many old feminists have a domestic worker at home, and they think they are doing this woman a favour. They completely forget that this woman has the right to a private life, they think; "As a white emancipated woman, I am doing you a favour as without me you would die of hunger"' (Bocca Rossa in ALI, *Colf* 30–31)

This tension between family work and paid work is clearly relevant to all women. However, while employing live-in domestic workers reduced this tension for some Italian women, employment as a live-in worker exacerbated this tension for African and Asian women. The subsequent *Libere, Insieme* debate, which addressed the issue of maternity, failed to explore the extent to which migrant women's maternal social identity was being negated as a direct consequence of their structural location within the domestic work sector. This issue was raised by only a minority of the round-table discussants and was never developed as a central issue.

The inability to explore the emegence of new models of family organization for migrant women stemmed partly from the adoption of a socio-sanitary perspective for the round-table discussion. Critically, this focus marginalized migrant women's *post-natal* experiences. The debate was in fact dominated by Italian medical practitioners (three gynecologists, one obstetrician, one pediatrician, one health visitor and a medical anthropologist). The ensuing discussion was framed in terms of whether the Italian social and health system was in a position to accommodate the cultural differences, traditions, and pathologies of ethnic minorities. It was left to the only non-Italian discussant, the Zairean gynecologist, Susanna Diku, to make the link between migrant women's difficulties with maternity and their employment niche:

> In our centre we know of women who have terminated pregnancies so as not to lose their jobs or of those who have continued their pregnancies and now have to find somewhere to sleep, because what was needed was an efficient person and not a pregnant person. . . . Once this woman has left hospital, she must start work as soon as possible and show her boss that despite the baby she can do what she was doing before and thus prevent her boss from employing somebody else. (Diku in ALI, "Il tempo della maternità" 47–48)

In addition, the issue of maternity highlighted further constraints to coalition building. Migrant women's effective exclusion from a Pds women's conference on maternity, held in 1992,[8] seemed to suggest that the theoretical and practical activities of Libere, Insieme were being restricted to a separate sphere of political activity that was peripheral to "mainstream" gender activism.

Conclusion

Although the Libere, Insieme association was undoubtedly an important political initiative, its activity in the early 1990s suggested that coalition building between Italian and migrant women would remain problematic. One difficulty centred around the fact that while this was a mixed association, it had been established to debate, discuss, and, possibly, improve the situation of migrant women. Any real scope for reciprocity was limited by the fact that Italian women's position was not at the centre of the agenda. The interventions by both round-table discussants and participants tended to confirm that migrant women and Italian women were pursuing dichotomous goals. Italian women, in the main, hoped to understand migrant women's situation and culture while mi-

---

[8] Area Politiche Femminili Direzione Pds (1992) Il tempo della maternità 9–10 gennaio.

grant women were centrally focused on improving their employment and living conditions in Italy.

A second problem concerned the association's inability to address the contradiction articulated in its founding document, namely that of migrant women's labor liberating some Italian women from domestic work. If this issue had been fully explored, Pds women's objective of politically representing (Italian) women was likely to have been jeopardized. This suggested that while a degree of receptivess to migrant women was possible culturally, at the political level, Italian activists were still primarily representative of the national gender constituency. The reluctance of Italian activists to explore the development of a distorted model of emancipation for Italian women underscored the importance of these issues. Any thorough analysis of the use of migrant women for domestic labor automatically questioned the perceived "success" of the Italian model of female emancipation.

Rather than viewing ethnicity as part of an interlocking paradigm of domination, along with factors such as gender and class, ethnicity was on a number of occasions subsumed under gender. In so doing, the *Libere, Insieme* association evaded critical questions concerning the model of Italian women's emancipation, the gendered and racialized division of reproductive labor and the negation of migrant women's multiple social identities.

Bibliography

Andall, J. "Catholic and State Constructions of Domestic Workers: The Case of Cape Verdean Women in Rome in the 1970s." *New Migration in Europe: Social Constructions and Social Realities*. Ed. K. Koser and H. Lutz. Basingstoke: Macmillan, 1998. 124–42.

———. *Gender, Migration and Domestic Service: The Politics of Black Women in Italy*. Ashgate: Aldershot, 2000.

Anthias, F., and G. Lazaridis. *Gender and Migration in Southern Europe*. Oxford: Berg, 2000.

Associazione Libere, Insieme. *Le identità culturali delle donne immigrate*. Rome, 9 May 1992.

———. *Donne migranti, condizioni di vita, diritti, aspettative*. Rome, 14 May 1992.

———. *Colf: Rapporto tra necessità e libertà; Voglia di emancipazione*. Rome, 14–19 May 1993.

———. *"Il tempo della maternità" in un paese straniero*. Rome, 14–19 May 1993.

Beccalli, B. "The Modern Women's Movement in Italy." *New Left Review* 204 (1994): 86–112.

Boccia. "Stare da donne nel Pci." *Reti* 1 (1989): 3–15.

Brah, A. *Cartographies of Diaspora.* London: Routledge, 1996.

Braidotti, R. "The Exile, the Nomad, and the Migrant. Reflections on International Feminism." *Women's Studies International Forum* 15.1 (1992): 7–10.

Caverero, A. "Towards a Theory of Sexual Difference." *The Lonely Mirror. Italian Perspectives on Feminist Theory.* Ed. S. Kemp and P. Bono. London: Routledge, 1993. 189–221.

Friese, M. "East European Women as Domestics in Western Europe: New Social Inequality and Division of Labor Among Women." *Journal of Area Studies* 6 (1995): 194–202.

Gregson, N., and M. Lowe. *Servicing the Middle Classes.* London: Routledge, 1994.

Guadagnini, M. "A 'Partitocrazia' without Women: The Case of the Italian Party System." *Gender and Party Politics.* Ed. J. Lovenduski and P. Norris. London: Sage, 1993. 168–204.

ISMU. *Migrations in Italy. The First Report 1995.* Milan: Franco Angeli, 1996.

King and Andall. "The Geography and Economic Sociology of Recent Immigration to Italy." *Modern Italy* 4.2 (1999): 135–58.

Libere, Insieme. *Documento politico dell'Associazione 'LIBERE, INSIEME,'* May 1991.

Morokvasic, M. (1983) "Women in Migration: Beyond the Reductionist Outlook." *One Way Ticket: Migration and Female Labor.* Ed. A. Phizacklea. London: Routledge, 1983. 13–32.

Parmar, P. "Other Kinds of Dreams." *Feminist Review* 31 (1989): 55–65.

Rollins, J. *Between Women: Domestics and Their Employers.* Philadelphia: Temple UP, 1985.

Rosenberg, D. "Distant Relations. Class, Race, and National Origin in the German Women's Movement." *Women's Studies International Forum* 19.1–2 (1996): 145–54.

Rossi Doria, A. "Primi appunti sulle donne dell'immigrazione." *Politica ed Economia* 22.7–8 (1991): 80–81.

Sezione femminile della direzione del Pci. *Dalle donne la forza delle donne – Carta itinerante.* Cles, Trento: Nuova stampa di Mondadori, 1986.

Thiara, R. "South Asian Women in Britain." Unpublished conference paper, ERCOMER, Utrecht University, 18–20 April 1996.

Yuval-Davis, N. "Women, Ethnicity and Empowerment." *Shifting Identities Shifting Racisms.* Ed. K. Bhavnani and A. Phoenix. London: Sage, 1994. 179–98.

ITALIAN AID IN NIGER
Women, Land, and Development: Gendered Paradigms of Tenure in the Rural Development Project of Keita (Niger)

Benedetta Rossi
London School of Economics

Abstract

The World Food Day theme for 1998 is "Women Feed the World," and contributors to the ceremony held at the FAO[1] headquarters in Rome on October 16 paid tribute to women's role, all over the world, as key food providers and skilled agricultural laborers. In the speech prepared for the occasion, FAO Director General, Mr. Jacques Diouf, mentioned that

> Although many developing countries have legally affirmed women's basic right to own land, they rarely exercise actual control of the land. The most problematic aspect of women's customary land rights is the lack of security, as secure land rights are important for access to credit, membership of rural organisations, extension assistance, technology and information.

In a similar vein, the intervention of the Italian representative, Sottosegretario Sen. Rino Serri, who was substituting for Prime Minister Romano Prodi, presented Italy's new approach to humanitarian aid and cooperation as primarily concerned with operations aimed at improving women's access to individual property of land and to credit. Sen. Serri explicitly referred to Keita's Rural Development Project as a case in point of Italy's cooperation with the United Nations and with the Republic of Niger to support women's access to land.

This paper illustrates the pilot-operation of this kind in the Italy-funded "Keita Project,"[2] which I have followed closely in repeated fieldwork visits to the District of Keita (Niger) since 1995. The operation

---

[1]Food and Agriculture Organization of the United Nations.
[2]The official name *Projét de Developpement Rural / Ader Doutchi Majiya* (PDR/ADM) is often simplified into "Keita Project" from the name of the District where it is located.

targeted the Women Group of Tinkirana Tounga, chosen for this innovative experiment because of its long-standing involvement in the Project's works of land-rehabilitation. It consisted in giving group members a credit, repayable in three years, with which they would buy from the (male) traditional landowners a rehabilitated parcel of land adjacent to their village.

The choice of this subject for a paper on Italy-Africa relations was not determined by fashionable new trends in international development policies, but by the direct consequences we can expect these very trends to bear for the people involved in rural development projects. My own observations and the accounts of others working in this field allow us to foresee some consequences of the interference of long standing development projects with indigenous gender ideologies and institutions dealing with property and access to land.

The paper is divided into four parts. The first part provides a description of the Project's origins and of the nature of its interventions. The second part highlights some aspects of local gender ideologies relevant to the questions discussed in the following sections. The third part is an account of Tinkirana Tounga women's acquisition of a rehabilitated parcel of land, of the spread of other similar operations, and of the establishment, within the PDR/ADM, of a division for the promotion of women's status. Finally, in the last part, I compare my evidence with other studies of the impact of rural development on indigenous social relations with regards to gender, property, and labor.

1. The "Projet de Developpement Rural / Ader, Doutchi, Majiya"

The Republic of Niger (capital: Niamey) is divided into seven departments that, in turn, are subdivided into 35 districts. It has a population of 9.6 million (last census 1988: 7,251,626) with an annual growth rate of 3.5 percent (*Coopération Française* 1998).

The District of Keita is one of the seven districts of the Department of Tahoua, located within 14`20 and 15`10 of North latitude and 5`20 and 6`35 of East longitude. It spreads over 4,842 SqKm.

In 1994 estimations, the District of Keita has 184,806 inhabitants, distributed in 205 villages, with an average density of 37 people per Sq.Km. Ninety-eight percent of the population is considered "rural." In 1993 figures,[3] the crude birth rate for the District is 27.1% and the crude death rate is 6.1%, with a natural increase rate of 2.1%, somewhat lower than the national figure of 3.5%. Life expectancy at birth is 48 years old. One quarter of the adult male population is estimated to have seasonally or permanently migrated to neighboring states or in the urban centres of Niamey and Tahoua (Bachar 20-ff).

"Official sources" cited by Bachar give the following distribution of the population according to "ethnic" (or socio-cultural) affiliation:

•	Hausa	36%	•	Tuareg	4.1%
•	Aderawa	29.2%	•	Peul (or Fulani)	1%
•	Buzu	29.1%			

However, with Bachar, this distribution on ethnic lines should be considered with particular caution, for two main reasons. First, the term "Aderawa" carries only a geographic connotation, but does not, in fact, say anything about the social affiliation of the communities to which it refers. Second, the term "Buzu," used locally in a denigratory way, identifies the lowest stratum of Tuareg society, i.e., the ex-slaves. If these two categories were included in the "Tuareg" group, as would happen if one took language as an indicator, the latter would result considerably increased, but settled villages of Tuareg ex-slaves resent defining themselves as members of Tuareg society. In fact, doing so would automatically place them at the lowest levels of a stratified social structure, still alive today in cultural representations of hierarchy and prestige.

The three most spoken languages in the District of Keita are Hausa, Tamacheck, and Fulfulde.

The PDR/ADM has entered the scene at a time when the ties of dependency and complementarity along which the local society was organized had reached an advanced stage of decay, initiated a century earlier with the advent of colonial power.

The Ader-Doutchi-Majiya region, where the District of Keita is situated, was severely hit by successive multi-year droughts occurring in the country as a whole at the end of the 60s, in 1973–1974, and 1984–1985.

---

[3]Source: *Tableau de Bord de l'Arondissement, SAP 1993.*

In December 1982, a joint identification mission, in which participated the Food and Agriculture Organization (FAO, UN), an Italian
team, and the CILSS (*Comité Inter-états de Lutte contre la Séchéresse dans le
Sahel*), laid out an outline of problems related to desertification, soil
erosion, and drought afflicting the Keita District in the Nigerian Department of Tahoua. This document contained the foundations for the
establishment of the *Projét de Développement Rural / Ader-Doutchi-Majiya*.

On Dec. 6, 1983, the Governments of Italy and of Niger signed an
agreement that assigned FAO as the project's executor. The area of influence of the PDR/ADM is characterized by the co-existence of Hausa
farmers and Tuareg (esp. sedentarized Buzu) and Fulani (or Peul) herders. In 15 years of intervention, based on the involvement of the local
population in all phases of planning and implementation, the PDR/
ADM has introduced new ways to relate to the environment and to act
upon it. The PDR/ADM started its activities in May 1984 under the
appellation "PIK" (Projet Integré de Keita"). During the second phase of
the project, between 1991 and 1996, the interventions were extended to
the adjacent Districts of Bouza and Abalak, to the North of Keita, and in
the recently started third phase, a further extension has been planned
toward the southern Majiya Valley (Cremona; Bayard).

The funds provided by the Italian government for each phase of the
project amount, respectively, to US $36,313,000; $18,700,000; and
$8,500,000 for the first two years of the third phase, which is expected to
end in the year 2001.

The interventions of the PDR/ADM can be divided into two main
categories: the first group is specifically aimed at the physical rehabilitation of the territory, the second one at the promotion of social welfare
and economic growth. Together, all operations are performed with the
purpose of restoring alimentary self-sufficiency.

The various actions undertaken on different environmental sites
consist in:

> *Plateaux*: subsoiling; sylvo-pastoral and sylvo-agricultural anti-erosion
> bunds; tree-planting on the bunds' sides.
> *Slopes*: reforestation trenches on hillsides; check-dams construction on
> small watersheds.
> *Glacis*: anti-erosion bunds and tree planting.

Valleys: rows of trees functioning as windbreaks; cement-lined wells on the valley-bottom.
Dunes: tree planting in three-rows-series.
"Live dunes": dense planting of trees and rows of millet-stalks.
Koris: dense tree planting along the koris-sides.

The following table resumes the results of some of the PDR/ADM's actions for the first two phases. The data are taken from the latest account on the PDR/ADM's achievements (Keita, July 1997).

Type of intervention	PHASE I	PHASE II	TOTAL
Land rehabilitation	Ha. 16,892	6,339	23,231
No. of seed-beds	33	55	88
No. of plants produced	8,845,000	5,788,845	14,633,845
No. of dams	11	24	35
No. of artificial lakes	–	2	2
No. of weirs	150	70	220
Km. Of tracks	113	151	264
Length of landing track (meters)	–	1500	1500
Deep bore (388 Mt.Depth)	1	–	1
Wells for watering camps	465	87	552
Village wells	52	31	83
Village shops	53	18	71
Mills	38	17	55
Slaughter-houses	4	–	4
Groundnut dryers	4	–	4
Veterinary posts	3	–	3
Vaccination Parks	4	–	4
Workshops	4	1	5
Onion deposits	11	–	11
Camps for women farmers	23	5	28
Animal-traction units	203	71	274
No. of goats	1,377	2,206	3,583
School locales	33	17	50

2. Gender Ideology and Gender Relations in the PDR/ADM: An Outline[4]

Local gender ideology and sexual division of labor vary across ethnic affiliation, social class, and main economic specialization of its inhabitants. The actual state of a village's gender relations is influenced by at least three further elements, intersecting in different ways with that village's social organization, as defined by the above mentioned factors: (a) relative adherence to Islamic values and dictata; (b) relative involvement in the project's activities; (c) rate of male out-migration.

The village of Tinkirana Tounga (TT) that will be discussed later is one of the many communities of settled ex-slaves of the Tuareg Kel Gress (Baier; Lovejoy and Baier; Bourgeot; Bernus, "L'Évolution"). A distinctive trait of the Kel Gress, the Tuareg "confederation" prevalent in the society living in the area influenced by the PDR/ADM, is the emphasis falling on the hierarchical relation between small groups of noble (*imajeghen*) landowners and variously classified dependent villages with usufruct rights over their lands (Bonte, "Structure de classe"). Among these, three principal categories can be distinguished: (a) semi-permanent camps of slaves working for their patrons; (b) villages of freed slaves (*iderfan* or *ighawellan*) owing their former patrons one tenth (*tamasadak*) of the agrarian produce[5] and various kinds of extraordinary contributions[6] on special occasions in the *imajeghen*'s life-cycle (marriage; birth of a child, war, etc.); and (c) villages of Hausa or Hausa-phone[7] peasants that had been progressively conquered and obliged to give a tenth of the produce and pay different kinds of tributes (*haraji*) to Kel Gress *Imajeghen*. TT seems to have belonged to the first or second kind.

According to Dunbar,

> The southern agricultural communities were able to establish some autonomy from their masters in that agricultural fields, unlike the animals they herded, came to be transmitted by the settled vassal commu-

---

[4]In this section, I shall deal only with aspects of gender relations in Keita that are strictly related to the discussion of the case study that will follow.

[5]Corresponding to the Islamic *zakat*, referring to 10% of the crop.

[6]For a detailed description of these contributions, see Bernus and Nicolaisen 120.

[7]Aderawa and Goberawa peasants, probably the original inhabitants of the Ader, are sometimes distinguished from Hausa communities *tout-court*, though from the eighteenth century they appear to have fully adopted Hausa lifestyle and social organization.

nities without direct interference of the Tuareg beyond the payment of tribute (an 80/100 Kg. Sack of millet/cultivator/year was typical). The pattern of transmission, however, apparently excluded women as it did amongst the neighbouring Hausa communities. (Dunbar, *Nigérian Women* . . . 15)

Notwithstanding the widespread and increasing adherence to Islamic norms, women often do not inherit half of the lands inherited by their brothers, as prescribed by Koranic law (Koran, sura IV). Women explain this deviation from Muslim norms on the basis of the locally established virilocal pattern of residence at marriage, which would take women away from the land inherited within their father's perimeters, while leaving their brothers as *de facto* owners of all paternal land holdings. They add, however, that in case of divorce a woman is free to return to her paternal household, and would then be allocated usufruct rights on familial lands, unless, of course, her relations with her family of origin are strained due to other reasons. This also holds true in the case that a woman's children decide to move to their maternal uncle's village. Flexibility in social arrangements concerning access to land, however, is likely to change, as competition over land holdings rises under population pressure and improved soil fertility calls back seasonal migrants.

Women hold usufruct rights upon their husband's fields, and my evidence is in line with other ethnographies reporting women's individual ownership of small *gamana*-type[8] parcels, sometimes called "kitchen gardens" to designate their main use in meeting household nutritional needs.

In the area under consideration, the primary form of capital held by women consists of small animals, which women are free to sell, and to dispose of the profits gained from the sale for purchasing gifts, clothing, and their own independent purchases and investments.

Despite the actual relative freedom enjoyed by women, also due to the high rate of male migrations, local gender ideology defines men as

---

[8]*Gamana* or *gayauna* are the Hausa terms referring to individually owned lands, as opposed to commonly owned and cultivated *gandu* fields. However, against the sharp distinction between "communal" and "individual" tenure, and for a critical assessment of the use of English terms such as "ownership," "property," "tenure," etc. in rural African contexts, see Shipton and Goheen.

primary responsible for all substantial economic activities, both with regard to agriculture and to cattle husbandry and commerce. Women, who provide an important input in terms of agricultural labor force, in addition to their key responsibility as water and food-providers, child carers, and, recently, as manual workers on PDR/ADM work-sites, do not, in the majority of cases, deal with the commercialization of agricultural output, nor with the purchase and sale of lands. All household major economic transactions are dealt with by male "household heads," especially in Hausa and Buzu villages, whereas Tuareg communities and the Fulani minority represent a case apart, which, for limits of space, cannot be treated in this paper.

This situation is consistent with the local habit of likening women to children, thus characterizing them as social actors unable to take responsibility for themselves and for others and dependent on the organizational and intellectual capacities of adult men. Although in contrast with the actual reality in which women take up multiple responsibilities in the absence of men away as migrant workers, this attitude was particularly evident with reference to the Project's "structural alphabetization" initiatives in favor of the *comité de gestion* of each *groupement féminin*.

When members of the Division for the Promotion of Women and of Socio-Economic Activities explained to the women of a *groupement* that their representatives would receive a two-week alphabetization training, almost inevitably a group of men would interrupt the meeting to complain about men's exclusion from this type of initiative. They would argue that the Project was wasting time and effort and, in a few instances, they claimed that "one single man could learn as much as ten women." The women listening to such comments would not give signs of indignation or resentment and, in a minority of cases, they actually seemed to acquiesce to men's perspectives. On one occasion the (male) elders of the village of Tinkirana Tounga expressed their view that, although the Project's efforts to support the women could only be approved of, trying to "educate" women was, in their opinion, a waste of time. Women are like "permanent children" and cannot put to any use the education received by the Project, because it is their nature to lack the "*ilimi*"[9] and the

---

[9]Hausa term for wisdom. It is often used as an attribute of old, respected men.

"hankali"[10] necessary to take initiatives and decisions as effectively as a man.

Muslim religion is not opposed to female education, as long as precautions are taken to ensure that it does not expose women to a situation of sexual promiscuity. Shehu Ousman Dan Fodio, the religious leader whose predicaments inspired the Fulani Jihad (holy war) that brought to the establishment of the Sokoto Caliphate at the end of the nineteenth century, is said to have supported female education. His disciples reported that his women relatives were highly educated and even authored a number of literary works. However, Dan Fodio predicated female seclusion (Hausa: *armen kulle)* that was not, instead, practised by pre-Islamic Nigerian societies. Wife seclusion is still rare in Keita because female labor represents a critical factor in household food production. This is particularly true for the poorest households, whose male adult members seasonally migrate to neighboring states and urban centers.

A substantial number (25%) of young and adult men rely on seasonal out-migration, which allows them to integrate the meagre returns of agricultural bad years with paid work, often petty trade, in Nigeria or in The Ivory Coast.

When a man can afford to remain in Keita for the whole year, he owns enough lands, in productive locations, to meet his family's subsistence needs through his own agricultural production, generally matched to small-scale herding. A successful farmer would not work on the Project's working sites, both in order to dedicate his time to farming his own lands, and to avoid the characterization of low social status that he would derive from doing so. Ideally, such a man would keep his wife/wives secluded at home, and rely on his agnatic kin or, more frequently nowadays, on paid workers, for the labor necessary on his fields. As is the case in other areas of West Africa, in the villages of Keita the higher a household's social status the greater the chance for its adult women members to be secluded.

---

[10]Hausa term for intelligence. It carries a connotation of mastery over practical and organizational problems. I do not think that it has any implication with reference to a person's age.

The district of Keita is situated in what used to be the heart of the Sokoto Caliphate, and Cooper's historical reconstruction of female seclusion in the Caliphate's area corresponding to today's northern Nigeria seems to suit closely the situation present in Keita.

> In the Sokoto Caliphate one way in which individuals could mark their status as Muslims and loyalists was to remove their wives and daughters from agriculture and replace them with slaves. Thus in Nigeria seclusion became associated with free-born status and agriculture with slavery. (Cooper 1994:67)

Keita's women's perspectives with reference to seclusion are controversial and non-homogeneous. Broadly speaking, it is possible to distinguish three main different approaches. The poorest women living in Buzu ex-slave villages tend to regard seclusion as a desirable option that would both liberate them from everyday heavy domestic chores and project-related activities, and raise their social status. A second group of women consists of the wives of local successful farmers, among whom seclusion is already practised, though not universal, and assumes different degrees of rigour. It varies from the generally observed rule that a woman may not leave her compound (*gida*) without her husband's permission, to permanent seclusion within the household's boundaries. These women are engaged in the typical Hausa women's petty trade of cooked food-stuffs, carried around and sold by a secluded woman's young daughters. The few secluded women I could contact did not complain about their status, but instead they highlighted the religious value of seclusion and underlined its aspects of flexibility rather than its constraining nature. However, I did not spend enough time with representatives of this group to be able to draw any well-founded conclusion on their perspectives. A third approach, which the majority of Keita's inhabitants would definitely regard as "revolutionary," is the one held by the young extension agents of the *Division pour la Promotion Féminine et Socio-Économique.* I was able to hold extensive semi-structured interviews with each of the thirteen *animatrices.* Only three of them declared themselves in favor of female seclusion, whereas the remaining ten clearly stated that they would not be disposed to give up their independence. Two among these ten asserted they would refuse to get married if they knew in advance that their husband would impose seclusion on them. These women's position is not representative of the mentality of village women, yet it is significant because it belongs to the very women who are most closely involved with the PDR/ADM's approach to gender. It is also noteworthy that, in contrast to village-women, they are partially literate and have received some "Western-style" schooling.[11] Through anti-conventional training these women have acquired a perspective which exhibits a different paradigm of judgement and action. However, they face the risk of social stigmatization, which might even prevent them from getting married, and ultimately exclude them from access to basic property rights. As has been suggested by different authors (e.g., Shipton and Goheen; Berry, *No Condition Is Permanent*; Platteau), access to property rights in sub-Saharan Africa depends not so much on the recognition of individual human rights, as on a person's belonging to a social network, often defined in the idiom of kinship. However, the social recognition of membership depends, as in societies elsewhere, on a person's good-standing within a group (Shipton and Goheen 312), and can be denied to members who choose not to comply with locally sanctioned norms and practices.

The following case study outlines the bargaining process that is going on between participants holding contrasting interpretations of women's role, and focuses on the connection between the outcome of this bargaining process and women's actual access to property rights.

3. Case Study: The Evolution of "Women's Role" within the PDR/ADM

The following account describes an operation started in July 1995 in the Village of Tinkirana Tounga (TT), aimed at giving the women of TT exclusive and inalienable control over a rehabilitated perimeter situated at their village's outskirts. At that time, project management considered this operation an "experiment."

The PDR/ADM had always relied consistently on women's work, due to male out-migration; to the fact that lower social standards for women's status would make it less degrading for the poorest among them to participate to the PDR/ADM's works; and because the payment

---

[11]I.e., they have attended Keita's "Western-style" school, as opposed to local Koranic schools that are, in any case, mainly frequented by boys; cf. Rossi, *Rapporto di Missione*.

in PAM[12] rations is seen as a particularly appropriate retribution for a woman's work, women being responsible for the preparation of meals for household consumption, and otherwise engaged in petty trading of foodstuff exceeding household requirements. TT's operation also responded to a growing international sensitivity to the adverse consequences of development interventions for women, reflected in the "WID[13]-focus" of successive consultancies by Italian and Nigerian sociologists (Cremona; Bayard, Gamatié 1995) the final outcome of which was the creation, in April 1997, of the "Division for the Promotion of Women" (Bayard, Paoletti, and Traoré).

In July 1995, with the help of a Project's extension agent, the women of TT bought 5 Ha. of rehabilitated land from the Village Chief and his Brother, the land's original owners, and redistributed the lot among themselves in sub-parcels of equal extension.

The women immediately started to cultivate spices and food crops on their individual parcels, and I learned recently that another strip of land, adjacent to the initial area, was rehabilitated later, and redistributed to the same women-owners.

The operation soon became very popular, and women from other villages started asking the extension officers of the PDR/ADM, with whom they had daily contacts on the sites of intervention (*chantiers*), to replicate the initiative in their villages. In a few cases the PDR/ADM received letters by the representative of pre-existing *groupements*, who had already selected a site and contacted its owner/s, and only awaited the Projects' agents to agree on the credit, convoke local administrative officers, and deal with the bureaucratic and technical aspects of the operation.

Tinkirana Tounga had set a template and, at the same time, international and local sensitivities to gender issues and "Women in Develop-

---

[12]*Projet d'Alimentation Mondial*. PAM contribution to Keita's Development Project consisted in 4,438,505 food rations for the Project's first phase and 3,522,428 for the second phase. Data are not available yet for the beginning of the third phase. The standard ration distributed in Keita has the following composition, with equivalent values in FCFA (PDR/ADM 1997): Millet, 2,250 Kg. / 248 FCFA; Sugar, 0,050 Kg. / 20 FCFA; Oil, 0,075 Kg. / 50 FCFA; Cow-peas (*niébé*), 0,200 Kg. / 28 FCFA; Tinned meat, 1 tin / 83 FCFA; Total value, 429 FCFA (approx. US $0,86).
[13]"Women in Development."

ment" discourses had reached their apex. In this intellectual environment, the Mission "Bayard-Paoletti-Traoré" (1996) charged with evaluating the preconditions and potentialities for the establishment of a new "Division for the Promotion of Women" found fertile ground for its recommendations. At the last moment, the name chosen for the Division was changed into *Division pour la Promotion Féminine et Socio-économique* (DPFSE), but the designation, as will soon become clear, was an unfelicitous one. It started its activities in April 1997 and in six months the newly established Division had replicated the Tinkirana operation in eight areas. The Division's yearly program foresaw the acquisition of 30 women-tracts, i.e., an average of 2.5 tracts per month (Traoré).

The DPFSE took over all the women-focused operations that had already been started by the PDR/ADM, and commenced new ones. Its activity, in September 1997, had reached the following state:

- 86 *groupements féminins* had been constituted, involving a total number of 6,254 women;
- 8 tracts had been bought by women through a Project credit and redistributed among the *groupement's* members, thus giving to 551 women individual ownership of a parcel (taking TT as a model);
- 27 *groupements* (653 women) were engaged in the production of new plants (*pépinières*), contributing to the reforestation target on the PDR/ADM's agenda, and gaining a total revenue of 25,000 FCFA (approx. US $50) in six months of business;
- 49 *groupements* had developed an economic activity linked to cereal processing at Project-supervised mills;
- 25 *groupements* were commercializing sun-flower oil;
- 27 *groupements* had formed a "committee of hygiene," and
- 19 *groupements* hosted a women-run "village-pharmacy."
- All of the existing *groupements* either had benefited or were benefiting from "functional alphabetization courses," run by an ad hoc Division within the PDR/ADM, aimed at instructing at least two members of the *groupement's* "comité de gestion" (president, vice-president, secretary, and treasurer) on how to fill in the forms illustrating the state of a *groupement's* activities at any time.

Therefore, in September 1997, women had become direct interlocutors of the PDR/ADM. This gradual but consistent shift in the project management's relation to local inhabitants, characterized by an increasing support to women's socio-economic activities, did not pass unnoticed by local men. At the time of my last research visit to Keita, men openly voiced their resentment with regard to what they perceived as an "unjust inequality of treatment" toward them.

The project management's reply to their remonstrations highlighted that the principal beneficiaries of the bulk of PDR/ADM operations are male land owners and farmers. Once rehabilitated through the kind of interventions described above, the Ader-Doutchi-Majiya lands would sustain increased agricultural production and cattle raising, and it would be the men who, individually or united in state-recognized co-operatives, would gain the major benefits from a "restored environment." According to the Project's staff, Keita's men did not need the extra-support required by women to organize themselves into producer groups and to gain access to exclusive property of land and "landed resources" (Riddel). The "project view" on this subject is that men rely on a pre-existing ideological substratum, undoubtedly not coinciding with "Western" capitalist relations of production, yet ideologically and practically supporting male entrepreneurial activities. Such a substratum is non-existent for women, and this is why it is women who should receive extra support by the "Division for the Promotion of Women and of Socio-Economic Activities."

However, the installation of the DPFSE coincided in time with a major "life crisis" in the PDR/ADM's evolution. In fact, the experienced Italian agronomist who had directed the PDR/ADM since its very start, and who was and is widely accepted as the "author" of the Project's success, retired from the position as Project manager and was replaced by a Nigerian agronomist. The passing over of project management to a Nigerian expert is in line with the orientation of the project's third phase, which foresees a gradual devolution of all interventions to local administration, in view of the forthcoming, if not yet established, "unmooring" of the PDR/ADM apparatus.

It is noteworthy that the incoming project manager graduated from the same Italian university as the previous project director. However, if there are elements of continuity in the "technical" understanding of the PDR/ADM's intervention on the territory, its "social approach" has inevitably taken a new course, as old and new management come from different social and cultural backgrounds.

Also within the DPFSE itself, tensions on issues of participation emerged with a new appointment to the office of vice-director of the Division. Before beginning to work for the PDR/ADM, the actual director had been an active member of the RDFN (*Ressemblement Democratique des Femmes du Niger*), a national organization originated from an internal division within the AFN (*Association des Femmes du Niger*). The latter was one of the ramifications of the *Société de Développement*, the institutional framework created by President Seiny Kountché in the early 80s to give a "new impulse" to Nigerian participatory development. The RDFN comprises the most anti-conformist tendencies of the AFN, and its policies are open to some "Western" feminist issues still rather unpopular among the majority of lobbying groups in Niger.

The activities of the newly established division, under the supervision of the director alone, had been primarily focused toward "women empowerment," reaching the results that have already been presented. The vice-director, a recently graduated socio-economist specialised in agricultural management, arrived at a time when men's disappointment with the "skewed tendency" of the DPFSE was at its higest. Interpreting the denomination of the division as suggesting that it should support not "women only" but all local "socio-economic activities," the vice-director started replicating in the villages the successful structure of the *groupement feminin*, with the only difference that, now, the participants involved were men.

That the new institution should be a "men only" prerogative was not explicitly stated, but it seemed obvious, women being already active and organized in the *groupements féminins*, presented as strictly open to women only, and because of the widespread local refusal, with few exceptions, to join into mixed *groupements*. Women resented such an initiative on the grounds that if they were to work together with men, the latter would make all decisions leaving them in a subordinate position. Men, on the other hand, emphasized a feeling of inappropriateness and "shame" in working next to women. The Hausa term used is *kunia*, but such a feeling is most emphasized by the members of Tuareg nobility, who use the terms *uksad* (to fear), or *takrakit* (shame), often associated with rules of sexual behavior (Nicolaisen and Nicolaisen 706).

This situation gave rise to tensions and misunderstandings within the Division, heightened by the fact that the director and her vice had separate working schedules and extension teams, a situation perceived, at the village level, as a "two-party structure" within the PDR/ADM, with one "party" advocating women's rights, and the other supporting men's initiatives. Several factors contributed to reinforce such a vision, three of which are particularly relevant.

First, in December 1998, men's fears of seeing their position weakened were not entirely unjustified, as, at that time, they were also facing the dissolution of the USRC (*Union Sous-Regional de Cooperatives*). A local-level branch of the UNC (*Union National de Cooperatives*), the USRC had been in charge of following the evolution of the cooperatives of producers, entirely constituted by men, which had been at first supported by the PDR/ADM, and then passed on to the UNC public structure. Keita's producers had invested a considerable subscription fee to join the USRC, and were justly preoccupied not merely with the sudden lack of support its dissolution would engender for their activities, but also with the likelihood that they would not be able to recover any money entrusted to the USRC. Therefore, while their women were gaining new forms of support thanks to the intervention of the DPFSE, they could see the supporting structures on which they had relied until then crumble to pieces.

Secondly, and adding up to their feeling of increased vulnerability, following the recommendations of the above mentioned Bayard-Paoletti-Traoré 1996 Report, which had laid down the premises for the constitution of the DPFSE, the PDR/ADM was considering the opening of a *Guichet de Credit aux Femmes*. The *Guichet*'s organization would be entrusted to the RDFN, and, apparently, the majority of micro-credit operations would be carried out in favor of women only.

Thirdly, the new project manager appeared to be sensitive to men's preoccupations, and interpreted the signs of gender turmoil as a "healthy" reaction of local society to excessive demands on the part of women, likely to undermine what he saw as the basis of Nigerian social structure, i.e., "familial solidarity."

On my departure from Keita, the scenario I left behind seemed to develop in two directions. On the one hand, the clash within the DPFSE was being steadfastly amended, as it was conducive to personal resentments and consequent organizational difficulties for the whole project. One of the measures taken to solve the question of who should take advantage of the Divison's support, was to change its name to *Division pour la Promotion Féminine*, in line with its original orientation as a specific structure to promote the role of women.

On the other hand, the "promotion of the role of women" formula was given a new "favored interpretation," which emphasized the "traditional" role of women in the household, and *as* household members. The vagueness of the term "traditional," however, makes it a formula that could easily be used instrumentally to limit, rather than promote, women's chances to improve their own independence and self-respect. An emphasis on "tradition" could lead to an increased male control over female activities through the practice of wife seclusion.

Seclusion is locally identified with culturally sanctioned values that go beyond the sphere of "gender ideology," such as religious piety and high social status, and mutually strengthen each other so as to produce an image of internal coherence ultimately backing patriarchal power. If women were to resist seclusion, they would appear to be opposing not just male supremacy, but also some basic religious and moral values, which are portrayed as the foundations of social stability. Wife seclusion was unknown in local societies' pre-Islamic background, but, as mentioned above, the Ader-Doutchi-Majiya area was situated at the heart of the nineteenth-century Sokoto Caliphate, and therefore directly exposed to the religious teachings of Shehu Ousman Dan Fodio.

As socialized members of their society, local women have internalized its values in their everyday habits, practices, and beliefs, and often subscribe to dogmas that, while apparently belonging to fields other than gender relations, are directly relevant to the sexual division of labor and women's independence.

The situation I have observed in Keita is consistent with Cooper's observation that

> the suggestion that men see seclusion as a means of limiting women's access to farmland should give us pause. Female seclusion has, particu-

larly recently, served as a locus of contestation between rural men and women over both female labor and women's access to land: women may acquiesce to seclusion in order to limit the demands upon their labor only to find that their husbands interpret their dependent status as a justification for denying them their traditional usufruct rights to land through marriage. (Cooper 1994:76)

4. Re-definitions and Re-distributions: Land, Property, and Gender

In his analysis of the Jahaly-Pacharr Irrigation Project in The Gambia, Michael Watts shows that, in a patriarchal system, the position of authority occupied by men endows them with a greater power to influence the outcome of ongoing bargaining and negotiations related to gender relations. He argues that "If successful, [. . .] male claims in effect transfer labor from personal, individually 'owned' property to domains directly controlled by men in the name of collective goods and domestic security" (Watts 187). The case described here is not entirely analogous to the situation presented by Watts, whose argument stands on the distinction between collective "*maruo*" lands and individually owned *kamanyango* parcels,[14] but it leads to similar theoretical implications for the study of development projects' impact on gender relations.

If Keita's men, supported by the new project management, are able to recast the meaning of "the promotion of women" into an understanding of "women" as primarily household members, then women's needs and rights will coincide with the ones ascribed to them by the dominant (patriarchal) ideology. This hypothesis is also supported by Dunbar's observation that

> [f]ear of social upheaval is an old theme of political discourse in Niger. Across Africa and elsewhere, improving the status of women is often linked in the minds of public officials with potential social upheaval. This places women in a double bind. On the one hand the State exhorts women to devote more energies to the development process. On the other, it holds back on substantive changes that might make it possible for them to improve the quality of their lives, unless it is tied to the

---

[14]Interestingly, Hausa land-tenure system is characterized by a similar distinction between communal lands (*gandu*) and individual parcels (*gamana* or *gayauna*), but my field research has not gone far enough to allow me to establish a parallel with Watts's evidence in Gambia.

economic good of the whole society [. . .]. Stated in the most positive manner possible, such ambivalence, a product of patriarchal tradition and contemporary development objectives, lends a two-steps forward, one step backward flavour to public policies concerning women. (Dunbar, *Nigérien Women* 5)

It is helpful to start from Bates's presupposition that ". . . property rights do not represent rights over material objects; rather they represent rights with respect to people: [. . .] to alter property rights is to redefine social relationships" (qtd. in Carney and Watts 217). The converse also holds true, namely that redefining social relationships alters pre-existing understandings of the needs and rights of different social factions. This appears to be all the more true in the sub-Saharan African context, where, as Sarah Berry pointed out, "the definition of property rights hinges on the demarcation of social boundaries" (qtd. in Watts 159). It follows that "struggles over land and labor [are] simultaneously symbolic contests and struggles over meaning" (Watts 161), and specifically, over the culturally sanctioned meaning ascribed to gender roles and relations.

In the example illustrated above, Keita's society, like Jahaly Pacharr's, had to face new visions of gender in the form of a renewed impulse of women-focused initiatives rooted in the spread of "Women and Development" and "Gender and Development" policies within the PDR/ADM.

Henrietta Moore has argued convincingly that social settings produce culturally accepted definitions of identities, which are stratified along axes of inequality. Otherwise stated, society is composed of various groups, each group holding different, often contrasting, and hierarchically ranked, interests. In Bourdieu's terms, different actors within any field (e.g., the field of gender relations; of marriage strategies; of ownership of land; etc.) hold different stakes of "Capital," and their capacity to influence the direction of events, as well as to produce visions and divisions of social reality, is not the same. In Keita, men detain a higher stake of "symbolic capital," as opposed to women, which allows them, in the absence of external interferences such as the PDR/ADM's operations, to find support for their own interpretations of the "promotion of women," i.e., to define what is appropriate for a woman to access, claim, own, and do.

However, women, and other subordinate groups, are not entirely passive, but are engaged in an ongoing process of bargaining and negotiation (Moore, *Anthropology and Africa*), which is primarily, with Carney and Watts, an interpretative struggle over meaning. If they succeed in altering local cultural constructions of gender, the women of Keita might be able to redefine their role in ways that sanction women's access to individually owned plots of land and to the sphere of economic entrepreneurship, or, more plausibly, to some local adaptation of these targets set up for them by the project.

Nevertheless, in addition to men's opposition, another obstacle to the women's task is the fact that their own perceptions of a woman's role and well-being might be, and my evidence suggests that in many cases it is, moulded by the dominant patriarchal ideology. Measures of well-being do not necessarily coincide with the fulfilment of perceived interests, as "in some contexts the family identity may exert such a strong influence on our perceptions, that we may not find it easy to formulate any clear notion of our own individual welfare" (Sen 125). Thus if, on the one hand, researchers advocate intra-household research methods that take into consideration the opposed interests of the individuals within a household, such views are still almost non-existent among Keita's women.

Seen from the perspective of Gidden's Structuration Theory, one of the elements that make possible a meaningful social world is the "contextuality" of action, i.e., the characteristic of human action to be rooted in shared structures of meaning. Shared definitions of objects, needs, rights, and identities, depend on the "indexicality of contexts" (Giddens 100), "indexicality" being the characteristic of social arenas to be organized through publicly recognizable institutions and concepts. Indexicality should not, however, be confused with context-dependency, but should instead be seen as both constraining and enabling, as individuals (e.g., Keita's women), through their "reflexive monitoring of action" (Giddens 98-ff.), can renegotiate their subordinate position, providing new interpretations of the roles ascribed to them by dominant ideologies.

The introduction of exogenous ideas and practices, which inevitably accompanies the intervention of international aid projects, adds new meanings to local discourses and "Power-Knowledge,"[15] in this case about gender.

The long-lasting presence of the PDR/ADM in the district of Keita makes it an ideal site for the observation of what Long has called "interface studies," characterized by

> the analysis of discontinuities in social life. Such discontinuities imply discrepancies in values, interests, knowledge and power, and typically occur at points where different and often conflicting life-worlds or social domains intersect. (Long 1996:55)

In such a situation, the relation of power, which defines the contrasting interests of different social groups, is rendered increasingly unstable by the interference of exogenous conceptualizations and understandings of gender roles and values. In the case illustrated above, the intervention of the new DPFSE introduced a new set of practices and ideas (e.g., land commoditization, credit to women, women as private land-owners, etc.) in pre-existing local gender ideologies. In so doing, it acted as a catalyst for the rearrangement of local gender relations, which is, in any case, a regular process determined by the ongoing bargaining in which different groups of situated actors are engaged.

In a syncretic way, exogenous ideas are re-interpreted and integrated in pre-existing ideologies, and therefore "amplify" the indexicality of the ideal contexts available for local actors to reflect upon, evaluate social reality, and act upon it. The development of such new interpretations is more frequent at "interface sites," where old moral codes and values are constantly being confronted with, and challenged by, new "imported" ones.

In conclusion, whether the women of Keita will ultimately see their independence increased or decreased depends on the interaction of two critical factors. First, on the support they will receive from the project management, which had initially been responsible for introducing new

---

[15]I am using Foucault's terminology here to indicate that such "knowledge" and "discourses" are never power-neutral, but, again, stratified and reflecting the perceptions and interests of their authors.

interpretations and understandings of gender, largely informed by "Western" development thinking and policies, but that has recently adopted a new line, à la Nigérienne, the direction of which is difficult to predict at this stage. Secondly, it depends on the reaction that their increased independence will generate among men, particularly in the short run, while the latter are still powerful enough to prevent women, even through physical coercion, but perhaps more effectively through moral stigmatization, from adhering to new "revolutionary" initiatives.

Works Cited

Bachar, M. *Étude en vue de l'aménagement d'un sous-bassin versant dans la zone d'intervention du projet Keita*. Mémoire de Maîtrise de Géographie, Département de Géographie, Université Abdou Moumouni de Niamey, Niger, 1996.

Baier, S. "Economic History and Development: Drought and the Sahelian Economics of Niger." *African Economic History* 1 (1976): 1–17.

___. *An Economic History of Central Niger*. Oxford: Clarendon, 1980.

Baxter, P. T. W. "Some Consequences of Sedentarization for Social Relationships." Monod 206–29.

Bayard, M. G. *Étude sur l'Analyse des Impacts Sociaux du Projet Integré de Keita. (Rapport Provisoir)*. Niamey: Unpublished Document, 1995.

___., P. Paoletti, and A. Traoré. *Rapport de Mission: La mise en place de la Division Socio-Économique et de la Promotion Féminine*. Rome: FAO, 1997.

Bernus, E. "L'Évolution recente des relations entre éleveurs et agriculteurs en Afrique Tropicale: L'exemple du Sahel Nigérien." *Cah. ORSTOM*, Ser. Sci. Hum., 11.2 (1974): 137–43.

___, and J. Nicolaisen. "Structures Politiques et sociales des Tuaregs de l'Air et de l'Ahaggar." *Études Nigériennes* (1982): 7–9.

Berry, S. *No Condition Is Permanent: The Social Dynamics of Agrarian Change in Sub-Saharan Africa*. Madison: U of Wisconsin P, 1993.

Bonte, P. "Structure de classe et structures sociales chez les Kel Gress." *Rev. Occ. Mus. Med.* 21 (1976): 141–62.

Bourdieu, P. *Outline of a Theory of Practice*. Cambridge: Cambridge UP, 1977.

___. *The Logic of Practice*. Cambridge: Polity, 1990.

Bourgeot, A. "Analyse des rapports de production chez les pasteurs et les agriculteurs de l'Ahaggar." Monod 263–84.

___. "Rapports esclavagistes et conditions d'affranchissement chez les Imuhag (Tuareg Kel Ahaggar)." Meillassoux 77–97.

Carney, J. and M. Watts. "Manufacturing Dissent: Work, Gender and the Politics of Meaning in a Peasant Society." *Africa* 60.2 (1990): 207–41.

Cooper, B. *The Women of Maradi: A History of the Maradi Region of Niger from the "Time of Cowries" to the "Time of Searching for Money" 1900–1989*. Ph.D. Thesis, Boston University, 1992.

___. "The Politics of Difference and Women's Associations in Niger: of 'Prostitutes,' the Public, and Politics." *Signs: Journal of Women in Culture and Society* 20.4 (1995): 851–82.

___. *Marriage in Maradi. Gender and Culture in a Hausa Society in Niger.* Portsmouth: Heinemann, 1997.

Cremona, L. *Étude du milieu. Résultats partiels des enquêtes villageois.* Document de Travail, PDR/ADM. Rome: FAO, 1985.

Dunbar, R. A. *Nigerian Women and Access to Productive Resources: an Assessment in View of the Projét du Code Rural.* Paper Presented at the XXXIII Annual Meeting of the African Studies Association, Baltimore, MD, 1990.

Foucault, M. *Madness and Civilization.* 1961. New York: Vintage, 1988.

___. *The Order of Things.* 1971. New York: Vintage, 1994.

___. *Discipline and Punish.* 1975. New York: Vintage, 1995.

Giddens, A. *The Constitution of Society.* Berkeley: U of California P, 1984.

Lovejoy, P., and Baier, S. "The Tuareg of the Central Sudan: Gradations in Servility at the Desert's Edge (Niger and Nigeria)." *Slavery in Africa: Historical and Anthropological Perspectives.* Ed. I. Kopytoff and S. Myers. Madison: U of Wisconsin P, 1977.

Meillassoux, C. *L'esclavage en Afrique pré-coloniale.* Paris: Maspero, 1975.

Monod, T., ed. *Pastoralism in Tropical Africa.* London: Oxford UP, 1975.

Moore, H. L. *Feminism and Anthropology.* Cambridge: Polity, 1988.

___. *A Passion for Difference.* Cambridge: Polity, 1994.

___, ed. *The Future of Anthropological Knowledge.* London: Routledge, 1996.

Moore, S. F. *Anthropology and Africa: Changing Perspectives in a Changing Scene.* Charlottesville: UP of Virginia, 1994.

Nicolaisen, J., and I. Nicolaisen. *The Pastoral Tuareg: Ecology, Culture and Society.* 2 vols. London: Thames and Hudson, 1997.

Platteau, J. P. "The Evolutionary Theory of Land Rights as Applied to Sub-Saharan Africa: A Critical Assessment." *Development and Change* 27 (1996): 29–86.

___. *Reforming Land Rights in Sub-Saharan Africa: Issues of Efficiency and Equity.* UNRISD Discussion Paper no. 60, 1995.

Riddel, J. C. "Dynamics of Land Tenure and Spontaneous Changes in African Agrarian Systems." *Land Reform: Land Settlement and Cooperatives* 1/2 (1988).

Rossi, B. *Rapporto di Missione, Keita 1998.* Roma: Ministero degli Affari Esteri, Cooperazione allo Sviluppo, Unità Tecnica Centrale, 1998.

Sen, A. "Gender and Cooperative Conflicts." *Persistent Inequalities: Women and World Development.* Ed. I. Tinker. New York: Oxford UP, 1990.

Shipton, P., and M. Goheen. "Understanding African Land-holding: Power, Wealth and Meaning." *Africa* 62.3 (1992): 307–25.

Traoré. *Tableau des réalisations par rapport au programme annuel.* Keita: FAO, 1997.

Watts, M. *Silent Violence: Food, Famine, and Peasantry in Northern Nigeria.* Berkeley: U of California P, 1993.

LAISSEZ-FAIRE, DYADIC KENYA-ITALY RELATIONS
A Critical Review of Past, Present, and Future Directions

Musambayi Katumanga
Institute of Policy Research and Analysis (Nairobi, Kenya)

Eric Edwin Otenyo
Miami University

Introduction

This paper is an attempt to explain and describe the nature of the relations between Kenya and Italy in the immediate past and present times. Specifically, Italy formerly established relations with Kenya after the latter's independence in 1963. Even then it must be observed that Italians had already made their impact in the territory that was to become Kenya. For starts it was the threats from Italy that influenced the British agreement with Ethiopia on the northern boundaries of the Kenyan state. Consequently, Italian war prisoners were also responsible for the construction of some of the key road networks in Kenya. In the social realm, Italian priests were already working in Kenya by 1940 as missionaries and many came to establish important centers of learning in the new African nation. Once formal contacts were established between the two States, business and cultural contacts began to evolve.

Traditionally, the relations between one country and another can be analyzed through various angles. Attention can be paid to trade relations, cultural interactions, and sometimes military operations. Relationships can also be visualized in terms of state to state or people to people — denoting a society-centered intercourse. Yet these categories are not mutually exclusive, but are mutually reinforcing and are in various ways part and parcel of the same phenomenon. Naturally, in a discourse of this nature, the temptation to apply the center-periphery frame of analysis is strong and this is the orientation in our investigation. However, our point of departure is not to de-emphasize the world systems approach that Wallerstein so ably articulates. The world system approach presupposes some form of dependency between the interacting sets of nations. Rather than focus on this important characteristic, a clearer picture in the relations between Kenya and Italy is reflected in a complex web of laissez faire and nonlinear dynamics.

Three strands of this dynamic can be discerned. First, the relationship is bilateral, between Kenya and Italy. Second, it is multilateral between Kenya and Italy as a constituent of the European communities. Third, Kenya interacts with Italy as a member of the Western hegemonic power belt under the tutelage of the United States. In all these situations, the center-periphery dynamics are not in doubt. Essentially, the core-periphery analogy as posited by Tarrow applies mainly in the case of Italy as a European power and one of the key seven industrialized states. When Italy relates to Kenya, in whichever form, for the most part, the African state assumes a subordinate role while the European state takes the superior position. This is not a new revelation; on the contrary, it is a restatement of European control and domination of Africa over the years.

Yet the cases specific to Italy are unique: Italy never colonized Kenya or a substantial part of Africa. Italy occupied Eritrea in 1885 and under Mussolini invaded Emperor Haile Selassie's Ethiopia in 1935 but lost control of the region in 1941. Its late entry and unsuccessful attempt in the horn of Africa did produce some legacy and ramifications on the Kenyan state. However, in retrospect, arguably the noncolonial Italy has been more influential. The latter consideration is important in one respect: Italian engagement in Kenya is intriguing especially because of the strong presence of an Italian community in post-independent Kenya. The aspects of the relations are threefold: aid, trade, and culture.

Italy as Donor State

There are three kinds of donors discernible in the current relationships between Kenya and the western countries, including Italy: the *hard*, *soft,* and the *no conditionality* donors (Ngunyi). These categories can be refined to include what, for lack of a better term, can be classified as "black list" or "red card" relationships that denote absence of diplomatic contacts. Such classifications should not give the impression of discrete categories. On the contrary, gray areas abound and may quite well explain the Kenya-Italy relationship. Regardless of the classifications, if we narrow our analysis to bilateral assistance, Italy together with France approximates the third group. The non-conditionality donors are those States that express no interest in making aid conditional on democratization and respect of human rights, issues that are synonymous with African politics.

Italian assistance to Kenya has been in literally all fields of human endeavor. Assistance has also been in matters of human resource development (for example in the Africover project on data management) and actual project assistance. Before 1984, Italian aid came mainly in the form of technical assistance and grants to finance feasibility studies in agriculture and agro-industry. After 1984, the focus changed to direct investment in agriculture, agro-industry, health and urban services, telecommunications, and health services. In 1985–86, Italy and Kenya agreed on the start of new projects in the area of food storage. This was in response to the request by the Kenyan government to move toward food security after a devastating drought and famine in 1984. More recently, in June 2000, Italy became among the first bilateral donors to contribute food aid to Kenya. The Italian government donated 2,500 tons of food as well as US$50 million to help Kenya cope with its worst famine (*Daily Nation* 14 July 2000).

Italy provided Kenya with a grant to construct cyprus bins for grain storage in Kitale and Nakuru. Through *Fondo Aiuti Italiani* (Italian Aid Fund), over 1.45M Kenya shillings were provided for the construction of 34 stores throughout the country.[1] Phase I of the project was a grant for building prefabricated steel structures especially in the food deficit northern regions of Kenya. By December 31, 1986, these were completed at roughly 13.16 billion Liras. Phase II entailed the construction of an additional 16 stores at places such as Malava, Kipkarren Salient, Karatina, Kwale, Kilifi, Tenges, Chavakali, Kapsokwony, Kimalel, Lessos, Makueni, Ndanai, Garsen, Bomet, and Sotik. Phase III of the project involved Italy providing 13,474,000 Liras for constructing a bulk Grain Silo Complex, planned in 1992 but shelved due to the failure of the government of Kenya to provide a suitable location for the project and also to the coincidence with policy changes that were negotiated within the

---

[1] One Kenyan pound (K£) equals 20 shillings.

European Community-funded program of the Cereal Sector Reform Program (CSRP) and the World Bank-funded Agricultural Sector Adjustment Operations (ASAO) that sought to reduce the role of the state in grain marketing. Nonetheless, phases I and II were successfully completed with the main contractor being M/S CISA Internazionale, Spa, of Udine, Italy.

Other aid projects funded by the Italian government were in areas such as refuse collection; brick and tiles project; the Western Kenya irrigation project; Telecommunications; commodity aid to supply rice, fertilizers, pesticides, and chemicals; and urban transport initiatives. Italy followed this latter project by providing several hundred buses to help set up the Nyayo Bus transport system for the urban and selected rural areas. Additionally, Italy supported the Kenya government with the donation of 15 ambulances and 12 equipped mobile clinic vehicles. These were presented directly to President Moi (*The Standard* 7 May 1987).

Also important are the Moi University computer project, Kuja river multi-purpose project, and the Rift Valley Institute of Science and Technology project (*The Standard* 2 June 1987). It is worth pointing out that assistance to Kenya began to increase in the tenure of Prime Minister Betino Craxi (*Kenya Times,* hereafter *KT,* 15 March 1989). Close to 95% of Italian aid is in the form of loans and is primarily linked to its commercial interests in Kenya. Currently Italy occupies the fourth position in the hierarchy of the ten leading aid donors to Kenya. Critical in the Italian funded projects was the Nol Turesh water pipeline that takes water from the Kilimanjaro to the Districts of Machakos and Kajiado. Other Italian supported projects in Kenya include: the Kirandichi water project, the Kitui water project, the Sigor Kerio Valley Weiwei project for hydro-Agricultural development, and emergency rehabilitation of Mai Mahiu Naivasha road constructed for K.SH.39.8 million. Italy also continues to assist the Rift Valley Technical Training Institute and the Kenyatta National Hospital (*Sunday Nation* 2 June 1996).

Trade Interactions

As one of the "no conditionality states," Italy did not impose economic sanctions on Kenya in November, 1991, a fact that was highly appreciated by Kenya (*KT* 21 July 1993). As a matter of fact, Kenya's exports to Italy increased from Kenya Pounds 20,447,000 in 1986; 16,978,000 in 1987; 32,763,000 in 1988; 26,951,000 in 1989; 39,291,000 in 1991; K£ 42,422,000 in 1992; K£ 66,108,000 in 1993; and 78,454,000 in 1994. At the opposite end, Kenya imported from Italy merchandize valued at K£ 48,845,000 in 1986; 48,391,000 (1987); 63,922,000 (1988); 100,128,000 (1989); 119,586,000 (1990); 91,919,000 (1991); 87,835,000 (1992); 228,089,000 (1993); and 175,326,000 pounds for 1994. (See comparative figures below.)

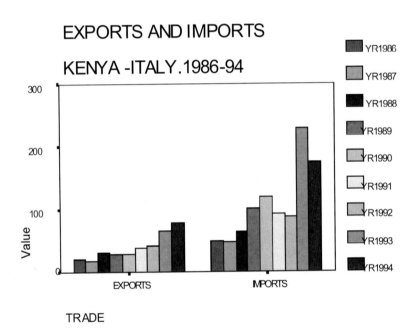

From the above figures, clearly a trade imbalance exists in favor of Italy. Today, the estimated figures indicate that Italy exports goods worth 5 billion Kenya shillings and imports only 2 billion Kenya shillings worth of goods (*Daily Nation* 7 August 1998). Incidentally, imports were high at the time when Kenya was facing a foreign currency crunch following the suspension of nonessential balance of payment support. This high trade could have been a function of credit facilities extended to

Kenya by the Italian government. For instance the Italian government gave Kenya a grant of 828 million, the bulk of which was to be used to purchase tractors for the Nyayo Tea Zones (*Daily Nation* 17 December 1993).

By 1995, trade between the two countries increased. For instance, during the first six months of 1995, Italian exports amounted to $87m compared to $89m for the whole of 1994. On the other hand imports from Kenya remained stable at around $46m. These mainly consisted of skins, fruits, frozen fish, coffee, and tea. Most of Italian exports to Kenya are mainly in plastic materials, agricultural and industrial machinery, spare parts, and chemicals. What emerges from the figures is that Italy remains an important trade partner for Kenya.

Investments and Cultural Issues

The discourse on trade and aid is incomplete without some reflection on the role and importance of Italian investments in Kenya. How Italy fits in the transnational and corporation world is of interest in the Kenya-Italy discourse as well. The starting point is that Italian multinationals are partakers of the "surplus value" from African resources. Maria Nzomo (444) takes a world systems-dependency approach to illustrate that Italy is also represented in the Kenyan political economy by, among other corporations, Brollo, Fiat Trucks, and Agip Petroleum products. Brollo in particular established itself in 1971 as a joint venture with Kenya. As a Multinational corporation (MNC), it "cheated the Kenya government of enormous amounts of money" through transfer pricing. By way of another illustration, Brollo sold Kenya goods that were over-priced by an average of about 100%. Besides, some of the machines it sold were obsolete and worthless in Italy (Nzomo 445). Treating MNCs in general as an avenue of exploitation is not confined to Africa alone but is a popular discourse in Latin American and Asian studies as well. Suffice it to say, Italian MNCs are important players in the entire MNC led industrialization regime in Kenya.

It is worth mentioning that today, Italy's main investments[2] in Kenya are in the area of tourism, particularly in Malindi — a Town of 45,000 on

---

[2]Other Italian investments in Kenya include Agip Oil, Alitalia, Alfa Romeo, Italcom (rep-

the Indian Ocean. Also, about 45,000 Italians visited Kenya in the last two to three years (*Daily Nation* 8 July 1998). So strong is the Italian influence in the town that out of every five people in the town two speak fluent Italian. Together with the significance of Italian Franciscan Catholics and other missionaries who have been an important feature in Kenya's rural settings, an elaborate Italian cultural export is also visible in the country through the Italian Institute of Culture in Nairobi. This center is important as a means of radiating Italian culture and also for affording Kenyans a chance to share their values with the Italian community in Kenya. Among the programs that have been popular are art exhibitions and musical shows. The center has been popular with the Kenyan youth and has witnessed painting exhibitions including the works of Rome-based artists Raffaele Ammavuta, Vanya Fornaciari, Giulio Greco, Cristiana Pucci, Valentina Ramacciottin, Marco Saviozzi, and an older painter Possenti. Several Italian Bands and musicians have performed in Nairobi, including pianist Ivano Borgazi, drummer Alessandro Lugli, trombonist Carlo Gelmini, and their Jazz Art Orchestra from Brescello, Italy.

Additionally, Kenyans have benefited from student exchange programs to Italy, including programs at Accademia di Belle Arti Vannucci in Perugia. Others have become members of Italian sporting clubs — particularly the world famous runners. So the interaction is significant as well.

The Hard Times of the Kenya-Italy Relations

Regardless of the locus of aid and trade in the relations between the two states and peoples, any evaluation of the impact of this relation cannot miss to discern the fluid nature of the intercourse. Consequently, it would be wrong to imagine that the dyadic relations between the two states have always been good. To a limited extent the converse is the case. As a matter of fact, these relations have at times been acrimonious, albeit with most of the crisis caused by Kenya.

---

resenting Italy's major telecommunicaters), Iveco, Olivetti, Fatta, Elianto, Farid, Fiat, Italtekna s.p.a (design and engineering services), Farmitalia Carlo Erba (pharmaceutical specialties), Cisa Internazionale, Telettra Telecommunications, and Enimont (E Africa) chemicals.

For instance, in 1989, the Malindi municipality rejected a request by some Italians to set up a K£180 million Casino arguing that such a step would push up the crime rate in the town (*KT* 3 March 1989). Malindi is an interesting town with a large presence of Italians in the community. Some commentators have argued that it is a haven for the Milan-based Mafia. The significance of this is that in the wake of the much touted globalization regime, parties such as *Alleanza Nazionale* and *Fiamma Tricolore* in Italy have bashed immigrants in Italy without mentioning the Italian presence in African countries. The presence of significant Italian populations on the Kenyan coast has been linked to crime, especially the Mafia. Our argument is that an immigration debate must take into consideration the totality of the issue.

Another area of concern with regard to Kenya-Italy relations is the association of Italian business concerns with dirty dealings. While this is not rampant, it must be put on the table. We say so because the nature of the Kenyan state is that it is on the verge of collapse due to endemic corruption among the state elite. A most illustrative example of this phenomenon is the saga surrounding the Kenya Chemical and Food Corporation (Kisumu Molasses) plant. In 1991, Italian investors featured prominently in the commission inquiry into the death of former Minister for Foreign Affairs Dr. Robert Ouko. It was increasingly pointed out that Dr. Ouko, who had at one time been Minister for Industrial Development, was assassinated by those who were opposed to his investigation of corruption, especially the molasses plant that was in his constituency.

According to accounts by Jonah Anguka, Ouko had opposed the deals that Ministers Nicholas Biwott, George Saitoti, and Elijah Mwangale made to operationalize the molasses and power-alcohol-making plant. Many non government Kenyan sources argue that the tender to rehabilitate the plant was given to rival Italian companies based on shady deals and bribes offered by one of the parties to the Moi establishment.

Anguka's thesis is that one of the reasons for the murder of Ouko was because of his whistle blowing activities against the corrupt Moi mafia. His book *Absolute Power* states that Ouko had mandated BAK, an international Italian-Swiss company, to identify a credible European firm to rehabilitate the molasses plant and also build a cement factory in Kisumu. BAK introduced Techint of Milan and Italy-Cement to do the job.

Yet, the work did not commence on the feasibility studies due to the insistence of the Moi administration on bribes and commissions. According to Mrs. Marriane Brinner Marten, the Chair of the BAK Group, Biwott demanded 15%, Vice President and Finance Minister Saitoti 10%, Kiptanui (State House Comptroller) 5–10%, Elijah Mwangale 5–10%, and Aslam, a banker, 5–10%. A Director with BAK, Domenico Airaghi got arrested and deported from Kenya on March 15, 1989, when BAK refused to yield to the pressure from the Moi administration and aides (Anguka part 3).

After Ouko's murder, Moi invited Scotland Yard detectives under Superintendent John Troon to investigate the murder. But this turned out to be mere window dressing, for the government made it impossible for Troon to "dig the facts." Troon was later to name Nicholas Biwott and Hezekiah Oyugi, a permanent Secretary in charge of Internal Security, as the key suspects in the murder. Throupe and Hornsby (59–60) reiterate the Anguka argument as does Smith Hempstone (68), the then V. S. Ambassador to Kenya. Throupe and Hornsby note that Biwott eventually received US$4 million from the Italian Contractor, the Italian branch of the International company Asea Brown Boveri, in return for securing the order to supply electrical equipment for the plant (59).

In the wake of increased pressure from the International Monetary Fund and the World Bank officials, the government of Kenya recently attempted to "clarify" the position regarding the Italian companies. We quote in detail:

> It has been alleged that there was rivalry between the Bak Group and the Tecnomasio Italiano Brown Boveri, a subsidairy of Asea Brown Boveri. The true position is that Tecnomasio Italiano Brown Boveri was part of the Bak Group. It was introduced to the Kenya government to replace Bak's earlier nominee, Techint, which had pulled out of the project as it was unable to fulfil its obligations to secure a grant from the Italian Government. It has been alleged that the rivalry between the Bak Group of companies and Tecnomasio Italiano Asea Brown Boveri led to bad blood between cabinet ministers Robert Ouko and Nicholas Biwott. There was no rivalry between the two Italian companies. They were all part of the Bak Group. . . . It has been alleged that Mr. Biwott influenced the removal of the Molasses Project from the agenda of the Kenya-Italy

bilateral talks held in November 1978. He hardly conspired with the cabinet colleague George Saitoti and Mr. Dalmas Otieno to remove the Molasses Project from the agenda. . . . As a matter of fact, the request to include this project on the agenda of the bilateral talks was made by the Bak Group to Kenya Government on November 3, 1987. (*Daily Nation* 27 November 1998)

The government of Kenya also stated that it did not award the contract to Tecnomasio Italiano Brown Boveri despite pleas from the BAK Group and Tecnomasio Brown Boveri itself. What is important from this narrative is that the alleged attempt by Minister Biwott to extort bribes from Tecnomasio Italiano Brown Boveri has featured significantly in the unresolved murder of Ouko — a stain that will forever be associated with Moi's long personal rule of this impoverished African state.

Regardless of the corruption case, nothing was more startling to the Italian population in Kenya than the allegations by the Kenyan president that Italian investors in Malindi were plotting to overturn his government in cohort with Raila Odinga, current chairman of the National Development Party (NDP), a son of Kenya's first Vice President, Oginga Odinga, and then Director of Elections in Forum for the Restoration of Democracy-Kenya Party (FORD-Kenya) (*Daily Nation* 23 May 1995). Significantly, the then Italian ambassador to Kenya Roberto di Leo denied these allegations (*Daily Nation* 6 April 1995). For some time the Italian community was viewed with suspicion. A partial explanation is that Raila's family have some residential investments at the Kenya Coast and an increasingly insecure Moi presidency may have spinned the news as a preemptive strategy. Nevertheless, the political culture in Kenya is riddled with conspiracies and lack of transparency. We may never be able to know the truth about this murky affair.

Raila himself had been detained by Moi on a number of occasions but has sprung back in recent times to become the leader of one of Kenya's important opposition parties, the National Development Party. The latter is currently "cooperating" with the ruling Kenya African National Union (KANU) in what is viewed by many to be an attempt by Moi's Kalenjin state elite to seek an alliance with the Luo-dominated NDP. The two, it is assumed, want to hedge themselves against the domination by the largest ethnic group, the Kikuyu.

Conclusion

Much scholarly attention has been provided with regard to the relations between Africa and Europe. Seemingly, the general patterns of intercourse continue to maintain as Europe provides aid while Africa receives it. Italy has provided substantial aid to Kenya and has also traded with it. In a nutshell, the thesis that the core provides the highly priced tools of modernization, such as machinery and other high tech equipment, while Africa sells cash crops and extractive raw materials holds in the case of the Kenya–Italy relations. The trade imbalance in favor of the core "penetrating" Italian state appears to fit into the profile of the Wallersteinian model of unequal exploitative relations. Notwithstanding the imbroglios, there are also vivid examples of infrastructures holding on as a monument to the association.

Yet, Italy remains an insignificant partner of the Western allies by its failure to condition aid disbursements to reforms in the African countries human rights practices. One gets the impression that the Italian government has lived up to Machiavelli's realist strategy of doing good and bad at the same time. On the one hand, the Italian government as a member of the EU and the Paris Club of Donors, voted to cut aid to Kenya, while at the same time celebrating contacts and business with an increasingly unpopular corrupt dictatorship. What we have argued is that the relationship between Kenya and Italy is significant and enduring, given the nature of assistance provided by Italy. However, pockets of a laissez faire attitude prevail in a true Machiavellian sense. The future, like the past, will continue to be business driven and Italy will make its calculations based on profit margins. Likewise, the Kenyan power elite will be hungry for any European patrons and will welcome Europeans as partners in its difficult search for modernization and economic growth, however skewed.

References
Anguka, J. *Absolute Power*. London: Zed Books, 1998.

Hempstone, S. *Rogue Ambassador: An African Memoir*. Sewanee: U of the South P, 1997.

Ngunyi, M. Unpublished Research Paper on "Donors in Kenya." IPAR Institute for Public Policy Analysis and Research, Nairobi, 1996.

Nzomo, M. "External Influence on the Political Economy of Kenya: The Case of MNCs." *Politics and Administration*. Ed. Walter O. Oyugi. Nairobi, Kenya: Konrad Adenaner Foundation and Editor, 1992.

Tarrow, S. *Between Center and Periphery. Grassroots Politics in Italy and France*. New Haven: Yale UP, 1977.

Throupe, D. W., and C. Hornsby. *Multi Party Politics in Kenya. The Kenyatta and Moi States and the Triumph of the System in the 1982 Election*. Athens: Ohio UP, 1998.

Wallerstein, I. *The Modern World System*. New York: Academic P, 1974.

___. *Africa and the Modern World*. Trenton, NJ: Africa World P, 1986.

THE LEGACY OF ITALIAN COLONIALISM

ITALY AND THE HORN
The Unbearable Weight of a Weak Colonialism

Giampaolo Calchi Novati
University of Pavia

From the outset of the colonial enterprise, Italian-African policy suffered a deficit of motivation and legitimacy. The Mediterranean with its familiar towns, harbors, and cultures, and plenty of Italian dwellers transplanted from the poor overpopulated lands of the Peninsula, was the main area of desirable expansion, but historical circumstances forced Italy to divert her attention from Tunisia and Egypt to the faraway and alien Horn of Africa. The Prime Minister, Benedetto Cairoli, did nothing to check the French occupation of Tunis, and the Foreign Minister, P. S. Mancini, author of well-known writings defending the basic rights of peoples and nations, declined the British offer to dispatch an expeditionary force against Urabi Pacha's nationalist uprising in Egypt. Africa was deemed not to be worthy of wasting the scarce resources of Italy, which was committed to building a nation, to establishing an integrated economy, and to working out a reliable network of alliances in Europe. The rising ambitions of some politicians did not meet a parallel commitment on the side of the business sector, still more attracted by investments and benefits in the newly reunified metropolitan state; in the entire story of Italian colonialism, dreams competed with interests almost making the authorities lose a sense of proportion. When the bell of conquests rang for Italy as well, Mancini, in January 1885, formulated a striking aphorism in a bid to convince a disoriented public opinion and hesitant parliamentarians: "The Red Sea is the key to the Mediterranean."

During the hectic years of the continent's partition, Italian territorial expansion in Eastern Africa attained its climax in the military confrontation with Emperor Menelik after his staunch decision to fight for the autonomy of the Ethiopian Empire. The defeat at the battle of Adowa in 1896 became the stain of blame that all Italian nationalists pledged to delete from the records of the Motherland, no matter what profits they expected to obtain by such a redemption. Obsession with Adowa had a strong impact on the fatal determination of the Fascist Government to initiate, in the mid-1930s, out-dated colonial adventures in Africa. Although Benito Mussolini focused his rhetoric on the Mediterranean, the *Mare Nostrum* of ancient Rome's historical memory, the target of his aggressiveness after all was Ethiopia. The founding of *Africa Orientale Italiana* (AOI) brought a large popularity to the *Duce* and spelt success for Fascism, making it easier to heal some of the negative consequences of the great world-wide depression.

Though Italy lacked the financial and technical resources, as well as the time, to effect a real transformation of the economy and society of AOI, from their headquarters in Haile Selassie's Palace, now the site of Addis Ababa University, Italian administrators hoped to achieve more far-reaching goals than mere imperialism. They believed that it was possible to change the very soul of Ethiopia by manipulating the hierarchical balance of power élites and major ethnic groups or nations. The Deputy General Governor, Enrico Cerulli, had always cherished as a scholar the idea to upgrade the peripheral nomadic Muslim peoples, if necessary at the expense of the Semitised Christian plateaux-dwellers, in order to gradually wear down Abyssinian resistance.

Due to the events of World War II, Italy lost all her possessions in Eastern Africa. The remaining colonial administration and military apparatus surrendered to British troops and to the Emperor's army in 1941. The AOI foundered and ceased to exist only five years after it had been pompously proclaimed. Italy left behind no credible legacy of influence and/or prestige that might have paved the way for the nation's return to Africa in any form whatsoever. The dismal reality was that Italy had been unable to establish any of those structures of mutual partnership and complicity that were normally the result of European imperialism, and that had often proved stronger and more resilient than direct colonial administration. It is possible to verify Italy's incapacity to carry out a consistent policy in the Horn of Africa, despite her virtual dominance in that region, in three crucial moments: (i) the disposal of Italian colonies as decided by the UN, (ii) the revolutionary changes in Somalia and Ethiopia following the seizure of power by the military, and (iii) the complete re-organization of power and authority that stemmed from the collapse of the established regimes in Somalia and Ethiopia and the affirmation of Eritrean national claims in 1991.

The terms of the 1947 Peace Treaty flatly demanded a formal renunciation of all Italy's colonies (of Libya beside the possessions in the Horn). No reservations existed as regards Ethiopia's legal status since the Peace Treaty recognized the full sovereignty of the Abyssinian empire and charged Italy with war damages. The conclusion of the war seemed to leave Italy no room to manoeuvre. Yet the Government did its utmost to fulfill a deep desire to regain the African empire, at least partly, possibly as a trusteeship. Italy prided herself for her colonial patrimony on the ground that her presence had been sustained by the hard work of many Italians rather than by capital investments. On the agenda of Italian foreign policy in the aftermath of World War II, the colonial issue was second in importance only to the dispute with Yugoslavia over Trieste. Even if almost all the Italian leaders who were working to build a democratic post-Fascist state paid lip-service to anti-colonial feelings, Government and opposition alike were committed to rescuing at least some colonies. Few if any at that time could have foreseen that the African continent would be so rapidly decolonized. In the meantime, Italy wished to preserve as many of the privileges and properties of the *coloni* [settlers] as possible, particularly in Eritrea.

The final destiny of the colonies would be determined by the so-called "four big powers" — America, Britain, France, and the Soviet Union — and if no deal was struck by September 1948, by the United Nations. In the end, Italy's residual aspirations, on the one hand, and the impending East-West confrontation, on the other, prevailed, overriding or baffling the rights of African peoples. The major powers were eager to make concessions or promises to Italy in an effort to secure the support of a state that was called to play a key role in the cold war thanks to its strategic location in the center of the Mediterranean. Great Britain and the United States had established sizable military bases and communication facilities in Eritrea and Libya. The Soviet Usnion envisaged the possibility of carving out a foothold in Africa indirectly through Italy if the left-wing coalition gained a majority in the April 1948 elections.

Italy's position during the discussions at the General Assembly was quite grim. Like all the defeated European nations, Italy had not yet been admitted to membership in the United Nations. Her former colonies were considered by many to be Arab countries and/or closely associated with the Muslim world, and they relied on the support of the Arab League as regards their claim for independence either at once or after a short period of administration under the aegis of the United Nations. The debate was dominated by the East-West dualism, and the main concern of the big powers was to prevent a widening of their counterparts' influence into the "grey areas" of the Third World. Britain and the United States were aware that hostility to Italy had spread throughout the Horn and feared that a pro-Italian verdict at the United Nations would step up unrest and riots that might be difficult to handle. Furthermore, Britain maintained strong reservations on pleasing an erstwhile enemy in both Europe and Africa. The Soviet Government was thoroughly sympathetic with the anti-colonial cause and in its mind the African territories were no exception. Italy was compelled to rely above all on the friendship of the Latin American countries with their twenty UN votes.

The outcome of the UN debate was disappointing in the light of Italian expectations, unless the real external goals of the Italian rulers were in Europe and not in Africa. Playing too many cards and pursuing too many ends, Rome lost almost everything. Libya obtained full independence, and Eritrea was proclaimed an autonomous unit federated to Ethiopia. Only poor and neglected Somalia was assigned to Italian administration as a trusteeship territory for a ten-year period. To make matters worse, the demarcation of the boundaries of Somalia, with the future of the Somali-speaking province of Ogaden belonging to the Ethiopian Empire as a major obstacle, was doomed to push Italy onto a collision course with Haile Selassie.

Official face-to-face contacts between Italy and Ethiopia were delayed until the conclusion of the United Nations discussions on the former Italian colonies. The first high-level meeting took place in New York in December 1950, on the very day after the vote over Eritrea. Some of the most prominent personalities of the regime in Addis Ababa took for granted that Italy was plotting to re-establish a semi-colonial presence in the Horn and openly disliked the fact that Italy was responsible for the administration of a territory on the borders of Ethiopia. Normal diplomatic relations between Italy and Ethiopia were restored in September 1951 as a result of the first visit to Addis Ababa since World War II by a high-ranking Italian official (Giuseppe Brusasca, Under-Secretary for African Affairs, who had a solid reputation as an anti-fascist). However the reciprocal mood was still lukewarm. The main source of difference was Italy's insistence on full respect for Eritrea's autonomy, whereas Ethiopia maintained that Italy was not entitled to look after the implementation of UN resolutions and disregarded any criticism. As a matter of fact, Italy did not succeed in inducing either America or Britain to look after the Eritrean question at the United Nations, and when Haile Selassie performed the unilateral annexation of the former colony as a province of the Empire, Ethiopia's abuse was tolerated by the international community and Italy was appeased as well.

These shadows in the relations between Italy and Ethiopia confirmed Rome's incapacity to reconcile different and possibly contradictory stakes. Did Italy mean to restore an implicit form of colonialism in the Horn? Or did she intend to make a fresh start by advocating the rights of the independent African states, and by dealing with the politicians in Addis Ababa on the basis of genuine equality? While disclosing Ethiopia's interference in Eritrea, did Italy seek to protect the integrity and national identity of her former colony, or was she just selfishly worried that the absorption of Eritrea into the Empire would jeopardize the assets of the Italian settlers and Italian business interests?

The Italian Trust Administration of Somalia (AFIS) reflected, at least to some extent, Italy's new democratic profile. Italian authorities put aside past hostilities and prejudices and took decisive steps in order to seek reconciliation with the most dedicated and militant nationalist movement, the Somali Youth League (SYL). In fact, their converging interests made it relatively easy to work hand in hand. Given the continuing blend of traditionalism, ethnicity, and modernization within a framework of representative institutions, Italy was confident that the SYL-led government would be bound to rely on financial assistance from Italy because of Somalia's craving for more goods, cash, and know-how. Having merged with what was formerly British Somaliland after independence in 1960, the Somali Republic (with Mogadishu as capital city) was the main if not sole beneficiary of Italian external aid throughout the

1960s and 1970s. Harmony would have been perfect if Italy had agreed to provide the arms and military training that the SYL regime desperately needed to support their campaign for a "Greater Somalia." Despite the traditional pro-Somali leanings of Italian diplomacy, the package deal put forward by the Government in Mogadishu was rejected as evidence of Rome's opposition to the pan-Somali irredentism that — threatening the territorial integrity of French Somaliland (Djibouti), Ethiopia, and Kenya — burdened Italy with an excessive responsibility.

The military *coup d'état* in September 1969 removed from power the SYL leaders whom Italy had helped to shape the Somali state. Some of the army officers that seized power in Mogadishu had been trained in the Soviet Union, and were therefore supposedly loyal to Marxism and the will of Moscow rather than to Western values and Italy's influence. But the new President, General Mohamed Siyad Barre, had spent several years in an Italian military academy, and the Council of Ministers appointed by the Supreme Revolutionary Council (SRC) included some specialists with Italian university qualifications who had acquired close links with the Italian Communist Party (PCI). Did the ideals that prevailed in the Somali Revolutionary Socialist Party (SRSP), lately founded by the SRC, arise from within the former metropolitan power, albeit via unorthodox channels?

Faced with a radical regime that had adopted the ideology and methodology of "Scientific Socialism" and had turned to the Soviet Union for hard military equipment, the Italian government decided to do what it could to prevent Somalia from relying completely upon the Eastern bloc in the bipolar system. Italy did not share in the US-imposed embargo on Somalia in retaliation for the use of its flag by ships delivering cargoes to North Vietnamese ports, but she did stop supplying military equipment until the disastrous war against Ethiopia in the Ogaden had ended in 1978. Out of the African nations, Somalia (as well as Nigeria) was the main buyer of Italian arms in the 1980s, and ranked sixth among customers from all developing countries. A prolonged infusion of financial and technical assistance was intended to promote economic linkages and strengthen political solidarity. The Somali National University, where lectures were given in Italian, provided powerful opportunities by creating an italophone intelligentsia and a West-oriented bureaucracy. Italy believed that her assistance was more palatable to nationalistic forces in Somalia, as elsewhere in Africa, than either American or British aid, not least because developing countries had little or nothing to fear from a middle-size power. Indeed, international weakness became a modest but significant asset since Italy could hardly be suspected of embarking on neocolonial arrangements.

In a period of about five years — from the 1969 coup of the Free Officers led by Muammar Qadhafi in Libya and the revolutionary upheaval in Somalia to the overthrow of the Ethiopian monarchy in 1974 — all the former Italian colonies passed through drastic changes that propelled the radicalized segments of the armed forces to power. Was this a simple coincidence? Certainly Italy proved to be a negligible factor in the political ups and downs of territories that were theoretically under Italian "hegemony." However, the shifting of the Horn regimes into the Socialist field and toward the Soviet bloc did not interrupt as such the flux of the Italian influence there. What is more ironical is that the demise of Western influence in a Third World country, highlighted for instance by Somalia's 1974 Treaty of Friendship and Co-operation with the Soviet Union (terminated in 1977) or by the strong alliance established in 1977–78 between the Ethiopian military regime and the USSR, was likely to foster Italian political self-promotion as a last resort for the West.

In principle, the revolution directed by the *Derg* against Haile Selassie's feudal autocracy was a hindrance for the left over Italian interests in Ethiopia and, above all, in Eritrea. The decision to close the Italian consulate in Asmara and the nationalization of Italian properties marked the end of an era. Nonetheless, Italy was ready as always to adapt her policy in order to forge ahead with the familiar strategy of being "present" and ready to deal with anybody regardless of their ideology or alignment. Perhaps the military junta in Addis Ababa was a bit too radical and its methods too violent, but having learned something of the Vatican's subtle diplomatic skills, those responsible for Italy's foreign policy knew how to wait for more suitable conditions.

A vast program of economic assistance was funded by Italy as a contribution to the growth and progress of Ethiopia under the leadership of President Mengistu Haile Mariam. Appropriate care was taken to reassure the Somalis that nevertheless they would still continue to enjoy

Italian aid and friendship. Officially, Italy was committed to a policy of strict equidistance — between Somalia and Ethiopia, as well as between Ethiopia and Eritrea — without embracing the cause of either side. Such multifaceted co-operation, within the framework of a more comprehensive Italian pledge to Eastern Africa as a favored region, was meant to temper the intransigence of rival regimes and guerrilla movements, and to urge the efforts of the nations in the Horn toward economic development rather than the arms race. The Government in Rome was racked by feuds — the two major partners in the Cabinet coalition, the Christian Democrats (DC) and the Socialists (PSI), sponsored Ethiopia and Somalia, respectively — and the general volatility made Italy's warnings and apparent goodwill far less effective.

The implications of these political differences and obvious ambiguity became manifest during the 1977–78 crisis, when Somalia attacked Ethiopia in an undeclared war. Because of Moscow's displeasure about Somalia's decision to send its regular army into the Ogaden, Siyad Barre made a U-turn and severed relations with the Soviet Union as well as Cuba. In Italy the invasion of Ethiopia was judged (and endorsed) by the standards of the cold war rather than by the merits of the Somali cause. The Socialists of PSI, especially, supported Somalia's adventurism — despite the reiterated official line of the Italian government, which was steadily contrary to Ethiopia's disintegration — because of their distrust of the Soviet Union and its allies. Italy was so tightly entangled in the Horn that the Somali-Ethiopian conflict embarrassed not only the government but the main opposition party, PCI, as well. As a minor partner of the Western bloc with a long-standing knowledge of the region's problems, Italy forecast that her own scope for action might be widened, and her possibilities of mediation enhanced, by the worsening of relations between the *Derg* and Washington. Basically Italy pretended to be neutral — friend to all, enemy to none — and sought to side with those regimes in the Horn that tried to evade the constraints of the alignments of the cold war. But this did not keep Italy from attending meetings with her Western allies to coordinate their actions vis-à-vis the Soviet and Cuban counteroffensive in the Ogaden.

The unresolved controversy concerning the status of Eritrea gave origin to even more marked and resounding rifts that likewise affected the coalition in power and all the various parties in Italy. While pan-Somali claims could be rejected as a threat to the stability and integrity of a state, the war in Eritrea was widely reckoned to be a legitimate struggle for national liberation to get rid of an anomalous form of internal colonialism. Apparently no one was concerned about the contradiction in formally sponsoring the unity of Ethiopia and simultaneously flirting with separatism and hosting semi-official rallies of Eritrean students living in Europe. Which principle ought to be put forward if the two were not compatible: the self-determination of peoples or the territorial integrity of states?

In order to preserve historical links and the legacies of her influence, Italy — both in Ethiopia and in Somalia — did not dare to support both governments and their oppositions. As armed resistance increased throughout the territory of the Ethiopian state, Italian workers and experts living in peripheral regions of the former Empire were repeatedly seized and held as hostages by opposition movements that wished to draw international attention to their fight, and to deter external support for the Ethiopian regime. It is significant that such actions were seldom labeled and condemned as "terrorism." In fact, Italy agreed to talk to the revolutionary fronts and accepted some of their demands perhaps to keep a path open for an alternative to the *Derg*. Apart from the political aspects, this comprehensive stance, seasoned with the questionable generosity of financial and technical assistance, was designed to assure a privileged place in markets that were relatively important for Italian exports.

Italy's potential or presumed advantages in the Horn evaporated abruptly when, in 1991, the established regimes were disrupted and broken down, first in Somalia and then in Ethiopia, with the overthrow of the *Derg*, giving way to the *de facto* independence of Eritrea and starting an unfinished period of civil strife and disintegration in Somalia. Italian policy had always considered "statehood" to be of fundamental importance, but the state was the first victim of the crisis, having collapsed or committed "suicide." What about consent, effectiveness, and viability? Africa at large was experiencing the effects of the great mutation that was overturning the very legitimacy, previously not contested, of nation-states, including those born with the blessing of decolonization. Was a centralized and bureaucratic state emulating Western models the best solution for societies, such as Somalia, in which the individualistic and clannish ethos of nomadic peoples is prominent? Was such an authoritarian state the best way to organize a peaceful *modus vivendi* among the different linguistic and ethnic groups in Ethiopia? And, if the "nationalism" of the Eritrean people had fought and defeated the multinational Ethiopia, how could the Eritrean independent state have concealed its own heterogeneous origins and composition as far as ethnicity, language, and religious faith?

While Somalia was ravaged by civil war, hastening the downfall of Siyad Barre in a dreadful crescendo of bloodshed and despair, Italy sought once more to cope with the crisis by offering her good offices. The aim was to promote an orderly transfer of power to a large coalition of forces, parties, and persons in which Barre would continue to play a role in order to avoid, so it was argued, a dangerous vacuum. But the President's enemies ostensibly refused to join such a deal, arguing that he must be held personally responsible for past human rights violations, malpractice, and political chaos. All attempts at an eleventh-hour agreement failed. The flight of Barre from Mogadishu in January 1991 marked the end of a regime that Italy had tried stubbornly, for over twenty years, to preserve as a token of stability. The University, the jewel of Italian technical assistance, was destroyed and vandalized. Aghast and bitter, a number of Italian expatriates in Somalia had to watch the final battle for control of the capital city as passive bystanders. Italy had been the last Western country to suspend economic aid to Siyad, and the Italian embassy was the last to be evacuated: a sign of responsibility and of the strong will to stay on, perhaps a pledge for the future, but also evidence — at least as viewed through the eyes of Barre's opponents — of a special link with the fate of the dying regime.

As anarchy and wild reprisals erupted in the entire country, wrecking the fragile coalition set up by the military factions that had seized power in Mogadishu, hardly any room was left for Italy's mediation. She could hope to profit in return for the backing given in the past to the United Somali Congress (USC), which had been founded in 1989 in Rome, but her connections with the new leadership remained precarious. Moreover, Italy had always had difficulty in dealing with the northern, anglophone Somalis, whose cause had been encouraged by British aspirations, and was scarcely able to dissuade the Somali National Movement (SNM) from proclaiming, in May 1991, the separate independence of the former British Somaliland — a move that was perceived in Rome as a further setback for its policy in the Horn. Nevertheless, Italy was asked to supply emergency aid and was prepared to reoccupy her traditional role in Eastern Africa. But was it possible to help Somalia without interfering in its domestic affairs? Given Ali Mahdi's quest for endorsements as a head of the state, would not external assistance be regarded as diplomatic acknowledgment of his besieged regime?

Ethiopia was supposed to be very different from Somalia, but in May 1991 Addis Ababa fell in somewhat similar circumstances though with less bloodshed and without such a turmoil of the central authority. Despite the Italian efforts in the preceding twenty years, the United States played the leading role that Italy had expected to be her own privilege thanks to her expertise in the intractable hornets' nest of the Horn. Americans had been active in Ethiopia during the negotiation sessions between the *Derg* and the Eritrean People's Liberation Front (EPLF) held by ex-President Jimmy Carter, and thereafter it was the US Assistant Secretary of State for African Affairs who virtually acted as the referee during the last days of the struggle that ended Mengistu's regime. The London conference that accompanied the dissolution of the *Derg*'s power had been supervised personally by Herman Cohen, and it was he who gave the green light to the Ethiopian People's Revolutionary Democratic Front (EPRDF) to enter and occupy the Palace as soon as it became clear that the *Derg* was no longer at the helm. An outstanding Italian diplomat (who had spent some years as ambassador in Ethiopia) had handled the talks between the *Derg* and the Tigray People's Liberation Front (TPLF) aimed at outlining a possible status of autonomy for Tigray, but these efforts were not enough to establish fruitful contacts with the new leaders of Ethiopia, most of whom were members of the liberation movement of Tigray, when the TPLF transformed its autonomist fight into a struggle for power in Addis itself. The final act of the long civil war clearly disclosed how groundless was Italy's belief that she was an indispensable go-between linking the *Derg* and the whole body politic of Ethiopia to the West. The outcome can be regarded as a diplomatic disaster for

Italy, not least when the interim president and ministers of the late government sought political asylum in the quiet premises of Villa Italia, the Italian Embassy in Addis Ababa, causing embarrassment and resentment. Only recently has Italy seriously made amends, returning the monumental stele that the Fascist regime had abducted from Axum to Rome in the 1930s to erect it in front of the planned headquarters of the Ministry of Colonies (where nowadays FAO, the Food and Agriculture Organization of the United Nations, is located), and that in vain all the Ethiopian governments reclaimed on the basis of the uncompromising wording of the 1947 Peace Treaty.

After the United States had agreed to take the lead in organizing the UN-sanctioned armed intervention designed to protect the delivery of humanitarian relief to Somalia in December, 1992, Italy was understandably anxious that her soldiers should also be involved in this multinational rescue mission. But after sharp disagreements with both the US Government and the UN commands about the ends and means of the peace-keeping operation in 1993, Italy withdrew her contingent from Mogadishu and relocated it northwards, to a less sensible area, despite the probable "correctness" of her views about the dangers of "enforcing" peace by measures that included retaliatory attacks by US helicopters and raids to kill or capture General Aidid, the arch-rival of the self-appointed President Ali Mahdi. After the vociferous and assertive "warlord" had been "rehabilitated," following a review of UN strategy, Aidid amicably traveled with the American special envoy on the US aircraft that carried them to Addis Ababa for talks with the other Somali counterparts, and Italy was again put aside.

Italy was not among the most enthusiastic supporters of Eritrea's independence despite traditional links with her beloved first-born colony. Nevertheless, as with Somalia and perhaps post-*Derg* Ethiopia, Italy cannot be totally ignored by any regime in the Horn, whatever their previous relationships. When the then provisional president of Eritrea, Isaias Afeworki, visited Rome in 1992, he was treated as a Head of State by the Italian authorities, major corporations, and the press. And when Eritreans celebrated their independence on 24 May 1993, the Italian Foreign Minister, Beniamino Andreatta, was an honored guest. Will historical heritage be stronger than political miscalculations? The usual ambivalence has definitely thwarted the attempt by the Italian government to effectively mediate between Eritrea and Ethiopia as they decided in May 1998 to start a war nominally because of a disagreement on the previous colonial border that Italy contributed to trace (on the maps rather than on the field).

From her earliest contacts with Africa, Italy had pursued and to some extent achieved a sort of pre-eminence in the Horn. Italian explorers were followed by missionaries, and these by ethnologists, linguists, and historians, with Ethiopia always as the main focus and target. The immense amount of scientific knowledge about the region's lands, peoples, languages, and civilizations became part of the nation's overall cultural wealth, but was exploited above all by the Italian state to gain its place in the world competition for resources and markets. Although defeat in World War II deprived Italy of her colonial possessions, she still asked to play a significant role in the new Africa, and where else but in the Horn?

As the last of the big or the first of the smaller European nations, Italy had many problems in fulfilling the tasks of power on a regional scale. Even the colonial conquests had been facilitated by the benign neglect of her informal ally, Britain, and Rome preferred not to openly challenge either Paris or London. The fact is that Italy was not powerful enough to implement the social, economic, and institutional transformations that had been the usual feature of European colonialism. Also for that reason, the special functions of Italian settlers had always been emphasized over finance. After the colonies' independence, Italy was unable to provide the economic and political assistance that is necessary to the periphery states to have a more profitable access to the international arena.

The reasons for the limitations of Italy's African policy, notably in the Horn, can be summarized as follows:

1. Italy tried to make up for her weakness as a virtual "half power" by multiplying initiatives and appeasing various partners at the same time. This strategy led to contradictions — including Somalia *versus* Ethiopia, as well as self-determination *versus* integrity of states, and sympathy with liberation fronts *versus* cooperation with governments — that she was in the end unable to resolve. Time after time it is nearly impossible to ascertain the real intentions of Italy's policy in Africa: to deal with states, nations, territories, peoples, political forces, classes, or individual

leaders? To respect local expectations, to improve political stability, or to pursue her own interests and stakes? The expedient course of action taken was often to delay making a definitive choice or to arrange an untenable synthesis of the possible options by preaching quite rhetorically the advantages of "conciliation," albeit often to those who were clearly irreconcilable.

2. Apart from the recurrent confusion concerning her goals in Africa, Italy often employed improper means. Given the sharp polarization of the country's political system, especially in the years of the cold war, when Italy was a very exposed outpost, and her political arena was characterized by conflicting East-West loyalties, it was simply not feasible to devise a bi-partisan policy, a policy that would be approved by both the opposition and the government; and in any case, the latter was itself divided. The result was rather a "partisan bi-policy," whereby the parties of the majority coalition — and sometimes organized factions within a single party — differed widely in their analyses and attitudes. Italian rulers, therefore, concentrated their efforts, and the funds made available by the allocations of the official aid policy, on a specific partner or issue, expecting profits in terms of political obedience, cronyism, lawful or illicit economic returns. This made it far more difficult to express a consistent and affirmative approach that respected the "rights" of African nations or even the regional balance of power.

3. Finally, with the crumbling of the military regimes that had been indulgently backed as *de facto* allies for many years by the Italian authorities, as well as of a number of private and public enterprises undertaken for their own particular purposes, it became clear that Italy could not manage the African emergency through her own economic and political resources. Due to her limited means, she could hardly support the local forces in rearranging their political institutions and economics in the era of globalization. Shelving as unrealistic the projects of autonomy and self-reliance dear to many of their founding fathers, dismantling their national enterprises in all sectors, and agreeing to replace collectivism with privatization and market-oriented reforms, African states have been incorporated into the world economy without further reservations. In the whole process, which is still ongoing, Italy has shown a very limited capacity to be active and positive, and in fact she

has been bypassed and eventually sidelined by the much more effective initiatives taken by France and later by the United States, frustrated in the long-awaited objective to be credited for taking the lead on her allies of the Western camp.

The overall difficulties through which Africa passed in the 1970s and 1980s have painfully unveiled that the continent lacked the conditions to obtain the benefits of interdependence that other developing regions have been able to grasp. The former Italian possessions appear to have been particularly vulnerable because of their isolation from the most significant economic and financial trends, and especially technological innovations, not least as the result of the weakness of their traditional European patron. In Ethiopia and in Somalia, ravaged by war and drought, the traumas of transition have brought catastrophe to the states, and Italian influence has not been a valid bulwark against any of their prolonged crises. Nevertheless, it is likely that the governments of Eritrea, Ethiopia, and Somalia will go on seeking Italian cooperation because of historical links and long-standing acquaintance, though their stabilization and sustainable development depend ultimately on factors that are beyond the scope of Italian possibilities and that require at least a European dimension.

In the meantime, Italy has been in trouble also in dealing with the dramatically increasing phenomenon of South-North immigration. Most of the refugees who land in Italy do not come from her former territories, and therefore, unlike the immigrants in France and Britain, they are not endowed with the general acculturation that colonialism brought about. Throughout her history Italy was accustomed to consider, and welcome, foreigners as tourists and/or travelers rather than as workers or new citizens. Now the arrival of multitudes of women and men, different in color, language, and religion, looking for safety, job opportunities, and integration, have overcome her capacity to provide.

*This paper is a revised and updated version of an article that appeared in *The Journal of Modern African Studies*.

Bibliography

Calchi Novati, Giampaolo. *Fra Mediterraneo e Mar Rosso: momenti di politica italiana in Africa attraverso il colonialismo.* Rome: Istituto italo-africano, 1992.

___. *Il Corno d'Africa nella storia e nella politica.* Turin: Società editrice internazionale, 1994.

Ciasca, Raffaele. *Storia coloniale dell'Italia contemporanea.* Milan: Editore Ulrico Hoepli, 1938.

Del Boca, Angelo, ed. *Le guerre coloniali del fascismo.* Rome: Laterza, 1991.

___. *Una sconfitta dell'intelligenza: Italia e Somalia.* Rome: Laterza, 1993.

Farer, Tom. *War Clouds on the Horn of Africa: The Widening Storm.* New York: Carnegie Endowment for International Peace, 1979.

Filesi, Teobaldo. *L'Italia e la conferenza di Berlino, 1882–1885.* Rome: Istituto italo-africano, 1985.

Korn, A. *Ethiopia, the United States and the Soviet Union.* London: Croom Helm, 1986.

Lewis, I. M. *A Modern History of Somalia.* Boulder: Westview P, 1988.

Marcus, Harold G. *Ethiopia, Great Britain and the United States, 1941–1974: The Politics of Empire.* Berkeley: U of California P, 1983.

Pastorelli, Pietro. *La politica estera italiana del dopoguerra.* Bologna: Il Mulino, 1987.

Poscia, Stefano. *Eritrea, colonia tradita.* Rome: Edizioni associate, 1989.

Rossi, Gian Luigi. *L'Africa italiana verso l'indipendenza, 1941–1949.* Milan: Giuffrè 1980.

Selassie, Bereket Habte. *Conflict and Intervention in the Horn of Africa.* New York: Monthly Review P, 1980.

Sforza, Carlo. *Cinque anni a Palazzo Chigi: la politica estera italiana dal 1947 al 1951.* Rome: Atlante, 1952.

Spencer, John H. *Ethiopia at Bay: A Personal Account of the Haile Sellassie Years.* Algonac, MI: Reference Publications, 1984.

Zaghi, Carlo. *P. S. Mancini, l'Africa e il problema del Mediterraneo, 1884–1885.* Rome: G. Casini, 1955.

MOTHERING THE NATION
An Italian Woman in Colonial Eritrea

Cristina Lombardi-Diop
Northwestern University

Italian colonial literature was born as a male genre. By the beginning of the twentieth century, its canon was already formed by narratives of exploration and diplomatic travels written exclusively by men. One exception to these male-authored texts was Rosalia Pianavia Vivaldi's *Tre anni in Eritrea,* published in 1901 and accompanied by the author's photos. Rosalia, wife of the colonel Domenico dei Marchesi Pianavia Vivaldi, can be considered a female colonialist pioneer. She resided in Eritrea from 1893 to 1895 and was able to chronicle, not only in writing but also in photography, the process of the making of the colony, established in 1890. She also witnessed the first Italo-Ethiopian wars of 1894–1895, whose detailed recollection appears in her memoir. This book is exceptional not only for its written text but also for the photographic work that accompanies it. Rosalia Pianavia Vivaldi was, to my knowledge, one of the few — if not the only — Italian women photographers operating in Africa in the nineteenth century.

This paper focuses on Rosalia Pianavia Vivaldi's travel narrative as a text in which the notions of motherhood and domesticity are symbolically evoked to serve an imperialist and patriotic agenda. The construction of domesticity and the maternal mediates colonial military violence, while helping establish a female voice within the male genre of colonial travel literature. Through close analysis, I illustrate how the maternal idiom coexists with a male militaristic one. This blending is made possible by the way in which models of womanhood circulating in turn-of-the-century Italy related woman to the nation. This paper also examines the author's philanthropic activities in the colony in favor of interracial children in relation to Cesare Lombroso's racialist theory. While philanthropy is understood here as a specific female activity that functions as surrogate colonial state politics, I argue that miscegenation threatens to disrupt Pianavia Vivaldi's careful staging of motherhood as a symbolic category necessary to sustain colonial authority.

The Patriot Mother

On her arrival in Asmara, Rosalia Pianavia Vivaldi writes in her diary: "ma come potrà passare il suo tempo all'Asmara una povera donna che, non è comandante delle truppe, non è ufficiale, non è soldato, non agricoltore?" ["how shall a poor woman spend her time in Asmara, if she is neither in charge of the troops, nor officer, soldier, settler?"].[1] Writing becomes a way to construct such a female identity in the colony as different and yet complementary to that of male officers, soldiers, and settlers. What the text affirms is the possibility of the existence of such a female role in a context where the imbalance of gender difference is mediated by the author's racial superiority. As I will discuss below, domesticity becomes a shifting ground of gender positioning, one that allows the writer to articulate different voices without completely disrupting the gender and racial balance that presides over Italy's imperialist wars.

When Pianavia Vivaldi settled in Eritrea, the colony had been in place for only three years. In England, many supporters of imperial expansion had already advocated pronatalist policies in order to fill the empty space of empire, and the *memsahib* had already become an icon of British untouchable femininity.[2] In Italy, this was a time when the *questione coloniale* seemed to be in everybody's mind: "Tutta l'Italia non parla che d'Africa. Si spasima per l'Africa. Tutti gli sguardi sono rivolti a Makalle', la cui eroica difesa forma l'ammirazione del mondo." [All over Italy people are talking about Africa. Everybody is yearning for Africa. All eyes are turned towards Makalle', whose heroic defense has earned us admiration worldwide.][3] In 1896, during the military campaigns in Eritrea, the front covers of the Italian magazine *L'Illustrazione italiana* were filled with things African. Illustrators, photographers, and journalists mobilized to cover the colonial enterprise. These were the first images

---

[1] Pianavia Vivaldi Boffiner 25. *Tre anni in Eritrea* is hereafter abbreviated "TAE." Unless otherwise specified, all translations are mine.

[2] Davin 204. For a discussion of the relations between white femininity and British imperialism, see Sharpe. Also in Chrisman and Williams 196–220.

[3] *L'Illustrazione italiana* 19 Jan. 1896: XXIII, 3.

that filled the Italian colonial imaginary. Yet Italian women had not yet discovered the newly founded colony. Although the right-wing deputy Antonino di Sangiuliano had already argued in 1885 in favor of a "re-placement" (cited in Mola 143) of the indigenous populations of Eritrea by Italian settlers, Italy seemed not yet aware of the potential use of women's reproductive function for the imperialist cause.

Motherhood lends itself as an ideological metaphor for colonialist propaganda in *Tre anni in Eritrea* only in so far as it serves in the contruction of the idea of the nation, a nation that is not yet expanding its boundaries but rather defining them. The concept of motherhood is here more closely affiliated with the *Risorgimento* ideal of the national mother than with the Fascist ideal of a prolific housewife.[4] Motherhood here is less a biological function necessary for the nation's expansion and more a symbolic category indispensable for the process of forming the nation. Moreover, the national revolution that brought about Italy's uni-fication in 1868 had resulted for women in a blurring of the boundaries between political activity and private life, so much so that traditional female roles had assumed political significance (see Jeffrey Howard). After unification, a new figure of woman emerged that envisioned the extension of women's domestic role within the public sphere, while me-diating the gender imbalance created by the war. This was the patriot mother, whom reformers portrayed as an educated, religious woman on the side of the liberal state and of the monarchy (Jeffrey Howard 238). This model — embodied in Cornelia Cairoli, mother of the famous na-tionalist heroes and example of civic responsibility and sacrifice — pro-vided a perception of motherhood as a private function that could nev-ertheless be enlisted for public purposes.

Differently from the Fascist image of woman as procreator, the patriot mother — whose roots could be traced back to the historical figure of Caterina Sforza — had made her own the moral mission of educating the nation's children.[5] Nameless but often represented as wrapped in the national flag, she was for Italy what Britannia was for England and Ger-

---

[4]For a discussion of the Fascist *donna-madre*, see Meldini. Also see Pickering-Iazzi, ed., *Mothers of Invention* for a recent articulation and contradiction of this model.
[5]For a reading of Caterina Sforza's presence in Italian cultural discourse, see Spackman.

mania for Germany (see Mosse). But in Italy, in the absence of a proper name, women participated in the life of the nation through symbolic figures, while leaving to men the privilege of "political contiguity with each other in the national community" (McClintock 355). Excluded from political life at home, middle-class women found in the colony a chance to be at the forefront of national and political events.

Mothers and Daughters

The lack of women's presence in political life did not mean their exclusion from public discourse. In turn-of-the-century Italy, as public opinion grew aware of its national identity, woman and nation became in fact intertwined in complex rhetorical schema and figures.[6] In *Tre anni in Eritrea*, nationalist rhetoric inevitably shifts to colonial propaganda:

> la Colonia Italiana potrebbe illustrare questa terra, facendosi pioniera della civiltà sorgente: perchè l'Africa ormai ha un avvenire, fa anch'essa il suo turno: l'Europa dopo l'Asia; l'America dopo l'Europa e l'Asia; l'Africa ora. E se ogni civiltà figlia ha sorpassato, per forza di progresso, la civiltà madre, quale splendida luce non deve venire dalla terra dei mori? (TAE 178)

> [The Italian Colony could illustrate this land, becoming the pioneer of a rising civilization. It is because Africa has now a future, her turn has also come. Europe after Asia; America after Europe and Asia; and now Africa. If every daughter civilization has surpassed, by the law of progress, her mother civilization, what splendid light must not come then from the land of the Moors?]

As the author cannot but choose images of light to signify Africa's future under colonial orderliness, the meaning of this passage is nevertheless obscured by the ambiguous syntax of the last sentence, where the future advent of Africa's "splendid light" is simultaneously affirmed and de-

---

[6]See De Giorgio, *Le italiane dall'Unità ad oggi*. On women's material and symbolic role in Liberal Italy, see De Giorgio, "Dalla 'Donna Nuova' alla donna della 'nuova' Italia." Also see Horn.

nied. Ironically, the entire passage is predicated on the possibility of a signifying activity, what Rosalia sees as the enlightening task of the Italians in Eritrea. The meaning of the verb "to illustrate" (to light up) tautologically attributes the origin of Africa's "splendid light" to the intervention of Italian colonialism in Eritrea and, by synecdoche, in the whole of Africa. The repetition of signifiers the verb engenders also suggests that Italy's agency over Africa is inescapably linked to the author's signifying activity. In other words, it is through colonial writing that Italy will establish the ideological forms of colonial governability in Eritrea.

Such an engagement in the imperialist project through writing gives European women a task that fits particularly well their national role as mothers. In the above passage, Pianavia Vivaldi's fantasy of world imperial development envisions a mother/daughter relationship in which "nations are symbolically figured as domestic genealogies" (McClintock 357). Again, the family trope offers nationalism and imperialism a single genesis narrative, one in which Europe prepares the way for Africa according to a hierarchy of power relations in which one nation "mothers" the other. In the author's wording, then, Italy will mother Africa as Asia mothered Europe, and Europe mothered America. The passage establishes a link between mothering and the process of empire building. As daughters grow up to become mothers within an endless chain of a reproduction of mothering function, so nations rise to become empires. The gynealogical metaphor naturalizes imperial genealogies, while emphasizing the social and political implications of motherhood.

The New Domestic Woman in the Colony

The idealization of the mother figure in the iconography of nationalism and imperialism came at a time when women's lives were nevertheless changing as a result of economic transformations. With their entry as consumers in the developing industrial market, Italian women also started to acquire a new public visibility within the social sphere. By the 1890s, we see the appearance in the press and in literature of the image of the *donna nuova* — the Italian translation of the British "new woman" that had much to do with the expansion of British imperialism in the Indian continent. And yet, while women entered the political and social realm, domesticity increasingly became a space where middle-class hegemony and sense of identity were redefined and contextualized. As a "political economy" (Tranberg Hansen 4), domesticity affirmed itself in Europe as a corollary of industrial capitalism. As a social and cultural form, it constituted a central dimension of the colonial encounter, being the locus where notions of labor and time, consumption and accumulation, body and clothing, diet and hygiene, sexuality and gender were defined and negotiated (see Comaroff and Comaroff).

How did the concept of a national and modern domesticity contribute to colonial propaganda, and what happened outside the national borders to women who ventured to the colonies? Scholars who have been studying how the ideology of modernity and progress shaped Italian discourses on women have focused primarily on the Fascist period (see de Grazia; Pickering-Iazzi, *Politics of the Visible*; Buci-Glucksmann; and Ben-Ghiat). To my knowledge, none of these studies have considered how discourses of femininity targeted women as bearers of civilization and progress in Africa. Among the many issues that remain to be assessed, is how the construction of womanhood and domesticity contributed to the consolidation of an imperialist discourse based on the alleged modernizing and civilizing mission of the Italians in Africa. In this sense, an investigation of how turn-of-the-century positivist culture hailed women as bearers of civic and modern values may yield productive responses.[7]

Italian colonial discourse incorporated a message of modernity and emancipation that was particularly attractive to women. During Fascism, Italian women were invited to go to the colonies to join their husbands and recreate the national domestic environment on colonial soil. Figures of female pioneers were celebrated in the press for their achievements as founders of farms and schools, activities that saw them at the forefront of the colonies' public life.[8] In *Tre anni in Eritrea*, the domestic environment where settlers and military ranks dwell epitomizes an attempt in progress and civilization in the midst of barbarity and backwardness. The process of its foundation, characterized by hardship and perseverance, reproduces the process of colonial settling. In this text, pictures of the

---

[7]This issue is only partially addressed in David Horn's *Social Bodies*.
[8]See "Figure di pionieri: Maria Fioretti," *Etiopia* 2.7–8 (July-August 1938): 109–13.

soldiers' quarters, of the Governor's residence, of the Catholic priest's home, and the military fort reconstruct the colonial space as organized around functions of command and coercion. Isolated within a single chapter, these images are structurally and ideologically separated from the native quarters and the market, center of Asmara's native activities and life. While both the colonial buildings and the native dwellings are photographed from the outside, the interior of the author's domestic space is the only one we are allowed to view through a photograph that portrays Rosalia Pianavia Vivaldi sitting at a desk covered with books and pictures, while the caption reads *salotto* [living room].

It is the conspicuous absence in Asmara of a proper *salotto* – the quintessential element of the Italian bourgeois home – that the caption is trying to fill. The obvious discrepancy between the image and the caption hints at the actual disruption of the domestic space effected by the displacement involved in the process of colonial settling, one that particularly affected middle-class women. The author never acknowledges this disruption. On the contrary, her diary is an effort to keep the Italian dimension of domesticity in place. Like an authorial signature, the picture portraying the author in the act of writing signals the importance of such an activity for the project of constructing a female colonial identity. While writing can be defined as a feminine activity here because it takes place within the domestic walls, it also constitutes a way of appropriating a male role within colonial discourse. Rosalia Pianavia Vivaldi also links writing to all the many other activities she undertakes in the newly founded colony that are not exclusively domestic, such as photographing; keeping up with her correspondence; overseeing soldiers', settlers', and natives' operations.

Rosalia's visits to the Abyssinian residences of Asmara are recorded in her diary in the form of revised ethnographic notes. These center on family ceremonies such as births, marriages, funerals, and social events such the festivity of the *maskal*. In her descriptions, the author never relinquishes the authority of ethnographic objectivity and yet also indulges in more personal comments that mark her writing as specifically feminine.[9] These are often centered on the incommensurability of women's

---

[9]See Pratt, "Fieldwork in Common Places." In this essay, Pratt explains that "personal

role in Abyssinian society *vis-à-vis* women's role in Italy. Significantly, the Abyssinian concept of domesticity is felt as non-existent, while family and the maternal are values the author finds lacking in Abyssinian culture. Her presence among the population thus aims at reforming their condition toward an acquisition of "material wealth" and "civil progress" (TAE 62) through the assimilation of the Italian way of life, on issues that are gender specific, such as cooking, household management, hygiene, and childbearing. Assimilation to Italianness — the text implies — begins at home. Significantly, it is a process that necessitates the disruption of indigenous social and cultural practices centered around women, family relations, and reproduction. As we will see in the last section, the author's philanthropic activities in favor of biracial children share the same goal.

Cesare Lombroso and Racial Inequality

This section investigates how Rosalia Pianavia Vivaldi's *Tre anni in Eritrea* articulates racial issues as a reflection of the anxiety miscegenation and racial contamination created in turn-of-the-century Italy. While most studies of Italian racial politics have focused on the Fascist imperialist project of the late 1930s, my analysis moves in an unexamined direction in the attempt to retrace their genealogical roots in turn-of-the-century racial discourses. For this purpose, Cesare Lombroso's racialist theories will be examined alongside *Tre anni in Eritrea*. As we shall see, while Lombroso's theory of race clarifies the ideological background of Italy's violent colonial encounter with Africa, Pianavia Vivaldi's narrative provides key elements for a better understanding of the role played by white femininity in the definition of racial identities and in the establishment of colonial relationships.

Cesare Lombroso's *L'uomo bianco e l'uomo di colore: letture sull'origine e la varietà delle razze umane* is an early and rarely cited work first published in 1871. Specifically addressed to a female readership, it was written as a tentative theory of the evolution of the races, well before Lom-

---

narrative persists alongside objectifying descriptions in ethnographic writing because it mediates a contradiction within the discipline between personal and scientific authority" (32).

broso reached his popularity with his studies on the criminal and deviant behavior of women and lunatics of the lower classes. Here, the Italian neurologist and criminologist dedicates the first of a series of lectures on racial inequalities to the issue of "interracial marriages" [*connubi tra le razze*]. Eager to dispel popular myths and fantasies of Biblical tradition, Lombroso emphatically states that on such matters "the only authority of our time is Science" (10). Ethnology is the human science on which Lombroso actually relies in order to support his ideas. Significantly, another important source of information is David Livingstone's exploration narrative, brought as scientific evidence on the issue of racial mixing. According to Lombroso and Livingstone, the mingling of different races produces degrees of degeneration, the highest of which occurring as a result of marriages between Negroes from Africa and "members of the Latin race" (Lombroso 14).

The objective of Lombroso's study is to answer the crucial question so widely debated a century earlier by French and British thinkers at the inception of the Atlantic slave trade, prelude to their imperialistic expansion, on the existence of inequalities among the races. As we know, the myth of the noble savage was one of the philosophical and ideological constructs emerging during this initial stage of the colonial encounter. At the time Lombroso was writing, social Darwinism and scientific racism had contributed to a different formulation of the debated question:

> Si tratta di sapere se noi bianchi, che torreggiamo orgogliosi sulla vetta della civiltà, dovremo un giorno chinare la fronte innanzi al muso prognato del negro e alla gialla e terrea faccia del mongolo; se infine, noi dobbiamo il nostro primato al nostro organismo o agli accidenti del caso. (Lombroso 10)

> [What needs to be assessed is whether the white race, which proudly towers at the height of civilization, will have to bow one day before the Negro's mug and the Mongolian's yellow and sallow face; finally, whether we own our supremacy to our organism or to mishaps of chance.]

The question Lombroso poses is no longer whether there are superior or inferior races but, rather, if the superiority the white race has proclaimed for centuries is either fortuitous or biologically determined, and if it will one day be questioned and subverted by the oppressed. Thus formulated, the question lacks all traces of the naïveté that Fascist colonial historians usually attributed to Italian racialist ideology. It, nonetheless, reveals the anxieties riding Italy's belated imperial discourse, at a time when imperialistic fantasies of easy conquest and domination had already been marred by native insurrections and domestic social crisis.

Lombroso's main thesis is that the anatomical differences among the races are a self-evident proof of the superiority of the white race. Using supposedly empirical drawings, and further unsupported considerations, Lombroso affirms that Black Africans (what he calls *Neri* and *Ottentotti*) have specific somatic traits also found in primitive men, idiots, and monkeys. Such traits are not limited to the physical realm, but extend to culture and morality: "Le scimie hanno commune, se non con noi, certo co'l negro, la continua mobilità di passioni e di muscoli, la gaiezza interrotta da bruschi ma brevi accessi d'ira e dispetto, e la maggiore alacrità intellettuale nell'età infantile"(Lombroso 147; What monkeys have in common with the Negro are the continuous mobility of muscles and passions, a cheerful disposition alternated with short but sudden fits of anger and spite, and intense intellectual liveliness in childhood). Lombroso's theory of race lacks the pseudo-scientific legitimization of eugenic measurements, eugenics being still unknown in Italy, and so it relies, for the most part, on hearsay information and, as we have seen, on travel literature.

In the absence of clear empirical proof, but striving to affirm the source of racial inferiority, Lombroso's home-made ethnology — already profoundly racist — also has recourse to theories, circulating at the time he was writing, of the degenerative influence of the climate on the development of physical and moral traits. This particular aspect of his theory poses a direct threat to white supremacy, because it posits racial inferiority as shifty and unstable. This may also explain why Lombroso's book had no echo in later theorizations of race. If, in fact, the traits of inferiority are not biologically determined but are contingent and localized, how can racial superiority be sustained in the face of changed environmental conditions? Notwithstanding this theoretical incongruity, Lombroso's geographic and climatic mapping of Italy according to the recurrence of what he calls "regressioni cretinico-melaniche" ["idiotic-melanitic regressions"] helps shift the focus from Africa to Italy. This gesture serves the specific purpose of targeting, together with Africans, the Italian peasant and lower classes: "io vidi nelle nostre vallate cretini che alla lunghezza del cranio, alla sporgenza del muso, alla grossezza delle labra e perfino all'oscuramento della pelle parevano Negri malamente imbiancati" (172; In our valleys I have seen idiots whose skull's length, face's protrusion, lips' size, and skin's darkness made them look like badly whitened Negroes). The areas Lombroso specifically mentions are Calabria and the islands, in short, *il mezzogiorno*. With this twist of theory, Lombroso goes full circle in racist imperialist ideology. The invention of race effects not only the dehumanization of Africans — ideological prelude to their enslavement — but also the identification, marginalization, and surveillance of the peasant and lower classes at home, of all the prostitutes, criminals, and lunatics, to whom Lombroso's career will be later entirely dedicated.[10]

Lombroso's idea of "idiotic-melanitic regressions" is a fear of contamination and degeneration that is at the root of the eugenic discourse spurred by the colonial encounter and centered around the question of miscegenation. The regressive traits — "cute scura, naso schiacciato, capelli corti, prognatismo, labbra spesse, denti incisivi prominenti, orecchie e braccia lunghe" (195; dark skin, flat nose, short hair, prognathism, thick lips, projecting incisors, long ears and arms) — are those employed in racist representations of black people everywhere; yet their geographical displacement adds an element of racial indeterminacy that hints at the idea of contamination and hybridity. Similar regressive characteristics, Lombroso tells us, are shared by other races "che nessun etnologo ebbe il coraggio di dire nere, ma nemmeno di dir bianche, la cui origine non si può derivare al di fuori dell'Africa" (177; which no ethnologists would ever call black, nor white, but whose origins cannot be derived outside Africa), identified as the Arabs, the Berbers, the Abyssinians, the Jews, "stadj della trasformazione del Negro d'Africa in bianco" (195; stages in the transformation of the African Negro into white).

---

[10]For a discussion of how British and French colonial discourses managed domestic preoccupations, see, respectively, McClintock and Lowe.

Not surprisingly, Lombroso's physiognomic descriptions of regressive types will widely inform not only Fascist eugenic studies on the degeneration of biracial children, but also Rosalia Pianavia Vivaldi's discussion of racial types. Sander Gilman defines miscegenation as "a fear (and a word) from the late nineteenth century vocabulary of sexuality. It was a fear not merely of interracial sexuality but of its results, the decline of the population" (193). Translated in Italian as *meticciato*, the term miscegenation appears in a 1916 dictionary as "La frequenza degli incroci di razza. Le persone nate da incroci di razza" (Migliorini and Cappuccini; The frequency of racial crossings. Persons born by racial crossings). Both cause and result of the same phenomenon — that is, racial crossings — the definition shows the anxiety of numbers that characterized the inception of eugenics and demography in turn-of-the-century Italy (see Horn; Pogliano).

For Italian male travelers, traces of ethnic mixing often define African women's beauty according to an aesthetic canon that re-affirms hierarchies of race and the parameters of European femininity. For the business man Pellegrino Matteucci — who took part in the 1878 commercial expedition in Abyssinia led by Gustavo Bianchi — it represented "il meglio che si possa desiderare; quella varietà di tipi e di razze, quella dissonanza di fisionomie e di idee danno al paese un aspetto fantastico" (38); the best you could ever desire; the variety of types and races, the clashing of physiognomies and ideas confer to the country its fantastic aspect). For the Italian female settler, the presence in Asmara of people of mixed origins is, rather, a source of profound anxiety. This represents a disruption of racial borders and a threat to the stability of her function as mother of the nation.

In *Tre anni in Eritrea*, special mention is nevertheless given to the *meticci* Kassa Zander and her sister Teresa Naretti, whose pictures appear in the text (105–06). In their portrayal, racial characteristics are presented as gender specific, but gender and racial differences finally collapse in the author's attempt to keep them apart. Angelo Del Boca often mentions Teresa Naretti — whom we see half reclined on a sofa in full Oriental regalia, her loose long black hair on her shoulders — for her important role as diplomatic mediator. According to the Italian historian, she acquired such a role because of the fascination she apparently exercised on

Italian officials as colonial *femme fatale*. The mysterious sexuality of the *meticcia*, enhanced by the typical ambiguity attributed to her race, constitutes an important topos of Italian colonial discourse through Fascism, one that certainly deserves further critical attention.[11] But as Del Boca's depiction of Teresa Naretti as colonial *femme fatale* — prone to intrigues and mischievous influences — shows, such a topos is still at work in postcolonial racial representations. This figure — whose indeterminacy conjures up a perfect mixing of sexual desire and fear of the unknown — embodies the repressed fear and desire exercised by interracial mingling, a fear that still lingers in contemporary Italian society.[12]

Teresa Naretti's crucial role in the political schemes of the Italians in Eritrea is undoubtedly linked to the influential figure of her husband, Giacomo Naretti, a real self-made man of Italo-Eritrean relations. A Piedmont artisan hired for his exceptional skills by King Yohannes, Emperor of Ethiopia from 1872 to 1889, he soon became one of his closest associates and political mediators. Between 1879 and 1886, Italian explorers, businessmen, and politicians had recourse to his vast knowledge of Abyssinia in order to bring forth diplomatic and commercial expeditions in the area (Del Boca 83–85). Teresa largely contributed to her husband's mediating position by offering interpreting services to Italians who visited King Yohannes's court. One of them was the businessman Pellegrino Matteucci, who describes Teresa as "la più intelligente dama abissina ... parla con molta correttezza il francese, l'italiano, l'arabo, l'amarico, il gallas, il tigre" [the most intelligent Abyssinian lady ... she is fluent in French, Italian, Arabic, Galla, and Tegregna]. Although impressed by Teresa's linguistic skills, Matteucci values above all Teresa's qualities as a model modern wife: "è una donna che conduce la sua casa come un orologio" (25–26; she conducts her household like a clock), he says in admiration. The traveler Peppe Vigoni describes her as

---

[11] For a discussion of stereotypical images of black women in advertising under Fascism, see chapter 2 in Pinkus.

[12] The 1996 election as *Miss Italia* of Denny Mendez, a black woman of Dominican origins, and the immediate reaction that followed are clear examples of how the dynamic of attraction and repulsion is still at work in contemporary Italy.

figlia ad una abissina e ad un europeo, prese dalla madre una leggera tinta delle donne del paese e dal padre i germi di civiltà che in un terreno così vergine trovarono campo propizio allo svilupparsi con tutto il rigoglio di una vegetazione tropicale. (27)

[daughter of an Abyssinian woman and a European man, she has her mother's light color — typical of the country's women — and her father's civilizing germs. These, in such a virgin soil, found a favorable field to develop with the luxuriance of a tropical vegetation.]

The botanic metaphor — which hides a sexual one — fits well the colonial background of Vigoni's description. Moreover, it also echoes Lombroso's idea of the climatic influence on character and morality, while highlighting how, in colonial discourse, the discussion of miscegenation is symbolically entwined with the political practice of colonial settling and land expropriation.

As we have seen, in Rosalia Pianavia Vivaldi's *Tre anni in Eritrea* Teresa Naretti finds the space of only a small picture and a footnote. While other male travelers focused on Teresa, the female author gives ample information on her brother, Kassa Zander, son of a German captain — possibly Teresa's father — and a Gallas woman. Defined as "mente tedesca ordinata all'abissina" (TAE 107; a German mind in Abyssinian form), Kassa Zander represents in the eyes of the female traveler a puzzling embodiment of the blurring of racial and cultural boundaries in the colonial context. Contrary to his sister — whose specific female role in the colonial gender system is outlined in her portrait by the languor of her reclined posture — Kassa Zander defies gender and racial roles and consequently, the power balance that sustains them.

In Homi Bhabha's terms, Kassa Zander is the typical "mimic man," "almost the same but not white," figure of a colonial desire that "reverses 'in part' the colonial appropriation by now producing a partial vision of the colonizer's presence" (129–30). Mimicry, as a form of colonial discourse, only partially represents and therefore recognizes colonial authority, and it is in the repetition of partial presence that it articulates difference, thus posing a menace to the wholeness of colonial representations of domination (129). In this text, Kassa Zander appears partially deracialized and desexualized, in a way that is only possible for a *meticcio*:

> Sa di mineralogia, di fisica, di chimica; dipinge; suona il piano; è cacciatore e valente imbalsamatore. Potrebbe e dovrebbe fare vita cogli ufficiali e vivere all'europea; ma il sangue ereditato dalla madre lo fa invece alquanto vagabondo, indolente, trascurato nel vestire. (TAE 106)

> [He knows about mineralogy, physics, chemistry; he paints, plays piano; he is a great hunter and embalmer. He could and should live among the military ranks like a European; but his mother's blood makes him instead idle, indolent, slovenly.]

It is in his clothing— a powerful site of cultural identification — that the ambiguity of colonial mimicry is revealed. A picture in *Tre anni in Eritrea* portrays him dressed in a rigorous Western uniform, but the author also provides a detailed description of his 'native' attire:

> Nelle grandi occasioni però indossa un ampio palamidone, soprabito bianco che gli arriva ai piedi; mette un berretto di pelo, con visiera alla prussiana che ha cura di calcar bene sulle orecchie; calza dei guanti bianchi enormi; mette un colletto lucido di gomma che, stando isolato, non avendo a dar niente col solino della camicia, lascia il collo scoperto e nudo. (106–07)

> [On special occasions he wears an oversize white overcoat, reaching down to his toe; a furry hat with a Prussian-style peak is crammed to his ears; he wears huge white gloves, and a slick rubber collar which, without a shirt, leaves his neck half-naked.]

As an ironic sign of partial representation, Kassa's dress represents a failed attempt at colonial assimilation. On him, the European sartorial signs of power have lost their signifying value and stand as a mocking reminder of the performative aspect of colonial control and domination. And yet, in the eyes of the female settler, Kassa also embodies the potential effects of racial mixing on the European progeny, especially if male.

Kassa Zander, rendered in her description a half-man, represents the degeneration resulting from racial contamination through miscegenation.

The discourse of miscegenation targeted children as the living evidences of the degenerative effects of racial crossings. In Lombroso's scientific racism, special mention is given to children as they are thought to embody the early stages in the developmental process of the races. In the newly founded colony of Eritrea, missionary schools — led by the French Lazarites — kept their traditional function of caring for orphan children by organizing native schooling and religious education. After the Batha Agos revolt — amply detailed in *Tre anni in Eritrea* — the colonial government expelled the Lazarites from the colony (see Battaglia 595-99). Although omitted from her narrative, Rosalia Pianavia Vivaldi's philanthropic activities in favor of biracial children coincided with this political event. In 1893, out of her own initiative, she founded the *Istituto degli Innocentini*, a shelter functioning also as a boarding school for abandoned or orphan children born out of wedlock to an Italian father and an Abyssinian mother. For this initiative, she received generous support from the colonial government and private and religious institutions. Pianavia Vivaldi's creation of a private institution specifically meant for biracial children suggests that miscegenation, in the absence of direct governmental and religious intervention, was becoming a concern for the settler community.

Philanthropy implies an extension of women's activities in the social sphere, but these tend to take place outside of the political domain proper. David G. Horn mentions philanthropy as an example of the confusion between the private and the public sphere effected by social discourses and practices during Fascism. Philanthropic initiatives often involve national public morality — as was the case during the two World Wars and during Fascism — but these are in most cases limited to "feminine" and private activities, such as knitting, nursing, and caring for the sick and poor. These are nevertheless undertaken with patriotic intentions. Pianavia Vivaldi's *Istituto degli Innocentini* is perhaps one of the best examples of how a female settler, in an authoritative and energetic move, crossed the boundary of the private sphere to which her position of wife confined her. This gesture nevertheless reinforced rather than transgressed patriarchal notions of feminine behavior. What motivated her public engagements was above all the conviction that the Italians, as she explains, were in Africa "per portare la civiltà" (TAE 312; to bring civilization).

The Italian settler is initially surprised at the living testimonials in Asmara of what she calls "le consequenze dell'amore non platonico" [the consequences of non-platonic love]. In her diary, she overtly declares her disgust for "il connubio fra il bianco e la nera" [marriages between a white male and a black female] — a sentence significantly similar to the title of Lombroso's lecture on miscegenation. She thus decides to take action. She contacts the Italian fathers of the children, and asks them to contribute to the institute's maintenance fee. As for the Abyssinian mothers, they are easily dismissed in one sentence: "l'indigena, passata ad altri amori facili, l'avrebbe lasciati al loro destino" (313; the native woman, involved in other affairs, would have abandoned them to their destiny). She thus feels entitled to baptize the children with Italian names, gives them frequent baths and clean clothing, and finally fashions herself as the new adoptive mother of the colonial innocents.

By substituting the Abyssinian mothers and community with her authoritative presence, Rosalia claims for herself the role of symbolic mother. If the presence of the little *mulatti* clearly points to the scant productivity of Italian women's biological functions in the colony, the author's political and policing intervention is meant to re-establish white women's authority as mothers and representatives of their race. Italian femininity thus assumes a political function that transcends the limits imposed on middle-class women at the end of the century. The Italian settler performs the policing task of the colonial state, and on such crucial a matter as sexual and racial relationships. Ironically, it is only outside the *madrepatria* that Italian women can claim full participation in matters regarding state politics. We do not know how long the *Institute for the Little Innocents* lasted and what happened to the children who lived there. What we know is that there, rendered clean, Christian, and almost white, they became the most visible sign of the triumph of Italian womanhood and civilization in Africa.

Works Cited
Battaglia, Roberto. *La prima guerra d'Africa.* Turin: Einaudi, 1958.

Ben-Ghiat, Ruth. *Fascist Modernities: Italy, 1922–1945*. Berkeley: U of California P, 2001.

Bhabha, Homi. "Of Mimicry and Man: The Ambivalence of Colonial Discourse." *October* 28 (1984): 129–30.

Buci-Glucksmann, Christine. "Catastrophic Utopia: The Feminine as Allegory of the Modern." *Representations* 14 (Spring 1986): 220–29.

Comaroff, Jean, and John Comaroff. "Homemade Hegemony: Modernity, Domesticity, and Colonialism in South Africa." *African Encounters with Domesticity*. Ed. Karen Tranberg Hansen. New Brunswick, NJ: Rutgers UP, 1992.

Chrisman, Laura, and Patrick Williams, eds. *Colonial Discourse and Post-colonial Theory: A Reader*. New York: Columbia UP, 1994.

Davin, Anna. "Imperialism and Motherhood." *Patriotism: The Making and Unmaking of British National History*, 3 vols. Vol. 1. *History and Politics*. London: Routledge, 1989.

De Giorgio, Michela. "Dalla 'Donna Nuova' alla donna della 'nuova' Italia." *La grande guerra: esperienza, memoria, immagini*. Bologna: Il Mulino, 1986. 307–29.

___. *Le italiane dall'Unità ad oggi: modelli culturali e comportamenti sociali*. Bari: Laterza, 1992.

de Grazia, Victoria. *How Fascism Ruled Women: Italy, 1922–1945*. Berkeley: U of California P, 1992.

Gilman, Sander L. "Black Bodies, White Bodies: Toward an Iconography of Female Sexuality in Late Nineteenth Century Art, Medicine, and Literature." *Race, Culture, Difference*. Ed. James Donald and Ali Rattansi. London: Sage/Open University, 1922.

Horn, David. *Social Bodies: Science, Reproduction, and Italian Modernity*. Princeton, NJ: Princeton UP, 1994.

Jeffrey Howard, Judith. "Patriot Mothers in the Post-Risorgimento: Women after the Italian Revolution." *Women, War, and Revolution*. Ed. Carol R. Berkin and Clara M. Lovett. New York: Holmes and Meirer, 1980. 237–58.

Lombroso, Cesare. *L'uomo bianco e l'uomo di colore: letture sull'origine e la varietà delle razze umane*. 1871.

Lowe, Lisa. *Critical Terrains: French and British Orientalisms*. Ithaca: Cornell UP, 1991.

Matteucci, Pellegrino. *In Abissinia*. Milan: Treves Brothers, 1880.

McClintock, Ann. *Imperial Leather: Race, Gender and Sexuality in the Colonial Context*. London: Routledge, 1995.

Meldini, Piero. *Sposa e madre esemplare: Ideologia e politica della donna e della famiglia durante il fascismo*. Florence: Guaraldi, 1978.

Migliorini, Bruno, and Giulio Cappuccini. *Vocabolario della lingua italiana*. Turin: Paravia, 1916.

Mola, Aldo. *L'imperialismo italiano: la politica estera dall'Unità al fascismo*. Rome: Editori Riuniti, 1980.

Mosse, George. *Nationalism and Sexuality: Middle-Class Morality and Sexual Norms in Modern Europe*. Madison, WI: U of Wisconsin P, 1985.

Pianavia Vivaldi Boffiner, Rosalia. *Tre anni in Eritrea*. Milan: L. F. Cogliati, 1901.

Pickering-Iazzi, Robin, ed. *Mothers of Invention: Women, Italian Fascism, and Culture*. Minneapolis: U of Minnesota P, 1995.

___. *Politics of the Visible: Writing Women, Culture, and Fascism*. Minneapolis, U of Minnesota P, 1997.

Pinkus, Karen. *Bodily Regimes: Italian Advertising under Fascism*. Minneapolis: U of Minnesota P, 1995.

Pogliano, Claudio. "Scienze e stirpe: Eugenica in Italia 1912–1939." *Passato e presente* 5 (Jan-June 1984): 61–97.

Pratt, Mary Louise. "Fieldwork in Common Places." *Writing Culture*. Ed. James Clifford and George E. Marcus. Berkeley: U of California P, 1986. 27–50.

Sharpe, Jenny. "The Unspeakable Limits of Rape: Colonial Violence and Counter-Insurgency." *Genders* (Spring 1991): 25–46.

Spackman, Barbara. *Fascist Virilities: Rhetoric, Ideology, and Social Fantasy in Italy*. Minneapolis: U of Minnesota P, 1996.

Tranberg Hansen, Karen, ed. *African Encounters with Domesticity*. New Brunswick, NJ: Rutgers UP, 1992.

Vigoni, Peppe. *Abissinia*. Milan: Hoepli, 1881.

L'ABBANDONO
Who's Meticcio/Whose Meticcio in the Eritrea-Italy Diaspora?

Laura A. Harris
Pitzer College

A widely circulated and variously phrased aphorism coined in Italy states that, "Italy ends at Rome and Africa begins at Naples." Scholars Pasquale Verdicchio and Gabriella Gribaudi have offered valuable analyses of the political use of the othering involved in the nation's North-South geographical divisiveness. Both locate one possible origin of the colloquial animosity within the historical construction elaborated through medical, anthropological, literary, sociological, and missionary documents that repeatedly pronounced the alterity of southern Italian culture and people from that part of the nation in relation to imagery of Africa. In this essay, I examine notions of race and cultural hybridity in relation to Africanness, meticcios, and black Italy in Erminia Dell'Oro's novel *L'abbandono* (1991). I argue for paradigm that perceives that African immigrants are caught between Africa's long history with Italy and recent global economic changes; I call into question the usefulness of the concept of immigration and the reactionary danger of a race-based hybridity.

Before I turn my attention to this project, I would like to take a moment to understand how burgeoning representations and studies of the African diaspora in Italy are sometimes entangled in a specific understanding of the above aphorism often solely linked to the impact of the recent unprecedented immigration of people of African descent into Italy as an engine of tremendous social change. As some scholars have suggested, this immigration has so changed the face of Italy that it is no longer possible to assume a monoracial or monocultural Italian national character. Quite the opposite, these scholars posit, Italy can now only be seen as an emerging multicultural nation.

Indeed, it is the 1996 public fuss over Denny Mendez's victory as Miss Italy, and her status as being both black and from the Dominican Republic, that has been cited more than once as illustrative of this so-called Italian multi-reality. However, in "Immigration and Social Identities," Vanessa Maher cautions that

> [t]he total number of recent immigrants amounts to no more than 1.8 percent of the Italian population, a much smaller percentage than that found in Germany, France, or Britain, but their presence has caused a degree of "social alarm" which can only be explained by taking into account the historical circumstance in which the immigration has taken place. (160)

Maher's percentage includes multiple categories of ethnic or racial immigrants — African, Middle Eastern, Asian, and Latin American — a generality from which we can conclude that those immigrants of African descent are an even smaller number within Italian society than the more inclusive statistic she cites. Maher's essay is not repudiating the social impact of the recent influx of immigrants. However, it does establish that the "historical circumstance" of this immigration is inextricably linked to Italian North-South geographical divisiveness and the omni-present social-political fragmentation of Italian identity. This contemporary wave of immigrants illuminates these historical tensions at the same time as it appears newly threatening to the changing structure of Italian society. As Maher states in her essay:

> The imagery evoked by the new immigration does not have an empirical referent. It is dissociated from its historical context. A sort of collective amnesia has swallowed up the experience of Italian emigration, of Italian colonialism, of Fascism, the knowledge of the complexity of Italian society itself. (168)

It is not my intent to dispute the social changes linked to immigration. This wave of immigration has indeed coincided with and incited many socio-political directions and effects reflected in the main of Italian society and culture. Instead, rather than understand the legal response, skewed media attention, and public sentiment against immigration as only due to the changes wrought by immigrant groups, it is also necessary to unravel how these discourses delineate groups and construct the "connection" between these groups and the social and economic changes. This discourse on immigration as one of race, otherness, and difference serves to distract from other factors causing global economic changes. This particular discourse wants to equate the changing racial and nation-face of Italy with the complex social and economic climatic unrest of the new European Union.

With Northern Italy historically functioning as the center of economic activity and growth, the current socio-political and perceived economic upset over African immigration can be understood as being motivated by the recent immigration of people of African descent not only to the South, but to Northern Italy. As evidenced by the Southern Italian labor emigration into Northern Italy in the late nineteenth and early twentieth centuries, a heightened Africanness is projected onto bodies as they move from the South of Italy into the North. Many of the African immigrants themselves follow this historical route from South to North. Geographically then, often it is within Northern Italy that substantial change is perceived. It is also within Northern Italy that the alarm of this change has sounded most loudly, as it once did with those so-called Africans of Southern Italy.

Therefore, it seems crucial to exercise a certain skepticism toward this newly assumed "multiculturalism." Further, it seems important to recognize that the same belief systems that cause xenophobic reactions in Italy, in both the North and South, in regard to people of African descent, undergird even liberal contemporary discourse surrounding African immigration into Italy. One of the promises evidenced by critical studies of this Africa-Italy diaspora and discourse is the deconstruction of xenophobic underpinnings and their antecedent historical constructions of African otherness within Italy. In other words, whether manifest in imagined bodily difference informing national definition or in the current immigration influx, Africa has always formed and defined the socially constructed myth of Italy as monoracial and monocultural.

Since subjectivity has been declared central to literary criticism, my audience deserves to know that I first heard the saying "Italy ends at Rome and Africa begins at Naples" in the United States. Whenever my Northern Italian grandfather argued with my Southern Italian grandmother he recited this common knowledge to her as proof of her intractable nature in whatever dispute had come up between them. During these moments of anger he also transmuted his frequent term of endearment for her into an epithet that signaled the end of the heated exchange: "Bedouina," he would shout at her as if that explained and settled all the trouble between them, and perhaps for him as a statement of both desire and anger, it did. What I came to learn later is that it additionally worked to silence her because it evoked her family's so-called hereditary scandal that results from the fact that her grandmother had come from North Africa and was of a Bedouin clan.

Of course, since subject-position is always multi-layered, this familial history of the Africa-Italy diaspora does not end there. It moves beyond my *nonna's* heritage to that of my African-American father who, while serving his tour in the Air Force, was stationed in Naples where he encountered my mother, fell in love, married, and brought her home to the USA. In short, what I am putting forth is that my literary perceptions of *L'abbandono* are filtered through a lived experience of an American-based understanding of the Africa-Italy diaspora, through Italian language as home-schooled Neapolitan slang and then formal study, and through my own specialization in African-American literature and culture in which I have exerted much critical effort on the literary representation of mulatto figures as a recurring trope informing all American literature and culture. The meticcio figure in Italian contexts — I am beginning to muse — can perhaps illuminate similar tensions such as those held in my grandfather's doubled use of "Bedouina."

Dell'Oro's *L'abbandono* serves as a literary model that contests any "collective amnesia" Maher described concerning the historic Africa-Italy diaspora through its narrative of the reign of Italian colonialism in Eritrea. This historically based narrative of colonialism, produced in the contemporary moment of increased African presence in Italy, can be viewed as mirroring the manner in which literary criticism must refuse a linear one-sided analysis of the "new" Africanness of Italy and its literature and culture. Instead, I argue, this critical project must recognize and begin with a similar narrative premise of a circular and multifaceted exchange between continent and nation, between nation and race, and between citizen and other.

Dell'Oro's novel relates the story of colonialism primarily through the struggles of Sellass, an Eritrean woman, and her daughter Marianna. In brief summary, Sellass falls in love with Carlo, an Italian in Eritrea during Mussolini's colonization project. During Carlo's years there, they live together and produce two children, Gianfranco and Marianna. Subsequently, Carlo leaves as the empire collapses and Sellass is left to fend for herself and her children. Both of her children, especially Marianna, grapple with their meticcio status in an Eritrean society that rejects them and an Italian heritage that ignores them.

Sellass's economic struggles cause her to feel utter degradation as she finally becomes a domestic for a white family. This position invokes daily her inability to adhere to the warning her own family had proffered, that she never be a slave to white people. Much like the colonial-period song that appears in the text, *Faccetta nera*, which likens African women to slaves at the same time as it promises that Italian soldiers would cherish them as slaves of love, Sellass must face the reality that her domestic slavery resonates with her failure to grasp the slavery imposed by the colonial dictate of her subordinate status in her romance with Carlo. Any contact with Italians in a society that erected legal sanctions against such contact could only invoke subordination and enslavement.

Sellas finds her "self" trapped between sexual service and domestic service. At this point in the narrative Dell'Oro has Sellass, in turn, become an abusive parent. Marianna suffers the brunt of this verbal and physical abuse as she reminds Sellass of Carlo. With Sellass's demise, Marianna then becomes the protagonist of the novel, ultimately acquiring an Italian surname and immigrating to Italy.

If subjectivity informs literary criticism, it is certainly equally active in literary production. Upon first reading this novel a couple of years ago, I knew one fact about the author's subject-position from the back-cover bio: "Erminia Dell'Oro è nata all'Asmara e vive a Milano" [was born in Asmara and lives in Milan]. That which I could not ascertain from this description, or assume as an outsider unable to grasp subtle nuances in the foreign languages of the standard Italian and Eritrean Tigre used in the novel, was if she was a white Eritrean or a black Eritrean or meticcio herself. From the perspective of an African-Americanist this was an unusual situation, as in the US literary identities are almost always a necessary context to the reading of the literary text. From my critical perspective, I had ambivalence about the text. I wondered who authored it. A bit of internet research revealed Dell'Oro to be an Italian woman of Jewish heritage with Eritrea as a lived experience. In this regard, I have come to understand Dell'Oro as a national meticcio herself, an Italian with a pronounced geographically hybrid experience of Eritrea at the core of her Italianness. Her subject-position, as one of national hybridity, comes to serve as a useful, albeit not unproblematic, critical model to situate the concept of an Eritrea-Italy diaspora as one of mutually porous boundaries of identity, nation, and race.

In *Playing in the Dark: Whiteness and the Literary Imagination* (1992), Toni Morrison writes in regards to the Africanness of a national US literature:

> For some time now I have been thinking about the validity or vulnerability of a certain set of assumptions conventionally accepted among literary historians and critics and circulated as "knowledge." This knowledge holds that traditional, canonical American literature is free of, uninformed, and unshaped by the four-hundred-year-old presence of, first, Africans and then African-Americans in the United States. It assumes that this presence — which shaped the body politic, the Constitution, and the entire history of the culture — has had no significant place or consequence in the origin and development of that culture's literature. Moreover, such knowledge assumes that the characteristics of our national literature emanate from a particular "Americanness" that is separate from and unaccountable to this presence. There seems to be a more or less tacit agreement among literary scholars that, because American literature has been clearly the preserve of white male views, genius, and power, those views, genius, and power are without relationship to and removed from the overwhelming presence of black people in the United States. This agreement is about a population that preceded every American writer of renown and was, I have come to believe, one of the most furtively radical impinging forces on the country's literature. The contemplation of this black presence is central to any understanding of our national literature and should not be permitted to hover at the margins of the literary imagination. . . . It has occurred to me that the very manner by which American literature distinguishes it-

> self as a coherent entity exists because of this unsettled and unsettling population. (5–6)

With a few historical revisions and factual adjustments, it strikes me that Morrison's point about American literature's self-defining process via opposition to Africanness equally illuminates the contentious connection between the Africa-Italy diaspora, a national Italian literature and identity. In Morrison's formulation of Africanness in American literature, diaspora comes to mean more than a racial category of literary identity. It posits a circuit of relay in which racial and national identities are not only intertwined, but interdependent. With Dell'Oro's novel this circuit of identity is put into effect through a narrative progression that focuses on the meticcio children produced in the colonial Eritrea-Italy diaspora.

This narrative progression is realized as the story moves from Sellass's search for self, as one that can only be inscribed by absence in relation to Italianness, to that of Marianna's search for an identity as a meticcio who is neither Eritrean nor Italian but racially both. This coming together of two races, as a facet of the hybridity inscribed in Dell'Oro's narrative is, in one example, exhibited in Marianna's ability to become literate in both standardized Italian and Tigre. Further, the resourceful Marianna, through use of legal constructions of identity that allowed Eritrean children with Italian fathers to claim Italian citizenship in the post-colonization period, manages to secure an Italian surname in order to immigrate to Italy. The story's focus on Marianna's meticcio status, as both inside and outside national identities, radically underscores the interdependent and politically embedded constructions of race and nation. At the same time, this focus obscures Sellass's subject-position as a racially unmixed woman. Sellass's experience of national hybridity as a colonial subject can no longer be articulated when the meticcio comes to serve as the sole definition of hybridity in relation to race and nation. Indeed, for much of the latter half of the narrative, Sellass articulates this erasure of her culturally hybrid experience in her oft-repeated refrain directed toward her Italian lover Carlo, "Ma come ha potuto? Come ha potuto?" [But how could he? How could he?] In other words, how could Carlo, as symbolic of Italy, fail to acknowledge that the desire for, as well as the rejection of, Sellass's Africanness were core to Italian national identity as it produced itself through imperial conquest and the brutal subjugation of an entire people.

Sellass's abject status in relation to Carlo-as-Italy is foreshadowed in an episode early in the novel in which Carlo emigrates to the US seeking economic opportunity. Once there, he befriends Wolf, an African-American residing in Harlem, New York, in the 1920s. Harlem, at this time, was considered the mecca of black cultural production, and to this day geographically symbolizes the height of the Harlem Renaissance literary and cultural movement — a movement that, some critics argue, was in great part premised upon a fashionable white vogue for all things black. Due to the 1929 stock market crash, Carlo fails in his economic pursuits in America and returns to Italy, from where he subsequently departs for Eritrea searching for yet another economic watershed. Dell'Oro's juxtaposition of an historical moment of US fascination and repugnance with "Africa" against Sellass's experience as colonial subject is central to understanding the complex interrelationships of race and nation in the novel. At the same time as the Harlem Renaissance found its demise in the stock market crash, Sellass's Africanness is positioned as the terrain upon which Italian desire and repulsion utilize colonialism to form national identity while rejecting claims to Italian culture and identity for colonial subjects.

Ironically, as Italy invades Ethiopia, Ethiopia becomes symbolic in the formation of an American black consciousness linked to international Pan-African communism. However, in the novel, it is only through the racially hybrid body of Marianna that diasporic resolution is found. This resolution, premised upon race essentialism, can only be realized by identifying the Italianness of the meticcio as a means of mediating African otherness. In Dell'Oro's construction of hybridity the meticcio functions much like the mulatto figure of US literature. The taboos of interracial contact are mediated by the mulatto's white Americanness as an expression of the shared national relationship between the races.

While Dell'Oro's narrative proves useful to contextualizing race in regards to nationality, its narrative construction of diaspora and hybridity threatens to become reactionary as it is ultimately predicated upon essentialized racial definitions. In *Colonial Desire: Hybridity in Theory, Culture and Race* (1996), Robert Young writes

> [t]here is no single, or correct, concept of hybridity: it changes as it re-
> peats, but it also repeats as it changes. It shows that we are still locked
> into parts of the ideological network of a culture that we think and pre-
> sume that we have surpassed. The question is whether the old essen-
> tializing categories of cultural identity, or of race, were really so essen-
> tialized, or have been retrospectively constructed as more fixed than
> they were. When we look at the texts of racial theory, we find that they
> are in fact contradictory, disruptive, and already deconstructed. (27)

Notions of cultural hybridity and multiculturalism are productive insofar as they work to undermine certain facets of nationalist-colonial hegemony. However, if they rely solely upon essentialized models of race
as opposed to including more elastic notions of nation and diaspora,
these formulations can also function to erase the complexity of identification and reinforce colonial hegemony. As Young points out, the radical
potential of hybridity can only exist in a conflictual paradox. He writes,
"Hybridity thus makes difference into sameness, and sameness into difference, but in a way that makes the same no longer the same, the different no longer simply different" (26). As Graziella Parati argues in "Italian
Fathers and Eritrean Daughters: Women Without Nationality," Del-
l'Oro's narrative creates a multicultural and hybrid literary sphere in the
Italophone canon. Parati's capacity to intertwine Dell'Oro's "white"
voice with that of Italian-Ethiopian writer Maria Viarengo, Senegalese
writer Saidou Moussa Ba, and her own western critical position allows
her to posit the possibility of a literary canon in which "multinational
and multiracial voices can become part of the Italian cultural tradition"
(196).

In concluding, I would like to suggest, that it is imperative for this
emerging literary scholarship to constantly interrogate and reassess the
criteria for membership in a so-called multi-sphere, when indeed the
colonial subject of Eritrea and the recent African immigrant are excluded
from this Italophone hybridity premised upon essentialism. These Eritrean and African immigrant bodies come to serve as examples for this
multicultural and hybrid diaspora. Simultaneously, as evidenced by the
character Sellass in Dell'Oro's narrative, these African bodies are exoticized, silenced, and exiled. It seems that it is not Dell'Oro's text but her

subject-position as an Italian national hybrid that creates this literary space. She is the privileged colonial body of an Eritrea-Italy diaspora that is permitted to exist between cultures, geographies, and literatures. Ideally, this new literary space should incorporate the national hybridity already present in Italian cultural traditions as a necessary part of complex racial and colonial identities. The anticipation of myriad and non-essentialized forms of hybridity finding voice in this sphere will depend upon Italian receptivity toward an African diaspora fulfilling its radical theoretical potential by reconstructing the power relations of difference, not re-inscribing or reappropriating sameness.

Works Consulted and Cited

Bekere, Ayele. "African-Americans and the Italo-Ethiopian War." *Revisioning Italy: National Identity and Global Culture.* Minneapolis: U of Minneapolis P, 1997. 116–33.

Dell'Oro, Erminia. *L'abbandono: una storia eritrea.* Torino: Einuadi 1991.

Gennari, John. "Passing for Italian." *Transition* 72 (Winter 1996): 36–49.

Gribaudi, Gabriella. "Images of the South." *Italian Cultural Studies: An Introduction.* Oxford: Oxford UP, 1996. 72–87.

Maher, Vanessa. "Immigration and Social Identities." *Italian Cultural Studies: An Introduction.* Oxford: Oxford UP, 1996. 160–77.

Morrison, Toni. *Playing in the Dark: Whiteness and the Literary Imagination.* Cambridge: Harvard UP, 1992.

Parati, Graziella. "Italian Fathers and Eritrean Daughters: Women Without Nationality." *Gendered Contexts: New Perspectives in Italian Cultural Studies.* New York: Peter Lang, 1996. 189–97.

Pinkus, Karen. "Ms (Black) Italy." *Black Renaissance, Renaissance Noir* 2.1 (Fall/Winter 1998): 80–93.

Verdicchio, Pasquale. "The Preclusion of Postcolonial Discourse." *Revisioning Italy: National Identity and Global Culture.* Minneapolis: U of Minneapolis P, 1997. 191–212.

Young, Robert. *Colonial Desire: Hybridity in Theory, Culture and Race.* London: Routledge, 1995.

AFRICA AND AFRICANS IN ITALIAN THEATER

ITALIAN AFRICAN *METICCIATO ARTISTICO*
IN THE TEATRO DELLE ALBE

Teresa L. Picarazzi
University of Arizona

The Teatro delle Albe in Ravenna stands out among contemporary multicultural representations in Italy and has received both national and international acclaim for its work. It was the first theatre company in Italy to adopt an interethnic ensemble based on the practice of *meticciato artistico,* or artistic métissage. With heavy emphasis placed on researching the two cultures that make up the theatre troupe, the Albe is one of the most significant avante-garde theatre companies in Italy that engages in *teatro di ricerca.* We can describe the Teatro delle Albe, in part, as *afroromagnolo*: its members are Senegalese and Italian.[1] While its artistic director and dramaturge Marco Martinelli is a white European male, the Albe is a cooperative made up of Romagnolo and Senegalese writers and actors (who are all equal members of the troupe).[2]

Since 1987 the Albe have been forging a poetics of border culture through their interethnic productions.[3] The troupe's works examine the relations between the North and the South of the world, beginning with their understanding that the "subsoil of Romagna is African," as depicted as well in the first *afroromagnolo* play by Marco Martinelli in *Ruh!*

---

[1] Many thanks to Albe Marco Martinelli, Mandiaye N'Diaye, Mor Awa Niang, Ermanna Montanari, Luigi Dadina, and Marcella Nonni for sharing their work with me. Thanks as well to Franco Nasi and Wiley Feinstein for their long-standing conversation with me about the Albe. This essay was made possible, in part, by two summer research grants from the University of Arizona: a Small Grant from the office of the Vice President for Research; and an HRI (Humanities Research Initiative) grant. This essay appears by courtesy of *Italica*; its original version first appeared under the same title in *Italica* 77.2 (Summer 2000): 224–45.

[2] In Italy the word "cooperative" carries with it a series of ideological connotations; cooperatives are generally non-hierarchical collectives in which all of the members decide on the group's decisions.

[3] Please note that when I refer to the Albe in the plural I am talking about the members of the company, who are also called Albe, *albe bianche*, and *albe nere.*

Romagna più Africa uguale (1988; Ruh! Romagna Plus Africa Means). Three plays make up what Martinelli calls an African trilogy: *Ruh, Romagna più Africa uguale* (1988), *Siamo asini o pedanti?* (1989; Are We Donkeys or Pedants?), and *Lunga vita all'albero!* (1990; Long Live the Tree!), all written and directed by Martinelli.[4] In addition to these three plays, others that engage in cross-cultural dialogue between the troupe's Senegalese and Romagnolo members include: the play *Le due calebasse* (1990; The Two Calabashes), by Mandiaye N'Diaye; *Griot-Fuler* (1993), by Luigi Dadina and Mandiaye N'Diaye; *I ventidue infortuni di Mor Arlecchino* (1993; Mor Arlecchino's Twenty-two Misfortunes), by Marco Martinelli; *All'inferno* (1996; In Hell), by Marco Martinelli; *Nessuno può coprire l'ombra* (1991; No One Can Cover Over a Shadow), by Marco Martinelli and Saidou Moussa Ba; *Perché mai uno? Credevo che ne fossero due* (1999; Why Ever Just One? I Thought There Were Two of Them), Marco Martinelli with Mandiaye N'Diaye.

This essay will briefly outline the Senegalese-Romagnolo experience, including members and performances, in the Teatro delle Albe. This spans an initial period between 1987, from its founding as an interethnic theatre company, to 1997 with the opening of its sister *casa di teatro* Guediawaye Theatre, on the outskirts of Dakar, and then from 1997 to 1999. As such it is reflective of the demographics of a specific moment or decade in the history of Italian-African immigration. The muticultural acts that characterize the Albe's work emphasize "a culture of links," in a *teatro di confronto* between two cultures in Ravenna — through research, representation, and performance.

The Albe practice their own unique form of avant-garde theatre, which they define as the practices of *teatro politttttttico* and *meticciato artistico*. *Teatro politttttttico* is written with seven t's to invite multiple interpretations of the word. Martinelli explains in a recent essay that the seven t's signal to the reader that the Albe's political theatre at the end of

---

[4]Marco Martinelli, *Teatro impuro* (Ravenna: Danilo Montanari Editore, 1997). This recently compiled collection includes the plays: *Ruh! Romagna più Africa uguale*; *Siamo asini o pedanti?*; *Bonifica*; *Lunga vita all'albero!*; *I refrattari*; *I ventidue infortuni di Mor Arlecchino*; and *Incantati*. Henceforth page numbers from some of these plays are cited in the text from this volume.

the millennium departs from a more traditional Marxist political theatre that provides answers and looks to the proletariat for solutions:

> Noi oggi queste certezze non le abbiamo, ma non siamo neanche ammazzati, instupiditi dal consumismo e continuiamo a porci delle domande. . . . Politttttttico perché l'orizzonte di questo fine secolo, di questo millennio è quanto di più caotica si possa immaginare e una risposta onesta a questo chaos non è nascondersi dietro gli slogan, dietro le risposte facili ma interrogarsi in profondità e insieme su che cosa fare. (Martinelli, "Il cammino dall'idea all'opera si fa in ginocchio" 63)

> [Today we do not have these certainties, but we have not been killed or turned into dummies by consumerism and we continue to question . . . Polittttttttical because the horizon of this end of the century, of this millennium is so much more chaotic than one could imagine and an honest response to this chaos is not to hide behind slogans and behind easy answers but to interrogate deeply and together about what to do.]

The seven t's thus suggest uncertainty. The assonance between the word political and polis also indicates that the company self-consciously derives much of its matter from the surrounding polis, with which it is also engaged through outreach cultural programs in the school system. Moreover, in addition to being a theatre of the polis in a cultural and political sense, the Albe is also a theatre that has the quality of a polyptych (*polittico* in Italian, and thereby another assonance), a painting or relief divided up into a variety of individual panels; in the Albe this is translated as a multiplicity of perspectives that form a whole. The practices of *teatro politttttttico* and *meticciato artistico* overlap.

The theatre advances the notion of reciprocity and engagement in the practice of *meticciato artistico*, which includes the dialogue, research, comparison, and celebration of differences between different aspects of the Senegalese and Romagnolo cultures that coexist in Ravenna (and in the theatre company). One of the troupe's stated goals for this *meticciato artistico* is the solidarity between different peoples against racism. By *meticciato artistico* I do not by any means intend to conjure up the American term melting pot, or of hybridized postcolonial identities, but rather the concept of syncretism where white is white, and black is black, like a kaleidescope, where the colors are still individual but form a variegated whole.[5] In very much this way the Italian and African Albe dig deep into their roots and their traditions in order to be able to dialogue with each other. One element of the Albe's *meticciato* is to recuperate lost or forgotten kinds of theatre — both canonical and noncanonical — as a way of integrating the past with the present. Another aspect recognizes the vital importance of cultural roots (from Aristophanes to Goldoni, to Senegalese and Romagnolo folklore and oral history), and aims at the renewal of traditions, oral histories, and dialects. For example, Luigi Dadina and Ermanna Montanari have done groundbreaking work in introducing the Romagnolo dialect and folklore on the avant-garde stage, as has Mandiaye N'Diaye done with his work in Wolof and his representations of Senegalese folklore.[6]

Prior to this, from 1977 to 1987, the Albe was a theatre troupe made up of four Romagnoli — Marco Martinelli, Ermanna Montanari, Luigi Dadina, Marcella Nonni — who addressed critical social and environmental issues through their performances. 1987 marks a pivotal moment in the Albe's history, when they attended a lecture by a geology professor (Franco Ricchi Lucchi) at the University of Bologna. The lecture, says Martinelli, provoked an earthquake in the imaginary of the Albe with the affirmation "il sottosuolo Romagnolo è africano, la Romagna è Africa" (Martinelli Gabriele 11; the Romagnolo subsoil is African; Romagna is Africa). This metaphor resounded for the Albe, who had recently seen the Italian Adriatic basin become a "border spiral," a site where different cultural and ethnic groups converge — more specifically, in the increasing numbers of Senegalese ambulatory vendors on the streets and beaches.[7] In response, the Albe set out to shift the company's borders —

---

[5]Joseph R. Roach discusses "the feasibility of theater as a mediator across boundaries of historical and cultural difference." His use of the word métissage is appropriate here: "métissage (or braiding), not a melting pot but a tactful weaving together of separate strands" (13).

[6]See, for example, a discussion of Montanari's use of dialect in Picarazzi, ed., "Ermanna Montanari's Voices Crossing the Borders Between Language and Magic" 41–43.

[7]Guillermo Gomez-Peña has theorized about the border spiral as a place where more than one culture converges; border culture is what is created as a result of such an encounter. See Guillermo Gomez-Peña, *Warrior for a Gringostroika* 45–54, especially 49; also in Guillermo Gomez-Peña, "The Multicultural Paradigm: An Open Letter to the National

linguistic, ethnic, and cultural — by placing the practice of interethnic exchange at the foreground of their aesthetics.

The *albe bianche* concluded that in order to highlight the disparities between the North and the South of the world and to theatrically inter-twine "white" culture with the culture of those "invading aliens" they needed to stage their new convictions: "Basta 'parlare' di Africa; mettia-mola in scena" (Martinelli, "Il cammino dall'idea" 51; Stop talking about Africa; let's put it on stage). The Albe, thus, became *afroromagnolo* by go-ing out to the nearby beaches and inviting three Senegalese ambulatory vendors to join their cooperative as actors. The first three men to join the troupe were: Iba Babou, Abibou N'Diaye, and Khadim Thiam. By 1989 these three men had left the company. Three other Senegalese men then joined the Albe, and remained in the cooperative through 1998: these men are Mor Awa Niang, known throughout Italy for his representation of the Mor Arlecchino figure; Mandiaye N'Diaye; and El Hadji Niang, a percussionist. Both Mor Awa Niang and El Hadji Niang are descendants of families with a griot tradition and both experience their work in the theatre as a return to the practice of griot. In certain parts of West Africa, the griot is an oral artist; advisor to the king; a live repository of knowl-edge and history; and the performer of song, dance, and music.[8] In 1998 Mor Awa Niang and El Hadji Niang decided to leave the Albe to pursue individual careers; Mandiaye N'Diaye remained.

All of the Senegalese Albe actors originally emigrated to Italy in order to make enough money as street/beach peddlars to send back home. In a recently published interview, Mandiaye N'Diaye talks about this painful and embarassing experience of trying to sell merchandise to half-naked and indifferent sunbathers. When the opportunity presented itself to try out for the Albe, he pretended to be a trained actor even though he had no experience and had never been inside of a theatre. For N'Diaye, the discovery of an Italian-African connection (and metaphor), as described by the already mentioned geography lesson, has been mutual. N'Diaye relates the experience of doing theatre in Italy as a discovery of his own African origins, as he confirms in that same interview: "Io l'Africa l'ho

Arts Community," especially 22–23.
[8]For a thorough discussion of the griot, see Okpewho.

scoperta in Romagna . . . le mie radici africane sono romagnole"
(N'Diaye, "Il drammaturgo dei miei sogni" 101 and 104; I have discovered Africa in Romagna . . . my African roots are Romagnole). N'Diaye
also attributes a heightened awareness of the actual conditions of French
hegemony in Senegal to his experience in the theatre, which functions as
a mirror:

> No, no! La vera storia tra la Francia e il Senegal l'abbiamo imparata
> vivendo qua. Da qui — solo da qui — puoi capire cos'hanno fatto i
> francesi in Senegal. . . . Vivi tutto questo sapendola un'altra storia, sim-
> ile, ma finché non ti vedi in uno specchio, è difficile vederlo.[9]

> [No, no! The true story between France and Senegal we learned living
> here. From here — only from here — you can understand what the
> French did in Senegal. . . . You live this knowing it to be another story, a
> similar one, but until you can see yourself in a mirror, it's difficult to see
> it.]

In the play *Ruh! Romagna più Africa uguale*, the interplay between the
Senegalese actors and their roles immediately reflects the lived experience of the three Senegalese actors who perform it. They play 'themselves' in the play, which actually stages the increasing numbers of African — mainly Senegalese — *vu-cumprà* (also the title of one of the chapters of *Ruh!*), on the beaches of Ravenna in the late 80s. They must also
contend with the hostile attitudes of the Italians who look down on
them. Subsequent plays increasingly portray this theme of the African
migrant who has made Italy his home, the problems he there encounters,
and the desire to return to roots and family in Senegal. Yet we often encounter a character in Martinelli's plays who finds a definitive return
impossible, and who must live between both cultures without ever feeling completely at home in one. These plays that treat the question of
immigration also raise the immediate and problematic issue of representation (who is writing these characters, and with what authority? —
questions which I shall address shortly), where real bodies on stage correspond in some way to real bodies in the community.

---

[9]Mandiaye N'Diaye, unpublished interview with author, June 1994.

The first *afroromagnolo* play, *Ruh! Romagna più Africa uguale*, articulates the Albe's new vocabulary and poetics in a performance that decentered its first spectators. For this reason I will quote at length from this particular play, which talks about Europe from the perspective of the Africans who have gone there to work, and not from the perspective of the European; it overturns the essentialized "Other" by making that other the whites. Before *Ruh!* began, the three Senegalese actors moved between the aisles peddling cigarette lighters as do the street/beach vendors in Italy. The audience at first could not understand why they were in the theatre, and were further caught off balance when the lights suddenly went out and the Senegalese men started to shout in Wolof. The *afroromagnole* Albe were thus initiated on stage. The play also points the finger at the figure of the industrialist, who like a leech or vampire, becomes "fat" at the expense of others; and it recasts the stigma surrounding the color black in the imaginary of the Italians. Martinelli describes this play as:

> Un lavoro su Ravenna, ancora una volta, e sul mare agonizzante, sui maiali di Raul e la svendita a basso prezzo del cristianesimo, sull'acida e insieme vampiresca angoscia che tiene bene in piedi il Nord e sulla vitalità disperata del Sud, sul nero, colore di lutto per gli europei, simbolo di fecondità, della terra fertile, e delle nubi gonfie di pioggia, per gli africani. (Martinelli, "Ravenna Africana" 11)

> [A work about Ravenna, once again, and about the sea in the throes of death, about Raul's pigs and the cheap selling out of Christianity, about the bitter vampire-like anguish that sustains the North, and the desperate vitality of the South, about black, the color of mourning for Europeans, and for the Africans symbol of fecundity, of fertile land, and of clouds swollen with rain.]

The titles of some of the key scenes in *Ruh!* clearly indicate the content. Act I is entitled "Vu cumprà?"; Act II, "Arriva l'uomo nero" [The Black Man Arrives]; Act XIV "La mia Europa" [My Europe]; and Act X, "Lezione di geologia" [Geography Lesson], articulated by a character who imparts that impressive geography lesson:

> La Romagna è Africa! Questa è Scienza, non fantascienza
> Qualità Costante nel Tempo. Il sottosuolo che regge
> Ravenna e Bagnacavallo
> Godo
> e le altre città romagnole è africano! (30)

> [Romagna is Africa! This is Science, not science fiction / A Constant
> Quality over Time. The subsoil that holds / Ravenna and Bagnacavallo
> / Godo / and all the other Romagnole cities is African!]

The motifs of cannibalism, excess, and waste mark the whole play, as do the themes of Eurocentrism, hunger, and the problems of the Third World. The characters of the Mother, played by Ermanna Montanari, and the three Senegalese actors metaphorically recount the hunger of the "Eurocentric Cow," the fatted calf of consumerism and materialism, who eats more than what more than 40 Senegalese would eat. Martinelli's depiction of this staged Eurocentrism (and intercultural issues) in the late 1980s was a novel innovation in Italian theatre that has since been adopted by other theatre companies and as such important to students of Italian cultural studies.

> from Act V: "Canto di invidia per la Vacca eurocentrica," Abib, Iba, Khadim e la Madre:

> La Vacca oh la Vacca
> la Vacca è eurocentrica
> la Vacca è intelligente
> la Vacca studia
> la Vacca è colta
> e sa parlare . . . inglese
> e sa parlare . . . inglese!
> (. . .)
> La Vacca mangia più di noi
> come quaranta senegalesi
> la Vacca ingrassa più di noi
> più di quaranta senegalesi.
> cantiamo la nostra invidia
> per la Vacca eurocentrica! (22)

[The Cow The Cow / The Cow is Eurocentric / The Cow is smart / The Cow studies / The Cow is refined / And can speak . . . English / And can speak . . . English! / . . . / The Cow that eats more than us / The Cow that eats more than us / Like 40 Senegalese / The Cow gets fatter than us / Fatter than 40 Senegalese / We sing of our envy / Of the Eurocentric Cow!]

Martinelli ironically couples this devouring Eurocentric calf with the figure of the industrialist Raul Gardini ("an authentic son of Romagna" who later committed suicide during the *tangentopoli* crisis of 1993), who never appears on the scene, but whose presence is felt throughout the play, and whose propensity to overeat is mentioned repeatedly. Gardini is ubiquitous but invisible, like a pesticide or "radionuclude": "Invisibile, ma odora . . . In certe zone della città la gente alza il naso per aria e non ha dubbi: quella è la puzza di Raul!" (25; He's invisible, but he smells . . . in certain parts of the city the people raise their noses in the air and have no doubts: that's the smell of Raul!).

Martinelli's biting irony is demonstrated again in Act XII, entitled "Bentornati" [Welcome Back], where the figure of the Mother, in an indictment against white bourgeois closed-mindedness, placidly comments on the historical ignorance and hypocrisy of those who live blindly in their comfort, in this case the Italian sunbathers who look at the peddlars of goods on the beaches and uncomprehendingly ask why they have come to Italy. In the following monologue, several voices are uttered by the Mother: the Mother's actual voice that says "and they steal the fish from your seas and rob the grain from your bowls"; the voices of the Italians on the beaches; and the voice of imperialism that justifies itself with the concluding words: "it's not our fault if we invented gunpowder before they did; even Ancient Greece had slaves." In addition to providing the spectator/reader with a creative representation of African ambulatory vendors, Martinelli is also critiquing the socio-economic conditions of exploitation and capitalism that have depleted resources in Africa and led to mass emigration:

Bentornati
a queste spiagge gremite di turisti.
Chi abita il nord del mondo

fuma Camel
e guarda il cammello sul pacchetto
e guarda voi
smerciare Lacoste a basso prezzo
e si dice
perchè vengono qui?
Perchè non se ne stanno a casa loro?
La gente ha sempre una domanda intelligente
da farsi
prima di addormentarsi.
E chiacchiera
chiacchiera sotto l'ombrellone
e compra le magliette false a basso prezzo
e gli orologi gialli e gli elefanti
e dice
il mondo va a rotoli
i neri sono belle statue in campo
e segnano tante reti
ma questi
cosa vengono a cercare qui?
Non hanno voglia di lavorare il campo
laggiù in Africa!
La gente ha sempre una frase storica
sul comodino
prima di addormentarsi.
E ruba al vostro mare tutti i pesci
e ruba alla vostra terra tutto l'oro
e ruba alla vostra scodella tutto il grano
e dice
non è colpa nostra se prima di loro
abbiamo inventato la stampa
non è colpa nostra se prima di loro
abbiamo inventato la polvere da sparo
non è colpa nostra se prima di loro
abbiamo inventato la mercatura
anche in Atene c'erano gli schiavi
e le statue perfette, dorate! (38–39)

[Welcome / to these beaches packed with tourists. / He who lives in the North / smokes Camels / and looks at the camel on the pack / and looks at you / pushing cheap Lacoste shirts / and he says / "Why do they come here?" / "Why don't they stay in their own homes?" / People always have some smart question / to ask themselves / before falling asleep. / And they chatter / they chatter under the beach umbrella / and buy fake cheap shirts / and yellow watches and elephants / and they say / the world is going to pieces / blacks are beautiful statues on the field / and they score a lot of goals / but these blacks here / what are they looking for? / They don't feel like working in the fields / down there in Africa! / People always have a ready phrase / on the nightstand / before falling asleep. / And they rob all of the fish from your sea / and they rob all of the gold from your land / and they rob all of the wheat from your bowl / and they say / it's not our fault if before they / we invented the printing press / it's not our fault if before they / we invented gunpowder / it's not our fault if before they / we invented commerce / even in Athens there were slaves!]

Act XIV, entitled "La mia Europa," is a creative and ironic reading of the relations between the West and Africa. This act infers and stages how the West discovered, conquered, understood, and "helped" Africa by the superimposition of culture, religion, education, and language. Martinelli rewrites Karen Blixen's descriptive appropriation of Africa into a Europe that has become increasingly sterile, and especially Italy with its *crescita zero*/zero birth rate. The Senegalese characters identify Blixen as the white European representative of power who paternalistically calls Africa "hers": the Senegalese characters predict that Europe will soon be "theirs." The rhetoric of a low birth-rate of Italians in Italy has been a topic for many right-wing groups, who like to sound the alarm that "pure-blooded" Italians will soon be in the minority if something is not done to stop immigration.[10]

> Iba: (in mano ha *La mia Africa* di Karen Blixen)
> Scriverò un romanzo.

---

[10]University of Massachusetts anthropology professor, Betsy Krause, has completed a manuscript in which she treats the issue of the low birth rate of Italians, as compared to recently emigrated African women living in Italy.

Abib: Come si chiamerà?

Iba: La mia Europa!

Khadim: L'Europa è bella.

Iba: L'Europa è libera.

Abib: Ci sono gli ospedali.

Khadim: Ci sono le discoteche.

Iba: La discoteca è bella.

Abib: Domani questa Europa sarà nostra.

Khadim: Domani quando?

Abib: Domani.

Khadim: Voi non fate più figli.

Abib: Le scuole chiuderanno.

Iba: Gli ospizi riempiranno.

Khadim: Siete vecchi.

Abib: Crescita zero.

Iba: Crescita zero.

Khadim: Noi siamo tanti.

Iba: La fame in Africa è brutta

Khadim: L'Europa è bella.

Abib: L'Europa è libera.

Iba: Noi non vogliamo fare i vu cumprà.

Khadim: L'Europa è bella.

Abib: Noi non siamo animali.

Iba: La fame in Africa è ancora più brutta.

Khadim: La nostra Europa . . .

Abib: . . . la daremo . . . ai nostri . . . bambini . . .

Iba: Voi non avrete figli, quel giorno.

Khadim: Crescita zero.

Abib: Poveri bianchi . . . non avete più sperma. (37)

[Iba: (he has a copy of Karen Blixen's *My Africa* in his hands) / I'm going to write a novel. / Abib: What's it going to be called? / Iba: My Europe! / Khadim: Europe is beautiful. / Iba: Europe is free. / Abib: There are hospitals. / . . . / Abib: Tomorrow this Europe will be ours. / Khadim: Tomorrow when? / Abib: Tomorrow. / Khadim: You don't make babies any more. / Abib: The schools will close. / Iba: The hospices will fill up. / Khadim: You are old. / Abib: Zero birth rate. / Iba: Zero birth rate. / Khadim: We are many. / Iba: Hunger in Africa is ugly. / . . . / Iba: We don't want to be *vu cumprà*. / Khadim: Europe is beautiful. / Abib: We are not animals. / Iba: Hunger in Africa is even more ugly. / Khadim: Our Europe . . . / Abib: . . . We'll give it to . . . our . . . children . . . / Iba: You won't have children, that day. / Khadim: Zero birth rate. / Abib: Poor white folks . . . you don't have any more sperm.]

The act "La mia Europa" demonstrates how Martinelli, through performance, provocatively attempts to raise the consciousness of the audience. Does he also empower the actors, by 'giving' them voice, or are the voices theirs? The above dialogue concludes with the words of Abib (played by Abibou N'Diaye): "Poor whites . . . you don't have any more sperm." Martinelli is attempting to shift the spectator's perspective concerning the birth rate issue, and African migrants in Italy, and the words are no less effective because they have been written by a man with white skin. Let me introduce a brief parenthesis here. Since we are on the topic of white appropriation of African identity and subjectivity it might be useful for us to establish a politics of location and ask ourselves at this point with what authority and legitimacy can Martinelli, a white bourgeois Italian, represent the experience of African immigrants, or can I, an olive-skinned daughter of Italian immigrants write about these matters? Are positive intentions enough; or sincere interest in intercultural dialogue and human relations? While representation risks misrepresentation at times, it is important to emphasize that speaking of another's experience does not always mean appropriation and objectification. The experience of the Albe is driven by the principal dynamic of constant collaboration and consent between the actors and the figure of the dramaturge, who writes the characters based on the personalities of the actors. While fictional — and at times caricatures — their personae or characters are 'custom-written' in what Martinelli calls a *teatro di carne*. Martinelli is not a director of someone else's texts, nor does he write plays for actors whom he does not know. Another critic has compared Martinelli's role as the poet of the Albe to the great Eduardo De Filippo:

> Penso alla dinamica drammaturgica di 'compagnia' che accomuna la scrittura di Edoardo a quella di Marco Martinelli, che come il Maestro napoletano, modella i personaggi e il loro parlare sulla maschera scenica dell'attore. (Guccini 4)

[I'm thinking of the dynamic 'theatre company' dramaturgy that Edoardo's writing shares with that of Marco Martinelli who, like the great Neapolitan Maestro, shapes characters and speech on the stage mask of the actor.]

The above ties in with the earlier mentioned dynamic practice of *meticciato artistico* based on respect, integrity, and exchange. Let me also suggest that one need not necessarily be African, or African American to look at African-Italian culture. End of parenthesis.

With the scope of continuing and deepening that dialogue already in motion between its members, and in order for the Romagnolo members of the Albe to step back and experience, at least in idea, the culture and lives of their Senegalese colleagues, in 1990 the Albe organized the Ravenna Dakar Project. The Ravenna Dakar Project included three phases: the first phase was the staging of a play called *Bonifica: polittico in sette quadri* [*Bonifica: A Polyptych in Seven Panels*]; during the second phase the Albe embarked on a trip to Senegal for two months; and the third phase was the writing and enactment of the play *Lunga vita all'albero!*, which marked the culmination of both the Ravenna Dakar Project and the Albe's African trilogy. The trip to Senegal was similar to previous experimental theatre companies' voyages of cultural exchange, like those of dramatists Peter Brook and Eugenio Barba's trips to Africa, Australia, and India. Both *albe bianche* and *albe nere* experienced the trip as a real cultural exchange. For example, the *albe bianche* understood what it means to perform as a minority as the Albe performed some of their work in front of a primarily Senegalese audience that proved a very different type of audience from that to which they were accustomed. Furthermore, Mandiaye N'Diaye describes how his own culture has been opened up to him through the trip to Senegal and through his work in the theatre:

Fare teatro mi è servito per fare tante cose: imparare la lingua, conoscere la cultura italiana, fare un lavoro onesto, ma anche conoscere meglio la mia cultura senegalese. In questo viaggio con i miei compagni ho visto delle cose che non avevo mai visto prima. Sono andato anche in Casamance, un posto dove c'è la cultura originale. Lì ho studiato tante cose che non sapevo. . . . (N'Diaye, "Albe teatro in bianco/nero" 32)

[Doing theatre has helped me to do many things: learn the language, know Italian culture, do honest work, but also to gain deeper knowledge of my Senegalese culture. With my companions on this trip I saw houses that I'd never seen before. I also went to the Casamance, a place where there is still original culture. There I studied many things that I didn't know.]

The first phase of the Ravenna Dakar Project was the creation and mise-en-scène of the play *Bonifica*, performed by two of the Romagnolo members of the troupe, Ermanna Montanari and Gigio Dadina, for the most part, in the Romagnolo dialect. The *albe bianche* explained this phase as a necessary looking back within themselves and their own cultural heritage, before confronting that culture with the Senegalese one projected in their trip. The characters, a mother and son, Daura and Arterio, are the owners of one of the many *bagni* lining Ravenna's beaches; the play thus focuses on the dying Adriatic from their microperspective. After reflecting that Italy is the fifth greatest industrial power, literally driven by its automobile industry, Arterio comes up with the scheme for the *bonificazione* of the whole Adriatic with cement, in order to make a parking lot out of it, and to connect the west with the east:

> Il mare non si riprende la notte lo sento ansimare respira pesante come una bestia che muore non c'è niente da fare. Anche i verdi e i loro amici lo sanno non c'è niente da fare gridano a destra e a manca ma anche loro lo sanno . . . i verdi vanno in macchina come tutti gli altri allora ad un certo punto bisogna chiedersi se vale la pena mettere in crisi l'industria padana per avere l'Adriatico pulito nessuno ci obbliga. (92)

> [The sea isn't recovering at night I hear it gasp breathe heavily like a dying beast there's nothing we can do about it. Even the Greens and their friends know that nothing can be done and they scream right and left but they too know . . . the Greens go by car like everyone else and so at a certain point you have to ask yourself if it's worth it to throw the Padana industries into crisis in order to have a clean Adriatic no one is forcing us.]

While one could read *Bonifica* within the very specific content of that summer of 1989 when the Adriatic was being smothered by the proliferaiton of mysterious algae, there is no denying that it is the black farce that Martinelli intended. *Bonifica* is about the cities of the West in decline and the economic exploitation of land and sea, by industrialists and environmentalists alike.[11]

The Ravenna Dakar Project proved fruitful in many other ways. One important testimony of this trip is the documentary video entitled *Il Ravenna Dakar*, which the Albe show to explain the history of *meticciato artistico* as experienced during their trip to Senegal. Furthermore, as a result of this trip N'Diaye and Martinelli for seven years held theatre arts workshops in Senegal while working with the Senegalese government to establish a sister Casa di Teatro that would be dedicated to the diffusion of Senegalese rather than French culture. This Casa di Teatro would also act as a center for intercultural exchange and dialogue, as is the *casa di teatro* in Ravenna, for the different ethnic groups living together in Dakar. The three Senegalese members of the Albe (Mor Awa Niang, El Hadji Niang, and Mandiaye N'Diaye) originally planned to spend six months of the year with Guediawaye Theatre, and 6 months with the Albe in Ravenna. That *casa di teatro*, the Guediawaye Theatre, finally opened its doors in October of 1997, with Mandiaye N'Diaye as the artistic director. Due to internal dissension and misunderstanding between the three Senegalese members of the Albe however, further work on Guediawaye Theatre remains temporaily suspended.

As a result of his work in the theatre Mandiaye N'Diaye is also active in outreach projects with the CEM (Centro di Educazione alla Mondialità), which promotes the diffusion of knowledge of, and mutual respect for, the differences between cultures, primarily through presentations and performances in elementary and middle schools. This work is an important aspect of the Albe's *meticciato artistico*, as it takes the dialogue and exchange out of the theatre and into the classroom space.

---

[11]The play *Bonifica* is still in production; in May of 1999 the Albe brought it to Budapest; it is also act four of the epic six-act Albe production called *Perhinderion* (pilgrimage in Breton). *Perhinderion* is very much tied to the six different performance spaces of the pilgrimage-play, and also to the city of Ravenna itself. It debuted the summer of 1998, and was repeated in the summer of 1999.

From 1990 through 1998 N'Diaye together with Mor Awa Niang participated in a program of cultural exchange by going to different schools in Romagna to teach young Italian students about African history and culture in the hope of presenting a more live and positive image of Africa and of Africans contrary to the one of war, famine, and exotic safaris that one often sees portrayed on television. During these workshops they performed two of the plays that have as their subject matter Senegalese legends surrounding a hare and an hyena: *Nessuno può coprire l'ombra*, coauthored by Martinelli and Moussa Ba, and performed by the three Senegalese members of the troupe, and *Le due calebasse*, written and performed by Mandiaye N'Diaye.

N'Diaye has been performing *Le due calebasse* since he wrote it in 1990 as a challenge to himself to write and perform a play that would be based on his childhood memories. I viewed (February 1999) this performance in a *centro sociale* in Bologna on an evening that had been organized by several groups, including the Bologna Cultural Commission and the Senegalese Association in Bologna. An interesting and relevant aspect of this performance was the co-existence of both cultures, both on stage and in the audience; N'Diaye maintains that if the theatre company is mixed (also *meticciato*), so then is its ideal audience. Because of this, N'Diaye actively recruits fellow Senegalese living abroad by writing to the different Senegalese organizations when the theatre company goes on tour.

On this occasion, N'Diaye performed in front of a mixed Senegalese and Italian audience, to a full hall of people sitting on the stairs and standing in the back. N'Diaye narrates the fable of two *calebasse* in Italian, with some Wolof interspersed, and with the active audience participation that is a common trait of performance in Senegal. The Senegalese spectators, well-familiar with the fable about *Leuk-la-lepre* and *Bouki-la-iena*, would shout out a comment in Wolof in agreement, or run down to the stage to challenge N'Diaye's performance capabilites during the dances at different points of the play. N'Diaye tells us that he learned this story about the hare and the hyena from an aunt of his who was the official story-teller of his village, Dioll Kadd, thereby highlighting the importance of the oral nature of the tale, and the continuity of story-telling from generation to generation. His own appropriation and representation of the Senegalese tale in Italy, in Italian and Wolof, is an extension of that oral practice, and through through this performance he spreads his own culture in Italy and Europe (Martinelli and N'Diaye 45).

Let us return to Ravenna Dakar Project intercultural trip in 1990, when the Albe visited the Casamance, a region in the Southern part of Senegal, where they heard about the legend of Alinsitowe Diatta, the self-proclaimed princess of the Diola ethnic tribe who led an uprising against the French colonialists between 1940 and 1943. She still exists as unwritten history and legend in the collective consciousness of some Senegalese, some of whom claim that she is still alive. (Martinelli tells us that in the 1970s an official investigation concerning Alinsitowe resulted with the news that she is dead [Martinelli, "Il cammino dall'idea" 55].) Her story was the inspiration for the play *Lunga vita all'albero!*, which Martinelli wrote upon return to Italy. In this play Martinelli returns to some of the thematics of *Ruh!*: an indifferent white colonialist presence in Senegal, as the culprit behind deforestation, and famine; the figure of the Italian industrialist figure; the idea of the invading *straniero*. In *Lunga vita all'albero!* Alinsitowe augurs that the imposition of the peanut monocrop by the French will bring about the destruction of the biodiversity that is necessary for self-sustenance, and she exhorts her fellow Senegalese to rebel:

> Avanti senegalesi rispondete
> chi è quell'uomo giovane e forte
> che permette a uno straniero
> di entrare nella casa
> come ladro nella notte (. . .)
> Guardate gli stranieri:
> non so quanti oceani hanno ingoiato
> per arrivare fin qui: ditemi
> vi hanno forse chiesto permesso?
> Invadono la nostra terra
> come bianca lebbra (. . .)
> gli uomini della tua terra tagliano gli alberi, danno tutto il raccolto ai bianchi, dimenticano il riso per far posto all'arachide. (119–20)

[Come forward Senegalese and answer / who is that young strong man / who allows a foreigner / to enter into the house / like a theif in the night (. . .) / Look at the foreigners / I don't know how many oceans they have swallowed / to arrive this far: tell me / have they perhaps asked your permission? / They invade our land / like white leprosy (. . .) / the men of your land cut down the trees, give all of the harvest to the whites, forget about rice in order to make room for peanuts.]

In *Lunga vita!* Martinelli resuscitated a now defunct theatre form, the *maggio epico*, with ancient origins in some parts of the Tuscan-Emilian Appennines. In a *maggio epico*, which would take place in May as part of the fertility rites of Spring, someone plants a tree in the middle of a piazza and different actors recite epic stories of knights and battles between Moors and Christians. Epic techniques typically emphasize the personal, individual experiences of characters and then widen the focus to include the community and its social, economic, and sexual relations. This particular *maggio epico* uniquely finds resonanace in both the structural and temporal schemes of the *Lunga vita all'albero!*, as 'Moors' and 'Christians' are reconfigured in the twentieth century.

Structurally, the play is divided into three acts: a "Prologo," a section entitled "Vita, visioni e presunta morte di Alinsitowe Diatta," and an "Epilogo." The play is further divided temporally. The aesthetic choice to adapt the *maggio* highlights the importance of the recuperation of legend and myth, and of a mythical pre-industrial culture still tied to nature. The initial scene takes place in a small farming town in Romagna at the end of the twentieth century. The narrative then shifts to Senegal, 1940 and the story of Alinsitowe. Another shift in the narrative transports us from Senegal to Romagna, and the year is 1943: the action has shifted to enact the story of Bruna, a young partisan fighter. In the *Epilogo*, time and place shift back to Senegal in the 1990s.

During the *Prologo*, a Narratore, a *cantastorie* or *fabulatore* whose family history of oral narrators goes back seven generations, announces that his story will be a descent into the past. The Narratore wants to tell the legend of Alinsitowe Diatta, but he does not know enough about her to execute it by himself. An African Arlecchino and his old uncle appear on the scene and Arlecchino announces that he is a griot; like the Narratore he has had his craft passed down to him generationally. They negotiate to collaboratively spin the tale. As early as the Prologue questions of identity politics are raised — who can tell the story? And with what authority? The double narrator and episodic structure will allow for shifting viewpoints and a multiplicity of voices and languages. Because these two custodians of collective memory and oral history are dying out in both cultures, their presence in the play also represents dying tradition and discontinuity. Furthermore, these figures raise the issue of artistic autonomy and truth within the context of a cultural mirage sponsored by the those in power, and by the media, in what Gomez-Peña describes as "the ideologically and aesthetically controlled spaces of the more established cultural institutions" (Gomez-Peña, "Multicultural Pardigm" 19).

In *Lunga vita all'albero!*, the Raul Gardini character from *Ruh!* is replaced by a Silvio Berlusconi type who appears in the mask of a Pantalone speaking Lombardo. This wealthy Produttore/Pantalone appears in the Prologo announcing that he has bought the entire town and all it contains, a mountain, a lighthouse, the man in the lighthouse, etc.[12] The Produttore offers to pay the Narratore and Arlecchino to recount the story of Alinsitowe, but wants to impose his own exoticized expectations of an African princess. Because the Produttore controls and owns everything, from the mountains to the newspapers, and because the Arlecchino character has already announced that he has 18 starving children to support back home in Senegal, we wonder how the Narrators will maintain their artistic autonomy. Despite the dangers in agreeing to sell their story to the Produttore (representative of officially sanctioned culture), the Griot and the Narratore, however, appropriate control over their narratives and recount the parallel stories of Alinsitowe and Bruna.

The discrete categories of black and white become subverted and challenged in this representation. Alinsitowe and Bruna are played respectively by Ermanna Montanari and Alimah Mamudu. Having a white woman play a Senegalese princess and a Senegalese woman play an Italian resistance fighter marks a typical convention of the Martinelli's

---

[12] See Martinelli's interesting *resoconto* of this experience in "Il cammino dall'idea" 54–56.

— *rovesciamento*. Another type of *rovesciamento* is articulated in the above-cited quote by Alinsitowe: in this case the white person is the *straniero* who has invaded her land, and not the black person *straniero* who is taking over Italy.

Incidentally, the play *Lunga vita!* led to further research of the two oral artist figures — the Italian *cantastorie*, known as a *fuler* in the Romagnolo dialect, and the griot. Romagnolo Luigi Dadina and Senegalese Mandiaye N'Diaye researched and co-authored the play *Griot-Fuler*, which they wrote in the Romagnolo dialect, Wolof, and Italian. The two men uncovered remarkable parallels between these figures of oral tradition, the griot and the fuler, and so the play traces the similarities between them. They also discovered that both cultures share a legend about the *orma* or footprint (or rather the dirt collected from someone's footprint), and the *maleficio* or curse that one can cast with that dirt. *Griot-Fuler* also presents contiguous issues of collective memory, roots, origins, and genealogies, as the two narratives unfold, one in Italy, the other in Senegal. *Griot-Fuler* debuted both in Italy and in Senegal in 1993, and was performed throughout Italy until 1998.[13]

The title immediately suggests a braiding of the two languages, Wolof and Romagnolo: both title and content are an example of the collaborative work that went into this work of cultural mirroring. One example of such mirroring, or *confronto culturale*, follows: the figure of oral history that exists in both cultures but that is in decline in both cultures (in Romagna, the figure of the fuler who traveled from home to home recounting stories for his meals and lodging died out in the 30s; in Senegal, where the griot's social function is ever decreasing, they say that when a griot dies it is as if a library has burned — such is the extent of the knowledge of which they are the bearers). Another issue that the play raises for both cultures is the value of oral culture and language; the linguistic choice of writing and performing the play in both Wolof and Romagnolo clearly indicates that often stories and legends are passed down orally, from family to family, around a table or fireplace, and that these histories belong to the realm of orality.

---

[13]See N'Diaye and Dadina. For more analysis of this play, see Picarazzi, "Roots, Footsteps and Dialects."

The following passage delineates a key motif of *Griot-Fuler*, that the future comes from the past. It underlines the impossibility of being able to have a sense of history and continuity without knowing one's origins, ancestors, and roots, and without understanding the power of the word that harbors and transmits those stories: "É la parola del padre di mio padre. Io vi diró la parola di mio padre come l'ho ricevuta . . . e ho insegnato a dei re la storia dei loro antenati affinchè la vita degli antichi serva a loro come esempip. . . . Perchè il mondo é vecchio, ma l'avvenire viene dal passato" (Dadina and N'Diaye 62; It is the word of the father of my father. I will tell you my father's word how I received it . . . and I have taught kings the history of their ancestors so that the lives of the ancients will serve as an example to them. . . . Because the world is old, but the future comes from the past).

Another motif, that of the footprint, is laden with meaning: it symbolizes roots, the traces one leaves, and suggests the moving from one place to another. Yet it also means that the loss, the erasure of one's footprints, leads to an erasure of history and identity: "Ho raccontato alla mia gente storie che non hanno età . . . ho raccontato, nei trebbi dentro le stalle, di orchi, folletti e streghe . . . ho raccontato storie alla mia gente, che da sempre lascia orme su questa terra" (88; I have told my people stories that have no age. . . . Gathered together in barns, I have told stories about ogres, fairies, and witches . . . I have told stories to my people, who have always left footprints on this earth).

In addition to the creation of *Griot-Fuler*, the Ravenna Dakar Project also served as a springboard for plays and conferences that were to follow: *I ventidue infortuni di Mor Arlecchino* (1993), the work, perhaps, for which the Albe have received the most international recognition (and to which I shall return shortly), and the annual three-day Vie dei Canti Conference (1993), in which most artistic ethnic communities in the area and throughout Italy have participated since its inception. The focus of the conference is on the themes *il nomadismo* and multiculturalism through music, dance and performance, with particular attention to the Adriatic as a place of transnational ferment.[14] Included as well is the

---

[14]In 1995 Beverly Allen spoke about the Adriatic as a place of transnational ferment at the MLA session that she organized and chaired: "Italia Adriatica, Italia Africana:

three year Progetto Grecia Africa and the play that Martinelli wrote as a result of this project, *All'inferno!* (1996).

The play *All'inferno!* is a co-production between the Teatro delle Albe and the Teatro Kismet in Bari. As such it is a crossing between classical Greek, Italian (more specifically, Romagnolo and Pugliese), and African cultures (Wolof Senegalese) within the context of an end-of-the-millennium Adriatic. For example, the play is framed by a story about two men who descend into the underworld in search of a god of gold. This convention was inspired, in part, by Aristophanes' satire in *Plutus* and the *Frogs*, and the West African legend *Kaidara*, which the Albe discovered to be similar in theme to the Plutus story. Martinelli injects this story into the end of the twentieth century by recasting Aristophanes' peasant figures, Chremylos and Carios, into two Senegalese men, Moussa and Dara, played respectively by Mandiaye N'Diaye and Mor Awa Niang. Their descent into the *inferi* in search of the *dio dell'oro*, the god of wealth, becomes a voyage to a hell on earth where they are forced to toil 24 hours a day "dalle sette di mattina alle sette di mattina"[15] [from seven in the morning to seven in the morning], in an *Autogrill* somewhere along the *Strada Adriatica*. Shortly into the play the audience realizes that the projected hell is the West, Italy, and the two men are African migrants in search of a fortune and future that will be denied them.

It is essential to emphasize here the amount of collaboration and exchange of information between the participants of this project, starting with the workshop sessions that were held on two consecutive summers on a *trulli* farm in Cisternino (Br) during which Martinelli introduced different aesthetic points to the group, from readings of Aristophanes aloud, to Martin Bernal's *Black Athena*. Martinelli invited the other participants to recount experiences of their own that might relate to the content from their own cultures and histories. Much of this information went into the final version of the script and performance. We should also note here that the image of the African immigrant in search of the *dio dell'oro* is not a mere conceit of Martinelli, but based on information that he received from the Senegalese members of the troupe and about which

---

(E)Merging Ethnicities." See also her "Transnational Italian Studies Today."
[15] Marco Martinelli, unpublished script *All'inferno!*

Mandiaye N'Diaye has spoken in an interview. N'Diaye recounts how he was advised by the local sorcerers in his town to emigrate to Italy in search of *il dio dell'oro* ("Il drammaturgo dei miei sogni" 86); during the workshop period he also remarks on the projected image that he had of the West based on watching programs like *Dynasty* and *Dallas*, and how that projected image fell short of expectations for him and fellow Senegalese.[16]

The theme of the African migrant in Italy and the problems and exploitation that he there encounters connects with the figure of Mor Arlecchino from the play *I ventidue infortuni di Mor Arlecchino*, and the problems that he has in trying to go back to Senegal.[17] Mor Arlecchino is burned in his sleeping bag and in the fireplace (in typical Arlecchino fashion dating back to the sixteenth century); racists, thieves, and bullies yell at him to go back to Africa. Mor Arlecchino nonetheless sings and dances a traditional Senegalese dance throughout this play, except for the final scene, when, in realizing that he is trapped in Italy forever as a servant, he loses all hope in returning home.

Before feeling that our political correctness has been offended by this portrayal of the offended black man we might also, for the sake of playing devil's advocate, say that placing the African figure in a white man's text is a double act of appropriation and exploitation — that is, first in a classic or canonical text, like Aristophanes and Goldoni, secondly in a writer like Martinelli. But we might say this only after considering the irony and social critique and specific Italian context behind such representations, as well as the already discussed dynamic relationship between character-actor-writer-director. As dramaturge, as *poeta di compagnia*, Martinelli writes characters and Masks together with the actors. With this regard, he often cites Goldoni himself:

---

[16]This information is based on an unpublished transcript that I wrote during the Cisternino summer workshop of 1995.

[17]For a more thorough analysis of this play, please see the anthology *An African Harlequin in Milan: Marco Martinelli Performs Goldoni*, ed. Picarazzi and Feinstein. This book contains a translation of the Martinelli play and of the Goldoni *canovaccio*, together with critical essays by Teresa Picarazzi, Wiley Feinstein, Franco Nasi, Bent Holm, Franco Fido, and Claudio Meldolesi.

Tutte le opere teatrali che ho poi composte, le ho scritte per quelle persone ch'io conosceva, col carattere sotto gli occhi di quegli attori che dovevano rappresentarle. (. . .) E tanto mi sono in questa *regola* abituato, che, trovato l'argomento di una commedia, non disegnava da prima i personaggi, per poi cercare gli attori, ma cominciava ad esaminare gli attori. (Goldoni 1: 694; cited in Martinelli, "Luce e mondo" 7)

[I wrote all of the theatre pieces for people who I knew, with the characters of those actors who had to perform them in sight. (. . .) And I became so used to this rule that, having found the subject of a play I did not first sketch the characters and then look for the actors, but I would start to examine the actors.]

Martinelli tells us that in writing the Mor Arlecchino character he had in mind both Mor Awa Niang and the original *zanni* of the Commedia dell'Arte of the sixteenth century, and not the eighteenth century French version of Arlecchino that may have been contemporary to Goldoni's time.[18] Struck by the modern appeal of the Goldoni *canovaccio*, Martinelli explains:

Quando mi sono imbattuto in queste sette otto paginette scritte da Goldoni sono rimasto colpito della loro contemporaneità. Per quanto riguarda Arlecchino bastava cambiare colore della pelle e passaporto per trasformarlo da bergamasco del '700 in africano di fine millennio. (Piccino 17)

[When I ran into these seven or eight pages written by Goldoni I was struck by their contemporary quality. With regard to Arlecchino all I had to do was change his skin color and passport to transform him from a person from Bergamo of the 1700s to an African at the end of the millennium.]

This quotation bears further scrutiny. What is so modern and compelling about the Goldoni *canovaccio*? If Arlecchino spoke Wolof in the 1990s he

---

[18]Marco Martinelli, ". . . di quando noi andammo a recitare *I ventidue infortuni di Mor Arlecchino* al Piccolo Teatro di via Rovello, e dei fatti che là avvennero" (Faenza: Filodrammatica Berton, 1998) 7.

might very well resemble the character that Martinelli has written. Martinelli is indignant but not tragic in his depiction of the the exploited migrants in Italy, and his social critique is presented generally through farce. In this play, Martinelli addresses the Italian context of immigration by comparing the northern Italian migrant (the Arlecchino mask or character) from Bergamo to Milan of Goldoni's times with the African migrant to Milan in the late twentieth century. He finds similarities between both of their plights as migrants in a hostile country where they have gone to seek work. There are also points in common between the all-consuming, cannibalistic, greedy (read white industrialist) father figures of Pantalone (also present in the Produttore of *Lunga vita!*) and il Dottore.

Goldoni's genius lay in his reform of the theatre, in his custom-written characters (together with and to suit the actors), and in his introduction of realism and realistic situations, through comedy and irony, onto the stage. In following this tradition Martinelli presents us a slice of Italian life from a specific moment in history; he is not making light of another's misfortunes, but presenting them alongside the joy that Mor Awa Niang/Mor Arlecchino imparts through two very important aspects of his culture, music and dance. Awa Niang did not lose that craft in Italy, as the quotation below attests; he developed it. This story of Mor Arlecchino is a story worth telling; it is a story about our times, because it is also Mor Awa Niang's story. That Mor Awa Niang's representation of Mor Arlecchino is light-hearted and comical does not take away from the relevance of this piece as an ironic and critical document against racism, and against the figures of the "fathers," the power-mongers, those who exploit.[19]

---

[19]At an international symposium dedicated to the study of Italy and Africa (Miami University, November 1998), Paul Jackson recently critiqued Martinelli and his portrayal of Mor Arlecchino in this play as insensitive and as upholding a racist literary tradition. Jackson related Arlecchino's misfortunes to the lynching of African Americans in the United States. Whether or not Goldoni himself was a racist, or if there exists documentation of African slaves in Venice in the late eighteenth century has little bearing on this argument. On the other hand, if Goldoni were racist, then we might indeed expand our discussion to talk about how the eighteenth-century Arlecchino was also a victim of oppression. Nonetheless, let us keep in mind that the context is Italian and African, and not American, and that the traditional figure of Arlecchino is known for a series of traits that

Let us consider briefly the relationship between the actor Mor Awa Niang and the Arlecchino Persona. There is more than a fortuitous correspondence between the names Mor Awa Niang and Mor Arlecchino, and more than a simple and reductive assignation of a caricature and identity onto a man. Mor Awa Niang himself identifies with his character or mask; he has spoken often of how his experience in the theatre has allowed him to connect to his own griot origins. Awa Niang views his work in a positive light because it has given him the distance and means with which to look back and learn about his country's traditions and his family's heritage by innovatively synthesizing them into his present day experiences. For example, in a published interview, Niang says of his persona:

> Il personaggio di Arlecchino riflette molte situazioni di oggi. Un immigrato che non riesce a tornare. Ma anche se potesse forse finirebbe per ripartire . . . Affrontarlo mi ha permesso di recuperare le mie radici, il patrimonio di una tradizione orale che era dei miei nonni, e che avevo perduto. (Piccino 17)

> [The character of Arlecchino reflects many of today's situations. He is an immigrant who cannot go back. But even if he were able to he might end up leaving again . . . Confronting him has allowed me to recuperate my roots, the patrimony of an oral tradition that my grandparents once practiced, and which I had lost.]

The above quote also suggests the impossibility of a return, and the ambivalence that often comes when living between cultures.

Niang has left the Albe though, in 1998, and with him has gone the *maschera* of Mor Arlecchino as he wore it, since it is indissolubly tied to the man. Mor Awa Niang and Mor Arlecchino are however linked, and Mor Awa Niang's own odyssey of immigration has been recorded in writing and performed in front of thousands of spectators, which makes the play *I ventidue infortuni* a potentially powerful document of a specific time and place. Nonetheless, his departure does not necessarily signal the end of the play *I ventidue infortuni:* just as Goldoni's plays hold a uni-

---

have no connection to race.

versal and lasting appeal, so does this one. What are the implications of this departure of the two griot figures, El Hadji Niang and Mor Awa Niang for the African Italian experience of the Albe? While it marks closure to one phase of the Albe's interethnic work, it has not brought it to a conclusion.

The Albe's interethnic commitment continues to play an important role on the Italian stage. During the summer of 1999, the Teatro delle Albe was recognized as the vanguard of *afroromagnolo* theatre at the 29th Festival di Santarcangelo, an annual theatre festival in the field of *teatro di ricerca*. One journalist wrote:

> Una dozzina d'anni fa un giovane gruppo teatrale romagnolo, Le Albe (poi divenuto Ravenna Teatro) lanciò una provocazione ironica: la Romagna, diceva Marco Martinelli, è un pezzo d'Africa . . . Quest'anno . . . il gemellaggio tra Romagna e Africa, quella che era insieme una visione e una provocazione, trova una consacrazione autorevole in un'edizione del Festival di Santarcangelo. . . . (Ponte di Pino 26)

> [A dozen years ago a young Romagnolo theatre group, the Albe (who then became the Ravenna Teatro) launched an ironic provocation: Romagna, Marco Martinelli said, is a piece of Africa. This year . . . the twinship between Romagna and Africa, that which was both vision and provocation, will enjoy an authoritative consecration in an edition of the Festival of Santarcangelo.]

Indeed, the nine-day Festival, comprised of over thirty theatre companies was entitled 'I tamburi nella notte' [Drums in the Night] and was dedicated to an exploration of a *gemellaggio* [twinship] between African theatre and Italian theatre, and of the *intreccio* [intertwining] of the two cultures in other interethnic theatre companies in Italy.

The Albe continue to work together in their *meticciato artistico*, with a recent production by Martinelli called *I Polacchi* (1998), based on the Ubu plays of Alfred Jarry, where Mandiaye N'Diaye, who plays Papa Ubu, speaks Romagnolo, Wolof, and Italian, and Ermanna Montanari plays Mamma Ubu. Mandiaye N'Diaye also dubuted in June of 1999 with a piece entitled *Perché mai uno? Credevo che ne fossero due* [Why Ever One? I Thought There Were Two of Them], based on the encounter between a

Senegalese prophet (called *Il profeta*) and a St. Francis-type character of the Murid, an Islamic Sufi order in Senegal. This play, written by Marco Martinelli with the collaboration of Mandiaye N'Diaye is particularly relevant because it marks the first known mise-in-scène of this powerful religious figure and of some of the tenets of Islam. Many of the Senegalese living in Romagna follow the Murid order. Because of this, the audience participation was keen, on the part of the Italians who were hearing about this story for the first time, and especially by the Senegalese who were there and who participated and intervened enthusiastically in the performance.

Before concluding, it is also important to recognize some of the dangers inherent in a theatre based on the practice of *meticciato artistico*. Joseph R. Roach writes:

> The very process of theatrical representation may unknowingly or knowingly impose the cultural values of one group upon the members of another — caricaturing them, even as it claims to respect their difference, erasing them, even as it purports to celebrate their existence. (13–14)

It is difficult to say whether or not there has been the unknowing imposition of Martinelli's cultural values in the characters that he has written for the Senegalese actors of the troupe, as they themselves have developed and changed during their ten-year experience with the Albe. I hope to have presented aspects of what is relevant and valid about the *afroromagnolo* experience of the Albe, and will let the reader decide for him/herself. At the Festival di Santarcangelo during the Summer of 1999, the Albe performed a piece entitled *Imperatore, tu sei negro*, which was a retrospective of some of the key scenes of many of the plays that make up the *afroromagnolo* experience. Artistic dialogue and exchange without the superimposition of one culture over the other is the foundation of the work of the Albe. The Guediawaye theatre project is still an important testimony to this dialogue, as well as one of its projected goals. At the same time the Albe are careful to point out that they are not out for an 'esperantic disney hodge podge' multiculturalism sponsored by the cultural mirage.[20] Nor do they, in Mandiaye N'Diaye's words, promote an unproblematic and happy multicolored society that looks like a Benetton ad.[21] Martinelli's own linguistic innovations integrate past and present, Wolof, Tuscan, Romagnolo, French, Pugliese, Lombardo, in his own rendering of Babel. When asked why, he responded:

> Si vuole rendere acusticamente la babele di fine millennio. Le nostre città sono piene di lingue, e puoi sentire senegalese e dialetto romagnolo accostati con naturalezza assoluta nella vita di tutti i giorni." (Arfelli 14)

> [We want to render acoustically the Babel of the end of the millennium. Our cities are full of languages, and you can hear Senegalese and the Romagnolo dialect alongside each other with absolute naturalness in everyday life.]

Works Cited

Allen, Beverly. "Transnational Italian Studies Today." *Symposium, Transnational Italian Studies Today.* Spec. ed. Beverly Allen. 49.2 (Summer 1995): 83–85.

Arfelli, Gianni. "Quello che abbiamo perso l'abbiamo recuperato." *Il nuovo ravennate* 22 Jan. 1992: 14.

Goldoni, Carlo. *Tutte le opere di Goldoni.* Milano: Mondadori, 1935.

Gomez-Peña, Guillermo. "The Multicultural Paradigm: An Open Letter to the National Arts Community." *Negotiating Performance.* Ed. Diana Taylor and Juan Villegas. Durham: Duke UP, 1994. 17–29.

___. *Warrior for a Gringostroika.* Saint Paul: Graywolf, 1993.

Guccini, Gerardo. "L'armonia dei suoni non nati: biografia d'una esperienza creativa." *Le opere senza canto di Giovanni Tamborrino.* Bologna: CLUEB, 1998.

Martinelli Gabrieli, Marco. "Ravenna africana. Il teatro politttttttico delle Albe." *Ravenna africana.* Ravenna: Edizioni Essegi, 1988.

Martinelli, Marco. "Il cammino dall'idea all'opera si fa in ginocchio." *Seminario sulla drammaturgia: Ferrone, Meldolesi, Marino, Martinelli, Molinari, Fo.* Ed. Luigi Rustichelli. West Lafayette: Bordighera, 1998. 48–64.

___. "Luce e mondo." *Lus*, by Nevio Spadoni. Faenza: Mobydick, 1995.

___. *Teatro impuro.* Ravenna: Danilo Montanari Editore, 1997.

---

[20]I modified the term from Gomez-Peña's "Multicultural Paradigm" 27.
[21]D'Diaye mentioned this during a demonstration he gave to the Concord Academy of Performing Arts in Ravenna, March 1999.

___, and Mandiaye N'Diaye. "Parla di Mandiaye N'Diaye: Teatro meticciato." *Africa* 10 (Nov.-Dec. 1998): 45.

N'Diaye, Mandiaye. "Albe teatro in bianco/nero." *Rivista anarchica* 173 (May 1990): 32.

___. "Il drammaturgo dei miei sogni: conversazione tra Franco Lorenzoni e Mandiaye N'Diaye." Interview with Franco Lorenzoni. *Saltatori di muri: la narrazione orale come educazione alla convivenza: esperienze interculturali di incontro tra stranieri e italiani, nella scuola e nel teatro.* Ed. Franco Lorenzoni and Marco Martinelli. Cesena: Macro Edizioni, 1998. 83–112.

___, and Luigi Dadina. *Griot Fuler.* Repubblica di San Marino: Guaraldi-AIEP Melting Pot Press, 1994.

Okpewho, Isisdore. *African Oral Literature.* Bloomington: Indiana UP, 1992.

Picarazzi, Teresa. "Roots, Footsteps and Dialects: Performing National Identity in *Griot-Fuler*." *Studi d'italianistica nell'Africa Australe, Special Issue: Margins at the Centre: African Italian Voices.* Spec. ed. Graziella Parati. 8.2 (1995): 83–99.

___, ed. "Ermanna Montanari's Voices Crossing the Borders Between Language and Magic." *Lus, The Light, Ermanna Montanari Performs Nevio Spadoni.* West Lafayette: Bordighera, 1999. 41–58.

___, and Wiley Feinstein, eds. *An African Harlequin in Milan: Marco Martinelli Performs Goldoni.* West Lafayette: Bordighera, 1997.

Piccino, Cristina. "Se Arlecchino parla wolof?" *Il Manifesto* 29 Oct. 1993: 17.

Ponte di Pino, Oliviero. "Lo 'strano intreccio' tra Romagna e Africa." *Il Manifesto* 25 June 1999: 26.

Roach, Joseph R. "Introduction." *Critical Theory and Performance.* Ed. Janelle G. Reinelt and Joseph R. Roach. Ann Arbor: U of Michigan P, 1992. 9–15.

REINVENTING HARLEQUIN IN END-OF-THE-MILLENNIUM RAVENNA

Wiley Feinstein
Loyola University Chicago

Between 1988 and 1993, the Albe Theater Company in Ravenna embarks on its great Afro-Romagnolo experiment. These are years in which Italy is forced to acknowledge that racist attitudes toward the new African Italians are leading to disconcerting public expressions of hostility toward migrants from North and West Africa.[1] It is during this period the sociologists Laura Balbo and Luigi Manconi move from talk about "possible forms of racism" ["*i razzismi possibili*"] to "the real forms that racism is taking" ["*i razzismi reali*"] in Italy.[2] But as racism takes firm hold, there are also counter-tendencies, politically correct ones if you will, to show open interest in learning who the new citizens of Italy are, and a number of new African-Italian authors begin to attract readers. The single most widely read book by an Italian-African writer is *Io venditore di elefanti* by Pap Khouma.

In the theatrical production of the Albe company during these years, a trilogy of plays *Ruh! Romagna più Africa uguale* [Romagna Plus Africa Equal], *Siamo asini o pedanti* [Are We Jackasses of Pedants], and *Lunga vita all'albero* [Long Live the Tree]"[3] develop the basic elements of the theater of cultural mixing (or "*meticciato artistico*") that are discussed by Teresa Picarazzi in her essay in this volume.[4] Picarazzi in her work on

---

[1] 1997 Government figures cited by Stefano Bellucci at the Africa/Italy Conference indicate that migrants from Morocco, Tunisia, Senegal, and Egypt comprise about one quarter of the total immigrant population in Italy. Migrants from Senegal — the country of origin of the African members of the Albe cooperative comprise about three percent of the total number of migrants — 34,831 out of 1,240,721. These figures, of course, do not account for workers that are not registered with the government.

[2] Balbo and Manconi's texts are: *I razzismi possibili, I razzismi reali,* and *Razzismi: un vocabolario.*

[3] All of the plays discussed in this essay are now included in a collection of Martinelli plays entitled *Teatro Impuro* (referenced as TI hereafter).

[4] Picarazzi has also addressed these issues in her introductory essay to the volume *An African Harlequin in Milan: Marco Martinelli Performs Goldoni* 1–16 (referenced as AH hereafter). This volume contains the translation of *Moor Harlequin's 22 Misfortunes* that

the Albe company emphasizes the collaborative nature of the project in which Marco Martinelli, playwright and artistic director, Italian actors — especially Luigi Dadini and Ermanna Montanari — and African actors — especially M'dyiaye Ndiaye and Mor Awa Niang — together develop a challenging theatrical system based on rediscovery of lost cultural roots of both Senegal and the Romagna region. In mixing the elements of both cultures, the Albe thus uncover some provocative points of comparison and contrast.

The trilogy lays the groundwork for the 1993 production of *Moor Harlequin's 22 Misfortunes* that earned the Albe a significant amount of attention throughout Italy and all of Europe. In this study, I will examine first the development of the Harlequin character in the context of the creation of the new project in the original trilogy and then go on to discuss the character in the late twentieth-century Moor Harlequin play derived from a mid-eighteenth-century Goldoni scenario for a *commedia dell'arte* performance in Paris.

After the introductiion of the new kind of "Afro-Romagnolo" theater in *RUH!*, as the next two plays of trilogy unfold, we note that an unexpectedly stimulating reinvention of Harlequin, the *Commedia dell'Arte's* most popular character becomes the key to the Albe theater company's exploration of questions of African and Senegalese cultural identity. It is a new Moor Harlequin, a new Black Harlequin, who becomes a key vehicle for pondering the reactions to blackness in white European society and culture in the 1990s.

But just who is Harlequin and what is it that so attracts both the European and the African actor-creators of the Albe Company? And once they have decided to feature a new Moor Harlequin incarnated by Mor Awa Niang, what precise new African and old Italian characteristics will he have? And once the character is created, what kinds of situations in Italy will he find himself in, and what reactions will be provoked in audiences throughout Europe?

---

will be cited in this essay as well as a translation of the Goldoni scenario that will also be referred to.

Part One: Who Is Harlequin and Why Is Africa His Ideal Country of Origin?

Harlequin, who is born either in the fifteenth or early sixteenth century, is a descendant of certain characters in ancient Roman farces. By the end of the sixteenth century, he assumes a fixed form and a fixed place of origin — from the mountains of Bergamo. Eighteenth-century theater historian Riccoboni gives an account of the early years of the character:

> The acting of the Harlequins before the 17th century was nothing but a continual play of extravagant tricks, violent movements and outrageous rogueries. He was at once insolent, mocking, inept, clownish and emphatically ribald. I believe that he was extraordinarily ribald and he seemed to be constantly in the air; and I might confidently add that he was a proficient tumbler.[5]

In the seventeenth century, two famous Harlequins, Tristano Martinelli of the Accesi Company and Domenico Biancolelli of the Riorelli-Locatelli Troupe, give the popular character a new richness, and the character acquires wit and wisdom on top of his ribaldry. Later characterizations of Harlequin will emphasize his new qualities:

> [Harlequin's] character is that of an ignorant valet, fundamentally naive, but nevertheless making every effort to be intelligent even to the extent of seeming malicious. He is a glutton and a poltroon, but faithful and energetic. Through motives of fear or cupidity he is always ready to undertake any sort of rascality and deceit. He is a chameleon who can take on any appearance. He must excel in impromptu and the first thing that the audience always asks of a new Harlequin is that he be agile and that he jump well, dance and turn. (From the *Calendrier historique des théâtres*, 1751, cited in Duchartre 133)

Duchartre gives an exemplary exchange between Harlequin and a master named Lelio (the same master the black Harlequin will have) to give

---

[5]Cited in Pierre-Louis Duchartre's excellent chapter on "Harlequin, His Ancestors and His Family" 125. Randolph Weaver's translations of the second edition of Duchartre's *La comédie italienne* originally appeared in 1929.

a good idea of the character who is a blend of bodily needs and practical wisdom derived from long experience:

> Lelio, the great lord asserts [to Harlequin] that he travels for the purpose of studying mankind:

> Harlequin: I' faith, it's a study which will teach you only of man's misery. There's little use in running about to study such rubbish. What will you gain from a knowledge of man? You will only find out the worst about him.

> Lelio: Than I shall not be deceived any more.

> Harlequin: No, but you will be spoiled

> Lelio: In what way?

> Harlequin: You will cease to be honest when you have learned all there is to know about humankind. For after you have seen so many scoundrels you will become a scoundrel yourself. Good bye. By the way, do you know which way to the kitchen. (152)

In the eighteenth century, Goldoni wrote both *canovacci* [rough sketches] for improvised *commedia dell'arte* stagings and also scripted comedies in which Harlequin figures as a character — such as *Il Bugiardo* (1748) and *Il Servitore di Due Padroni* (1753). Goldoni's Harlequin was from the city of Bergamo in Lombardy — a place known for bumpkins — and had come to Venice to eke out a meager living in serving members of the fading aristocracy or rising bourgeoisie. In reading the particular scenario *Le vingtdeux infortunes d'Arlecchino*, Marco Martinelli was struck by how the eighteenth-century Harlequin's situation reflects that of a late twentieth-century migrant in Italy:

> When I happened across these seven or eight short pages by Goldoni, I was struck by their contemporary appeal. As for Harlequin, all one had to do was change the color of his skin and passport in order to transform him from a Bergamasque of the 18th century to an African at the end of the millennium. (cited in Picarazzi AH 2)

But what first attracted Martinelli and M'dyiaye Ndiaye and Mor Awa Niang was the precise look of the traditional character. Harlequin always wore a black mask that some suggest may be a revival of the look of actors in Roman farces who put soot on their faces when playing foreign slaves (Duchartre 124). In some reproductions of Harlequin from *commedia dell'arte* scenes, the mask gives the character a strikingly authentic African look. And his costume also seem to be just right. Harlequin's famous colorful costume — usually consisting of triangular patches — seems to have uncanny resemblance to the shirt worn in traditional West-African dress.[6] Once Harlequin's look has drawn Martinelli and Mor Awa Niang to the character, they find that everything else is uncannily appropriate to their specific theatrical needs. They want a character who speaks a foreign language on stage, and Harlequin is known for speaking his native Berqamasque dialect. They need a character who is often hungry, and Harlequin is known for his habitual and voracious hunger. They need a character who is often the butt of insults and beatings, Harlequin is well-known for being hit with sticks and being otherwise abused. In the second and third plays of the African trilogy and in *Moor Harlequin's 22 Misfortunes*, Harlequin's unsatisfied hunger will represent all the hunger of Africa, and the insults and beating he receives will evoke the insults and beatings reported with great frequency in the Italian press throughout the 1990s.

Part Two: Enter: Harlequin Moor

In the Albe theater company, the working assumption is that characters are not abstractions in a playwright's mind but living stage presences that will be brought to life "in the flesh" by the specific actors who create them.[7] The Harlequin Moor character will be created specifically to tell Mor Awa Niang's personal story of lost and recovered identity. The Italian name of the character "Mor Arlecchino" is derived di-

---

[6]The original edition of Pap Khouma's *Io venditore di elefanti* was accompanied by a book jacket with a photo of Pap Khouma in a multi-color shirt that seems very similar to a traditional Harlequin costume.

[7]For a full explanation of the "theater of the flesh" concept, see Franco Nasi's discussion in Picarazzi 111–14.

rectly from the actor's name: Mor Awa Niang, identifying him as both a Moor and a Harlequin character.

But before the Black Harlequin can be introduced, the Albe must first introduce their new kind of theater in the first play of the African Trilogy. The strange title of the opening play, *RUH! Romagna Plus Africa Equal,* is explained by a mid-play "prologue" speech, in which an old-fashioned kind of artificial narrator explains: "according to the latest advanced geology research, Romagna is a piece of Africa that drifted away in ancient eras, a dark raft that split off of the mother continent and sailed all the way here" (TI 30; my translation). The play itself opens powerfully with three Senegalese street vendors, Abib, Iba, and Khadim, hauling rugs over their shoulders as they circulate among the audience and hawk their wares aggressively and annoyingly: "Nonna vu compra" — hey gramma wan buy" (TI 17), as they try to sell watches, lighters, and, of course, elephants. Martinelli's characteristically exuberant stage directions indicate the anticipated hostile audience reactions that Abib, Iba, and Khadim are supposed to provoke in tonight's ticketholders. Specifically the playwright imagines the murmuring internal monologue of a typical member of the audience:

> What are these peddlers doing here? Has the theater-manager gone nuts? What? Are they grabbing a percentage of sales of this shit? But, you know a thousand lire for a lighter isn't all that bad. Do these cigarette-lighters really work; at the Tobacco store, they're 2000 lire. All right I'll take it; how bout 500 lire, will that do? No? Just listen to these little black guys; what is this? They speak Italian with a Romagna accent! Where do you come from? You look just like Gullit, the football star with the dreadlocks? From Dakar? Like how many people would there be in Dakar? (TI 17)

This opening sequence of *RUH!* thus emphasizes forcefully the uneasiness that the presence of itinerant peddlers from Senegal provokes and that an audience would not expect that African peddler characters could possibly be characters in an Italian play. *RUH* thus boldly proclaims from the outset that the new research theater company (*"teatro di ricerca"*) is attempting to move the African presence in Italy from the public spaces of scorn to a serious public encounter with men and women from a rich cultural tradition whose vitality can help Romagna learn much more about its own cultural traditions. *RUH* will later, in Act V and VII — entitled respectively "Canto di invidia per la Vacca Eurocentrica" [Song of Envy for the Eurocentric Cow] and "Nera" [Black] — present the basic political economic conflict over resources between Africa and Europe and between Africans and Europeans. In the "Song of Envy" (see Picarazzi in this volume for complete text), the mother played by feature Albe actress-writer Ermanna Montanari, together with Iba, Abib, and Khadim, sings of the "Cow that eats more than us / like 40 Senegalese / the Cow that gets fatter than us / fatter than 40 Senagalese." In "Nera" they return to sing a paradoxical song in praise of blackness as Iba spreads dark earth on the legs and hands of the mother. Following this, she sings a song in which it is repeatedly asserted that "nera è Venere" [black is Venus].

After *RUH*, which in some ways can be considered a manifesto for a new kind of theater, the second play of the foundational trilogy is entitled *Siamo asini e pedanti* [Are We Jackasses or Pedants] and establishes more precisely the kind of characters and situations that will characterize this new theater of culture mixing. The Italian characters are generally farcical or caricatural presences, such as Fatima (Ermanna Montanari), the talking visionary donkey with a political conscience, and the racist man in the suit, the obtuse average Italian. The more affirmative search for Romagnolo roots, featuring the characters Daura and Arterio, will take place in plays such as *Bonifica* and *I refrattari* that are also produced in these years. The African characters, on the other hand initially play only themselves — vendors struggling to get by — and they keep their own names and will often use their own language, Wolof. But an audience that cannot understand Wolof needs a theatrical representation in order to understand the Senegalese characters and it is the association of the central African character with Harlequin that will prove to be the vehicle for a new perspective for cross-cultural understanding.

In *Are We Jackasses or Pedants*, Fatima the jackass narrates as Abib assumes the role of Harlequin-Botochio and, to the rhythm of rolling drums, does a "low dance" in which his body moves sensually and caresses the ground, laughing and giving the impression he wants to devour the earth (TI 61). Fatima narrates for the dancer,

> I am Harlequin come from the mountain where hunger is black black
> black . . . I am Harlequin come to the city because they've told me
> there's' work, there's work there's work, I am Harlequin with a face
> that's black black black and when I walk the streets they said dirty Ne-
> gro. I am Harlequin looking for a master / who's a kind and sweet
> honey tiramisù / mascarpone, English truffle, wedding cake.

(This first Abib-Harlequin played by Abibou N'Diaye is later played by
Mor Awa Niang who takes over the role in the third play of the trilogy
and then establishes the role in all its dimensions in *Harlequin Moor's 22
Misfortunes*.)

The third play in the trilogy, the 1990 *Lunga vita all'albero* [Long Live
the Tree] is defined as a "May Epic," which the playwright Martinelli
explains as

> one of the most ancient existing forms of traditional Italian folk theater.
> Rooted in certain areas of the Apennine regions of Tuscany and Emily,
> the May-Epic derives from the ancient fertility rites of spring: acted
> outdoors, constructed theatrically around central antagonisms (the
> struggle of Good versus Evil, Christian and Moors). (TI 136)

In *Long Live the Tree*, the company conceives the ancient and now forgotten May Epic as a way of introducing and celebrating the cultural
traditions of the Senegalese actors. The play begins with Harlequin
Moor/Mor Awa Niang carrying a torch and singing a Senegalese song
that is an invitation to feasting and dancing. During the course of the
play Mor will give us his real biography: he is from a family of "griot"
who "used to go to villages and used to dance at feasts, and used to sing,
and tell so many stories to people." His grandfather was a "griot" but his
father could not earn enough as storyteller and boarded an airplane
heading for the cities of the white men (TI 108). We thus understand, that
in the play we are seeing, *Long Live the Tree*, Mor Awa Niang through the
Harlequin character is reassuming an identity he had lost when his father was forced to emigrate. The character is thus adapted to allow Mor
to rebecome an African storyteller-entertainer, and in fact he sings traditional Senegalese songs, and his Harlequin dances are Africanized and
accompanied by traditional African rhythmic drumming. Commenting

on his being given the opportunity to become a new kind of griot, Mor Awa Niang has in fact reported in an interview cited by Teresa Picarazzi that, "Taking up the challenge of becoming Harlequin has made it possible for me to go back to my roots, to the heritage of my grandparents' oral tradition which I had lost" (AH 14).

But the African Harlequin is not only an African griot, he is the Italian Harlequin: a very hungry, servant character looking for a master to feed him. As we have seen, the voracious appetite of the always-hungry Harlequin is a key characteristic of the traditional character, and in the Albe's Afro-romagnolo theater, Harlequin's hunger stands for the hunger of both African and other migrants in Italy and in crisis-ridden and famine-scourged Africa itself.

Like the old Harlequin, the new Black Harlequin has a lot of wisdom and a lot resources at his disposal — he knows languages and is good talker who can win some people's sympathy — but like the traditional Harlequin, he seems to have a penchant for arousing the anger of masters and would-be masters as in fact happens in *Lunga vita all'albero* with the TV mogul who is not about to hire a traditional Senegalese storyteller who could hardly be expected to get decent ratings. He would need the African character to be titillatingly exotic in the manner he thinks his viewers will respond to. The producer from Lombardy with the mentality of Silvio Berlusconi — Italian TV magnate and conservative politician — has fixed notions about exotic Africa: "mysterious Baobab jungles Elephant cemeteries exotic beauties with breasts hanging out, palm on the beach, leopard men, drums in the night" (112) and has no inclination to move away from old stock fantasies. *Long Live,* in fact, centers on the story that aroused the producer's sexual appetite when he heard the term "African Queen," the story of Alinsitowe who lead resistance against the French colonial government in Dakar in 1943–45.

We can now turn to the play in which Harlequin Moor becomes the title character and assumes fully his role as poetic and dramatic representative for millions of African and other scorned legal and illegal "guest workers" in the wealthy Europe of today. The eighteenth-century Goldoni scenario that Martinelli discovered is the source of the basic situations, characters, and the misfortunes that befall Moor Harlequin, but there are additions (Spinetta) and subtractions (Coraline) of key characters, and most notably the ending is drastically altered: Martinelli drops the happy ending with the wedding of Harlequin and Coraline of the scenario and substitutes an ending in which Harlequin's misfortunes must inevitably continue.

In the Martinelli-Mor Awa Niang version, the title character makes a dramatic entrance in the middle of the first act. He enters to the sound of African drums as he again performs a traditional Senegalese dance, this time, the "Deiung," a dance of Senegalese wrestlers when they make their entry into the ring. And he confirms the African aspects of his identity when at first he speaks Wolof, in a warm greeting to El-Hadiy, the musician (AH 26). (In the staged versions, Mor also gives a long monologue in Wolof that is not written out in the published play or its translation.)

Soon after his entrance, Harlequin says his first words in Italian to the chauffeur character Spinetta, mistaking her for a "him," speaking in Italian, and also mistaking her social status, taking her for the motel owner:

> Good evening Mr. patron! Ah, what a nice face . . . attractive . . . oh yes, I know what I'm talking about, I know what I'm talking about, I can tell everything from a face . . . you are certainly not the type of white man that turns his back on those in need. . . . (AH 26)

Here the character is quickly demonstrating the traditional *commedia dell'arte* character's calculating charm that would seem to coincide perfectly with the tone needed for a successful sales pitch used to soften a potential purchaser of watches, lighters and elephants on an Adriatic beach. But Mor is also a Harlequin who is out of place — like his eighteenth-century ancestor from Bergamo — and shows lack of complete mastery of Italian language. His uses of the term "patron" ("patrone" in Italian) in place of "padrone" or "proprietario" for "motel owner" also calls attention to his foreign-ness. And he also asks the wrong person for protection, a mistake also typical of a standard Harlequin.

Shortly afterwards Harlequin finds out that Scapino is the motel owner. This surprising piece of information that a black Senegalese man has prospered in white Italy makes him quite happy and he instantly reverts to his slick salesman mode and resumes the campaign for free lodgings he had mistakenly started with Spinetta. Whereas when he spoke to Spinetta, Harlequin had played on her potential feeling of guilt as a white "man," with Scapino, he appeals to his countryman's sense of solidarity with people from his country of origin. As one would expect of any shrewd Harlequin, Mor shows an impressive ability to shift his tone to suit the person he is trying to get something out of.

But Moor Harlequin was wrong to think his special appeal to a fellow African would do any good. Scapino rejects Harlequin's plea as soon as he finds out Harlequin is not planning on paying for his room. And from this point on, after the initial promise of happiness, things sour rapidly and Moor Harlequin — in the long tradition of his ancestors — will be subjected to calamitous beatings and general abuse and ridicule. Scapino kicks Harlequin out of his motel onto the street and before long Harlequin's five stuffed suitcases are stolen by thugs who beat Harlequin up and scream, "Go back to Africa! Go back to Africa," while they beat him almost senseless. In the typical beating-of-Harlequin sequence, the relation between what happens to the *commedia dell'arte* character in the Goldoni scenario coincides perfectly with the real life robbings and beatings of African migrants in the Italy of the 1990s.[8]

When the disconsolate Harlequin returns after the luggage theft to Scapino's motel, Scapino can only drag him away, because he fears that Harlequin's presence might be bad for business. And this second rejection of Harlequin will lead to the next huge calamity that assails him — the theft of his Koran-carrier and the money he has set aside for purchasing a ticket home to Djourbel, Senegal.

In Act II, Moor Harlequin reverts to his traditional, comically hunger-crazed self after his arrival at Pantaloon's house in contemporary Milan. And as often happens to his ancestors from previous centuries, the new Harlequin's plates of food will be whisked out from under his nose just when he is about to dig in and enjoy. After this comic interlude in the middle of Act II, this long act of the play will conclude with the greatest

---

[8]For the early 1990s, an extensive thirty-page bibliography, provided by Balbo and Manconi in *Razzismi: un vocabolario*, cites numerous studies of the reaction to new migrants in the various regions of Italy.

misfortune — when Harlequin is literally burnt by the fire Pantalone made Spinetta light in the chimney where Moor was hiding. Here again the burning that was a Harlequin gag in the Goldoni scenario seems an all-too real possibility, given the frequency of anti-immigrant violence in contemporary Europe.

The short third act of *Moor Harlequin* leads to the pessimistic conclusion that conditions in Italy make it difficult for any sort of happy ending to the story of a 1990s black Harlequin. In the background in Act III the African drums that had accompanied the character's entrance beat to conjure up a fantasy of Africa. But Harlequin's dream of returning home cannot come true. Moor will have to go on getting by as best he can in an indifferent, complacent-cow Europe in which cynicism, greed, and selfishness triumph uncontested.

We are now in a position to make some general reflections on the new Harlequin and the reactions he provokes. Like all of the African characters in the trilogy and also in *Romagna più Africa Uguale* [Romagna Plus Africa Equal], Moor Harlequin finds himself in a hostile and cynical world with people in power who revel in their ignorance and have no interest in his struggle for economic and spiritual survival. The key powerful white characters — "the Man in the Suit" in *Are We Jackasses or Pedants,* the Lombard Producer in *Long Live the Tree,* and Pantaloon and Horace in the *22 Misfortunes* — are all completely uninterested in assisting Moor. Not all Italians are so thoroughly ignorant and close-minded as the "typical Italians" we meet — some are even relatively sympathetic and inclined to help in some ways — especially a character like Spinetta in the *22 Misfortunes,* but the general outlook remains bleak.

In conclusion, we note that although the plays give ample space to positive presentation of African culture and identity, they all show an Italy that feels little need to integrate her new citizens and guests or to create a new multicultural society. End-of-the millennium consumer-society Italy is spiritually impoverished and there is little hope of rooting out the racism that is engendered by media-manipulated ignorance and complacent close-mindedness.

Ultimately what Martinelli and his actor-authors discover together in the Harlequinesque explorations is a bleak truth that has always lurked

beneath the surface frivolity and exuberance of the *Commedia dell'Arte*:
As George Sand wrote in the nineteenth century:

> The *Commedia dell'arte* is not only a study of the grotesque and the face-
> tious . . . but also a portrayal of real characters traced from antiquity
> down to the present day in an uninterrupted tradition of fantastic hu-
> mor which is in essence quite serious and, one might say, even sad, like
> every satire which lays bare the spiritual poverty of mankind. (Duchar-
> tre 17)

Mor Awa Niang uses the age-old Harlequin character to tell his own
end-of-the-millennium story and that of millions of migrants like him.
The Albe company has made explicit the hidden sadness that Sand refers
to, and their Harlequin's suffering even acquires a Christ-like dimension,
that Martinelli has sometimes made clear. But the Albe company never
forgets Harlequin's sense of humor and his long-admired irrepressibility
and his resilience.

Works Cited

Balbo, Laura, and Luigi Manconi. *I razzismi possibili*. Milan: Feltrinelli, 1990.
___. *I razzismi reali*. Milan: Feltrinelli, 1992.
___. *Razzismi: un vocabolario*. Milan: Feltrinelli, 1993.
Duchartre, Pierre-Louis. "Harlequin, His Ancestors and His Family." *The Italian Comedy*. New York: Dover, 1966.
Khouma, Pap. *Io venditore di elefanti*. Milan: Garzanti, 1990.
Martinelli, Marco. *Teatro Impuro*. Ravenna: Danilo Montanari Editore, 1997.
Picarazzi, Teresa. Introductory Essay. *An African Harlequin in Milan: Marco Martinelli Performs Goldoni*. Ed. Teresa Picarazzi and Wiley Feinstein. West Lafayette, IN: Bordighera, 1997. 1–16.

THE DECENTERED SPECTATOR:
Imagining *Moor Harlequin's 22 Misfortunes* Cross-Culturally

Paul K. Bryant-Jackson
Miami University

Weird? Not at all. Neither the laugh nor Danforth's reference to it. Every black person who heard those remarks understood. How necessary, how reassuring were both the grin and its being summon for display. It is the laughter, the chuckle, that invites and precedes any discussion of association with a black person and certainly to continue it. The ethnic joke is one formulation-the obligatory recognition of race and possible equanimity in the face of it. — Morrison, *Race-ing Justice, En-gendering Power*

I first learned of the conference prior to my arrival at Miami University from Alphine Jefferson, Professor of History and Chair of the Black Studies Department at the College of Wooster. Our friendship developed through an 8-week intensive study of Portuguese at Michigan State University followed by an in-country stay in Salvador, Bahia, during the summer of 1994. One of the defining aspects of our relationship has been an abiding affection for Diaspora Studies. During our stay in Salvador, the colonial capital of Brazil during enslavement, we spent many hours discussing and observing race and its construction in the country that saw the largest population of forced African migration. Much of our conversation focused on the representation of people of African descent in various aspects of popular culture. We were often amazed at that representation. Much of it resembled images, icons, and commercial representations of African Americans, "Negroes," during the 1950s and early 1960s in the US. European Brazilians often chided us for bringing our US perspectives on race, while more militant factions of African Brazilians encouraged us. Ultimately we felt that global social, cultural, and political constructs of race are often contradictory, complex and problematic. Equally, the performance and reception of race, or racialized performance, mirror that same complexity. The lasting aspect of this experience was the knowledge or potential possibility of an elasticity of racial constructs. In Brazil this elasticity revealed itself in both cultural production and political reality. As Alphine spoke of the Africa Italy Conference little did I know that these perceptions would prove again valuable.

The Africa Italy conference, of which my friend spoke, would set out to explore geographic, cultural and racialized borders and interchanges through a variety of academic paradigms. The conference was to be held at Miami University an institution located in the US Midwest. As such each geographic entity involved in such a conference, primarily Africa, Italy, the United States, and Miami University, and each participant assembled would negotiate voice and authority and thereby bring a very complex *histoire* and discourse to the conference.

A few days later, I received a call asking me if I would be interested in participating in the conference. I was asked to stage a production of *Moor Harlequin's 22 Misfortunes*. (Both Feinstein and Picarazzi refer to the history and synopsis of *Moor Harlequin* in this volume.) Upon first and later readings of the play, it became clear that a dramaturgical investigation of an African Harlequin would precede any reading, or performance of which I would be a part. The multi-layered cultural complexity of *Moor Harlequin's 22 Misfortunes*, its reception by an audience in the US Midwest and my ability to theatrically conceptualize this text would preface any production. Ultimately I would be unable to stage a performance of *Moor Harlequin's 22 Misfortunes*. Staging a premiere, in translation, in a little over three months, and attending to the many cultural and dramaturgical concerns would not be possible in such a short period of time. For the conference, I was able to develop a presentation that moved me closer to the text than I was upon my first encounter. This presentation involved visual materials that historicised the relationship of Italy and Africa in the visual arts, music, and popular iconographic representations of that relationship, and African American plays and images that could be read contrapuntally and alongside *Moor Harlequin's 22 Misfortunes*. Now, after almost two years, I would like to share my thoughts about the issues surrounding such a US performance of such an Italophone work, and the potential issues that might accompany such "border" theatre.

Teresa L. Picarazzi's important introduction to *Moor Harlequin's 22 Misfortunes* unveils compelling issues related to the play.

> The objection might possibly be raised that Niang, in "rebecoming" someone he never was in a play rewritten by a white artist for a bourgeois theatre-going audience, is taking part in a type of disturbingly colonialist operation. This returns us to the question of whether or not people from the hegemony can be a part of a counter hegemonic movements. Another question one might ask is whether the author Martinelli eradicates or appropriates the voice of the oppressed or voiceless through his work, and in this play in particular. Does he engage in analyzing his own subjectivity within the parameters of his work? How interactive and collaborative are the work, goals and motivations and intent of the Teatro? What is their target audience? And in which ways is community imagined, recreated, and presented and to which end?
>
> I hope to have presented one aspect or level of the community-based nature of the Ravenna Teatro. (Picarazzi, Introductory Essay)

I am interested in many of these same issues and how they might perform, and subsequently be received, within a cross-cultural context. Encountering *Moor Harlequin's 22 Misfortunes* has been difficult. Even now issues such as colonial discourse, claiming text, and cultural signifiers continue to disrupt relationships that I seek to develop with *Moor Harlequins 22 Misfortunes*. As I read the translated text and read myself in relation to the text as potential dramaturg/Diasporic theorist, director, producer, or audience member, I often find myself decentered. You can imagine my added concern when a letter from Mascherenere, another Italophone theatre troupe, was shared with me:

> We are a cultural association concentrated mainly on the theatre based in Milan and working with African immigrants now resident in Italy. Mascherenere was founded in 1990 by Italian and African artists: the main goal was to make Black African culture more widely known throughout Italy. At the moment we are witnessing the birth of what we can call Italophone culture. In even the most hidden corners of the Italian artistic panorama, there are novelists, poets, actors, playwrights and so on that although they have no Italian mother tongue express themselves in the Italian language. It's a historic moment without precedent

because we are talking language that is borrowed, through hospitality and not enforced by colonization. It's a very important moment for Italian culture that thereby embraces artistic richness coming from other populations, which will prime the process of cultural synthesis, the driving force of transformation. The theatre philosophy of Mascherenere arises from studies done in West Africa on vernacular forms of drama and non-ritual performances. [It has been discerned that when these forms] come in contact with western theatre expressions, a "contamination" (or alteration) takes place within the African actors and within the projects themselves. So the structure of African traditional representations is soiled by western elements such as dialogue. Mascherenere searches for an expressiveness where survival is still at the root of any thought and action and where a strong sense of belonging to the land together with the acceptation of a continuos migration, but always accompanied by the essence of the land that has been abandoned, reveal hidden sources of humanity. Mascherenere recognizes that cultural languages that are put alongside in the same plan produce the contamination that is necessary for theatre in continuous mutation.

I include this letter to underscore the complexity and the abundance of such "continuously mutated theatre work" throughout the Diaspora, and to problematize voice and authority and to recognize the presence of other such work even though it may not be discussed in this specific paper.

Approaching Image

The Tunisian Foreign Ministry summoned the Italian ambassador to Tunisia, to protest against accusations by Rome that it is not fulfilling its role in halting illegal immigration.

Italian Foreign Minister Lamberto Dini stated Wednesday that Tunisia has abandoned its role of responsibility for illegal immigration.

One day after the deaths of five Tunisians in a fire that took place on board a ship, on which the Tunisians were traveling illegally in the Italian harbor of Genoa, Tunisia demanded that the Italian authorities investigate the circumstances concerning the deaths of these five Tunisians.

The number of illegal immigrants to Italy who were caught in July reached 3,000, most of them from north Africa. The Italian Foreign Minister had just concluded a trip to Morocco where an agreement was signed to deal with Moroccans residing illegally in Italy.

Meanwhile, Spanish non-governmental association "SOS Racisme" warned Spanish authorities against the upsurge of racist acts targeting Moroccan nationals living near Madrid where there have been complaints of discrimination against night clubs barring entrance to Moroccans. (Arabic News.Com 7/31/98)

Reading and visualizing a US performance of *Moor Harlequin's 22 Misfortunes* remains very problematic and are the first steps toward any theatrical presentation. Questions arise. How do we talk about image within a performance text that crosses borders, has been mutated, and is multi lingual and multi visual within a cross cultural spectator analysis? I find myself confronted with several obstacles. Many are in the images. Imagine my feelings when I encounter this dialogue early in the play —

Angelica: These shoes that you gave me . . . are so tight . . .
Lelio: They are shoes fit for a lady!
Angelica: My feet are swollen up like watermelons. (*Harlequin* 19)

And then there are Spinetta's words:

Spinetta (*to the audience*) That Black man is such a pain. But I would have to say that black people in general . . . in general . . . I mean . . . I like them. The blacks in commercials: tall . . . slender . . . smooth . . . with really white teeth. The other night on the television there was a girl who was engaged to one of them. . . . She said that when she changed . . . from white to black she came out ahead! They sure know how to treat a woman. . . . Even if she's wearing pants . . . even if she's small. They sure know how to say just the right sweet words; the words our men don't remember any more. (*Harlequin* 25)

Cultural representation in a given society weighs heavily upon the imagination, perceptions and receptions of both the party represented and the group(s) who receive that representation. Many commercial representations of people of African descent would not be welcomed in the US. Yet such representations are frequent outside of the US. [During this section of the presentation at the conference I showed many images from the contemporary Italian media of people of African descent that would not be acceptable to a US audience.] Questions surrounding hegemony, history, migration and xenophobia play a great part in the acceptance of such images. The same holds true of staged representations and these representations are not limited to people of African descent. Accompanying these "visual" images is the issue of language.

Language

> You taught me language and my profit on't is I know how to curse.
> The red plague rid you for learning me your language. (Shakespeare, *The Tempest*)

The presence, manipulation and symbolic function of language in *Moor Harlequin's 22 Misfortunes* is underscored by the fact that the characters of African descent are multi lingual yet powerless. This recalls observations about language and its relationship to culture, authority and identity made by noted border theorist Guillerrmo Gomez-Pena.

> There are many misconceptions related to the use of language in the border. I think that these misconceptions generate mistrust from one group to the other. Mexicans have traditionally been seen as extremely oral: Chicanos, having a culture of resistance and not a culture of affirmation like the Mexicans have developed an extremely minimal dialect and confrontational way of relating intellectually. Right there you have two modes of utilizing language that generates incredible mistrust. The Mexican is seen as flowery and talkative. The Mexican perceives the Chicano as rude and as too direct. Another opposition that we find that generates a lot of tensions and problems is that California is extremely anti-intellectual. It is in an outdoors and easygoing culture. There is a basic distrust of cultures that use language as intellectual inquiry and as pleasure- the whole notion of conversation as pleasure, as dialogue, as intellectual inquiry, as social event, as ritual is very foreign to Californians. When Californians and Mexicans try to sit at the same table it's very difficult to communicate. For the Mexican, the language has extreme connotations of plasticity, of texture, of sensuality and of communication. For the Californian it's very pragmatic. (Fusco 156)

The Moor's journey is one that is linguistically choreographed across many borders, physical, symbolic, and spiritual. In another instance, Pena observes:

> To cross the linguistic border implies that you decenter your voice. The border crosser develops two or more voices. This is often the experience of Mexican writers who come to the United States. We develop different speaking selves that speak for different aspects of our identity. I am very interested in the epic genre because I believe that the Mexican immigrant experience is of an epic nature. The journey is linguistic, cultural, political, and geographical. The journey goes from the past to the future, from the south to the North, from Spanish to English, from pre-Columbian American to high tech, from folk art to new technology. (Fusco 156)

The function of the native tongue as a centering device functions both intratextually as well as within the performative realm of the spectator. For Harlequin language informs without empowering. The issue of language, with its subtle flexibilities, nuances and understandings, in production and in its relationship to the general US spectator, who has trouble with Shakespeare in performance, warrants much consideration in a preproduction dramaturgical context. The question of language is central when considering staging *Moor Harlequin*. It is language that informs Moor Harlequin's multiple realities and potentially embodies his multiple selves. If we represent him on the stage in the United States, how would he be interpreted? Would he be received and understood? The "eating scene" would emerge as a complex cultural critique, and as such the impact of the critique would be heightened in performance.

How might audience members who bring a different social and cultural context and *histoire* translate the information present in these scenes? How might they balance the scene with the chicken, while simultaneously recalling the incident of the money being stolen from the Koran carrier in an earlier scene? Ultimately how will that culturally and socially constructed imagination receive the image and thereby translate the performance?

Cultural and Social Positioning: The Spectator

> If the slave no longer belonged to a community, if he had no social exis-
> tence outside of his master, then what was he? The initial response in
> almost all slaveholding societies was to define the slave as a socially
> dead person. . . . In the intrusive mode of representing social death the
> slave was ritually incorporated as the permanent enemy on the inside-
> the "domestic enemy," as he was known in medieval Tuscany. He did
> not and could not belong because he was the product of a hostile, alien
> culture. He stood, on the one hand as a living affront to the local gods,
> an intruder in the sacred space. . . . (Patterson, *Slavery and Social Death*)

Ostensibly Harlequin and Scapino are both dislocated. Each character
represents a site or interpretation of border crossing. Scapino actively
denies his African ancestry. Harlequin on the other hand seeks to return
but will never get there. Orlando Patterson, author of *Slavery and Social
Death*, would argue that Harlequin and Scapino are examples of cultural
enslavement — both are alienated and are alienated because they lack
authority. Authority rests in law, charisma, and tradition. As outsiders
inside a hostile environment, authority is unattainable. Additionally the
Africans are also alienated from "due process." Harlequin lacks access to
law and is victimized throughout the play. In the course of the play he is
beaten, robbed, burned, and ridiculed. The question that arises within a
dramaturgical spectator analysis is ultimately that of interpretation and
how does that appeal "play," alongside or contrapuntally, against the
obvious charismatic power brokers in the text: Lelio, Pantalone, and
Doctor?

How might a US audience member, given US multiculturalism, receive Harlequin's traditions, especially traditions that are out of US nor-
mative processes? For example in the "chicken scene," what emotions do
we experience and how are they read within a multicultural audience
context? Do we seek refuge in Aristophanic, western, comic traditions?
What if Aristophanes is not within the dramaturgical consciousness? If
so, do we then essentialize performance by assuming the aesthetic reception of given western traditions? Do we "laugh" at someone who is
both intruding and socially dead? Is he an animal? What happens to
comedy, other dramatic forms, or the performative in general for that
matter, at the (Africa Italy) site of the border? These issues reveal an as-

pect that must be considered when producing this play cross-culturally. In fact at the close of my presentation at the conference, an African woman spoke to me about our session devoted to the Martinelli experiment. In the process, she informed me that one of the fears of Africans who slept in the train station in Rome was that they might be burned. She thanked me for my reading my paper.

Yet in *Moor Harlequin*, constant references are made to hanging and burning in the text and most are made to Harlequin with the exception of one that is made to a member of the lower/servant class.

> Scapino enters, and brings out a mattress in very poor condition. He lays it down inside the motel, makes a sign to Moor: sleep right there. He comes in again, and goes out with a bowl of rice. He's done his duty. And this time he can really get back to sleep. Spinetta also comes back. Moor stretches out on the mattress. The notes of "Nisi Dominus" slow and heavy. In the background there appears a black figure, cloak, three-cornered hat and oil lamp. He slips out Harlequin's Koran-carrier and disappears. After a few seconds . . . fire! Harlequin is burning. Moor snaps to his feet, shouts and tries to put out the fire. He succeeds. But then he realizes that he has lost his treasure: the Koran-carrier! and he shouts, shouts, shouts!!! Exit. Scapino and Spinetta. (*Harlequin* 35)

and

> Harlequin: A good man. An intelligent man. So, listen . . .
> Spinetta: So just who do you think I am?
> Harlequin: Well . . . the manager of this motel!
> Spinetta: (*entering the motel*) Oh, go hang yourself. . . . (*Harlequin* 26)

There are throughout the play references to hanging and at the close of each act the Moor is set afire. Such constant occurrences of so vivid and controversial an image would need dramaturgical preparation before being produced on the US stage.

In the introduction to the *Moor Harlequin*, Marco Martinelli, artistic director of the Ravenna Teatro, is quoted as saying:

> When I happened across these seven or eight short pages by Goldoni I was struck by their contemporary appeal. As for Harlequin, all one had to do was change the color of his skin and his passport in order to trans-

form him from a Bergamasque of the Eighteenth Century to an African at the end of the millennium. (Picarazzi 2)

Imagining a production of *Moor Harlequin* cross-culturally necessitates much dramaturgical and cultural consideration. If a play is a material product, that is to say one that self locates historically and culturally, then does a simple alteration of skin and legal document simultaneously achieve material dramaturgical transformation? Are these constructs transhistorical? To what degree do native, materially-based cultural traditions construct the performance and reception of such work? For example does Moor Harlequin remain Moor Harlequin staged and situated within a contemporary cultural context of the US? Or, does he transform, yet again before our very eyes and, if so, what is the nature of that transformation?

Works Cited

Fusco, Coco, and Guillermo Gomez–Pena. "Bilingualism, Biculturalism, and Borders." *English Is Broken Here: Notes on Cultural Fusion in the Americas.* Ed. Coco Fusco. New York: The New Press, 1995. 147-59.

Harrison, G. B., ed. *William Shakespeare: The Complete Works.* New York: Harcourt Brace and World, 1968. 1471–1501.

Martinelli, Marco. *Moor Harlequin's 22 Misfortunes.* Trans. Wiley Feinstein. Picarazzi and Feinstein, eds. 17–73

Morrison, Toni. Introductory Essay. *Race-ing Justice, En-gendering Power: Essays on Anita Hill, Clarence Thomas and the Construction of Social Reality.* Ed. Toni Morrison. New York: Pantheon. 1992. vii–xxx.

Patterson, Orlando. *Slavery and Social Death: A Comparative Study.* Cambridge MA: Harvard, 1982. 182–213.

Picarazzi, Teresa. Introductory Essay. Picarazzi and Feinstein, eds. 1–15.

___, and Feinstein, Wiley, eds. *An African Harlequin in Milan: Marco Martinelli Performs Goldoni.* West Lafayette, IN: Bordighera, 1997.

AFRICA AND AFRICANS IN ITALIAN CINEMA

SHOOTING A CHANGING CULTURE
Cinema and Immigration in Contemporary Italy

Graziella Parati
Dartmouth College

Pier Paolo Pasolini's *Notes on an African Oresteia* (1975) is a collection of cinematographic notes that was never made into the film Pasolini had envisioned. At the center of these notes is a dialogue, or what appears to be a dialogue, between Pasolini and a group of African students at the University of Rome with whom he shares ideas about his African *Oresteia*. Pasolini's oral exchanges with his African audience are dominated by Pasolini, his project, his ideas, and his body, which is free to move while his audience sits and listens, only marginally involved in his narrative. Pasolini controls the conversation and dismisses any attempt to question his inscription of Western paradigms into an African cultural landscape. His controversial role in this project, and in Italian culture in general, is a useful introduction to this study, which is devoted to contemporary films that portray what Homi Bhabha has called "the irremovable strangeness of being different" (34). Immigration, difference, strangeness, and otherness are the focus of a body of contemporary Italian film production that attempts to change the terms of the relationship between Western and non-Western, dominant and subordinate, that are still encoded in Pasolini's experimental project, and in his very traditional exchange with his African audience.

In 1989 a short documentary entitled *Stranieri tra noi* [Strangers among Us] explored the physical and cultural locations of strangeness and foreignness in Italy at the time when the legal debate over immigration was at a turning point because of pending immigration laws (Legge Martelli). At the center of this visual narrative is Pap Khouma — his story, his life, and his ideas. He is interviewed throughout the documentary, and narrates both his arrival in Italy as an illegal immigrant and his struggle to survive in Italy where he later became a spokesperson for the Senegalese community. The interviewer plays a discreet role as a listener. Employed as an educational tool in schools, *Stranieri tra noi* has also marked Pap Khouma's experience in Italy by allowing him to become visible through exposure outside the Senegalese community he represented. His body appearing in each frame occupied a "space" that was very different from that of the audience in Pasolini's film notes. This experience motivated Pap Khouma to explore other narrative forms that would allow him to experiment both with the oral tradition with which he was familiar and the demands of the Italian narrative tradition, in which he wanted to inscribe his voice. The resulting autobiographical text, *Io, venditore di elefanti* [I am an Elephant Salesman], was published in 1990 by Pap Khouma and Oreste Pivetta. This text is the translation into practice of the theoretical framework Pap Khouma had in mind; in it, he authored his life story by employing narrative techniques that relied on both orality and Western narrative traditions. His life story was in fact recorded on tapes that Pivetta transcribed, edited, and then gave back to Khouma, who corrected and "censored" those parts he did not want made public. This collaboration, in this "split authorship" (Portelli), the process of narrating at the intersection of different cultures, becomes the locus of an exchange, often a difficult one, that has created a model allowing for a revision of cultural and literary paradigms. It is a transitional model that is abandoned when the role of the linguistic expert is no longer necessary, as in Khouma's second, still unpublished novel.

Khouma's approach to film and literature focuses on orality, on translating a tradition from his past into a present that allows the use of different media. Saidou Moussa Ba started at the opposite end in his acts of cultural hybridizations, by moving from a novel to film. The stress in this context is on agency, on the active intervention in the construction of meaning and paradigms. *La promessa di Hamadi* (1991; The Promise of Hamadi) begins with a chant modeled on the Senegalese oral tradition and tells of two brothers' journey from Senegal to Italy. The story is narrated by a dead man, the older brother, who is killed shortly after seeing his younger brother. The younger brother came to Italy in search of his older sibling who, after migrating to Italy, had severed contacts with his Senegalese family. By engaging in acts of cultural translation, both Khouma and Ba are able to construct their identities as mediators between past and present cultural identities.

Translation is not a limit or a limiting strategy for Ba: translation becomes a border that he crosses and recrosses repeatedly, changing the language — and therefore the culture — that sits at the center of the text created by his acts of translation. Ba is Peul, fluent in Wolof, French, and at ease in Italian, which is the language of co-authoring for him. In his collaboration with Alessandro Micheletti, Ba has written two novels; he insists that he wishes to pursue their collaboration in future projects. Italian is the language in which he has become a teacher, a playwright, an author, and an actor; it is the language in which he authors his daily life. Languages have become his way of unsettling borders, as his collaboration with the theater group Ravenna Teatro now frequently takes him back to Dakar. His latest project, a film entitled *Waalo Fendo* (*La, où la terre gèle,* 1997) embodies his revisionist agenda, which looks at translation as a necessary cultural act that permeates daily life. Ba rejects any attempt to privilege one dominant language into which all other languages must be translated. Even while living and writing in Italy, Ba works on the possibility of destabilizing the dominant linguistic location of Italian.

Before engaging in a discussion of *Waalo Fendo*, I need to retrace my steps to Pasolini's Orientalist discourse. In his *Oresteia*, language plays a pivotal role in his exchange with the African audience. He shows them his cinematic notes, which tell the story of Aeschylus's Orestes, a hero who "discovers" democracy after leaving barbaric, religious Argos and moving to Athens. There he is put on trial by his peers for killing Clytemnestra for her murder of Agamemnon, Orestes's father. In his geographical move from Argos to Athens, Orestes symbolizes the birth of a new, "better" era of democracy in which the Furies, who had tried to punish him for his violent act, are transformed into Eumenides, "the Kindly Ones." The geographical and political displacement in which Orestes inscribes himself tames the Furies and "civilizes" the future. Pasolini's plan to write this evolutionary teleology in the Africa of independence in the 1950s and 60s is opposed by Pasolini's captive audience. What is questionable is the discovery of "democracy" as a Western model to be imitated. It is also questionable that Pasolini talks about "Africa" without paying attention to one of his guests, who stresses the cultural differences to be taken into account when talking about Africa as a

continent and points to the fact that African tribal societies are functioning societies. Pasolini talks about looking for "characters" in Africa, in
Uganda, Tanzania, and Kenya — characters who can embody an already
carefully scripted text based on intellectual and ethnic hierarchies. It is a
text closed to other interpretative voices originating from the cultural
locations that are supplying "color" and both human and geographical
landscapes that "lend themselves," according to Carrie Tarr, "to the neo-
colonialist project of repossessing the colony in fantasy through the visual recapture of its reified landscape" (63). Pasolini's film notes portray a
muted dialogue in which "color" is represented, but has no impact on
shaping a narrative in which those who are silenced function as object in
a narrative that tells the myth of a linear evolution to perfection.

Twenty years later, film talks back to Orientalist discourses. *Waalo
Fendo*, for instance, becomes the location in which those voices silenced
in Pasolini's creative space can turn the tables and construct their own
audience. *Waalo Fendo* is a film project originating from a cross-national,
cross-cultural collaboration. Saidou Moussa Ba wrote the script and was
the actor-protagonist of the film. Mohammed Soudani, an Algerian living in Switzerland, directed the film with Italian, Swiss, and French
funding. The story narrated is closely linked to the plot in Ba's first
novel, *La promessa di Hamadi*. Neither want to be autobiographical texts;
however, they focus on immigration experiences in Italy. At the center of
this film there is a man, his story, and, in the end, his death, but above all
there is language. The film is in Wolof and Pulaar with French subtitles,
which will be translated into Italian once the film is distributed in Italy.
The choice of creating a film for a Western audience in a non-Western
language radically changes the terms of the cultural relationship between North and South, and shifts the attention from the linguistic hybridizations brought by colonial languages to a reversal of roles. Ba and
Soudani also articulated the possibility of creating a film for a European
audience grounding it in the ideology of language found in Ousmane
Sembene's work in film: that is, using the non-Western language as subject in the narrative and subordinating the translation into a European

language to, literally, a marginal script on the screen.[1] As Laura Mulvey affirms in her discussion of Sembene's work:

> The cinema can speak across the divisions created by illiteracy and language and is therefore, a perfect mechanism for a cultural dialectic. It can participate in the oral cultural tradition; it can produce a culture in which the Wolof language plays a major role; and it can bring Wolof [and Pulaar, in Ba's case] into the modernity of the post-colonial. (518)

In "The Alchemy of English," Braj Kachru analyzes the impact of English in Asia as it

> has provided a linguistic tool and a sociopolitical dimension very different from those available through native linguistic tools and traditions. A non-native writer in English functions in two traditions. In psychological terms, such a multilingual role calls for adjustment. (293)

Exposing an audience to the unfamiliar sounds of Wolof, Ba and Soudani demand an adjustment on the part of the European viewers, who are confronted by the familiar, easily legible landscape of urban Milan, which is destabilized by the story of a migration as expressed in the language of the migrant. In a conversation (13 Feb. 1998), Ba justified the motivation behind this linguistic choice by stressing that this story is about immigrants and that the actors portraying them feel "comfortable" with languages other than Italian. It is their story, their life, and turning it into Italian would make the narrative artificial. In addition, this film was created with the express purpose of being marketable in Italy, France, and Switzerland; therefore the foreignness of the text is a unify-

---

[1]On this subject, Laura Mulvey writes: "As a Wolof, Sembene came from an oral tradition in which the *griot* functioned as poet and storyteller. As the son of a fisherman, he was self-educated. . . . Sembene's cinema is more the product of popular, Senegalese traditions and his films are directed towards the cultural needs of the Senegalese people through the specific possibilities offered by the cinema. . . . Sembene's commitment to promoting and transforming traditional culture [is] to using the cultural developments of Western society in the interests of Africa. Sembene was more interested in finding a dialectical relationship between the two cultures than in an uncritical nostalgia for pre-colonial pure African-ness" (517).

ing rather than a separating element between the different audiences, who are confronted with the same displacement of a linguistic center. Broadcast by Swiss TV on a Saturday night and by French television, this film has also reached Ba's family in Senegal and has crossed the linguistic cultural boundaries between Europe and Africa. It embodies the possibility of a return home that involves an intellectual journey without demanding a Manichean choice between past and present.

This film also comes after Ba's experience as an interpreter of Italian texts about immigrants. As an actor, Ba performed with Piero Mazzarella, a well-known Italian actor, in *La tempesta* (1993; The Tempest), a play by Emilio Tadini that intertwines the life stories of a black immigrant and an old Italian man. Tadini's split text is a space shared by two different identities at the margins; it offers a valuable commentary on contemporary life in a Western world where old people and "new" immigrants are placed at the margins. In *Waalo Fendo*, the cinematic narrative space is filled by a character similar to Tadini's character, whom he named "il Nero" [the Black] in his play. In Ba and Soudani's film, the screen is filled by his voice, his language, his life, and his marginal identity.

Collaboration between Italian linguistic experts and immigrant writers is at the center of the discussion on contemporary Italophone culture. It can be condemned as exploitation and as an exercise in control. But it is at the same time an exploration of both difference and similarities, carried out by both the immigrant and the local cultural expert. David Ward affirms that in Italy,

> racist strategies bear now not so much on the fear of difference, but the fear of equality [and sameness, not difference]. For racist groups, the threat now posed by the immigrant is to the integrity of the host country's culture, which they fear risks being diluted by the bearers of other, antithetical cultures. (91)

These processes of uncovering similarities within differences, and therefore shifting from a discourse on distance to its opposite, emerge from collaborative projects between immigrant writers and linguistic experts, but also in those texts, such as Angioni's *Una ignota compagnia* (1992; An

Unknown Company) or Tadini's *La tempesta*, authored by Italians who attempt to combine an Italian's marginal position in his own culture with an immigrant's experience of cultural exile. Mohammed Aden has recently stressed that, following the new phenomenon of migration to Italy in recent years, Italians have begun to confront their own colonial past, buried for a long time and absent from educational curricula. In his article, Aden cites the African American Marcus Garvey, who in 1935, following the Italian invasion of Ethiopia, condemned Italian colonialism by stating that Mussolini "claims to be a white man [an apparent ahistorical belief about Italians still held by some] although the Italian race cannot be called purely a white race" (123). In "'Italy' in Italy: Old Metaphors and New Racism in the 1990s," David Ward describes a cartoon published in Italy in 1991 that "shows a bemused Italian being pursued by a German Neo-Nazi while pursuing a black immigrant." It refers to episodes of violent racism taking place a few days apart: one in which Italians were attacked by Nazi-skins in Germany, and another where Italians attacked immigrant workers in Italy. The caption reads: "I do not know whether I am chasing the black man or running away from the German." Those texts that present a double difference in a shared space of marginality contribute to a discourse that uncovers the off-whiteness of Italian identity; they have opened a discourse on difference based on sameness that, as Ward states, is perceived as more threatening than traditional discourses on separations, differences, and the intrinsically inferior nature of otherness.

Ba, who privileges both discussions on difference and sameness, continues working in the same collaborative relation with an Italian, a coauthoring process that led him to write *La memoria di A.* (1995; The Memory of A.) with Alessandro Micheletti. This novel focuses both on the difference of immigrants in Italy and on the perceived sense of difference of the young protagonist, who is a racist in Italy, but who experiences racism against himself in Germany, where he also witnesses episodes of violence against Jews. Ba's work is based on a non-exclusionary pattern of collaborations and experimentations among genres. His ongoing collaboration with Micheletti, who is the linguistic expert, is complemented by his collaboration with Soudani, an Algerian immigrant living in Switzerland with whom Ba can move from theater to film and from fiction to script writing. This collaboration among immigrant intellectuals destabilizes the inevitable hierarchical relationship that is established between the linguistic expert and the immigrant writer.

In his acting, novels, film script, and plays, Ba experiments with translating his own experience into texts that are never completely autobiographical. He is a true multilingual nomad, who hides his identity even in a film, *Waalo Fendo*, which uncovers the mechanisms and strategies inherent in presenting a life in exile in the original language. Ba's native tongue is Pulaar, not Wolof. Khouma has noted that while he is Wolof, and only speaks Wolof, Ba can move easily between the two languages, and from there to French and Italian. This interplay between revealing and concealing one's identity is at the basis of Ba's autobiographical construction, which never becomes openly autobiographical, but is rather a fragmented combination of his life story and other people's experiences. However, Ba stresses the presence of an "accent" when he speaks Wolof, and insists that his identity as a Peul is easily recognizable by other Senegalese. His stress on his foreignness, even within the boundaries of the familiar languages, establishes this film as an exercise in linguistic transgressions that destabilize the separations between original and adoptive languages, between past and present. The linguistic and cultural "accent" is already a structural component of his Senegalese identity that was constructed before and outside of the dislocation created by the act of migration. While Wolof is the language more often used in this film project, the title of the film is in Pulaar, which is also the language employed in some exchanges between characters in the film. This film, which represents the visual and visible location of strangeness for Western viewers, also offers a complex interplay of linguistic texts for Pulaar and Wolof speakers. The stress on the illegibility of difference for a European audience connotes the need to create a film that crosses the boundaries between audiences' cultural and linguistic identities. This film contains a plurality of texts according to the "reading" abilities of the viewers. In *Waalo Fendo*, a Western world signified by Pulaar, Wolof, and Italian words, Ba and Soudani succeed in constructing a cultural accent that can be re-translated back into the cultural context where Ba's migration began.

While Ba's first novel began with a griot chant, *Waalo Fendo* explores the oral tradition by representing the narrative as told by a collective voice embodied by two narrators: Teo, who is Yaro's (the main character, played by Ba) friend, and Demba, Yaro's brother, who survives at the end of the narrative while Yaro dies. A griot who sings the Senegalese diaspora is also inscribed in the narrative, which moves from Italy to Senegal. Through repeated flashbacks, it moves back again to Senegal, and bears witness to the complex acts of leaving a country to move toward *Waalo Fendo*, the land where the earth freezes. In these repeated and destabilizing shifts between two continents, the film teases the audience by employing the same stereotypes that the West has constructed about Africa. Before leaving the village, Demba is asked by an old man to take a letter to the old man's son, who migrated to Waalo Fendo. It is a letter with no precise address: in *Waalo Fendo* the West becomes the generic entity that Africa was in Pasolini's film.

It is the migrant, the nomad, who has the privileged position of bearing witness to the two worlds and to the transitions or mediations between the different cultural contexts. Ba's character seems to theorize his interpretative position by embodying an identity torn between past and present. In fact, Yaro stands up for his rights and fights the people who want to exploit the immigrants. He constructs a life with his Italian friends who help him in a difficult situation, but he still sets boundaries to his belonging to *Waalo Fendo*. In a dialogue with his brother Demba, Yaro reprimands Demba for being attracted to a white woman, a friend whom Yaro sees only as an obstacle to Demba's construction of an independent identity in Italy. As in many French films by ethnic minority filmmakers, Ba has focused on "the immigrant as victim and [has] taken a pessimistic line on the possibility of integration" (Tarr 69). In this context, the linguistic and cultural experts found in the country of migration are represented as obstacles, not facilitators, in the process of redefining one's identity in translation.

The process of identity construction is at the center of *Waalo Fendo*. In a national context in which identity cards are issued in one language only and can bestow the right to belong to a Western country, Ba plays with the concept of legal identity cast in Italian by scrambling identity papers and using many languages to do so. The result is the description of a journey from Senegal to Italy, where the main protagonist cannot survive. In Italy, Yaro inscribes his diversity within the already fragmented sense of Italianness that permeates contemporary Italian culture. He mocks Umberto Bossi and his Northern separatist agenda ("La Savania libera, noi della Savania libera marceremo su Roma" [Free Savania, we of free Savania will march on Rome]), by replacing the slogan "Padania libera" [Free padania] with "Savania Libera." He also draws Italian historical memories into the equation, threatening a black march on Rome that mocks Mussolini's black shirts' march of 1922. These film segments address an Italian audience and temporarily interrupt the "European" and "Non-European" dialogue that is both Ba's and the director's agenda.

The protagonists of *Waalo Fendo* are closely connected with particular migration issues in Italy, and their life in the West is marked by experiences developed in confronting Italian culture, society, language, and intolerance. Italy becomes, therefore, the location in which their new identities are being shaped in that initial moment when the country of migration is completely new and uncharted. At the end of the film, Yaro disappears as a guide for the newcomers. His death represents the disappearance of a separatist way of reading and approaching a new culture. His heroic death in the name of an ideal is replaced by a new movement, a new journey on other people's terms, people who become independent interpreters. After Yaro's death, the final shots of the film focus on a moving streetcar and reintroduce the concept of the cultural and geographical journey that his death cannot interrupt. By moving away from a representation of the immigrant solely as victim, Ba and Soudani separate themselves from the production in French cinema portraying "ethnic minorities in subordinate roles as the (relative) helpless victims of aggression [as it] can be hardly empowering for minority audiences" and the viewers in Senegal.

Yaro's disappearance also defines the changes in the communities of immigrants in Italy from a polarized to a more dispersed group identity: immigrants have first portrayed their life in Italy as centered around immigrant communities, and then on identity categories that become more fragmented in later narratives. Pap Khouma, Saidou Moussa Ba, and others have stressed the role of the "group," which supplied support and a link with the familial and familiar country, language, and culture. These initial reflections on group identity, which characterize those autobiographical narratives published in the early nineties, have changed into narrative explorations of issues that contest and reinterpret any essentialistic identification with one identity as representative of one group, or one origin. This movement toward a plurality of identities that describe migrating selves even within communities has been facilitated by the production of narratives created independently of the intervention of linguistic or cultural experts — intervention that was necessary at a time when the authors were not familiar with the Italian language and the Italian publishing industry.

These processes of collaboration and dual authorship are revealing aspects in contemporary Italophone culture. The Tunisian Mohsen Melliti wrote *Pantanella: Canto lungo la strada* [Pantanella: Song along the Road] in 1992. Originally written in Arabic, the novel was translated into Italian by Monica Ruocco and became public only in Italian, while the Arabic version was never published. In 1995 Melliti wrote his second novel, *I bambini delle rose* [Children of Roses], in Italian without any mediating intervention on the part of an Italian expert. In 1997, Melliti collaborated with the director Massimo Guglielmi on a film project entitled *Verso casa* [Homeward]. Broadcast by Italian television, *Verso casa* documents the trip back home of a number of Moroccans who board a bus at the central station in Milan and return "home" for disparate reasons, traveling by bus through France and Spain. The camera follows them into their Moroccan homes and investigates the difficult processes of return to what was once home but can no longer be defined as such. A very successful project, Melliti and Guglielmi's documentary contributes to a discussion on separations and borders in the emergence of Italophone voices within Italian culture.

Accessibility within dissemination is the aim of the authors within Italophone culture who are documenting the location of "strangeness" as the irremovable strangeness of being different within fortress Europe (Bhabha 34). They confront the concept of cultural borders by searching for a creative space that can be linguistically — as is the case of Ba and Soudani — and thematically appealing to large, geographically disseminated audiences.

Directly and indirectly influenced by Italophone culture and by the innovative projects of Italophone authors, Italian filmmakers have confronted the issues that immigrants have placed at the center of their narratives. Giovanni Maderna's *Jahilia* locates itself at the intersection of different cultures. Inspired by Flannery O'Connor's "The Life You Save May Be Your Own" (1953), Maderna replaces the main character in the American short story with a religious immigrant from Northern Africa to Italy. The story unfolds similarly to O'Connor's: a man arrives at a farm run by two women. The mother is well off and has raised a daughter, Antonia in Maderna's film, who appears to have mental problems. In O'Connor's narrative the man is a con artist who covets their car and succeeds in getting it. In O'Connor's story, marrying the daughter leads to the revelation that the man only wanted to take advantage of the women since he abandons his bride by the road side and disappears with the car. In Maderna's version, instead, there is an attempt to link two identities at the margins: that of the immigrant man, who only has a dirty towel as his prayer mat, and who covets an old car that reminds him of his work in a car factory in Northern Africa; and that of a defenseless young woman who is unable to choose for herself. In fact, the narrative ends when the new couple leaves in the car after the wedding ceremony. The final shots narrate their silence, the impossibility of communication between them, underlined by the music he has chosen and by her sobs. This final twist, which modifies O'Connor's unhappy ending, shows the influence of other European films that focus on immigration. In particular, Maderna's film seems to dialogue with Fassbinder's *Angst Essen Seele auf* (1976; Ali, Fear Eats the Soul), in which a young Northern African develops a relationship with a much older German woman. These encounters at the margins within the narrative structure of Maderna's short film point to the processes of cultural hybridizations that define the flexibility of borders and boundaries on which immigrant authors are also focusing. An example is Pap Khouma's *Io, venditore di elefanti*, whose literary model is the German *Ganz Unten* (1985), a narrative about a German journalist who disguised himself as a Turk and lived among a Turkish community so that he could write autobiographically about his experience as an immigrant. Khouma chose this German text, which he read either in French or Italian translation, as a model for his autobiography in Italian.

I began this essay by talking in unflattering terms about *Notes on an African Oresteia*. In fact, Pasolini's film is not about Africa or an African *Oresteia*, but rather about Italian culture and its relation to (its own) otherness, which is kept at bay through strategies of distancing. I have, however, moved my discussion from an Orientalist discourse to a hybrid analysis of contemporary film by minority and non-minority filmmakers. My methodology and theorethical framework are grounded in the assumption that it is in a double and nonseparatist discussion that we can locate Bhabha's "strangeness of being different." This dissemination of strangeness and difference that encompasses immigrants and Italians alike allows us to discard the question: "who can speak?" or "who is allowed to speak?" because it is in the hybrid area of sameness and exploration of difference that the work of minority and non-minority filmmakers and writers that this discussion takes place in theory and practice.

In this light I will consider a particular film project carried out by RAI, that is Italian state controlled and a subsidized television channel, in an attempt to break the visual silence on immigration. As Alec Hargreaves stresses in analyzing the French case, state controlled television broadcasts have not devoted much air time to the representation of immigrants and immigration outside of the "emergency" and "invasion" dominated discourse of news broadcasters. In 1997, RAI commissioned Pier Giorgio and Marco Bellocchio and their production company Filmalbatros to make four films in a series entitled "Another Country in My Eyes." The films deal with the experience of immigrants in Italy. Until then RAI had paid little attention to immigration, allowing a program such as *Non solo nero* [Not Only Black] to broadcast for a couple of years, then to disappear during one of the many restructuring turnovers at RAI.

Created as films to be shown on the big screen and not only for television, *The Apartment*, directed by Francesca Pirani, *The Tree of Pending Destinies* by Rachid Benhadj, *Torino Boys* by Marco and Antonio Manetti, and *From One Sky to the Other* by Roberto Giannarelli represent a partially successful attempt to investigate immigrants' lives between and within two cultures from the point of view of both minority and non-minority filmmakers. The two films I will not discuss at length are *Torino Boys* and *From One Sky to the Other*. *Torino Boys* is a not very successful attempt to portray youth culture in the Nigerian communities of Torino and Rome. *From One Sky to the Other* is based on Hassan Itab's autobiography entitled *The Hyena's Den*. It narrates Itab's incarceration in Italy, brought about by his terrorist bombing of the British Airways office in Rome in the mid eighties. The book focuses on his training as a Palestinian fighter, his mission in Italy, and his incarceration; the film portrays his life, divided between his nights in prison and his days working in a cafeteria, and his attempt to create a new life in Italy, complicated by his memories of the past, which create obstacles in his relationship with an Italian woman.

The two films I want to discuss here, although briefly, are Rachid Benhadj's *The Tree of Pending Destinies* and Francesca Pirani's *The Apartment*. The former is directed by an Algerian who has lived and worked in Switzerland for many years; the latter allows me to introduce a discourse on gender and on the still not very visible role of women in the discussion on migration issues.

The Tree of Pending Destinies is a film about identity construction and migrancy intended as a "movement in which neither the points of departure nor those of arrival are immutable or certain" (Chambers 5.) Sami, the young protagonist of Benhadj's film, works as a cook for a community of Moroccan men who earn their living in Italy as construction workers. Sami hates to be enclosed in a domestic sphere that limits his life and his experience as an immigrant. The realm he inhabits belongs to a separate, suspended, sphere of in-between spaces. He works with familiar people who use the language and meta-language with which they grew up because they all originate from the same Moroccan village. This space, however, is located in Italy where, as a man states, Sami does not even need to learn the local language to accomplish the daily shopping for the community. These communities of men, which Khouma, Ba, and Melliti had so eloquently described in their autobiographical texts in the early nineties, find their translation into visual language in Benhadj's film.

Sami is a true nomad who rejects suspension in between cultures and tries to explore the linguistic intricacies of his new country of residence. He does so by acquiring a language-acquisition course on tapes which he listens to while taking care of his daily chores. The oneiric component in the film takes place in dream-like sequences that are a very effective satire of language-acquisition material. The dialogues he listens to are in Italian and take place between a hypothetical Mrs. Bell and a Mr. Rossi. Mr. Rossi talks to her while they are dancing and Mrs. Bell tries to get to know him. Mr. Rossi turns out to be a gigolo from Calabria who tangos with the American Mrs. Bell in order to learn English. This ridiculous situation efficiently brings in a discussion on stereotypes by looking at the Italian migration to the Americas and the subsequent stereotypical representation of Italian men. This parallel between migrations, which is at the basis of Sami's language acquisition, contributes to that discourse on sameness, previously discussed in this presentation, which becomes more evident in the visual representation of a generic Mr. Rossi from Calabria who resembles the Moroccan protagonist Sami.

Sami's language acquisition through stereotyping is interrupted by Yussef, the son of the village chief who has come for a routine visit. Yussef functions as a go-between between the immigrants in Italy and their families in Morocco: he brings letters and takes money and presents back for relatives in Morocco. Yussef embodies the identity Sami would like to acquire, an identity closely connected with geographical and cultural mobility. Sami aspires to betweenness and not in-betweenness and wants to appropriate that possibility of mobility between Italy and Morocco. This mobility would allow him to live in both places and certainly to acquire a privileged identity for his Moroccan community, as he would embody the link between the migrants and their family, the past and the present, Morocco and Italy. When Yussef dies of a heart attack and the rest of the community does not want Sami to take his place because they consider him too young, Sami takes action and leaves for the trip back to Morocco in Yussef's car, loaded with presents.

Sami's return is partial and echoes Ba's intellectual journey back to Senegal thanks to his film project. In both cases, mobility is preserved, as are the protagonists' double identities. Sami's trip is complicated by the presence of a traveling companion, an Italian woman he has met when she was taping a lipstick commercial in a supermarket. Named Maria, this young woman embodies Italianness for Sami as he has seen it on posters and television, the Itanianness he has imagined in daydreams while listening to those inane language lessons on tape. Maria is pregnant, alone, and in need of a friend. They travel together to Morocco, but a love relationship, eagerly desired by Sami, cannot be established between them. There are what I would call cultural disturbances between them. In the segment of the trip from Milan to the French border, they find shelter from the rain in an abandoned and crumbling church. Maria feels comfortable there and invites Sami to join her, but he cannot enter a Catholic shrine that still has religious images hanging on its walls. In contrast, Maria finds the church a comforting cocoon that contains her past (the film has a flashback to the memories of her first communion) and her unhappy present. Standing in front of the image of the virgin Mary, Maria finds both her namesake and a representation of troubled motherhood that speaks to her. Maria sleeps inside the church, while Sami remains outside in the car that belonged to Yussef.

It is in the strategy of locations that Rachid Benhadj constructs the pattern of strangeness in his film. Once in Morocco, Sami attempts to kiss Maria, but raising his eyes he sees a Muslim religious symbol and it is only with uneasiness that he can approach Maria. In Morocco, Maria becomes a more legible text. Sami finally is told by a doctor that Maria is pregnant and their romantic interlude comes to an end. However, Sami leaves Maria when he has almost reached his village and has driven through Morocco seeing it through the eyes of a Western woman. The director has chosen to portray that side of Morocco familiar to tourists: glamorous hotels and mud palaces. Poverty is talked about and visualized only once, when they visit an abandoned village. Sami's village is often at the center of the conversation between him and Maria, but it only becomes visible at the end of the film when Maria is literally out of the picture and Sami enters the village carrying gifts, becoming Yussef, welcomed by a festive atmosphere. Only then does Sami return to the hotel where he left an ailing Maria, only to find her gone, replaced by a text, a letter she has left for him expressing her desire to see him again.

Benhadj proclaims the impossibility of a happy ending, and the possibility only of an open end to Sami and Maria's story. However, the happy ending lies in the fact that Sami ends up acquiring the same mobility across borders that Maria seems to have. In this context, Maria represents a Westerner who can easily cross borders; we see her deciding to join Sami in the trip to Morocco at the very last minute. It is Sami who always knows where his passport is, where his identity is, because he had to document himself and prove his identity. Maria always has trouble finding her identity card, lost at the bottom of her bag, unaware of what it symbolizes for those who have experienced migration. Ba and Soudani's *Waalo Fendo* originally had the working title *Senza visto* [Without a Visa], as the film begins with an undocumented migration and ends with the disappearance of the protagonist. Benhadj's film ends with the acquisition of mobility through borders, but also with the impossibility of creating a relationship with the woman who takes such mobility for granted, even though the woman of Sami's daydreaming, the woman he imagines while listening to the exchanges in his Italian lessons on tape, now has Maria's face.

Rachid Benhadj's film, *Il cantico delle donne di Algeri* [The Canticle of the Women of Algiers], connected the director to his Algerian identity; his short film *L'ultima cena* [The Last Supper] tells of the memories, the dreams, and the experiences of a group of immigrants in Verona. The film, *The Tree of Pending Destinies*, explored an other otherness in Sami's story. Benhadj is working on another film, *Mirka*, in which he focuses on Bosnia's ethnic cleansing and, as in his first film, on women. At the center of *Mirka* is a rape and a pregnancy. This film confirms Benhadj's particular attention to gender issues: "Il film e' dedicato alla figura femminile," states Benhadj "Anche contro la donna la storia si ripete, da sempre, in ogni situazione di guerra o di emergenza; diventa oggetto di violenza e di ricatto." [The film is dedicated to the role of women. Even against woman history repeats itself, from the beginning, in every situation of war or emergency; she becomes the object of violence and blackmail.][2] *Mirka* is produced by the Italian Filmart in collaboration with France and Spain and has, unexpectedly according to the director, actors such as Vanessa Redgrave and Gérard Depardieu and the Oscar-winning Vittorio Storaro as director of photography.

---

[2]This is from an interview with Rachid Banhadj by Maria Pia Fusco (1998).

If Benhadj moves his experimentation in the representation of strangeness from Algeria, to Italy, to Morocco and the ex-Yugoslavia, Francesca Pirani, director of *The Apartment* (1997), circumscribes otherness in a very enclosed and at times claustrophobic space. The protagonists in Pirani's film live in Rome but originate from Egypt and Eastern Europe. The woman comes from the former Yugoslavia, where she was a school teacher, but cleans apartments in her exile in Italy. The director focuses on her loneliness and on the economic struggles that occupy most of her time. Emotions caused by displacement and marginality are at the center of a narrative that eloquently portrays the tragedy of involuntary exile experienced by a woman. Gender issues are subtly treated by Pirani as part of a complex system of relations connecting two different cultures.

The apartment becomes the tangible location of difference and foreignness shared by two strangers for a limited amount of time. The male protagonist, an undocumented Egyptian called Mahmud, encounters the woman while he is on the run. The viewer is confronted, at the beginning of the film, with the representation of a stereotype: an immigrant committing a crime. He snatches a baby from the cradle and sneaks out of the institution where the child lived, waiting for adoption. The plot does not give any plausible explanation and the viewer follows the protagonist's wandering in search of shelter and a place to hide. The opportunity arises when he sees a wealthy family leave for a vacation. He breaks into their apartment and sets out to take care of the baby. In the apartment he encounters the "cleaning lady," Lajila, who reluctantly allows him to stay for the night. Everything happens in a very short period of time, at night, because a safe location is impossible to find and they both have to come to terms with their identity as others who are watched by "those who belong" and must protect their wealth. The police intervene, called by a nosy neighbor who has seen a stranger in the apartment, and the Egyptian man is arrested for trespassing. However, the baby girl remains in the apartment, and the "cleaning lady" is left with her. She already knows the story; he has told her; the baby is his daughter, born from a relationship with an Italian woman who refused to raise her and left her in an orphanage. He illegally reclaimed her in order to raise her because as an undocumented immigrant without a home he could not be granted custody. The short truce found in the apartment is only temporary, and the ending leaves us with a powerful image of a present in which otherness can only be defined by problematizing it, and the future is being constructed by a young woman and a baby girl thrown together as strangers but also as reflections of each other's difference. Lajila is, in fact, a Muslim woman from hard hit Mostar who left her family there and has embraced the safety and loneliness of exile.

I would like to use Laura Mulvey's definition of African film in order to conclude by summarizing the impact that new films by and about immigrants have on contemporary Italian culture: these films "should not be seen as a 'developing' cinema," or as new temporary expressions of creativity stimulated by these moments of "emergency" in Italy. These are films that "are now making an original and significant contribution to the aesthetics of contemporary cinema." These films are now creating the revisionary groundwork in representing otherness with which film-makers will have to come to terms in future representations of a culture whose skin is revealing its darker color.

Works Cited

Aden, Mohammed. "Italy: Cultural Identity and Spatial Opportunism from a Postcolonial Perspective." *Revisioning Italy: National Identity and Global Culture*. Ed. Beverly Allen and Mary Russo. Minneapolis: Minnesota UP, 1997. 101–15.

Angioni, Giulio. *Una ignota compagnia*. Milan: Feltrinelli, 1992.

Ba, Saidou Moussa, and Alessandro Micheletti. *La promessa di Hamadi*. Novara: DeAgostini, 1991.

___. *La memoria di A*. Novara: DeAgostini, 1995.

Bhabha, Homi K. "On the Irremovable Strangeness of Being Different." *PMLA* (Jan. 1998): 34–39.

Chambers, Iain. *Migrancy, Culture, Identity*. London: Routledge, 1994.

Fusco, Maria Pia. "Intolleranza un male che conosco." *Repubblica* 19 Aug. 1998: 43.

Hargreaves, Alec, and Mark McKinney, eds. *Post-Colonial Cultures in France*. London: Routledge, 1997.

Kachru, Braj. "The Alchemy of English." *The Post-Colonial Studies Reader*. Ed. Bill Ashcroft, Gareth Griffiths, and Helen Tiffin. New York: Routledge, 1995. 291–95.

Khouma, Pap. *Io, Venditore di elefanti*. Ed. Oreste Pivetta. Milan: Garzanti, 1990.

Melliti, Mohsen. *Pantanella: Canto lungo la strada*. Rome: Edizioni Lavoro, 1992.

___. *I bambini delle rose*. Rome: Edizioni Lavoro, 1995.

Mulvey, Laura. "*Xala*, Ousmane Sembene 1976: The Carapace That Failed." *Colonial Discourse and Post-Colonial Theory: A Reader*. Ed. Patrick Williams and Laura Chrisman. New York: Columbia UP, 1994. 517–34.

O'Connor, Flannery. "The Life You Save May Be Your Own." *The Complete Stories*. New York: Farrar, Straus and Giroux, 1972. 145–56.

Portelli, Alessandro. "Mediterranean Passage: The Beginnings of an African Italian Literature and the African American Example." *Mapping African America*. Ed. Carl Pedersen and Maria Diedrich. New York: Oxford UP, forthcoming.

Tadini, Emilio. *La tempesta*. Turin: Einaudi, 1993.

Tarr, Carrie. "French Cinema and Post-Colonial Minorities." Hargreaves and McKinney 59–83.

Wallraff, Günter. *Faccia da Turco: Un "infiltrato speciale" nell'inferno degli immigrati*. Salerno, Tullio Pironti, 1986.

Ward, David. "'Italy' in Italy: Old Metaphors and New Racisms in the 1990s." *Revisioning Italy: National Identity and Global Culture*. Ed. Beverly Allen and Mary Russo. Minneapolis: Minnesota UP, 1997. 81–97.

NERO SU BIANCO
The Africanist Presence in Twentieth-Century Italy
and Its Cinematic Representations

Chandra Harris
Brown University

Introduction

Despite the attention paid to present-day immigrants to Italy from African nations such as Senegal, Nigeria, and the former Italian colonies in East Africa, there has been no systematic analysis of the appearance of Blacks, either Africans or African Americans, in Italian culture to date, and the limited discussion of Africa or Africans in literature and cinema has revolved primarily around works produced during Italy's colonial expansion in the Fascist era. Media representations echo the beliefs of Italian society, conveying the attitudes and preconceived notions of its people, and the appearance of "blackness" in Italian cinema reflects the conceptions historically held by Italians about people of African descent. I have divided these cinematic representations into four categories in order to better circumscribe these conceptions: films in which the action takes place in an Africa, real or imagined, *without* Africans; films in which the plot involves Africans, on or off the continent, including films in which Italian actors portray Africans as historical characters; films in which the plot involves African Americans; or lastly films in which Africa or Africans are mentioned by the characters in any context. In order to compose a thorough picture of the Italian perceptions of themselves as a nation in relation to Africa, it is necessary to provide a detailed content analysis of the images of "blackness" in various Italian films, in addition to pertinent images in literature, advertising, and television.

Since its origins in the late nineteenth century, cinema has served as a powerful tool for propaganda and the communication of national values, as well as for entertainment. During the Fascist period, in particular, governmentally approved films, specifically designed to convince viewers of the merits of the Fascist cause, were released. These films also encouraged support for the Italian campaign to colonize Ethiopia. Fascist images portrayed Africans as weak and barbaric, meriting subordination to foreign rule. This supplanted the previous representations in literature, cinema, and print media of Africans as "noble savages" and of Africa as a locus of fertility and exoticism.[1] Black Americans who were represented as subservient and accommodating toward whites or as buffoons displaying exaggerated movements and facial expressions in films exported to Italy, like *Birth of a Nation* (1915), Al Jolson's *The Jazz Singer* (1927), and *Gone with the Wind* (1939), added to the already stereotypical notions of Africans that Italians possessed. With the appearance of sympathetically portrayed African Americans in Italian-made films about the aftermath of WW II like *Paisà*, *Vivere in pace*, and *Senza pietà*, these notions were somewhat dispelled.

In the post-WW II "economic boom" of the 1950s, television came to Italy and an "Africanist presence"[2] appeared there as well, although with different connotations from those propagated by Fascism. These representations were more influenced by the music and literature that had stemmed from African-American culture since the Harlem Renaissance of the 1920s, but still contained many stereotyped images of Africans. Cinematic "Africanist presences" possess a specific historically-grounded significance for Italians and demonstrate former racial attitudes that continue to affect the nation's relationship with African immigrants and African Americans today.

Late Nineteenth-Century Italy, History, and Cinema

> The history and culture of the Italian peninsula — and by extension all of Europe — has been shaped by its contacts with African cultures: from the Punic wars between Rome and Carthage in Classical times, to the Crusades on the threshold of the Renaissance, to the colonial wars of the

---

[1] I have in mind writings by Arnaldo Cipolla (*L'Imperatrice d'Etiopia*, 1922) and Guido Milanesi (*La sperduta di Allah*, 1927) and films like *Cabiria* with Maciste as the "noble savage."
[2] Toni Morrison coins this term in *Playing in the Dark: Whiteness and the Literary Imagination* (New York: Vintage Books, 1992).

Fascist regime. The current renewed contact between Africans and Italians, with the flow of African migrants moving into the Italian peninsula, presents a new set of issues, problems, and opportunities that have important implications not only for the future of Italian society but for intercultural and interracial relations throughout the world. (Sante Matteo, Program notes for Africa Italy Symposium)

Much attention has been given in recent years to the subject of African-Italian relations in the news media as well as in Italian cultural studies in the United States and Italy. Books, such as *Io, Venitore di elefanti* by Pap Khouma (Milano: Garzanti, 1990), and films, such as *Strangers Among Us* (Davide del Boca, 1989), *Waalo fendo* (Mohamed Soudani, 1997), and Massimo Guglielmi's *Homebound* (1997) trace the African immigrants' encounters with the native population on the peninsula, while allowing the Africans to use their own voices and language to describe their personal experiences. This presents a new era in Italy's relationship with the African continent where previously Africans were spoken for and depicted stereotypically as they were in English, French, and other European colonial representations.

Italian writers referred to Africa in nineteenth-century Italian travelogues as a location of exoticism, and the concept of an underdeveloped, unenlightened Africa (the physically and intellectually "dark" continent) was used by the positivist anthropologist Cesare Lombroso in 1871 (*L'uomo bianco e l'uomo di colore: letture sull'origine e la varietà delle razze umane*) to justify the inferiority of Africans to the Europeans. Italian historians of the late nineteenth century had defined the southern portion of the newly united Italy as "Africanized" in its relationship to the North since the rise of the "southern question" in 1859, supposedly as a result of the rampant banditry and criminality prevalent in the region.[3] The

---

[3]Southern Italian immigrants to the US were negatively represented during their initial immigration and the subsequent decades of acclimation due in part to the propagation of such "Africanization." They were often referred to as "swarthy" to denote their darker skin. The opinions of Anglo-Saxon immigrants were twofold: Italy had a reputation as a seat of culture in art and music, but this image was marred by the criminality of its inhabitants — the people of the North were more influenced by the white "culture" of Europe while the southern Italians, who had a closer proximity to Africa and generally were of a darker skin color, were more associated with organized crime. Many of these

view of Italian superiority in relation to the African continent continued its influence in the peninsula as Italy formed its national identity immediately following the Unification and into the twentieth century. Southern Italians were referred to as *"marrocchini"* [Moroccans] during the Italian economic and industrial boom of the 1950s and were allied with Africa in the rhetoric of the 1990's Lega Nord leader, Umberto Bossi (Forgacs and Lumley 162). Although Italy's history of colonialization was not as extensive as that of other European nations, the rhetoric of colonialization began immediately following the Risorgimento. Italy's history of colonial enterprise in Africa since the late nineteenth century has contributed greatly to past and present Italian-African relations and the formation of misconceptions and stereotypes about people of African descent. The historical treatment of Africa and people of African descent has also served in Italy's own self-definition. Africa and its people have become a measure of comparison for the Italians to view themselves as more civilized and closer to the northern European standard; if Africa is portrayed as backward and barbaric, then the people of Italy are justified in colonizing, educating, and civilizing it:

> There is still much ill-gotten gain to reap from rationalizing power grabs and clutches with inferences of inferiority and the ranking of differences. There is still much national solace in continuing dreams of democratic egalitarianism available by hiding class conflict, rage, and impotence in figurations of race. And there is quite a lot of juice to be extracted from plummy reminiscences of "individualism" and "freedom" if the tree upon which such fruit hangs is a black population forced to serve as freedom's polar opposite: individualism is foregrounded (and believed in) when its background is stereotypified, enforced dependency. Freedom (to move, to earn, to learn, to be allied

---

people of Anglo-Saxon descent could not reconcile the Italy about which they read and saw romantically depicted with the deplorable behavior of its apparently "barbaric" citizens: "The dichotomous picture of how Americans beheld Italians is not new, for it was also true of the pre-1880 period. During that era Americans could read popular accounts about Italy in which they quickly learned that it was a land of beautiful scenery, ancient ruins, and old churches. They also learned, however, that it was a land of ragged beggars, voracious *banditi*, and violent feuds. Thus, Italians were pictured as a people whose distinguished achievements in the arts went along with an unsound character" (Salvatore LaGumina, *WOP!* [San Francisco: Straight Arrow Books, 1973] 14).

with a powerful center, to narrate the world) can be relished more deeply in a cheek-by-jowl existence with the bound and unfree, the economically oppressed, the marginalized, the silenced. The ideological dependence on racialism is intact and, like its metaphysical existence, offers in historical, political, and literary discourse a safe route into meditations on morality and ethics; a way of examining the mind-body dichotomy; a way of thinking about justice; a way of contemplating the modern world. (Morrison 64)

From 1881 to 1915 about five million and a half Italians fled the poverty of southern Italy, the majority settling in the United States. The large numbers of Italians leaving the continent to find prosperity in the Americas caused great concern in the Italian government, and a campaign in Africa became a means to encourage national feeling while discouraging emigration and providing more land and resources to the peninsula. The focus on Africa as the object of Italian expansion inspired the creation of African stereotypes similar to those found in French and British cinema.[4] In light of the extensive historical interaction between Italy and Africa, further study of this relationship is necessary to understand the past and present place of Africa in the Italian consciousness and how it has become an intrinsic part of Italian culture.

The last decades of the nineteenth century saw the meeting of technological innovation and political change in Italy. After the completion of Italian unification in 1870, much still needed to be done to create a feeling of national identity between the different regions of the peninsula. In 1885 Italy occupied the port city of Massawa on the Red Sea coast and pressed inland without success. Italy's attempts were again thwarted two years later with defeats in Eritrea and Somalia. This entire period of colonial enterprise culminated in the embarrassing Italian defeat at Adua in 1896. This period inaugurated the first Italian colonial move on Africa, and its failure would not soon be forgotten. Although

---

[4]See Kenneth M. Cameron, *Africa on Film: Beyond Black and White* (New York: Continuum, 1994); Alfred E. Opubar and Adebayo Ogunbi, "Ooga Booga: The African Image in American Films," *Other Voices, Other Views: An International Collection of Essays from the Bicentennial* (Westport, CT: Greenwood, 1978); and Dina Sherzer, ed., *Cinema, Colonialism, Postcolonialism: Perspectives from the French and Francophone World* (Austin, TX: U of Texas P, 1996).

this defeat curtailed the Italian colonial enterprise for the time being, Italy had gotten its first taste of ruling others instead of being the pawn of foreign powers as it had been for so many centuries.

During this same time, the photographic innovation of Thomas Edison's kinescope led to the invention of a similar product patented by the French brothers Auguste and Louis Lumière in 1895 and then to the Italian patent granted to Filoteo Alberini also in 1895. These inventions, in turn, made possible the development of a medium that continues to influence the modern world — the motion picture. In the early years of its development, Italy, a leader in cinematic production until the 1920s, created documentaries, many of which were filmed in the Italian-occupied territories of the Eritrean coast.

Italy's Second Colonial Attempt and Its Cinematic Representations, 1910-1920

The years 1911–12 saw the Italo-Turkish war in Libya, and two years later a full-length feature Italian film. Giovanni Pastrone's *Cabiria* (1914), the monumental Roman epic, gained widespread international acclaim. *Cabiria* features Maciste, a character created by writer Gabriele D'Annunzio and based on the concept of the "*superuomo*" [superman] prevalent in his writings. The Carthaginian slave of a Roman soldier who identifies more with the Roman characters than with his fellow Africans, Maciste remained an Italian cult hero until the 1930s. The Roman soldier was in love with Cabiria, a Roman girl kidnapped by the Africans to be sacrificed to their god, Moloch. Maciste helps save Cabiria from the "savage" Africans, thereby aligning himself with Rome/Italy. In its evocation of the myth of Rome, this film succeeded in entertaining its Italian viewers while emphasizing the importance of Italian nationalism.

Maciste, portrayed by Bartolomeo Pagano "painted" in dark makeup to simulate blackness, became a popular hero as a man of strength and action — the vision the Fascists would later encourage for its men. It is very interesting that an African character should become an important vehicle for transmitting Italian nationalism (Cameron 64), but this is also due to the establishment of Africa as the locus for the birth of Filippo Tommaso Marinetti's version of the superman contained in *Mafarka il futurista* (1910). Africa as a locus of rebirth for Italians who travel there will reach its apex in the literature and films of the 1930s when the Fascist movement more fully establishes the social characteristics of its ideal man. Mafarka, a light-skinned African in the midst of darker-skinned barbarians, represents the dynamism and heroism of the southern European. The Africans portrayed in *Cabiria* were represented as barbaric and uncivilized, worshipping idols and practicing human sacrifice. Only the African who links himself with the more civilized Romans is represented as a hero, with admirable qualities.

The 1920s saw the establishment of the Fascist Italian state, the election of Benito Mussolini as prime minister, and a renewed policy of aggression toward Africa. Libya was the focus of the many colonial films made in this decade. Two such films include *Maciste contro lo sceicco* (1925) and *Kiff tebbi* (1928), both directed by Mario Camerini. During this period, literature in which Africa is a major focus was inspired by travel reports and exotic accounts and gained increasing popularity. Guido Milanesi's novel *La sperduta di Allah* (1927) alludes to Africa as the origin of the Italian civilization, and Mario dei Gaslini's 1926 *Piccolo amore beduino*, portrays Africa as the ideal object of Italian colonial expansion. Mainly designed for younger male readers, these works contained several themes that continued to be found in the cinema of the 1920s and 1930s: travel to the primitive, virgin Africa as a voyage of rebirth and development of manhood, the civilization of Africa as an Italian missionary goal, and the liberation of the African people from barbarism. One of the most common narrative typologies goes as follows: the Italian male hero leaves Europe for Africa; he meets an indigenous woman, with whom he often falls in love; an Italian woman appears on the scene; and the hero returns to Italy where he experiences "mal d'Africa" (Pagliara). This early colonial literature promoted the growing idea that European "civilization" produced apathy and mental and physical laziness, but Africa was the perfect location for European men to reenergize physically and psychologically.

The Fascist African Campaigns: Two Images of Africa

Italy's campaigns in Africa in the 1930s culminated in the war against Ethiopia in 1935–36, which in turn ended in the Italian proclamation of the Empire on May 9, 1936. Mussolini's desire to create public consensus in order to justify the large amount of State funds being channeled into the colonial effort in Ethiopia required the Fascist regime to represent Italy's African campaign to the public in a positive light. Cinema proved to be a powerful force in this period, and Mussolini realized its potential for public influence early on in his administration through the propagation of ideology in newsreels and feature films. Film was the most popular form of entertainment, although only a small percentage of the films produced during the Fascist period could actually be called Fascist or propaganda films. Popular cinema functioned more as a source of diversion for the public than as a propagandistic tool (Bondanella 24). As an incentive for private studios to produce works commensurate with the regime's ideology, the government offered subsidies of up to 60 percent of production costs for scripts that had already been approved by the Ministry of Press and Propaganda.

One of the most famous of such subsidized films was Augusto Genina's *Lo squadrone bianco*. The focus of *Lo squadrone bianco*, released in 1936, may appear at first sight to be the failed love affair between the protagonist and the object of his affection, but, as its conclusion reveals, this film centers around the protagonist's development into the Fascist ideal of the "new man" as previously seen in colonial literature of the 1920s and 1930s. Partially filmed in the Libyan desert, *Lo squadrone bianco* demonstrates the coming of age of an Italian male on the African continent in the service of Italian imperialism. The film begins with an establishing shot featuring the protagonist Marco Ludovici's vehicle speeding along a deserted road accompanied by music reminiscent of chase scenes, with trees passing quickly on either side. Ludovici arrives home the day before he begins his service as a lieutenant for the Italian forces in Africa. He telephones Cristiana, speaking extremely fast and demonstrating impatience, and insists upon seeing her that night. Despite her refusal, Marco arrives at the static, bourgeois setting of Cristiana's apartment and attempts to make love to her by force. She toys with his affections and fends him off, but when she decides to give in moments later, Cristiana discovers that Marco has already left. The focus on Marco's speed and impatience exemplifies the love of motion and violent action made popular by the futurist movement in the first two decades of the twentieth century and that carried into the Fascist period. His desire for action and pending service in Africa establish Marco as a man with qualities valuable to the fascist regime: an energetic spirit and an active body. He lacks only a willingness to serve his country.

Demoralized by Cristiana's rejection of his advances, Marco arrives in Africa deflated and less active than at the beginning of the film. He salutes the captain upon his arrival without enthusiasm and mopes around the camp while off-duty, recollecting his past with Cristiana and attempting to write letters that he never completes. When the captain asks Marco whether he requested to serve in Africa out of a *"vera passione coloniale,"* to his dismay Marco says "no." It is as if his association with the bourgeois environment and Cristiana's manipulation has sapped his innate activism, but the African continent provides a suitable location for the rebirth of Marco's enthusiastic imperialist spirit. The scenes shot in the Libyan desert contrast in their solarity and openness with the cold interior of Cristiana's apartment. The desert heat represents a male sphere of creative activity, which contrasts with the staleness of the apartment and the frigidity of its female inhabitant.

The Fascist movement focused primarily on the position of young men in Italian society, emphasizing masculinity and activities that were considered appropriate for the "new man" that Fascism strove to create. Captain Santelia, who commands the troops at the outpost, represents an ideal fascist man "squarely rooted in the traditional values of renunciation, sacrifice, and service, values associated with Christian morality" (Landy 118) and contrasts with Marco who possesses instead a lackluster attitude toward serving the Empire. Santelia's tireless dedication is thrown into relief when he refuses to join a card game with fellow officers during a moment of repose. He prefers instead to check on his troops. Moreover, according to Marco's African attendant, the captain is a great leader who is as strong as iron (*"forte come ferro"*) and makes men tremble when they hear his name. He is the perfect specimen to head a squadron in the new colonies Italy had established. Throughout the film, Santelia's strength in command is accentuated by the deference shown to him by both the Africans troops and the Italian officers whom he supervises. He berates Marco for being a ladies' man and for not dedicating himself heart and soul to the Fascist struggle to expand the empire. It will take exposure to the African "elements" and participation in the colonial effort for Marco to realize his full potential as a "new man" in Fascist terms.

Stereotypical images of Africa are present throughout the film: men with turbans, a plethora of camels, and a powerful sun beating down on a great expanse of hot desert sand provide a stock view of the continent and create an appropriate atmosphere for Marco's conversion to a "new man." The theme of conversion, a component of Fascist colonial literature as well as cinema, often appears in the form of an Italian man who tires of the apathy and laziness created by the languor of European middle class "civilization" and finds instead that the primitivity and innocence perceived to be found on the African continent inspire a rebirth of his physical and mental activity.[5] In order for Marco to become a "new man," he must leave Italy and go through the "fire," that is the heat of the African desert, on a mission for his country. In fact, Marco does not completely fall into line with the Fascist conception of the "new man" until, while he recovers from a fever, he symbolically lays to rest the bourgeois aspirations of his old persona by symbolically burying the cigarette case given to him by Cristiana. According to film critic Marcia Landy, "disguises, name changes, symbolic death and rebirth, or actual death and apotheosis are common features of the narrative of conversion" (141). At the end of the film, Cristiana, who has come to Africa in the hope of reconciling their relationship, greets Marco upon his return from the field and notices that he has changed. Marco replies that he buried his old self in the desert with Captain Santelia who died honorably in battle and that he will remain in Africa "con la terra che amavo così tanto" [with the land I loved so much] and continue to help the colonial effort. By rejecting Cristiana and her stifling bourgeois environment in exchange for an active life in the service of the State, it is as if Marco has been reborn with the renewed zeal for the colonial struggle characteristic of his dead captain.

Genina represents the Africans in *Lo squadrone bianco* as subservient and submissive people who display an eagerness to please the Italian

---

[5]For more on fascist colonial literature, see Giovanna Tomasello, *La letteratura coloniale italiana dalle avanguardie al fascismo* (Palermo: Sellerio, 1984) and Maria Pagliara, "Il romanzo coloniale," *I bestseller del ventennio: Il regime e il libro di massa* (Rome: Editore Riuniti, 1991) 365–457.

officers whom they serve. Ironically, the film's title is *The White Squadron* though the squadron is composed of mostly Africans. The Africans are dutiful followers of the Italians, even fighting against other Africans in the name of Italy, and their tacit acceptance of Italian rule, indeed complicity in it, is demonstrated in their solemn salute to the Italian flag as if it were their own. Colonial newsreels produced by the LUCE studios were often staged for the benefit of the public and occasionally featured such feigned shows of support for the regime by Libyans and Ethiopians "consisting of a small group of natives giving the Fascist salute and cheering in front of the camera" (Mancini 138). In *Lo squadrone bianco* there seems to be no question in the native's minds as to whether the Italians have the right to rule in Africa. The relationship between the inhabitants and the colonialists is friendly and occasionally inspires cultural exchange; one example appears when Marco's designated African manservant makes a talisman to help the lieutenant recover from his fever in the desert. This scene also stresses the Africans' primitive nature. In contrast, the Italians believe they have made important cultural contributions to the Africans' standard of living by, among other things, introducing them to the latest wartime technology: airplane flight. A search plane, sent on a reconnaissance mission to locate the lost squadron, flies over the outpost while Italian guests, including Cristiana, await indoors and socialize with the officers. A man makes a toast saying, "Il deserto, signori miei, non esiste più; la civiltà l'ha ucciso" [The desert, ladies and gentlemen, does not exist anymore; civilization has killed it"]. The Italians have arrived, he implies, bringing in their wake peace, well-being, and technological advancement to a backward people. This beneficent, paternalistic attitude was followed by a more belligerent one as Italy struggled to maintain supremacy in its African colonies.

Historical dramas constituted the largest proportion of the cinematic works produced during the Fascist era (Bondanella 14) and provided excellent opportunities to create metaphors for the Fascist regime. The Second Punic War is a "thinly veiled allegory" (Landy 194) for the Fascist campaign in Ethiopia in Carmine Gallone's 1937 film, *Scipione l'Africano*. This large-scale production features crowd scenes and elaborate sets that hark back to Giovanni Pastrone's *Cabiria* not only in technique but also in subject matter. This is perhaps no coincidence as Pastrone's film was also released in a period of dynamic Italian colonialist expansion — three years after the war against Libya in 1911. As in *Cabiria*, the setting for *Scipione l'Africano* was intended to inspire nostalgia for the ancient empire of Italy's glorious Roman past while simultaneously mustering the public's patriotic feeling in favor of Mussolini's imperialist policies in Africa, represented by Carthage in the film.

Gallone's film presents a more racially antagonistic view of Africa than *Lo squadrone bianco*. As the opening title recounts, in 218 BC, Hannibal invaded Italy over the Alps and the only way to stop him, according to Scipio, was to invade Africa. Carthage is designated "enemy territory" that merits repression by the Romans. This move is justified by portraying the Carthaginians as cruel and murderous with dangerous, primitive beliefs. In a scene reminiscent of *Cabiria*, Hannibal, who has taken a Roman woman prisoner, attempts to shake her courage with threats of sacrifice to his god, Moloch. Those who have seen *Cabiria* will remember the enormous and terrifying statue of Moloch to whom the Carthaginians sacrificed children. These depictions were designed to distance Italian viewers from any sympathy toward Africans during the colonial enterprise. The overall effect of the representations in *Scipione l'Africano* "is to highlight the brutality of the enemy and thus portray the Roman [and therefore Italian] war effort as a defensive gesture against barbarians who would violate innocent women and children" (Landy 196). In contrast to *Lo squadrone bianco*, where the Africans salute and smile at them and exchange friendly banter with some of the Italian officers, *Scipione l'Africano* contains no scenes in which Italians mingle peacefully with Africans. In general, the film characterizes the Carthaginians as disorganized barbarians with long hair while the Romans are clean-cut and march in organized columns. Though Scipio does express admiration for Hannibal as a powerful leader in battle, this African gains respect from the Romans due solely to his past victories against them. The battle scene pits black against white as each army advances, Scipio and his troops on white horses and Hannibal and his contingent on black steeds. This color coding reduces the Italy-Africa relationship to a simplistic moral question of "good" and "evil."

Post-WWII and Neorealist Film

During World War II, Black American soldiers arrived in Europe for the first time disembarking in Italy, which gave many Italians their first direct personal contact with Blacks. Apart from Italian soldiers serving in the African colonies, the only contact the majority of Italians had with Blacks prior to this period and for many decades following it was on the screen. Jazz music had arrived on the continent with the Harlem Renaissance of the 1920s but Italians did not connect the people of its origin with the music and had much to learn about this subset of American culture.

In 1946, Rossellini released *Paisà*, whose episodic form, divided into six segments, focuses on Italy during the period of Liberation by the Allies beginning in 1943 until the final German defeat in April of 1945. All of the episodes in *Paisà* involve personal encounters between Italians and the Americans, including soldiers, chaplains, and medical personnel, who come as part of the Liberation. The initial segment treats the first encounter of a Sicilian town with American soldiers, ending in tragedy for an Italian girl and a hapless American soldier named Joe; the second, which takes place in Naples, deals with the interaction between a Neapolitan street urchin and an African-American MP, also called Joe by the boy. The Roman and Florentine episodes are stories of failed love affairs, due to the implied American corruption of Italians in one instance and a partisan captain's death in the other; the episode in the Franciscan monastery confronts American and Italian intellectual differences, in particular regarding Roman Catholicism and its American counterpart. The episode that ends the film portrays the last stand of a group of American soldiers and Italian partisans against the retreating German forces in the Po valley.

By creating two characters named Joe and placing them in the first two episodes, Rossellini reveals an awareness of two Americas in the 1940s, one Black and the other white, and the vast differences between them. In the first segment, a white soldier introduces himself as "Joe from Jersey" to Carmela, an Italian girl who agrees to guide the Americans through a minefield. He has all the attributes of "Americanness": His name is "Joe"; he drinks milk and is involved in the milk industry; he uses a Zippo cigarette lighter; he shows Carmela pictures of his family back in the States. Joe from Jersey represented what America embodied for most Italians. The late 1930s and 1940s brought an enormous influx of American films into the peninsula, and the arrival of the American military in Italy marked the first encounter with Americans outside of the silver screen for the overwhelming majority of Italians, though migrant workers and visitors to American relatives already had first-hand impressions. American cinema, more than any other medium, conveyed to Italians an idea of the United States. Yet Joe is identified with rural New Jersey, which was familiar to Italian immigrants who arrived in New York. He describes his family in minute detail, creating a cheerful, prosperous picture of life in America.

In the segment immediately following this one, however, the audience is presented with another "Joe," an African-American. Although direct Italian encounters with African Americans were still more rare than with white Americans, at the time the film *Paisà* was made, Italians were still more likely to personally encounter Black Americans than Africans. Any previous knowledge on the part of Italians of African Americans came overwhelmingly from films eagerly received by the Italian public in which the American Blacks were portrayed in stereotypical roles or as displaying stereotypical behavior.[6] Sitting atop a pile of rubble that was once a house, "Joe" rambles on in a drunken stupor to the young street urchin Pasquale. In a monologue possibly improvised by the actor himself, "Joe" imagines a homecoming where he figures as a hero and receives honors like the ticker-tape parade and a dinner at the famed restaurant, the Waldorf-Astoria. As he becomes sober, "Joe" remembers that such accolades and celebrations will most likely *not* be open to the returning Black soldiers. Thus, Rossellini's use of the name "Joe" creates a relationship between the white and Black characters that necessarily emphasizes their different roles and different treatment in American society. They are both identified with America as the name

---

[6]Later, the US government would make some attempts to counteract the legacy of racism against Blacks in American film, albeit with limited success. For an interesting account of American liberals in US studios attempts to change racially biased representations of African Americans in American films, see Thomas Cripps, "*Casablanca, Tennessee Johnson* and *The Negro Soldier* — Hollywood Liberals and World War II," *Feature Films as History*, ed. K. R. M. Short (Knoxville: U of Tennessee P, 1981).

"Joe" confirms, they both risk their lives in the war, but they do not equally share in the bounty promised by the United States.

In the case of *Paisà*, Roberto Rossellini dedicated the entire second segment of the film to the interaction between a Black soldier with the American Liberation forces and a poor Neapolitan street urchin. The film has been analyzed from the point of view of increased communication and humanity between Italians and the American Liberation forces, but the segment with "Joe" has rarely been spoken of from the perspective of a person of color. Rossellini was present in Naples in 1943 during this time and witnessed the aftermath of the seaport city's destruction and the arrival of American soldiers, including the segregated Blacks. In the film, the Black MP makes specific references to the differences in treatment between white Americans and Black Americans at the time and the inequities of a racially divided American society. There are references to Africans as slaves or chattel. When "Joe" takes the side of the Moor against the Christian Orlando in the puppet show scene, Rossellini sets up a parallel between how Black Americans were treated by whites and how Italians treated Africans during the colonial campaigns. In extant critical analyses of this film, the character of "Joe," the African-American soldier, is examined only superficially, completely erasing the color crucial to driving Rossellini's point home. If "Joe" is simply mentioned as "a Negro soldier," the critic has failed to elaborate on the deeper meaning of including a Black American soldier in an Italian film. Other critics, while often referring to "Joe" as Black or "Negro" do not connect his color directly with Rossellini's commentary on the American and Italian societies during the 1940s.

Dots M. Johnson, the actor who plays the character of the African-American "Joe," established the role of Black Americans in Italian postwar cinema and although these roles reflected stereotypes primarily from American films (the loud-talking, drunken musician being one), at least they did not represent them with the same "colonized" perspective that Africans were shown in Fascist film of the previous years. Not only does Rossellini comment on the race divisions in American society of the 1940s, he also challenges the negative Italian perceptions of Africans propagated by Fascism. This film signifies a turning point in the representation of Blacks in Italian cinema. These images are shown with compassion and sympathy; they still possess some stereotypical characteristics, but they are no longer simply the dutiful servants of the Italian colonists as portrayed in *Lo squadrone bianco* or the enemy Africans in *Scipione L'Africano*.

In addition, Rossellini comments on the American involvement in Italy's destruction and in the devastation of its citizens' lives during the Liberation with Joe's realization that Pasquale's poverty mirrors his own. During the monologue, "Joe" says, "Goin' home! Goin' home? I don't want to go home. My house is an old shack with tin cans at the doors!" Later, he recognizes Pasquale as the boy who had stolen his shoes. He takes Pasquale home to retrieve them and discovers that the youth lives in a shanty town, built in the protection of a cave, together with other Neapolitan families. The children of the town cheer at the soldier's arrival, giving "Joe" the "homecoming" he seeks, but only because he represents to them the Italian perception of America's abundance. He asks Pasquale to call his parents, but when the boy explains that his home was destroyed by the bombing and his parents are dead, "Joe" understands that Pasquale lives in the cave. The GI, moved by such abject conditions, drops his shoes and leaves. He comprehends that, because he is a part of the American forces, he has helped subject Pasquale to the same level of poverty in which he lives as an oppressed African American. He sees his own living conditions back in the US reflected in the shanty town and realizes that he has taken part in creating a society of impoverished people. Film critic Peter Bondanella analyzes *Paisà*'s structure as a gradual progression toward a greater understanding between the two cultures, and according to him, "Joe has taken the first step, that of understanding, toward becoming Pasquale's *paisà*" (46). More specifically, Rossellini uses the American soldier's "blackness" as a means to make a comparison between oppression of African Americans in the US and Italian victims of World War II and America's "Liberation."

In their analysis of the appearance of Blacks in Italian films, critics often overlook or avoid completely any reference to a character's race or the importance of the character's race in the film's plot. One must wonder why an Italian director in the 1940s, for example, would dedicate an entire segment of a film to a story about a Black American soldier that then influenced other characterizations of Black Americans in Italian film. Because the histories of Italy and Africa are so intrinsically linked, writers and filmmakers cannot help but be influenced by the stereotypes and conceptions held by the culture in which they live. Whether the individual intent is to search for the exotic, recycle stereotypes, or make a statement about negative conceptions of race both in Italy and America, critics need to examine more closely how Black characters, both African and African American, are portrayed, and how they reflect the culture at large. Because the images that the Italians saw most frequently were based on stereotypes and portrayals of Blacks as an inferior race, these views served as the "realistic" portrayal Italian audiences expected.

Claudio Camerini, in examining the film *Senza pietà*, notes that,

> La presenza dell'americano nella parte del negro Jerry è, nell'economia del film, il veicolo di due referenti: uno realistico (grazie all'analogia dei tratti caratterizzanti l'*attore* e il *ruolo*) e uno cinematografico (per la partecipazione al film *Tombolo paradiso nero* realizzato da Giorgio Ferroni l'anno prima). (28)

> [The presence of the Black American in the part of Jerry is, in the economy of the film, the vehicle of two referents: one realistic (thanks to the analogy of the traits which characterize the *actor* and the *role*) and one cinematographic (for his participation in the film *Tombolo paradiso nero* made by Giorgio Ferroni the year before). (translation mine)]

The actor John Kitzmiller is indeed a former African-American army officer who portrays an African-American army officer in the film, but the audience has no way of knowing the actor's original occupation. How, then, does Kitzmiller's presence further the audience's sense of realism? Why would an Italian audience, the vast majority of whom never encountered any other Americans personally, let alone a Black American, consider his presence realistic? What makes such a statement even possible? What perceptions of Black Americans were created by Kitzmiller's representations or other actors' representations before him? It is not necessary to discuss theories of realism at this point, but it suffices to say that cinema itself has the effect of making the events on the screen appear realistic. Playing on the term *"neorealismo rosa,"* Tatti Sanguineti's article, "Neorealismo nero: John Kitzmiller" discusses the actor's short-lived but popular career in Italian film and provides some possible responses to the previous questions. Described as the "palo americano della banda italiana del neorealismo" (Camerini 143; the american pole of the Italian band of neorealism), Kitzmiller appeared first in Luigi Zampa's 1946 *Vivere in pace* (first as an injured soldier then later as a drunken, trumpet-playing, boogie-woogie dancing Black American army officer), then in Giorgio Ferroni's 1947 *Tombolo paradiso nero* (where he played a Black army officer), followed by *Senza pietà* (when he portrayed a cognac-drinking, boogie-woogie dancing Black American officer), and a few years later in Federico Fellini and Lattuada's 1951 production of *Luci del varietà*, where Kitzmiller played a trumpet-player. The similarity of these roles, combined with stereotyped images of American Blacks as singers, dancers, and musicians, well-known to Italian audiences from American films exported to Italy (Noble), made Kitzmiller's representations "familiar" and therefore more realistic in the view of an Italian public. Furthermore, the actor owes his own "familiarity" to his predecessor Dots M. Johnson (there is a similarity in both actors' physical traits) who portrayed the Black American MP in Rossellini's *Paisà*. Johnson came to Italy as the result of an American talent search by Rod Geiger who claimed that he was a new American star, better than Paul Robeson (Faldini and Fofi 108). Johnson's character was also drunk in *Paisà*, a stereotype that later became a common characteristic of Kitzmiller's characters. In fact, Zampa, searched for Johnson to play the role of Jonny in *Vivere in pace*, but he could not be found and was presumed to have returned to the US. Fortunately, the Italians had access to other African Americans who remained in Italy with the US forces still stationed there in the years after the Liberation and located Kitzmiller among them.

The 1960s to the Present

In examining other films produced after World War II, the viewer sees many similar portrayals of African-American characters. Federico Fellini, for example, utilizes various nightclub scenes in his films. The performers in these nightclubs are most often African-American — jazz musicians, dancers, roller skaters. Portrayals such as these, although lacking derogatory overtones, still perpetuate Italian stereotypes of people of African descent. If Black characters appear predominantly in films to serve some need or desire of the Italians — colonization of African land, reinforcement of Italian masculinity, entertainment for the Italian people — then they never can achieve equal status in the eyes of the viewers. People of African descent in some way continue to represent an opposite perspective, that which is farthest from the northern European ideal. A close study of Italian film from its beginning to the present reveals how the many attitudes toward Africa in the Italian mind have become a vital part of Italian culture and history.

Bibliography
General Sources on Italian Cinema
Antonioni, Michelangelo. *The Architecture of Vision: Writings and Interviews on Cinema*. Venezia: Marsilio Editore, 1994.
Aristarco, Guido. *Antologia di cinema nuovo 1952-1958: dalla critica cinematografica alla dialettica culturale*. Rimini: Guaraldi Editore, 1975.
Arrowsmith, William. *Antonioni: The Poet of Images*. New York: Oxford UP, 1995.
Bondanella, Peter. *Italian Cinema: From Neorealism to the Present*. New York: Continuum, 1990.
Brunetta, Gian Piero. *Storia del cinema italiano*. Roma: Riuniti, 1993. 4 vols.
Burke, Frank. *Federico Fellini:* Variety Lights *to* La dolce vita. Boston: Twain, 1984.
Camerini, Claudio. *Alberto Lattuada*. Firenze: Il Castoro Cinema, 1981.
Dalle Vacche, Angela. *The Body in the Mirror: Shapes of History in Italian Cinema*. Princeton, NJ: Princeton UP, 1992.
Darretta, John. *Vittorio De Sica: A Guide to References and Resources*. Boston, MA: Hall, 1983.
Faldini, Franca, and Goffredo Fofi, eds. *L'Avventurosa storia del cinema italiano: raccontata dai suoi protagonisti, 1935–1959*. Milano: Feltrinelli, 1979.
Fellini, Federico. *Fellini on Fellini*. Delacorte Press, 1974.
Leprohon, Pierre. *The Italian Cinema*. Trans. from the French by Roger Greaves and Oliver Stallybrass. New York: Praeger, 1972.
Lizzani, Carlo. *Il cinema italiano dalle origini agli anni ottanta*. Roma: Riuniti Editore, 1992.
Miccichè, Lino. *Il cinema italiano degli anni '60*. Venezia: Marsilio Editore, 1976.
Mida, M., and L. Quaglietti. *Dai telefoni bianchi al neoralismo*. Roma: Laterza (Biblioteca di Cultura Moderna), 1980.
Nowell-Smith, Geoffrey (with James Hay and Gianni Volpi). *The Companion to Italian Cinema*. London: British Film Institute, 1996.
Rohdie, Sam. *Antonioni*. London: BFI, 1990.
Rossellini, Roberto. *The War Trilogy:* Open City, Paisan, Germany — Year Zero. Trans. Judith Green. New York: Grossman, 1973.

Sitney, P. Adams. *Vital Crises in Italian Cinema: Iconography, Stilistics, Politics.* Austin, TX: U of Texas P, 1995.

Sorlin, Pierre. *Italian National Cinema: 1896–1996.* New York: Routledge, 1996.

Vermilye, Jerry. *Great Italian Films.* New York: Citadel, 1994.

Witcombe, R. T. *The New Italian Cinema: Studies in Dance and Despair.* London: Secker & Warburg, 1982.

Sources on Italian Fascist Cinema

Gili, Jean A. *L'Italie de Mussolini et son cinéma.* Paris: Veyrier, 1985.

Landy, Marcia. *Fascism in Film: The Italian Commercial Cinema 1931–1943.* Princeton, NJ: Princeton UP, 1986.

Mancini, Elaine. *Struggles of the Italian Film Industry during Fascism, 1930–1935.* Ann Arbor, MI: UMI Research P, 1985.

Zagarrio, Vito. "Ideology Elsewhere: Contradictory Models of Italian Fascist Cinema." *Resisting Images: Essays on Cinema and History.* Ed. Robert Sklar and Charles Musser. Philadelphia: Temple UP, 1990.

Sources on Italian Neorealist Cinema

Aristarco, Guido. *Neoralismo e nuova critica cinematografica: cinematografia e vita nazionale negli anni quaranta e cinquanta tra rotture e tradizioni.* Rimini: Guaraldi Editore, 1980.

Brunette, Peter. *Roberto Rossellini.* New York: Oxford UP, 1987.

Farassino, Alberto, ed. *Neorealismo: cinema italiano 1945–1949.* Torino: E.D.T. (Edizioni di Torino), 1989.

Marcus, Millicent. *Italian Film in the Light of Neorealism.* Princeton, NJ: Princeton UP, 1986.

Overbey, David. *Springtime in Italy: A Reader on Neorealism.* London: Talisman Books, 1978.

Sources on African Images in International Cinema

Cameron, Kenneth M. *Africa on Film: Beyond Black and White.* New York: Continuum, 1994.

Opubar, Alfred E., and Adebayo Ogunbi. "Ooga Booga: The African Image in American Films." *Other Voices, Other Views: An International Collection of Essays from the Bicentennial.* Westport, CT: Greenwood, 1978.

Sherzer, Dina, ed. *Cinema, Colonialism, Postcolonialism: Perspectives from the French and Francophone World.* Austin, TX: U of Texas P, 1996.

Sources on African-American Images in US Cinema

Ashton, Charlotte Ruby. *The Changing Image of Blacks in American Film: 1944–1973.* Ann Arbor, MI: University Microfilms International, 1981.

Cripps, Thomas. *Slow Fade to Black: The Negro in American Film, 1900–1942.* New York: Oxford UP, 1993.

___. "*Casablanca, Tennessee Johnson* and *The Negro Soldier* — Hollywood Liberals and World War II." *Feature Films as History.* Ed. K. R. M. Short. Knoxville: U of Tennessee P, 1981.

Guerrero, Ed. *Framing Blackness: The African American Image in Film.* Philadelphia: Temple UP, 1993.

Jones, G. William. *Black Cinema Treasures, Lost and Found.* Denton, TX: U of North Texas, 1991.

Noble, Peter. *The Negro in Films.* Port Washington, NY: Kennikat, 1969.

Sampson, Henry T. *Blacks in Black and White: A Source Book on Black Films.* Metuchen, NJ: Scarecrow, 1977.

Smith, Valerie, ed. *Representing Blackness: Issues in Film in Video.* New Brunswick, NJ: Rutgers UP, 1997.

Sources on Africa in Italian Literature

De Donato, Gigliola, and Vanna Gazzola Stacchini, eds. *I bestseller del ventennio: il regime e il libro di massa.* Rome: Editore Riuniti, 1991.

Licari, Anita, Roberta Maccagnani, and Lina Zecchi. *Letteratura, esotismo, colonialismo.* Bologna: Cappelli, 1978.

Piccinato, Stefania. "La letteratura afro-americana in Italia." *Studi Americani* 17 (1971): 473–505.

Tomasello, Giovanna. *La letteratura coloniale italiana dalle avanguardie al fascismo.* Palermo: Sellerio, 1984.

Other Sources

Buchanan, A. Russell. *Black Americans in World War II.* Santa Barbara, CA: American Bibliographical Center — Clio Books, 1977.

Davis, Lenwood G. *A Paul Robeson Research Guide: A Selected Annotated Bibliography.* Westport, CT: Greenwood, 1982.

Del Boca, Angelo. *Gli africani in Africa orientale: Dall'unità alla marcia su Roma.* Roma: Editore Laterza, 1976.

Duggan, Christopher. *A Concise History of Italy.* New York: Cambridge UP, 1994.

Fabre, Michel. *From Harlem to Paris: Black American Writers in France, 1840–1980.* Urbana: U of Illinois P, 1991.

Forgacs, David, and Robert Lumley. *Italian Cultural Studies: An Introduction.* New York: Oxford UP, 1996.

Gordon, Lewis R. *Bad Faith and Antiblack Racism.* Atlantic Highlands, NJ: Humanities, 1995.

___, ed. *Existence in Black: An Anthology of Black Existential Philosophy.* New York: Routledge, 1997.

___. *Her Majesty's Other Children: Sketches of Racism from a Neocolonial Age.* New York: Rowman & Littlefield, 1997.

Hargrove, Hondon B. *Buffalo Soldiers in Italy: Black Americans in World War II.* Jefferson, NC: McFarland, 1985.

Kros, Jack. *War in Italy: With the South Africans from Taranto to the Alps*. Cape Town, S. Africa: Ashanti (division of Ashanti International Films), 1992.

LaGumina, Salvatore J. *WOP: A Documentary History of Anti-Italian Discrimination in the United States*. San Francisco: Straight Arrow Books, 1973.

Marinetti, F. T. *Mafarka il futurista*. Milano: Sonzogno, 1920.

Morrison, Toni. *Playing in the Dark: Whiteness and the Literary Imagination*. New York: Vintage Books, 1992.

Osur, Alan M. *Blacks in the Army Air Forces During World War II: The Problem of Race Relations*. Washington, DC: US Government Printing Office, 1977.

Pinkus, Karen. *Bodily Regimes: Italian Advertising under Fascism*. Minneapolis, MN: U of Minnesota P, 1995.

Quaglietti, Lorenzo. *Ecco i nostri: L'invasione del cinema americano in Italia*. Torino: Nuovo ERI (Centro Sperimentale di Cinematografia), 1991.

Robertson, Esmonde M. *Mussolini as Empire-Builder: Europe and Africa, 1932–36*. New York: St. Martin's P, 1977.

Shindler, Colin. *Hollywood Goes to War: 1939–1952*. Boston, MA: Routledge & Kegan Paul, 1979.

Sklar, Robert, and Charles Musser, eds. *Resisting Images: Essays on Cinema and History*. Philadelphia, PA: Temple UP, 1990.

Sorlin, Pierre. *The Film in History: Restaging the Past*. Totowa, NJ: Barnes and Noble Books, 1980.

Wynn, Neil A. *The Afro-American and the Second World War*. New York: Holmes & Meier, 1976.

Zavattini, Cesare. *Totò il buono*. Milano: Bompiani, 1943.

Filmography

Alessandrini, Goffredo. *Luciano Serra pilota*. Aquila, 1937.

___. *Abuna Messias*. REF, 1939.

Antonioni, Michelangelo. *La Notte*. Emmanuele Cassuto-Nepi Film-Sofitedip.-Silver Film, 1961.

___. *L'Eclisse*. Interopa-Cineriz-Paris Film, 1962.

___. *Zabriskie Point*. MGM, 1970.

___. *The Passenger*. 1975.

Brignone, Guido. *Sotto la croce del Sud*. Mediterranea, 1938.

Calzavara. *Piccoli naufraghi*. 1939.

Camerini, Mario. *Maciste contro lo sceicco*. Fert Film, 1926.

___. *Kiff tebbi*. Adia, 1928.

___. *Il grande appello*. Artisti Associati, 1936.

D'Errico, Corrado. *Il cammino degli eroi*. Luce, 1937.

De Sica, Vittorio. *Miracolo a Milano*. Vittorio De Sica-ENIC, 1951.

___. *La Ciociara*. Carlo Ponti-Titanus, 1960.

Fellini, Federico. *Luci del varietà*. [Variety Lights (w/Lattuada).] Capitolium Film, 1951.

___. *Lo sciecco bianco*. The White Sheik, Pdc, 1952.

___. *Le notti di Cabiria*. Nights of Cabiria, Dino DiLaurentiis-Les Films Marceau, 1957.

___. *La dolce vita*. Riama Film-Gray Films- Pathé Cinéma, 1960.

___. *Otto e mezzo*. [8 1/2.] Cineriz, 1963.

___. *Giulietta degli spiriti*. [Juliet of the Spirits.] Federiz, 1965.

___. *Fellini Satyricon*. PEA, 1969.

___. *I Clowns*. RAI-Ortf, 1970.

___. *Roma*. Ultra Film — Les Productions Associés, 1971.

___. *Ginger e Fred*. PEA-Istituto Luce, 1985.

Ferreri, Marco. *Non toccare la donna bianca*. [Don't Touch the White Woman.] Mara Film-Les Films 66-Laer Production-PEA, 1974.

Ferroni, Giorgio. *Tombolo paradiso nero*. 1947.

Lattuada, Alberto. *Senza pietà*. [Without Pity.] LUX Film, 1948.

___. *Luci del varietà*. [Variety Lights (w/Fellini).] Capitolium Film, 1950.

Marcellini, Romolo. *Sentinelli di bronzo*. Fono Roma, 1938.

Pasolini, Pier Paolo. *Appunti per un'Orestiade africana*. [Notes on an African Oresteia.] 1970.

Pastrone, Giovanni (Piero Fosco). *Cabiria*. Itala Film, 1914.

Pontecorvo, Gillo. *La battaglia di Algeria*. [The Battle of Algiers.] 1966.

___. *Queimada!* [Burn!] PEA, 1969.

Rossellini, Roberto. *Paisà*. [Paisan.] Ofi-Foreign Film Production Inc.-Capitani Film, 1946.

Zampa, Luigi. *Vivere in Pace*. [To Live in Peace.] LUX Film, 1946.

BLACK SKIN

Maria Silvia Riccio
Cattolica, Italy

I went back to Italy this past summer. For me it was both a trip that I had anticipated for one year and yet a rather banal one but, at the same time it was for hundreds of Africans the first stop on an adventure and possibly, unfortunately, the last one.

The news concerning this "African invasion" welcomed me as soon as I got to Italy and, following the typical wanderings of an Italian on vacation in her own country, it kept piling up both on TV and in newspapers as the days went by. One day I was having coffee at the train station bar of my hometown, and despite the varied polyglot noise of the place, I heard a part of an interview on the regional news broadcast by Rai Tre Marche. The topic was immigration, of course, and the woman who was being interviewed, a young African who has been living in the Marche region for several years, whose name I did not catch, was commenting in a calm but rather severe tone, that the Europeans who decided to go and colonize Africa were not asked for a passport, nor was their stay restricted by any limited permanence permit. Naturally enough, the Europeans have no intention of returning the favor. Rather, they try to keep their borders very difficult to cross for those who, even if in peace, come not as tourists but with the intention of settling down, temporarily or permanently, and of looking for a job.

There was a lot to think about.

The nineteen hundreds are a dense century, maybe too dense. During the last almost hundred years, progress has accelerated history to a vertiginous speed that has changed the face of the world. Now it seems to be willing to mix colors from one pole to the other, and it is finding resistance. After one century, those who, willingly or not, had to accept the foreign rule imposed on their countries; those who had to learn traditions and languages that were not theirs; those who were dazzled by the wealth proposed and flaunted by their invaders, have decided to go and look for that very wealth in the lands where their governments resided in colonial times. Imperialism, though, understands only one direction: it is always ready to go and break through the boundaries of other countries in order to expand and pile up new riches, but it fights tooth and nail to defend its own, not to share its properties with anybody. I read of the notion of the "civilized mission," which the imperialists always use to justify their status as role models, and I find these verses by Rudyard Kipling:

> Take up the White Man's Burden —
> Send forth the best ye breed —
> Go bind your sons to exile
> To serve your captives' need,
> To wait in heavy harness,
> On fluttered folk and wild —
> Your new-caught, sullen peoples
> Half-devil and half-child.

Cynically enough I would like to reply that the so-called savages, half-devils and half-children, have learned their lesson and are trying to pay back their teachers in the same currency, but it is not so. The western world is living through times of — relative — peace and the Africans who try to gain our coasts come in peace: they come to look for the wealth that the invaders promised, then stingily refused to share. It would be good for them to get back what was extorted out of them. They look for a way to support their families and they are not afraid of working. These are the very premises that pushed Italians to Belgium, Germany, overseas, when Italy was not yet one of the major industrial powers in the world. Maybe a full stomach is directly proportional to a short memory.

Being in the center of the Mediterranean Sea, and as the theater of socio-political messes that slow down the law and leave its coasts almost unguarded, Italy is the best landing place for those who try to reach Europe, especially in a clandestine fashion. Therefore Europe becomes severe and asks Italy for severity, for organization in preparing to intercept, contain, and repatriate the *clandestini* [illegals]. Italy conforms;

grumbling, it sends reinforcements to the shores where illegal immigrants are most likely to land, it improvises reception centers, tries to do whatever it can, and complains.

Italy has its own problems, especially one of non-existent cohesion, as a nation that seems such only on paper; there is the so-called southern issue, *la questione meridionale*, dealing with that leaden burden, the South, Italy's internal Africa. Northern Italy has given up on colonization; rather, it preaches secession. And now the Africans are coming, together with the Albanians, with the Yugoslavs, with the Russians.

Italy is already an overcrowded country, nearly 190 inhabitants per square kilometer, with a high unemployment rate, an enormous number of college graduates, high school graduates, in short with too many bourgeois-wanna-bes who wanted to leave behind the rural past of their country and yet do not find any office desk at which to sit, any school desk from which to teach. The foreigner comes, he has got black skin, it is all his fault, he must be stopped. He takes away our jobs, our houses, our profits; it costs us money to care for him, to cure him, to educate him. He is ignorant, uneducated, savage, poor; he is not elegant, he does not buy anything, he does not reinvest, he does not produce wealth; he steals, he deals drugs, he rapes, he kills; he is already a criminal. It is right to take advantage of him, he does not understand anyway. And even if he did understand, we are still doing him a favor because at home he would not even have anything to eat.

The foreigner, non-European or *extracomunitario* as the politically correct term defines him, is the scapegoat. The politicians campaigning in the Italian provinces know it very well and they fan the flames: there are no jobs; too many immigrants; salespeople do not sell enough; there are too many unauthorized peddlers; taxes increase; there are too many immigrants who do not pay for them.

Fortunately the movies are still there. Sometimes with irony, sometimes with bitterness, but almost always with serious intents, they filter through the commonplaces and reveal them as such so that reality can show through.

During the time I spent in Italy this summer, which is a dead season for movies, the theaters were showing films that had been hits during the winter. One of these, *Tre uomini e una gamba* [Three Men and a Leg], filmed by and starring Aldo, Giovanni, and Giacomo, a comic multire-gional trio, comments on and exemplifies what I have been saying so far. The film is the story of a trip between Milan and Gallipoli, in the Apulia region. Aldo, Giovanni, and Giacomo work together in a hardware store, *Il paradiso della brugola,* owned by Aldo and Giovanni's father-in-law. The reason for the trip is the imminent wedding between Giacomo and the youngest of their boss's daughters. The three men also have to bring along a wooden sculpture representing a leg, which has suddenly and enormously increased in value because of the unexpected death of its sculptor. Needless to say, the leg will become the *deus ex-machina* in the movie and it will modify the path and the outcome of the whole trip. On the way, the group increases: a tourist on her way to Greece is given a ride to Brindisi after a collision with the men's car. Unavoidably, Gia-como falls in love with her.

Even though it is a comedy, the movie does not spare anybody. It mocks, with the favorite theme of the comic trio, the opposition between Northern and Southern Italy — even the composition of the group is representative of it, since Aldo is Sicilian and Giacomo and Giovanni are from Lombardy, and there are many allusions to the pseudo-racism of the Northern League; it ridicules the problems that are typical of the Italian system, first of all the bad health system; and there is plenty of irony about the Italian mentality. What interests us here though is a spe-cific episode during which, half way through their trip, the four travelers stop by a river. Giovanni walks down to the water in order to wash the leg that has just been territorially marked by a dog that they picked up. Once on the riverbend his cell phone rings and the habit — nearly the obsession — of answering it makes him lose his balance and conse-quently lose hold of the leg. Caught by the water, the leg flows away from Giovanni and soon disappears from sight. Panicking, Giovanni gives the alarm and he and his friends all jump in the car and follow the river in search of the leg. Discouraged and worried by the costly loss, they eventually catch sight of their sculpture on the seashore. A group of *extracomunitari* playing soccer is using it to mark one of the goalposts. In order to get the leg back they have to play and win a soccer match against the young Moroccans. Naturally enough, the match ends ten to three for the Moroccans, who walk away singing and dancing, proud of their victory and brandishing the leg as a trophy.

Aldo, Giacomo, and Giovanni cannot leave without the sculpture, though, and they decide to steal it from its new owners. During the night, their faces covered with masks representing the last three Italian Presidents and Nilde Iotti, they sneak into the building yard, which is the Africans' headquarters. They gain possession of the leg, but, on their way out they get stopped by the whole group of their antagonists, who were waiting outside in order to catch them red-handed. They end up at the police station where the *maresciallo* [marshal] of the *Carabinieri* [national police] severely rebukes them: he does not understand the reason for such a theft and exhorts them to thank the Moroccan engineer who not only does not intend to press charges, but also leaves them the sculpture that he actually finds rather ugly: "With thirty thousand lire a carpenter would make you a better looking one, maybe even with toe nails!"

This episode, which seems only to provoke laughter at first, has instead, in my opinion, a much deeper meaning. First of all, the masks of Scalfaro and Co. are an obvious reference to the saying *"governo ladro,"* or "thieving government," the traditional Italian saying that is both an insult and an accusation. They also seem to refer more specifically to the Italian government that stealthily tries to control the immigrant flow by taking away their possibility of finding the means of sustenance (represented by the leg) necessary for their survival. It is worthwhile to stop and consider the value of this sculpture as a meaningless item, both from an artistic and an objective point of view. Through the whole film everybody keeps hinting at the dullness of that piece of wood, often adding the remark that thirty thousand lire would be enough to have a carpenter do a better job. Nevertheless, together with Aldo, Giacomo, and Giovanni, the spectator knows that the market value of that very piece of wood has just been enormously increased by the death of the sculptor, therefore not because of an intrinsic quality of the work of art, but by virtue of purely commercial reasons attributed to it by social custom, by a calculation that has nothing to do with the mastery of the execution nor with the pseudo-philosophical thought that might have inspired it. The spectator knows that the value attributed to the leg is an arbitrary value.

In the very same way, somewhat misled by the movie, the spectator does not expect the Africans' status to be any different from what their black skin and their improvised sleeping quarters suggest. When the four friends are caught after they think they have escaped it, the spectator expects the Africans to lynch the thieves, but is surprised by their appeal to the police. He is surprised because he has to realize that appearance can be misleading; he has to face the fact that the equation, black skin = primitive = tribality, does not work. Like a Frenchman, a German, or a Belgian, an Italian meeting an African often does not see the person in front of him; rather, s/he perceives a mixture of prejudices, suppositions, and common images imposed by the outside, suggested by what mass imagination proposes. Finally, s/he sees her/his own ignorance, without being able to recognize it. At this precise point the movie stresses that the impossibility of any understanding is tightly linked with the issue of ignorance.

Pummarò, the first film made by director Michele Placido in 1990, also stresses the blinding effect of ignorance. The movie tells the odyssey of Bacù, a young medical doctor from Ghana who goes to Italy with the intention of finding his brother who has disappeared. Bacù's search takes him northward through Italy. He eventually gets to Verona, where he spends some time and falls in love. During his first stroll with the woman, she takes him to Juliet's balcony, a character in a great English writer's tragedy, she says. Smiling, Bacù replies by reciting the balcony scene by heart, and in English. It is hopeless to try and describe the confusion and the surprise of the young woman, who, while presuming to educate the good savage, ends up being instructed about her own ignorance. Western culture, which barely manages to hide its arrogance, always sets itself up as the depository of knowledge and is astonished by the knowledge of others.

At other times it denies it, or refuses it. In a 1993 movie by Maurizio Zaccaro titled *Articolo 2,* the protagonist and his family are repeatedly confronted by widespread ignorance and indifference. The film tells the story of Said, an Algerian who has settled down in Milan with one of his wives and their three children. He eventually has to face the problems set forth by the unexpected arrival of his other wife accompanied by their three other children. Said, as well as his family, is always hastily referred to as Moroccan, *marocchino*, despite his real nationality and his attempts to draw attention to the obvious difference; his right to worship his religion is denied him the moment when the Italian law insists on considering him a bigamist; his identity is ignored even when his dead body is repatriated in a coffin that bears the Christian symbol of the cross.

There is an Italy that recognizes only one reality and only one truth, and it not only contents itself with those but shields itself behind them, to defend itself against anything that represents a threat to its well-being and to its stability. Times are economically difficult and the instinct becomes protectionist: we mark our territory, we become somewhat racist, we avoid foreigners. Of course there are different kinds of foreigners:

> Il razzista è più portato a diffidare di un operaio africano che di un miliardario americano. Meglio ancora, se un emiro del Golfo viene a passare le sue vacanze in Costa Azzurra è accolto a braccia aperte, perché non è l'*arabo* che si riceve, ma il *ricco* che è venuto a spendere soldi. (Ben Jelloun 14)

> the racist is more inclined to be suspicious of the African worker than of the American millionaire. Better yet, if a Gulf emir goes on vacation on the Côte d'Azur he is heartily welcomed, because it is not the Arab who is welcomed, but the rich man who is going to spend money.

The average person's way of thinking, of feeling, of reacting is influenced by shallow mass morality. One listens to the news while having breakfast or preparing dinner, between telephone calls; one reads the newspaper at the bar while waiting for her/his espresso, keeping an eye on the time, and often the only pieces of information s/he gathers are contained in the titles that are disquieting by their very nature. The average person lacks the vast and precise information to explain concepts in detail and to soothe her/his defensive instinct. Tahar Ben Jelloun is right when he says that racism is substantially a lack of culture: as with the leg in the movie, one laughs every time a reference to the ugliness of the sculpture is made because it is understood that the value given to it is foolishly arbitrary; and yet it does attain real market value. One laughs less willingly and even feels bad when the images reveal that the *extra-comunitari* are not the assumed *vuccumprà* [street vendors] with their goods consisting of fake Cartier watches and lighters, sleeping on fake Persian rugs, but they are instead a foreign company's engineers and construction workers. The fact that one feels bad is already a positive sign, a hope that integration may take place and that the success in those places where it is already happening may spread. I read in an old issue of the magazine *Grazia* that in Milan there is a multiethnic school in which basic education is combined with a series of activities aimed at including and bringing out the value of non-Italian traditions and cultures in order to give the children the notion that diversity is positive and fun.

For the adults there is no life-training place as efficient as school, but it is not impossible that children may not help to open the eyes of those who do not want to see that diversity means culture and enrichment. I am convinced that cinema helps in this endeavor because it is a spectacle aimed at the general population, comprehensible to anybody, and more and more *engagé*, even when it tries primarily to entertain.

I would like to conclude by recalling the scene that ends the trial against the rebelling slaves of the *Amistad* in Steven Spielberg's movie of the same name: finally free, Cinqué shakes the hand of his lawyer in the western way that he has taught him; consequently, the lawyer reciprocates with the thanking gesture that Cinqué used with him. It may be a somewhat rhetorical image, but it is nonetheless a symbol of a fellowship among people willing to mutually learn from each other, open to the outside and always hospitable, even to those who come without legs that are worth three hundred million lire.

Work Cited

Ben Jelloun, Tahar. *Il razzismo spiegato a mia figlia*. Trans. Egi Volterranni. Milan: Bompiari, 1998.

AFRICA AND AFRICANS IN ITALIAN LITERATURE

BETWEEN HEROES AND PEASANTS
Levi and the Political Consciousness of the Abyssinian War in *Cristo si è fermato a Eboli*

Pina Palma
Southern Connecticut State University

> History is fashioned on the basis of written documents, of course. When there are any. But it can and must be fashioned even without written documents if none is available. Then it can be made up out of anything that the historian's ingenuity may lead him to employ. . . . Words, signs, landscapes, titles, the layout of fields, weeds, eclipses of the moon, bridles, analysis of stones by geologists and of metal swords by chemists, in a word, anything which, belonging to man, depends on man, serves him, expresses him and signifies his presence, activity, tastes and forms of existence. (Febvre 34)

Lucien Febvre's words propel us immediately into the world of *Cristo si è fermato a Eboli*. Beyond describing the reality of that world, Febvre's assertion reminds us that, contrary to appearance, phenomena that on the surface may appear insignificant can attest to the unfolding of human history and can also reconstitute the emotional life of a given period. As an exile from the north, and within the limited horizon of his "confino," Levi uncovers a new anthropological landscape in Lucania, where "la storia (è) senza storia e il tempo (è) fuori dal tempo" (viii; history is without history and time is outside of time). It is the discovery of this world untouched by time that impels him to portray its peasants and to objectively describe the socio-cultural characteristics permeating and shaping the fabric of the southern villages in which he is forced to reside. Centered around atavic traditions, the villages of Gagliano and Grassano represent an immobile universe — the world of peasants — that vibrates with its own regulated rhythms, extraneous to and unaffected by external temporal structures and political oscillations. *Cristo* attests to this, in Levi's compelling portrayal of the peasants and their lives.

The events unfolding in the villages are recounted alternatively by a subjective "I," which represents the narrating author (Corti 39). This is a "unitary self" engaged in mnemonically re-capturing the people and predicaments of his experience in exile (Gottlieb 21). The other, more collective "I," represents the impoverished peasants whose world is shaped by their struggle for survival. Through their descriptions of events, Levi's peasants give "voice to the voiceless, breaking the silence of the silenced" (Lincoln 42). These two "I's" transform the novel into a two-dimensional but mutually inclusive text. First, as the peasants be-come "subject voices," they move both literally and metaphorically from the margins of society to its center,[1] thus acquiring the prominence that has historically been denied to them. Second, as Levi discovers that world of Southern peasants and makes public the conditions under which they exist, he creates a powerful document to voice his acerbic criticism of local social injustices and national political failures. As he evaluates the historical and socio-economic traits coloring the period and the society in question, Levi illustrates the peasants' disillusionment with the governing class and their dissatisfaction with their miserable life. These are evidenced in psychological submissiveness rather than in feelings of unrest and disquiet. This passivity dominates those passages of the novel in which the colonization of Africa intersects the lives of Levi's characters.

Chronologically, the narrator's arrival in Gagliano corresponds to the beginning of the Italian invasion in Ethiopia (October 1935); in fact, the village's *Podestà* Don Luigi mentions the war the first time the narator meets him. Don Luigi zealously oversees those men who are forced to reside in his village. Like a Dantesque Minotaur regulating the sinner's afterlife and the bolgia he must occupy, Don Luigi cautions the new exile regarding the limits of his freedom during his residence in Gagliano. At the same time, he asks the educated doctor why he has been exiled. Don Luigi's curiosity is accentuated by his belief that such a penalty must necessarily be a severe one, since it takes place at a time when "la Patria diventa così grande" (12; our country is on the road to greatness). His haughty reference to the "expansion of the fatherland" suggests the en-

---

[1] In this I have followed Herrington and Curtis.

thusiastic and conceited rhetoric of a man whose self-identity and self-respect are directly intertwined with and dependent upon the success of the Fascist conquest of Africa, as well as his disdainful disregard for the well-being of his fellow-citizens and the accompanying preoccupation with his personal advancement.

In effect, Don Luigi's attitude mirrors the regime's indifference to the peasants' welfare and exemplifies its ineptitude in ameliorating the condition of their lives, even as it pursues an aggressive foreign campaign to establish an Italian empire in Africa. Through this initial juxtaposition, the reader draws an immediate analogy based, on the one hand, on Mussolini's inability to administer Italian national affairs and, on the other hand, on his eagerness to colonize the distant regions of Africa.[2] Through this inferred paradox, Levi launches a piercing denunciation of Don Luigi's attitude and — by extension — of the Fascist beliefs he embodies.

During their initial meeting, the narrator detects a hint of fear in his new guardian's voice: "la guerra d'Africa è appena all'inizio. Speriamo che tutto vada bene" (12; the war against Abyssinia has hardly begun. Let us hope that all goes well). With his ego inflated and inflamed by Fascist propaganda, Don Luigi appears to believe in a war of colonization that can empower him and enrich his country. These expectations, however, are belied by the apprehension detected in his voice that, when combined with his auspicious "let us hope that all will go well," denote a moment, if fleeting, of disbelief in his own words. As the Fascist *Podestà*, representing the regime's ideology, he can satisfy his craving for power. His endorsement of the war in Africa therefore epitomizes not his ideological position but rather his loyalty toward the regime that lends him his authoritative identity. With this "borrowed" public identity Don Luigi is able to maintain complete control over the lives of his townspeople. It is precisely between Don Luigi's stated public beliefs and his

---

[2]See Mussolini 283. On October 27, 1930, Mussolini declared "oggi io affermo che il fascismo in quanto idea, dottrina, realizzazione, è universale: italiano nei suoi particolari istituti, esso è universale nello spirito. . . . Il fascismo oggi risponde ad esigenze di carattere universale. Esso risolve infatti il triplice problema dei rapporti fra stato e individuo, fra stato e gruppi, fra gruppi e gruppi organizzati." With this discourse Mussolini inaugurated a universalistic Fascist ideological perspective which sought to be convalidated through the imposition of its model on different cultures. See Tomasello chapter 5.

unspoken private fears that his hypocrisy lies. Like no other character in the novel, he is aware that within his own family, participation in the African campaign, although it masquerades as duty and patriotism, in reality represents a practical manner to escape from personal problems while acquiring material gains.

The notion of patriotism and of nationalism (see Breully), as advocated by the official propaganda and dutifully espoused by Don Luigi, eclipses the fundamental nature of both ideals. Embracing the distortions implicit in Fascist extreme nationalism,[3] the *Podestà* unconditionally promotes the war in Africa without demonstrating any inclination to make personal sacrifices, either on behalf of his country or on behalf of his townspeople (see Nathanson, *Patriotism, Morality, and Peace*), who he claims will directly benefit from the war. With unerring accuracy, Levi portrays the *Podestà* as engrossed exclusively with solidifying his agrandizement, a description fitting many Fascist bureaucrats of the period. Absorbed solely with his own momentousness and with the prosperity of his immediate family, this man remains thoroughly unconcerned with the validity of his country's motive for the war and with the divisiveness and destruction it will engender. His uncritical attitude toward the conflict and his negligence toward his own community illustrate his lack of moral commitment to both his country and his village. While he masquerades as a patriot behind an ambiguous and self-serving form of nationalistic fanaticism, he is able to manipulate the uneducated peasants by continually limiting their autonomy while at the same time forcing upon them his enthusiasm for the imperialist expansion of Italy.

For men like Don Luigi, patriotism — or their interpretation of it — often serves to disguise personal, and therefore less aggrandizing, realities. This is the predicament in which Nicola Cuscianno, Don Luigi's brother-in-law, finds himself. His wife, convinced that he is having an affair with the pharmacist's young daughter, accuses Nicola in private — thus "avoiding" a public scandal — of plotting with his young lover to poison her. In a private subversion of the public perception, Cuscianno,

---

[3]In "Nationalism and the Limits of Global Humanism," Stephen Nathanson discusses extreme nationalism. People who adhere to this ideology, he argues, "seek to dominate other nations, believe that their own nation is superior to others, and think that any action that promotes their own nation's interest is justified" (184).

who in public is a feared secretary of the Fascio, is at home the insulted and persecuted victim of a despotic wife. After six months of this private misery, he decides that the African war represents the only escape from his torment:

> finchè apparve la sola possibilità di salvezza e di redenzione: la guerra d'Africa. Il delinquente umiliato chiese di andare volontario, pensando che avrebbe così espiato le sue colpe, si sarebbe conciliato, al ritorno, con la moglie, e intanto avrebbe preso lo stipendio di capitano, assai superiore a quello di maestro di scuola; e partì. (51)

> [until there appeared a chance for redemption: the war with Abyssinia. The humiliated sinner enrolled as a volunteer thinking that in this way he might expiate his sins, reconcile himself with his wife when he returned, and, at the same time, obtain the pay of a captain, which was considerably higher than his salary as a school teacher.]

Nicola has a practical — if less than honorable — motive for volunteering to serve in Africa. Reflecting neither an ideological belief nor an ethical commitment, his interest in the conflict stems from his desire to advance his interests as well as his hope of simultaneously escaping his domestic difficulties. These selfish incentives — the prospect of a higher pension and moving away from his petulant wife — become the only rationale for his willingness to enlist and to depart for Africa, while he ignores any objective consideration of the war's ethical validity. Not inadvertently, Levi portrays the two Fascist representatives of the village as prisoners of a self-serving web, which for them is crystallized in the Italian colonialist enterprise in Africa. While in the literal sense they maintain authority over other people — both local and foreign — by imprisoning them within the boundaries of political rules, metaphorically they are themselves both captives of their sheer craving for power.

In the political isolation that sheathes the lives of the villagers, only two other people volunteer for war. One of them is *tenente* Decunto who yearns to leave behind the misery of Grassano, which — in his words — is ruled by the "questura, carabinieri, and the secretary of the Fascio," all of whom are "ambiziosi, ladri, disonesti, and violenti" (21; ambitious, thieves, dishonest and violent). If Decunto's candid assertion to the narrator indicates the degree of his exasperation with the impoverishment and injustice asphyxiating life in his village, his pronouncement also reflects the sentiment of one who warily and objectively recognizes the uncertainty of the war's results:

> Pazienza se tutto andrà in rovina. . . . Giochiamo il tutto per il tutto. . . . Questa è la fine, mi capisce? La fine. Se vincessimo, forse si potrà cambiare qualcosa, chissà. Ma l'Inghilterra non lo permetterà. Ci spaccheremo la testa. . . . Andrà male vedrà. Ma non importa. Così non si può continuare. . . . Quando avrà visto che cos'è la vita in questo paese, mi dirà che avevo ragione. (21)

> [Never mind if the whole venture will turn out badly. . . . We are gambling it all. . . . This is the end, do you understand? The end. If we win, perhaps we will be able to change something. But England will not allow it. We will break our heads. . . . He will not succeed, you'll see. But it does not matter. We can't continue on like this. After you will have seen what life here is like, you will concede that I was right.]

These words illustrate Decunto's deep skepticism toward the Italian colonization of Africa. Nonetheless, his pessimistic acknowledgement that even a ruinous loss in Africa can be an expeditious solution to the inequities engulfing Grassano, attests to his willingness to evade his responsibility. His desire to flee from the village ruled by little despots and tormented by petty enmities without attempting to rectify them — along with his forthright criticism of the political system that he recognizes as unjust — reveals him to be as selfish as Cuscianno. These two men choose the war in Africa as an antidote to their personal anguish. Although at first it would appear that a distinction could be drawn between Decunto's decision — which is prompted by the social inequities that lacerate his town — and Cuscianno's decision — which is inspired by the circumstances of his private life — ultimately their actions are dictated exclusively by their selfish needs. Because their personal motivations do not coincide with any ideological convictions, both Decunto and Cuscianno become "disguised heroes." This process demonstrates that as individuals they regress to a state of moral involution rather than developing into ethical men: "e la guerra diventava una fuga, la fuga in un mondo di distruzione" (25; and war became an escape from a world of destruction). They are solely concerned with fleeing the source of their afflictions and wholly unconcerned with the devastation that the war will cause.

This point is central to understanding the dichotomy between those who rule, embodied by the village's presumptuous bureaucrats, and those who are ruled, embodied by the unpretentious peasants. Two parts of the same impoverished and exploited universe, these two classes are paradoxically separated by the belief, deeply embedded in the consciousness of both groups, that the social superiority of one group is necessarily held at the expense of the other. Based upon this theory, each group maintains the illusion of its distinctiveness, even while it is part of the same impoverished milieu. To the bureaucrats, the occupation of Africa is part of the official propaganda[4] and their acceptance and advocacy of it, regardless of its amoral ramifications and trappings, assures them an unquestionable identification with the potential nation's success. Moreover, it holds for them the possibility of profiting from the economic gains[5] that may be achieved in the process (see McKim).

To the peasants, the African war is a distant reality, devoid of any benefit that could ameliorate their existence. Although they lack a clear knowledge of the logic of this war, the peasants are fully cognizant of the aberrant conditions in which they live. Thus, they remain skeptical about the future imperialistic grandeur proclaimed by the Fascists and equally skeptical about the promise that they will share the promised wealth that Africa represents. In light of their poverty, to which they are forcibly relegated by their own government and to which they are accustomed to submit, any notion of their country's superiority "uber Alles" appears virtually preposterous. The implications of a military war outside their village do not coincide with their idea of nationalism. The only "war" with which they can identify and in which they are the perpetual victims, is the struggle against Rome. This city, and the government it symbolizes, is synonymous with the taxes that ceaselessly threaten their live-

---

[4]See Del Boca, in particular the chapter "L'Italia e la spartizione dell'Africa."

[5]"L'Etiopia con I suoi altopiani fertili . . . le sue miniere d'oro e di platino . . . più che un paese era un pianeta, capace di accendere e di stimolare ogni varietà di appetiti," Del Boca 32.

lihood. The African war is Rome's concern and not theirs, an event that must be endured but that cannot serve their cause. Their simple reasoning reveals clearly that Rome and its bureaucrats support the war only in order to profit from it.

Their ideological indifference to the war in Africa is in large part dictated by this logic and to a lesser extent by the amorality inherent in any war. Submerged in the sea of daily necessities, they are politically lethargic, grasping neither the structure nor the programs of the government, and certainly not its political metamorphoses. The peasants unanimously maintain an attitude that is apolitical and disengaged both from the Podestà's and from Rome's pursuits and that superficially appears to prevent the emergence of any individual political consciousness. Aware that Rome is not concerned with ameliorating their living conditions and that, to the contrary, it proclaims laws aimed at thwarting any such improvement because "non vogliono che noi si viva da cristiani" (67; they do not want us to live like Christians [human beings]), the peasants maintain an affected indifference to the regime's propaganda for the African colonization. With words that affirm their submissiveness "Ci fanno ammazzare le capre, ci portano via i mobili di casa, e adesso ci manderanno a fare la guerra. Pazienza" (67; they force us to kill our goats, they take away furnishings from our houses, and now they will send us to war. Patience!), they exclude themselves from the established State and unwittingly forge for themselves the very identity which separates them from the more cosmopolitan Fascist adhesion to the war. Their impassive acceptance of Rome and its laws is a conscious act, however, in which is reflected their "comune accetazione" (69; common acceptance) and to which corresponds their solidarity. Powerless individually against Rome, they collectively retain the self-determination of their indifference toward a government, in retaliation for its indifference to their plight.

The collective uniqueness of the peasants is manifested through their stubbornly affected apathy toward the official government; ironically, this empowers them with a collective dignity. Undaunted by the fanatical loyalty their leaders must show toward the regime, the peasants possess both scope and strength to manifest their indifference as well as their cynicism toward the purported merits of the Fascist enterprise in

Africa. In this atmosphere, they maintain a "collective independence" from the village despots, retaining a self-respectability stemming from their conscious detachment from the regime's policies. For this reason, the *Podestà*'s town meetings, which are punctuated with radio broadcasts aimed at stirring the war's ardor in the listeners, are met with utter passivity by the few who attend. Because the meetings are announced the night before to assure maximum participation, many peasants resort to leaving for the fields much earlier than usual in the mornings, in order to avoid attending. Their indifference toward the war in Africa emerges more vividly when the Italian troops reach Mareb. As the *Podestà* blasts the village with the notes of "faccetta nera, bella Abissina," interspersed with words saturated with the rhetoric of power and hegemony in a foreign land, the only reaction he obtains from the villagers is a more profound alienation from and distrust for the political system.

Accurately, the peasants recognize the moral repercussions of an Italian supremacy in Africa. Unlike the village's educated fascist leaders, the uneducated peasants see the Italian appropriation of the African land as an offensive act. This act has as its direct correlative the abuses that the peasants themselves suffer at the hand of the same government that now claims that the fertile lands conquered in Africa will enrich the villagers. Impervious to these promises, because they evoke the familiar pattern of the injustice of misappropriation and the forcible imposition of the hegemony of a dominant elite, which "embodies" the national ideology, the peasants distrust the whole idea of the war. Correctly they perceive that it will be fought not for a common good but for the benefit of a few others "la guerra è fatta per quelli del nord" (117; the war is fought for the northerners). In view of this, their silent criticism of and passive resistance to the war attest to their ethical stand and their universalism, two fundamental tenets that are lacking in the more worldly Fascist leaders.

The peasants' disdain toward the war evokes Tolstoy's argument regarding patriotism, particularly the passages in which he argues that national patriotism, rather than cohesively uniting people, foments civil fragmentation and the enrichment of the few.[6] For Levi's peasants, living

---

[6]Tolstoy 74f. For Tolstoy one way to prevent war is to root out patriotism and replace it

on the geographical and cultural fringes of a society that has all but forgotten them, their actions and beliefs have no resonance in the official
arena of the militant government. Throughout the novel this notion
clearly defines the peasants' attitude toward the Italian colonization of
Africa. Interestingly, the peasants' apathy with respect to the government's actions and their submissiveness with respect to its rulings never
produce a moment of social awakening. If this occurred, it would be a
concrete delineation of the critical passage from the state of making accusations against the Fascist rulers to the higher state of active involvement against the laws ratified by them. From this perspective, it would
represent the transition from political idleness to ethical activism.

In this universe of dominating political forces, the priest Don Trajella
becomes the self-appointed spokesman of the African war. In so doing,
however, he too has a personal interest. The occasion for his public
speech presents itself on Christmas Eve when, arriving late and drunk
for the Mass he is to celebrate, he claims to have lost the sermon he
originally prepared. To the assembled congregation, he proposes to read
a letter received from Abyssinia and written by the other man enlisted
from the village. After an unpretentious incipit, imbued with the con-
ventional rhetoric of absence and distance from one's hometown, the
sender expresses his wishes for peace to his fellow-villagers. The letter
continues with the soldier's description of the Italian mission in Africa:
"Qui noi combattiamo per portare la nostra Santa Religione a queste
popolazioni infedeli, combattiamo per convertire alla vera fede questi
pagani, per portare la pace e la beatitudine eterna" (178; here we fight to
bring our religion to the savages, to convert the pagans to the true faith,
to bring them peace and eternal happiness). The soldier's explanation,
suggesting that the Italian invasion of Abyssinia has as its fundamental
objective the conversion of the pagans,[7] not only distorts historical reality
but directly contradicts the *Podestà*'s earlier expansionistic assertions.
More importantly, the letter serves to thrust Don Trajella into a progressively more aggressive invective against the peasants, rather than against

with a universal commitment to the well-being of all human beings. "Patriotism promises
men nothing but a terrible future, but the brotherhood of nations represents an ideal
which is becoming ever more intelligible and more desirable to humanity" (87).
[7] Del Boca, particularly the section "In nome della fede," 23–29.

the war itself and against its intrinsically heinous nature.[8] The intoxicated priest's sermon reveals his twisted interpretation of the juxtaposition of war and peace. He embraces the theory that the Italian war in Africa is an effort to convert non-believers.[9] Paradoxically, he supports his belief by distinguishing between the "African pagans" and the "village pagans." The priest in fact affirms that, while the conversion to Catholicism will bring the "foreign pagans" the peace they now lack, the "local pagans" will be denied that same peace to which their religion would otherwise entitle them. He states that the reason for this is that the peasants have not fulfilled their customary Christmas obligation of gifts and offerings for him. Having received no gifts, and having no care for the poverty of his flock, the village "shepherd" concludes with the syllogism that the peasants are pagans — like the Africans — and that therefore they deserve all the sufferings that may befall them.

Don Trajella's words expose his human selfishness; while they focus on the distinction between war and peace, they lack the moral concerns inherently befitting the religious office he occupies. In his position, he should recognize the destructiveness engendered by all war. Nonetheless, from his pulpit Don Trajella neither advocates the sacredness of all creatures nor speaks against a war that champions the usurpation of other people's rights; rather he explodes in an accusation against those who have failed to adulate his authority. Daring to equate the celebration

---

[8]The assertion of another Italian writer can help understand the manner in which Levi flawlessly portrays Don Trajella's attitude that plainly reflects the Church's position. Specifically, Ignazio Silone affirms: "se avessi dovuto attenermi al magistero morale della autorità religiosa nei confronti del fascismo e di tutti i suoi errori, avrei dovuto aspettare parecchi anni, Durante la guerra d'Abissinia le lettere pastorali dei vescovi di cui leggevo i titoli o i brevi cenni di riassunto su "L'Osservatore Romano," trattavano generalmente problemi di morale privata: I costumi da bagno delle donne, i balli popolari, la bestemmia e così di seguito. Non una parola sulle ignominie statali. Sì, sì, conosco e apprezzo in tutta la loro gravità le cause che allora limitavano fortemente la libertà del magistero morale della chiesa. Ma se è così, se circostanze storiche, specialmente nei paesi a maggioranza cattolica, possono imporre al magistero della chiesa il silenzio su fatti gravissimi come la guerra d'Abissinia, allora bisogna ammetterlo lealmente, non resta per gli individui che il 'si salvi chi può,'" ("Ignazio Silone tra testimonianza e utopia," *Atti del seminario di studi* [Assisi: Biblioteca Pro Civitate Christiana, 1972] 8).

[9]Interestingly, Don Trajella's belief of the religious mission to colonize Africa corresponds to one aspect of the colonization. See Betti.

of Christmas with the gifts he expected to receive, the priest shamelessly projects not only the imperfection of human institutions but also the greed that gnaws every representative of the Fascist ruling class.

His public sermon clearly highlights his hypocrisy, revealing him to be no different from the *Podestà*, Cuscianno, or Decunto. Don Trajella, like the *Podestà*, Cuscianno, and Decunto, holds a position of influence over the villagers and, also like them, he is concerned only about the personal enrichment he expects to receive. His egoistic speech, delivered on the night that consecrates the quintessence of human fellowship, pulverizes any respect for him and for the office he represents, deepening the abyss between rulers and subjects, between Rome and the villages, and between a war in Africa and the peasants in Lucania.

In the opening, Lucien Febvre's words reminded us that through the historian's ingenuity, phenomena that may appear irrelevant at first, are the essential — if small — rivulets feeding the grand river of History. It is they that allow us to delve into the psychology of History, permitting us to glimpse at the way in which "ordinary people" view and react to events sanctioned by "official leaders." *Cristo si è fermato a Eboli* is a poignant document, capturing the pivotal difference between "war heroes" and "village peasants." In tracing the social consciousness of "unimportant people" with regard to the colonization of Ethiopia by Fascist Italy, this novel reveals that History is made by peasants and not by political figures. This occurs because it is the peasants who refuse to be drawn into the vortex of conceited political fanaticism, choosing instead to live their lives according to their deeply felt moral convictions.[10]

Works Cited

Betti, Claudio Mario. "Le missioni religiose." *Fonti e problemi della politica coloniale in Africa. Atti del convegno Taormina-Messina, 23–29 ottobre 1989.* Roma: Ministero per i beni culturali e ambientali, 1996. 702–27.

Breully, J. "Nationalism and the State." *Nationality, Patriotism and Nationalism in Liberal Democratic Societies.* Ed. Roger Michener. St. Paul, MN: PWPA, 1993.

---

[10]In V*ino e Pane* (Milano: Mondadori, 1970) Silone has a remarkably appropriate assertion which mirrors the attitude of Levi's peasants "Si può vivere anche in un Paese di dittatura ed essere libero, a una semplice condizione, basta lottare contro la dittatura. L'uomo che pensa con la propria testa e conserva il suo cuore incorrotto, è libero. L'uomo che lotta per ciò che ritiene giusto, è libero" (67).

Corti, Maria. "Risposta a Giovannetti." *Carlo Levi nella storia e nella cultura italiana.* Ed. Gigliola De Donato. Manduria: Lacaita, 1993.

Del Boca, Angelo. *L'Africa nella coscienza degli italiani.* Bari: Laterza, 1992.

Febvre, Lucien. *A New Kind of History.* Trans. K. Folca. Ed. P. Burke. New York: Harper & Row, 1973.

Gottlieb, Alma. "Behind the Lonely Anthropologist: Collaboration in Research and Writing." *American Anthropologist* 97 (1995): 21.

Herrington, A. J., and M. Curtis. "Basic Writing: Moving the Voices on the Margins to the Center." *Harvard Educational Review* 60 (1990): 489–96.

Levi, Carlo. Letter to Giulio Einaudi editor. *Cristo si è fermato a Eboli.* Torino: Einaudi, 1981.

Lincoln, Yvonna S. "I and Thou: Method, Voice, and Roles in Research with the Silenced." *Naming Silenced Lives.* Ed. D. McLaughlin and W. G. Tierney. New York: Routledge, 1993. 29–50.

McKim, Robert. "National Identity and Respect among Nations." *The Morality of Nationalism.* Ed. R. McKim and Jeff McMahon. New York: Oxford UP, 1997. 258–73.

Mussolini, B. *Opera Omnia.* Ed. E. and D. Susmel. Firenze: La Fenice, 1958. Vol. 24.

Nathanson, Stephen. "Nationalism and the Limits of Global Humanism." *The Morality of Nationalism.* Ed. R. McKim and Jeff McMahon. New York: Oxford UP, 1997.

___. *Patriotism, Morality, and Peace.* Lanham, MD: Rowman & Littlefield, 1993.

Tolstoy. "On Patriotism." *Tolstoy's Writings on Civil Disobedience and Non-Violence.* New York: New American Library, 1968.

Tomasello, G. *La letteratura coloniale italiana dalle avanguardie al fascismo.* Palermo: Sellerio, 1984.

Two Italians and Two Africans
Moravia, Volponi, Komla-Ebri, Wasswa

Peter N. Pedroni
Miami University

A review of Italian fiction of the twentieth century reveals an almost complete absence of Black or African characters. This absence may be explained by the preference on the part of writers to write about what they know best. Some exceptions found in the work of Alberto Moravia only serve to underline the fact that Blacks and Africans are unknown and therefore exotic and unexplainable. In *Agostino* the author wants to make a political statement by contrasting the middle-class life of the protagonist with that of a group of lower-class boys who function like a primitive community with a natural and brutal order. They are for the most part intended to be socially and psychologically typical of their class. Tortima is the oldest, the strongest, and the most vulgar. Berto is sly and cunning. Sandro is blond and apparently for this reason seems more intelligent and sensitive to the bourgeois Agostino. The unexplained exception is Hommes who is black and homosexual. Since Hommes is not essential to the plot and not essential to the class contrast that Moravia was representing, one wonders why it was important for Moravia to include this character, if not simply to make a peripheral negative statement. In the same novel when Moravia wants us to understand how difficult it is for Agostino to imagine what goes on in a bordello he uses the following analogy, "Like a poor savage who has heard about the palaces of Europe, and can only picture them as a slightly larger version of his own thatched hut" (69) suggesting a rather condescending attitude toward non-Europeans.

Probably the most dramatic and most determining episode of *La Ciociara* [*Two Women*] is that in which the protagonist and her daughter are raped by a group of Moroccan soldiers. This violent crime is made to be especially abhorrent because it is committed in a church beneath a Marian icon that has no apparent significance for the rapists. What is most important for our purposes is that this crime happens without a comprehensible word being spoken by the Moroccans. None of them speaks a word of Italian. Only one is distinguished from the group because he attacks the mother rather than the daughter. They are in effect an amalgamated mass of dark beings. There is no explanation either before or afterward as to why they committed this crime. From the viewpoint of the protagonist, the attackers are no different than wild animals that might have attacked them in a jungle with no need for explanation. One might argue that this is because Cesira, the first-person narrator-protagonist is simply unable to understand and that this does not necessarily reflect the viewpoint of the author who does nothing to alter the impressions.

This situation must then be evaluated in context with the way enemy German soldiers are presented. They have certainly earned the despise of the local population through their military law, their forced evacuations, and their military searches. Nevertheless there are several individual Germans who distinguish themselves for some human aspect of their character. For example there is the friendly soldier who plays the accordion and sings "Lili Marlene" and the gentlemanly captain who had thought to send a goat to his children in Germany (albeit a goat that might have provided milk for Italian children). But even the German lieutenant who says, "War is an experience for which there is no substitute, and lacking which, a man cannot call himself a man" and who experienced an esthetic sensation when he "cleared out a cave full of enemy soldiers with a flame thrower" has an intellectual side. He had studied Italian literature in Rome and had translated an Italian novel. More significantly this otherwise negative character seems to understand and correctly identify Italy's basic problem in its distinction between the classes.

> Do you know why Italy has lost the war and why we Germans now have to waste precious soldiers on the Italian front? It is precisely because of that difference between soldiers and officers, between the people and you gentlemen of the ruling class. The Italian soldier doesn't fight because he thinks this is *your* war, not his. And he shows you his hostility precisely by not fighting. (198)

In response to his Italian interlocutor he says,

> You Fascists and anti-Fascists are all bound to one another because you're all of the same class . . . and this government is the government of the whole lot of you, both Fascists and anti-Fascists, because it's the government of your class. Facts speak for themselves and all the rest is nonsense. (198–202)

Whether we agree with him or not, whether we despise him or like him, this German officer is recognizable as a human being. He is a known, even if feared, quantity. What is most significant is that, unlike in the case of the Moroccans, Moravia chose to present these examples of humanity. And furthermore he chose to make Cesira capable of remembering and quoting verbatim the somewhat legalistic speech of the German lieutenant. Each of the Germans is able in some way to communicate. They are for Moravia, after all, Europeans, and therefore known and explainable. The same can be said for the various Englishmen who are not always friendly and sometimes bad, but who are nevertheless explainable. Even the Americans, who are somewhat strange from the protagonist's and author's point of view, are nonetheless explainable and explained.

Even after Moravia's travels in Africa in the sixties and seventies and in the three travel books and one novel that result from them, there is no evidence of a changing attitude. In fact, these books reveal the author's apparent need for Africa to be unknown, mysterious, and different. He often refers negatively to modernized cities as "Europeanized" or "Americanized" and positively to undeveloped areas as the "real Africa." He also shows little interest in contemporary African writers whose works might serve to diminish his sense of inexplicability regarding Africa. Instead his interest is in the primitive beauty of a dangerous and irrational nature. In the novel, *La donna leopardo* [the leopard woman], "woman," incarnated in the irrational and unexplainable wife of the protagonist, is a reciprocal metaphor for "Africa," as explained by Giuseppe Stellardi in his excellent article on this subject.[1]

---

[1]For a thorough discussion of these works see Stellardi, and Moestrup. The works referred to were all published in Milan by Bompiani. The travel books are: *A quale tribù*

In Paolo Volponi's novel *Il sipario ducale* [*Last Act in Urbino*] Africa seems to evoke a similar prehistoric religious mysticism for Vives. "She thought nostalgically about Africa, . . . She had seen how it was even easier to die in Africa . . . and as soon as he was dead he did not become a cadaver, but a monkey . . . or a little bagpipe . . ." (144). Here too a concept that has little to do with any African reality seems to satisfy a need for a European intellectual no longer capable of mysticism within a European context.

A reading of the short story, "Quando attraverserò il fiume . . ." [When I Cross the River] by Kossi Komla-Ebri from Togo, reveals a different attitude toward death. The narrator explains that "è credenza da noi che la vita e la morte si trovino sulle due sponde opposte di uno stesso fiume, e morire non è altro che attraversare il fiume" (60; it is believed among our people that life and death are found on the opposite banks of the same river, and dying is nothing more than crossing the river). This is of course a religious concept that makes dying easier for a believer in the same way that the Christian Paradise makes dying easier for Christian believers. But the same story reveals that this religious concept does not apply anymore necessarily in the African context than in the European context. The plot of the story is based on the fact that Nukuku, who is dying, had, many years before, after a furious argument with her daughter, said, "quando attraverserò il fiume . . . tu attraverserai il fiume con me" (60; when I cross the river . . . you'll cross the river with me). Now it is up to the young narrator to win his place among the village leaders by convincing the old woman before she dies to forgive her daughter and thus save her from dying with her. He succeeds and is a hero because he indeed saves the younger woman from premature death. The name Nukuku means "dead thing" and, as the narrator explains, her mother gave her this name "per farla vivere perchè chiamandola così era sicura che la Morte non l'avrebbe portata via. Che se ne fa la Morte di una cosa morta?" (58; to make her live because by naming her that way she was sure that Death would not take her away. What would

---

appartiene? (1972) (trans. Angus Davidson as *Which Tribe Do You Belong To?* [London: Secker and Warburg, 1974]); *Lettere dal Sahara* (1981), and *Passeggiate africane* (1987). The novel is *La donna leopardo* (1991). Other important references regarding Moravia's African experiences and writings are found in: Siciliano, and Elkann.

death want with something dead?). This would certainly suggest that
death is something more than a change of identity or the crossing of a
river; that instead death is an active spirit that "takes us away" just as in
the European tradition, and that it is certainly something to avoid. By
reading this short story, by delving beneath the title, we learn something
about Africans that we might not have learned through superficial observation or superficial reading. But perhaps this knowledge is disappointing because we would have preferred to think that Africans were
somehow different, perhaps to be envied, but nevertheless different.

In the short story "La mia tradizione in valigia" [my tradition in a
suitcase], the Ugandian writer Sinan B. Wasswa expresses the sense of
exclusion that he feels in relation to the European world. He talks about
the "circo bianco dei cavalieri della tavola rotonda, la stirpe che ha dato
origine a un popolo nobile, di cuore trasparente e di spirito puro come la
neve" (179; white circus of the knights of the round table, the stock from
which descended a noble people, of transparent heart and spirit pure as
snow). And he goes on to say that "Dentro si entra solo quando si fa
parte del clan a tutti gli effetti, fino nei minimi particolari. Finora nessuno ha mai potuto osare metterci i piedi dall'esterno. Da lì si è originato
tutto quello che noi viviamo oggi" (179; you get to enter only when you
become a full fledged member of the clan, in every minute detail. No one
has ever yet gotten a foot in from the outside). He uses the term "extracir-
colari" with obvious reference to the Italian political term "extracomunitari" to define his own African world where the dominating law is
"l'ugualianza fra tutti" (182; equality for all). Wasswa's text seems to
suggest that the European need that Africa remain different and unknown is based on its need for moral justification of its social-economic
exclusiveness. The more familiar the "cavalieri" become with the "ex-
tracircolari" the more difficult it is to remain exclusive.

There is an interesting similarity between Wasswa's "circo" and Paolo
Volponi's metaphorical use of the circus. While Wasswa's circus is one
that he would like to enter but cannot, Volponi's circus is a symbol of
captivity, humiliation, and degradation, from which he would like to
escape. It is the prison in which the "cavalieri" keep the rest of society
and deny us the freedom to seek self-fulfillment, which is undoubtedly
what Wasswa also seeks. In Volponi's *Memoriale* [*My Troubles Began*] the

factory and the sanatorium are a kind of *"circo"* where everything is provided for but where the possibilities for human development are stifled. Crocioni, the protagonist of *La macchina mondiale* [*The Worldwide Machine*], works in a circus where he must perform dehumanizing chores like cleaning animal excrement from the show floor. In *Last Act in Urbino* the "circo Universal" refers to a traveling circus in which some tropical snakes die in the cold of the Apennine winter. But the circus concept and escape from it are best expressed in the short novel *Il pianeta irritabile* [*The Irritable Planet*] that takes place around the year 2293 immediately after the last atomic explosion that nearly destroys the earth, drastically altering its physical characteristics and leaving very few survivors. Among these are the four protagonists of the novel: a baboon, a talking elephant, a trained goose, and a human dwarf. All four belonged to a circus before the explosion. The explosion that destroyed the circus opened their cages and gave them their freedom, albeit freedom to live in a world of terrifying adversity, that is, in the world imagined by Gerolamo Aspri, the autobiographical protagonist of Volponi's *Corporale* [corporal]. And perhaps it is also the opportunity desired by Crocioni for the creation of a new world. Freed from their cages the four protagonists organize themselves according to a natural order and set off on a journey toward an unidentified destination. The group functions very well because each member has a mission that is essential to the well-being of the group. I would suggest that this is an idealized version of the kind of society that Wasswa would like to leave in order to enter the circus that he in turn idealizes.

Gian Carlo Ferretti, in one of the few reviews of *Il pianeta irritabile*, noted that "con tragico paradosso, infatti, l''orrido scoppio' ha segnato l'autodistruzione degli uomini non-umani, e la liberazione dei diversi" (19–20; in a tragic paradox, in fact, the 'horrendous explosion' marked the auto-destruction of the non-human men, and the liberation of the deviants). However for Volponi there does not appear to be any paradox. There is instead a terrible logic. The tendency of society to organize itself into structures that are increasingly oppressive, inflexible, and militaristic can lead only to self-destruction. Perhaps this is what Wasswa had in mind when he wrote, "I nostri anziani dicono che prima o poi il circo cadrà in pezzi e i cavalieri dovranno smascherarsi, e la spada nelle loro mani non sarà più invisibile" (181; Our elders say that sooner or later the circus will fall apart and the knights will have to unmask themselves, and the sword in their hands will no longer be invisible).

Wasswa theorizes that the origin of the "*circo bianco*" is based on the formation of the alphabet: "L'alfabeta è ciò che apre l'accesso alla filosofia, alla fisica, alla scienza e alla tecnologia" (181; The alphabet is what opens up access to philosophy, to physics, to science and to techcnology). In *Il pianeta irritabile*, Volponi gives similar importance to a fundamental level of communication. The amorous relationship between the dwarf and the "suora di Kanton" [the nun from Canton] develops silently in a hospital and fulfills itself still silently in the latrine of the same hospital, silently, but certainly not without communication. It is a language of living signs left in the latrine to be read by the other member of the courting pair. However here the use of language seems to be in a declining phase suggesting the ending of a civilization rather than the beginning as would be the case with Wasswa's theorized alphabet.

In another story within the novel, a young technician called the "imitatore del canto di tutti gli uccelli" [imitator of the song of every bird] attempts to keep alive an element of the culture of his decaying society by memorizing and distinguishing between the calls of all the birds that had already become extinct two centuries previously, but had been recorded on tape. It is an activity similar to that of an African "griot" who has the responsibility of remembering and passing on the accumulated knowledge of his community. However because of this activity he is accused of spying and condemned to forced labor. He succeeds in fleeing and arrives in the enemy state where he is valued as a good musician, if not as a real imitator, and is assigned to the circus where he enjoys great popular success, suggesting a devaluation of the historical culture that only he possesses.

In the final episode of the novel the dwarf achieves absolute freedom by abandoning his nostalgic love for the "suora di Kanton." His memory of this love survives on a sheet of rice paper that he had preserved with the greatest care. Now this last linguistic connection, that is, this last chain linking him to the past, is broken when he tears apart the rice paper in portions that are socialistically proportionate to the needs of his companions and he begins to eat his portion. It would seem that the "*circo*" that Wasswa would enter has ceased to exist, much as he predicts in the final paragraph of his story. It is in this collapse that the imaginations of the Italian and the African intersect. Both see in the destruction of the "*circo*" the opportunity for a new beginning.

Perhaps this new beginning would lead to the kind of future world imagined by Komla-Ebri in his short story "Sognando una favola" where an African grandfather and Italian grandmother, using the grammatical "remote past" tell their incredulous grandchildren about the old days when Italy

> non era preparata ad accogliere tutta questa gente, Arrivò gente dalla ex-Jugoslavia in guerra, dall'Est-europeo, dall'Albania, dai paesi asiatici, dal Bacino mediterraneo e ovviamente dall'Africa. L'Italia che per anni era stata un paese di emigrazizone, si accorse di colpo di essere considerata, senza saperlo, un paese ricco, una specie d'America. (146)

> [was not prepared to take in all those people. People arrived from the former Yugoslavia at war, from eastern Europe, from Albania, from Asian countries, from Mediterranean countries and obviously from Africa. Italy, which for years had been a county of emigration, suddenly realized that it was considered, without knowing it, a rich country, a kind of America.]

Works Cited

Elkann, Alain, and Moravia, Alberto. *Vita di Moravia.* Milan: Bompiani, 1990.

Ferretti, Gian Carlo. "Anno 2293: dopo l'apocalisse." *Rinascita* 35.21 (26 May 1978): 19–20.

Komla-Ebri, Kossi. "Quando attraverserò il fiume. . . ." *Memorie in valigia.* Ed. Ramberti and Sangirogi. Rimini: Fara, 1997.

___. "Sognando una favola." *Destini sospesi di volti in cammino.* Ed. Sangiorgi and Ramberti. Santarcangelo di Romagna: Fara, 1998.

Moestrup, Jorn. "Moravia — viagggiatore nella preistoria." *Studi d'italianistica nell'Africa australe* 6.2 (1993): 36–50.

Moravia, Alberto. *Agostino.* Trans. Beryl de Zoete in *Two Adolescents.* New York: Farrar, Straus & Giroux (Bantam), 1969.

___. *Two Women.* Trans: Angus Davidson of *La Ciociara.* New York: Manor Books, 1974.

Siciliano, Enzo. *Alberto Moravia.* Milan: Bompiani, 1982.

Stellardi, Giuseppe. "L'Africa come metafora femminile (e viceversa) ne *La donna leoparda* di Alberto Moravia." *Studi d'italianistica nell'Africa australe* 6.1 (1993): 74–93.

Volponi, Paolo. *Last Act in Urbino*. Trans. Peter N. Pedroni of *Il sipario ducale*. New York: Italica, 1995.

Wasswa, Sinan B. "La mia tradizione in valigia." *Memorie in valigia*. Ed. Ramberti and Sangiorgi. Rimini: Fara, 1997.

BUSTER KEATON GOES TO AFRICA
Gianni Celati's *Avventure in Africa*

Charles Klopp
The Ohio State University

One point of travel, it has been observed, is not so much to explore other places and see other people as it is to discover oneself. This is the goal of at least some of the better known recent travel literature in Italian. For instance, thanks to his geographical and spiritual voyage back to his personal and ancestral origins in Sicily, Elio Vittorini's Silvestro is able, by the conclusion of that modern writer's 1941 *Conversazione in Sicilia*, to attain a fresh assessment of who he really is and what is important to him. Similarly, at the climactic conclusion of his voyage across the Indian subcontinent in Antonio Tabucchi's *Notturno indiano* of 1984, the narrator of this post-modern work confronts a Xavier who is at once his Other and at the same time — and this to chilling effect since the man involved would seem to be a criminal and moral outcast — his double and brother: an encounter that forces the narrator to examine the potential for evil latent within himself and, perhaps, all of us.

Even before he published *Avventure in Africa*, Gianni Celati had showed interest in tourism and tourists — whether Italians in foreign lands or foreign tourists in Italy. In "Baratto," one of the most interesting of his 1987 *Quattro novelle sulle apparenze*,[1] the title character overcomes a personal crisis and attains spiritual tranquillity thanks to his alliance with a group of Japanese tourists he meets in Mantua and then follows to Germany. Even though Baratto and the Japanese share no common language, at the story's conclusion, it has been pointed out,

> l'impossibilità della comunicazione, dovuta oggettivamente alla differenza linguistica esistente tra il protagonista e i giapponesi si tramuta paradossalmente nella prima forma di comunicazione possibile per Ba-

---

[1] In English as *Appearances* (London: Serpent's Tail, 1991).

ratto muto. Baratto riesce a comunicare perchè scopre se stesso come straniero, come altro da sè. (Novero 316)

[The impossibility of communication, due in objective terms to the linguistic difference that pertains between the main character and the group of Japanese is paradoxically transformed into the first form of communication possible for the mute Baratto. Baratto succeeds in communicating because he discovers that he is a foreigner, an Other in regard to himself.]

In Celati's new book set in Africa — *Avventure in Africa* (1998) — the author has cast the autobiographical narrator himself as a tourist, foreigner, and "Other" and in this way produced a highly unconventional, often hilarious but at the same time provocative travel book.

There is a good deal in *Avventure in Africa* about being a tourist. Toward its conclusion, in fact, the narrator decides that since the "primitive populations" of the Africa he has been visiting are now little more than, in his words, "sbandati straccioni o comparse esotiche" ["wandering beggars or exotic walk-ons"], and concluded that what is needed today is not further documentation of Africans and their ways of life, but a new ethnography of the demographically more vigorous, healthy, English-speaking, and expanding tribe of white European tourists who by now also inhabit Africa.[2] After all, he points out, this group of homogeneous individuals constitutes an ethnic grouping that has "elaborato un proprio sistema di credenze, una mitologia molto complessa, dei propri modi di vestirsi, mangiare" (163; "worked out its own beliefs system, an extremely complex mythology, its own ways of dressing and eating"). It is also the tribe to which — as if to answer the question posed by Alberto Moravia in his 1972 book about Africa, *A quale tribù appartieni?* ["What Tribe Do You Belong To"] — Celati himself belongs.

What do tourists do, exactly? They look at things, usually quite ordinary things that they observe with extraordinary wonder. To the natives who are observing them, in turn — whether these are the inhabitants of

---

[2]*Avventure in Africa* 163. The English translation of this work, *Adventures in Africa*, came out after this article was written. All translations, consequently, from *Avventure in Africa*, like those from Celati's other works included here, are my own.

the Mali, Senegal, and Mauritania where Celati pursues his "African Adventures" or those of his native Italy, that land par excellence of tourists and tourism — they mostly look foolish. In Africa, Celati points out, European tourists with their white or sunburned skins, the short pants that they favor after the manner of children world-wide but that no African adult would be caught dead in, and their wallets bulging with money and credit cards, are especially conspicuous and bizarre. It is thus no wonder that their African hosts look on these "toubabs" as exotic prey — "penguins," or "white cows ready for milking."

On the simplest level, *Avventure in Africa* is an irreverent account of the journey made in January, 1997, by two such "white penguins" through West Africa from Bamako to Bandiagara and Dakar and then back to Bamako. The account of their wanderings by the sometimes-pixilated Celati is remarkably similar to that contained in his 1989 *Verso la foce* [*Toward the Estuary*], which describes a trip through some of the remoter reaches of the Po valley. A first conclusion about *Avventure in Africa* is that the African book is a rewriting of Celati's earlier travel book about northern Italy, with West Africa and its indigenous peoples the equivalents of the Valpadana and its natives. As in *Verso la foce* where the narrator was accompanied on his journey by a series of professional photographers, in the new book Celati's traveling companion is also a picture-taker: in this case the documentary film-maker Jean Talon. This is appropriate, for in both works Celati himself is a kind of writer as photographer — "Io faccio le foto scrivendo" (37; "I take pictures writing") he confesses while in Africa — in that he limits himself to describing what he encounters without ascribing a narrative or dramatic structure to it. Instead, Celati, deadpan, simply records what he see — an attitude reminiscent of the silent movie actor Buster Keaton whose talent for implicit expressiveness the Italian author much admires.[3] For Celati in this book the visual is more important than the psychological. This is why such ordinary activities as waiting for a bus to leave or finding a hotel (the book's two travelers, for a variety of reasons, invariably choose their lodgings very badly) are as significant as meeting a beautiful and exotic woman, or a visit to the homeland of an ancient civilization, or a botched

---

[3]For Celati on Keaton, see his "Su Beckett, l'interpolazione e il gag."

encounter with the Italian director of the Center for Traditional Medicine who was supposed to be the subject of Talon's film. Because of his commitment to recording rather than analyzing, a good bit of the prose in Celati's descriptions in this book consists of noun phrases without verbs — descriptions of reality deliberately unmediated by a governing syntax of hierarchical arrangement and subordination.

Many of the Africans encountered in *Avventure in Africa* are themselves at loose ends, individuals who seem to be reinventing their lives: starting from scratch in their new roles as tourist guides or hotel attendants or bush taxi drivers instead of the farmers, herders, warriors, or magicians they were or might have been in the old days. In the same way, Celati and Talon themselves seem bereft of a personal past. At Bamako, when he runs into someone he knew from his student days in Paris, Celati makes no attempt to rekindle memories of this part of his life. "Non ho voglia," he tells us about this, "di parlare del passato, memorie, racconti ecc. — qui non c'è che il benedetto presente, e quello è l'orizzonte degli eventi, il resto un polverone di fantasmi" (105; "I have no desire to talk about the past, memories, stories, and so on — here there is nothing but the blessed present, and that is the horizon for events, everything else a huge dusty cloud of phantoms"). In the same way, although mention is made from time to time of the Sovietophile and French periods in the recent history of Mali, the Africa of this book is a land as historically deracinated and free-floating in a nebulous present as are the natives and tourists who wander across it in Celati's pages.

Unlike, say, Moravia in *A quale tribù appartieni?*, Celati is chary about making judgments regarding the people and social practices he encounters in West Africa. Although he does not hide his interest, for example, in the several beautiful women he meets in the course of his travels — including the hotel prostitutes, though not the "prostitute bambine" who bedevil him in Dakar — he tells us nothing about whatever feelings he may have for the way they make a living in these circumstances of postcolonialism. When he does remark, in regard to the sex-tourism that he finds in Dakar, that "niente scappa al traffico di carne umana tra bianchi e neri" ["nothing evades the traffic in human flesh between whites and blacks"] he quickly adds "ma io sono rimasto a corto di giudizi morali" (139; "but I am fresh out of moral judgments"). In another part of the book, similarly, he dismisses his own ruminations about what he has seen in another context, styling these "pensieri così poco edificanti" ["such not very edifying thoughts"] that he believes they are better left "allo scrittore di grande impegno sociale" ["to some writer of great social commitment"] — is he thinking once again of Moravia? — "che spiega l'Africa con infinito paternalismo a forza di concetti generali" (160; "who thanks to broad general concepts is able, with infinite paternalism, to explain Africa").

In Africa, then, as earlier in the Po valley, the narrator moves through empty spaces that are suddenly and without apparent reason interrupted by vacation villages, housing complexes, or supermarkets (Italy) or by Europeanish cities on the one hand or traditional African towns on the other (Africa). In neither place is there any apparent rationale for constructing habitations in one location rather than another. In both environments, instead, there is a powerful sense of estrangement between the human constructions and the surrounding landscape — what the critic and translator of Celati, Bob Lumley, has described as a lack of harmony between a place and those inhabiting that place (46). But then, even back in Italy, as Celati noted in *Verso la foce*, "viaggiando nelle campagne della valle padana è difficile non sentirsi stranieri" (9; "travelling through the fields of the Po valley it's difficult not to feel a foreigner").[4]

Alienated, then, from the language, social practices, and the landscape that surround him, the narrator of *Avventure in Africa* cannot be said to master the situation in which he finds himself. This is partly because for Celati, being controlled by an inherited situation is inevitable — whether those concerned are tourists or members of some other social group. "Siamo qui," he says about Talon and himself in Africa,

> a rappresentare non quello che siamo o crediamo d'essere, ma quello che dovremmo essere in quanto bianchi (ricchi, potenti, moderni, com-

---

[4]Lumley has spoken of the importance throughout Celati's fiction of "people who would otherwise be labeled deviants and marginals who do not want to or cannot conform, and those, like autodidacts and immigrants, who try hard to master conventions not their own, thereby drawing attention to the unspoken rules governing social interaction [and whose function] is also to show that normality itself is a fiction that everyone is busy sustaining" (466).

pratori di tutto). E portiamo in giro questa rappresentazione come uno scafandro, ognuno nel suo scafandro che lo isola dal mondo esterno. (11)

[We are here not in order to represent what we are or think we are but what we are supposed to be as white people (rich, powerful, modern, ready to buy up everything). And we are carrying this representation around with us like a diving bell, each one of us in a diving bell that isolates him or her from the external world.]

In this book, Celati is the deviant who acts to expose the conventionality of behavior not only in African society but everywhere. "Più resto qui," he says about his stay in Africa,

più mi sembra di vedere dappertutto ruoli che conosco, comportamenti che mi ricordano qualcosa. E' come se tutti i segreti degli uomini fossero esposti là fuori, nel funzionamento generale alla luce del giorno, nelle recite che ognuno deve fare per essere quello che è. (70)

[The longer I stay here, the more I seem to see roles that I recognize, behavior that reminds me of something. It's as if all of mankind's secrets were revealed right out there, in the general functioning of the light of day, in the play-acting that everyone must do to be the person he or she is.]

What roles have other people assumed in this book? The Africans who appear in it are a disorganized, thieving, and highly sexed lot. The Europeans, by contrast, are often organized to a fault, sexually inhibited, and while not thieves on a personal level, certainly complicit in a global system of neocolonial exploitation. Struck by these differences between the two peoples, Celati cannot help thinking about what will happen to the Africans he has met and admired in a possible future of greater economic development and personal well-being. "Diventeranno scomposti, pedagogici, romantici, depressivi, maniaci di tutto sotto controllo?" he wonders.

Crederanno nella privacy, nelle vacanze, nei progetti, nella testa proiet-
tata verso l'avvenire e mai nel presente dov'è? Si vergogneranno della
deperibilità dei corpi, del vecchiume, degli scarti, del rimediato,
dell'aggiustato? Bandiranno il disordine naturale delle cose, il contatto
non legalizzato dei corpi, le mescolanze del nuovo e del vecchio, del fresco e del putrido? (175)

[Will they become agitated, pedantic, romantic, depressed, maniacal
about keeping everything under control? Will they believe in privacy,
vacations, long-range plans, in keeping their heads faced toward the
future and never toward the present where they in fact are? Will they be
ashamed of physical decline, of old stuff, of rejects, of what has been re-
cycled or fixed up? Will they outlaw the natural disorder of things,
contacts between bodies unauthorized by law, the blending of the old
with the new, the fresh with the rotten?]

If Africans do become Europeanized in this way, Celati seems to be saying, something important and deeply human will have been lost.

Like the Italy of the Po valley, the Africa that Celati describes is awash
in the detritus of global capitalism. This leads to some striking cultural
contrasts: Tuarogs in Ray-bans, for example, young African men who
have never left their villages sporting haircuts based on those popular in
North American ghettos, and Africans everywhere in shirts with mottoes
in English that either come or pretend to come from America. Like it or
not, Africa and Europe are bound together with each other and with
America through fashion trends and marketing schemes that leapfrog
across national frontiers and easily tumble local traditions. One especially striking manifestation of the ubiquity of this throwaway consumer
civilization is the garbage that the narrator encounters — especially the
discarded plastic bags and worn-out tires that fill Africa as they do the
ditches of the Po valley.

In Africa as in Europe, moreover, distinctions between the sacred and
the venal and between country and town have been increasingly blurred
if not eliminated. In the same way that the countryside of the Po valley
has become impregnated with "un'aria di solitudine urbana" (Foce 9; "a
feeling of urban loneliness"), the boundaries between what used to seem
the very distant space of Africa and the familiar space of Europe have

been similarly effaced. No matter how remote the sites that Celati and Talon visit, there are always tourists there: typically tourists very much like them. But this is only to be expected since "ogni turista va nei posti dove vanno degli altri un po' simili a lui" (159; "each tourist goes to those places where tourists in some ways like them also go"). Even though far from home, tourists cannot exist outside the roles that they collectively imagine for themselves, indeed cannot even imagine such alternative roles.

Such an effacing of boundaries and "Americanization" of the planet is nowhere more evident than in the elimination of a sense of the sacred from human existence, a draining of awe from everyday life that is also a theme in many of Celati's Italian stories. In *Avventure in Africa,* the two travelers visit the land of the Dogon. But, except for references to writing about these people by the French ethnographer Marcel Griaule, almost nothing is said about the more direct experiences these men have. Now that it has been explained and categorized by such scholars as Griaule — whose *Masques Dogons* is meticulously arranged into categories and sub-categories with lots of tables and plates including those of Masks, Rhythms and Dances, Animals, Plants, Formulae in the Sigui Language — for Celati the Dogon religion has been evacuated of meaning, its system of signification banished to some inaccessible connotative space beyond the ethnographic descriptions and categorizations that have been accumulated about it over the years. For his part, Celati insists that he has learned nothing about this celebrated people during his travels. "Quando torno" his narrator claims, "dovrò dire che di questi villaggi non ho visto quasi niente, tutto quello che posso dire l'ho letto nel libro di Griaule" (86; "When I get home, I will have to say that I saw almost nothing of these villages; all that I will be able to say is what I read in Griaule's book").

For observers like Celati, Africa is not really "available" except as mediated by the tendentious print and electronic media. "La televisione trasmette notizie sui massacri di Ruanda," Celati notes at one point, "la mancata civilizzazione delle tenebre africane, lasciando anche intendere che in Europa si vive invece tranquilli e pacifici" (15; "The television is transmitting news of the Ruanda massacres, the lack of civilization in the African darkness, leading one to understand that in Europe, by contrast, one lives peacefully and quietly"). But the Africans too, with their Americanoid garb and haircuts and radios blasting rock and rap music, are prisoners of mediated notions of Europe and America, insouciant inhabitants of a grotesque "global village" that has reduced civilization everywhere to the lowest commercially practicable common-denominator.

What, then, has the narrator of this book learned in his travels? What have his "adventures" added up to? First of all, Celati has had the sheer fun of traveling: the exhilaration derived from breaking loose from the usual constructions of identity and expected behavior through "un'intensa osservazione del mondo esterno [che] ci rende meno apatici (più pazzi o più savi, più allegri o più disperati)" (*Foce* 9; "an intense consideration of the external world that renders us less apathetic [crazier, wiser, happier, or more desperate"]). The very confusion that travel engenders is an important part of this transformation, since "se hai la sensazione di capire tutto, passa la voglia di osservare" (95; "if you have the feeling that you are understanding everything you no longer feel the need to look at it"). In Africa, moreover, Celati has learned to be "patient" with life. One of the meanings he assigns to the two men's adventures is that of a tale of "due europei che a poco a poco si calmano e dopo non hanno mai più fretta per tutta la vita" (149; "two Europeans who gradually calm down and for the rest of their lives are never in a hurry").

But the most important achievement of this book so suspicious of "achievements" is the narrator's perception of the "niente" or "nothing" that lies at the heart of things everywhere — both in Africa and in the very un-African Paris that he returns to, for example, "dove vedi tutto pulito, ordinato, levigato, glossy, flashing, rifatto a nuovo, neanche uno scarto troppo vistoso" ["where you see that everything is clean, kept in order, polished, glossy, flashing, remade, and with no rejects in evidence"]. "Ma poi si sa" he goes on at the book's conclusion,

> che quando uno è lasciato dietro un vetro, tende a sentire che gli manca qualcosa, anche se ha tutto e non gli manca niente, e questa mancanza di niente forse conta qualcosa, perché uno potrebbe anche accorgersi di non aver bisogno davvero di niente, tranne del niente che gli manca davvero, del niente che non si può comprare, del niente che non corri-

sponde a niente, il niente del cielo e dell'universo, o il niente che hanno gli altri che non hanno niente. (179)

[But of course one knows that when someone has been left behind glass they tend to feel that something is missing, even if they have everything and nothing is missing, and this nothing missing maybe counts for something, because you can sense you really miss nothing, except for the nothing that you are really lacking, the nothing that it is impossible to buy, the nothing that corresponds to nothing, the nothing of the sky and of the universe, or the nothing that those who have nothing have.]

This "niente" that Celati has encountered in Africa is quite unlike the "horror" described by Joseph Conrad in his well-known 1899 novella, "Heart of Darkness."[5] Unlike Conrad's story, which is a "quest" tale of the sort that— as Rebecca West has noted[6] — Celati abhors, *Avventure in Africa* is not a quest but an account of usually quite aleatory wandering. The story's action is not organized into a crescendo that penetrates climactically into the heart of a mystery. Even Celati's prose seems underwritten when compared to Conrad's more flowery and frequently metaphorical writing. Above all, there is no sense in Celati's post-modern work of the modernist Conrad's "horror" — an emotion that for the earlier writer was associated with a sometimes-exceptionally brutal colonial exploitation and the darkness within the human heart. Instead of this horror, Celati has found "nothing" in Africa, though this nothing is not unique to Africa but endemic to the human condition. Instead of the appalling difference that Conrad found in Africa and attempted to define or at least describe as "darkness," Celati finds an increasing effacement of difference that is appalling too, though in a different way.

Celati's is a book about what can happen to a traveler who relinquishes control and refuses to strive, colonialist-like, to present a master narrative of what Africa is really like. "Come sanno dormire bene da queste parti!" he exclaims toward the end of *Avventure in Africa*, "Quella è una cosa da desiderare, altrochè la conquista del pianeta" (143; "How

---

[5]Conrad is an author Celati has translated.
[6]West, "Gianni Celati and Literary Minimalism" 17. See also, now, her *Gianni Celati: The Craft of Everyday Storytelling*, especially 257–69.

well they know how to sleep in this part of the world! That is something worth desiring and never mind the conquest of the planet"). Is this "weak writing," then? Perhaps, but not from a position of moral feebleness.

Works Cited

Celati, Gianni. *Avventure in Africa*. Milan: Feltrinelli, 1998. In English as *Adventures in Africa*. Trans. Adria Bernardi; Foreword Rebecca West. Chicago: U of Chicago P, 2000.

___. "Su Beckett, l'interpolazione e il gag." *Finzioni occidentali. Fabulazione, comicità e scrittura*. Turin: Einaudi, 1975. 53–80.

___. *Verso la foce*. Milan: Feltrinelli, 1989.

Griaule, Marcel. *Masques Dogons*. Paris: Insituts d'Ethnologie, 1938.

Lumley, Bob. "Gianni Celati: 'Fictions to Believe in.'" *The New Italian Novel*. Ed. Zygmunt G. Baranski and Lino Pertile. Edinburgh: Edinburgh UP, 1993. 43–58.

Novero, Cecilia. "'Baratto' di Gianni Celati e l'affermazione passiva del pudore." *Romance Languages Annual* 4 (1992): 314–18.

West, Rebecca. "Gianni Celati and Literary Minimalism." *L'anello che non tiene* 1 (1989): 11–29.

___. *Gianni Celati: The Craft of Everyday Storytelling*. Toronto: U of Toronto P, 2000.

AFRICAN IMMIGRANT LITERATURE IN ITALY

Some Remarks on African Immigrant Literature in Italian
My Homeland Is Literature

Carla Ghezzi

Istituto di Studi Italiani per l'Africa e l'Oriente, Rome

> I went up onto the quarter-deck to see my sixteen hundred travelling companions for the last time. A few minutes later the official and the Uruguayan doctor, the captain, the officers and the ship's doctor arrived. And the sad procession began. Sad, not only in itself but because the crowd was simply numbered off like a herd with no-one interested in knowing their names. The impression was that they were being counted up like goods ready for sale, as if these were not the citizens from a European state filing past us but victims of a slave-trader's raid on some African or Asian shore.[1]

The 1600 third-class passengers on board the "North America," who had embarked at Genoa bound for Latin America, were immortalized in these words by Edmondo De Amicis, who had sailed with them in 1884 and who had used his diary of the journey as the basis for *Sull'Oceano* [On the Ocean], published by Treves in Milan 24 March 1889. The book was the subject of an exceptional advertising campaign for those times that caused it to become a literary event even before publication.[2] One hundred and ten years after the event, this work by De Amicis, along with his tale "Dagli Appennini alle Ande" ["From the Appenines to the Andes"] in the collection entitled *Cuore* [*Heart*],[3] is considered a classic of Italian emigrant literature.

Let us move on from the Italian literature of emigration to the literature of immigration into Italy. In my country there is only a partial

---

[1]De Amicis 252 (the quotation refers to the edition by Giorgio Bertone [Genova: Herodote, 1983]). The book had ten editions in two weeks.

[2]See *L'Illustrazione Italiana* 11.11 16 marzo 1884: 167; 13.29 11 luglio 1886: 22; 14.7 13 febbraio 1887: 129; 14.10 6 marzo 1887: 182; 15.33 5 agosto 1888: 93; and 16.12 24 marzo 1889: cover picture, 186–87, and 190.

[3]Milano: Treves, 1886. Two months after publication the book got its 41st edition; they had published 500,000 copies in 1910 and 1,000,000 in 1923.

overlap between colonialism and immigration — compared to France and Great Britain — and so the Italian language has the advantage of neutrality compared to French or English, which are colonizing languages. For the immigrant, however, Italian has the disadvantage of a loss of identity, the identity of the colonized, which in extreme circumstances may serve as an antidote against feeling extraneousness to completely new cultural references and against the isolation it brings. The Italian language must rise to the challenge posed by new tones and standards from which we can legitimately expect its form and content to diversify and broaden. One of the earliest expressions, if not the first, in the new immigrant vocabulary, with strong pejorative connotations, is *vu' cumprà*, which some interpret as a corruption of the French *vous* [you] and Italian *comperare* [to buy].[4]

In the early stage of immigration it was in fact trade that imposed its own vision, with the classification of all non-Europeans as unlicenced hawkers. Today, however, the worrying equation of immigration with crime is asserting itself. The individual immigrant, who from the outset tended to conceal his own identity as far as possible, nowadays aspires to proclaim his set of traditions to his host society and to display his own diversity, sometimes through writing.

The first immigrant writings in our country represent a literary genre on the borderline between autobiography and fiction. The fact that they were written in the language of the host country signified the presence of Italian editors or co-authors or of a partnership, as in the case of the tried-and-tested duo Tahar Ben Jelloun and Egi Volterrani. The influence of real-life situations on this particular genre is clear: suffice it to consider one crime report, the murder of South African refugee Jerry Essan Masslo, which took place on the 24th of August, 1989, at Villa Literno, a community in the province of Caserta known for offering immigrants seasonal work harvesting tomatoes. In his collection *Dove lo Stato non c'è* [*Where There Is No State*], Ben Jelloun devotes a story to this episode, conscious of the importance of the role of literature when working on mate-

---

[4]This idiom in fact appeared the first time in 1925, in Raffaele Viviani's poem "O' tripolino," referring to a Neapolitan emigrant to Libya as a hawker (see Micheletti and Moussa Ba 157).

rial drawn from real life. But also in *La promessa di Hamadi* [*The Promise of Hamadi*] Alessandro Micheletti and Saidou Moussa Ba make the murder at Villa Literno the starting point of the incident related in their book. Finally Salah Methnani, author of *Immigrato* [*Immigrant*], the first novel(?) or autobiography(?) of immigration written in Italian, reveals that only after that crime did the weekly magazine *L'Espresso* decide to publish an inquiry and, for the first time, entrusted it to a protagonist: an immigrant. The initial idea was later distorted by Methnani who opted for the form of a travel diary, taking over other people's stories as his own and attributing his own to other people (Methnani 6–7; quoted in Valgimigli 26–27).

Reaction to the episode was strong in real terms too: the demonstration on the following 7th of October testified to a solid anti-racialist conscience, a perhaps rather confused set of demands but, certainly, a unanimous claim for a new law to replace the existing one.[5] It is difficult not to discern a link between these events and Decree Law no. 416 of December 1989, which later became Law no. 39 of 28/2/90, known as the "Martelli law," after the name of the socialist Minister of Justice who promoted it. Since then declarations of principle and pragmatism have not found their balance, partly because a large proportion of the Italian right wing uses its intransigence over the immigration question as an electoral trump card. We are probably the only country of immigration in which two public bodies, the Home Office and the National Institute of Statistics, provide conflicting figures for the number of foreigners on Italian soil (Bonifazi 258). The result of this uncertainty is limited knowledge, at all levels, of the immigrant population, which causes one Palestinian to declare:

> Wherever I go I can feel the name of foreigner written on my face. . . : I am not in my own country. I don't feel I am a citizen. . . . When you are a citizen you can choose where you want to go but in the end you know where your grave well be. (Carlini 54)

---

[5]The first organic law on immigration was no. 943 of December 30, 1986, an innovative but badly fulfilled one. A brief *excursus* of Italian set of rules on immigration is to be found in Ghezzi, "Una politica dell'immigrazione" 61–74.

Ignorance also creates imprecise terminology, which is why immigrants are collectively referred to as "*marocchini*" [Moroccans]: "*Marocchino* is a word I dislike . . . it's a kind of insult, a word which as far as I am concerned lacks humanity" (123); and he goes on: "For Italians *marocchino* is synonymous with a scruffy illiterate" (145).[6] The lines by Moroccan poet Aziz Bouzidy spring to mind:

> (. . .) Qui cara madre
> siamo più o meno tutti uguali,
> lo sporco lava-vetri
> il deliquente spacciatore
> e il "vu cumprà" ignorante
> siamo tutti in uno
> e non siamo nessuno (. . .) (Bouzidy 27–28)

> [(. . .) Here dear mother / we are more or less all the same / the filthy fellow washing windscreens / the crooked dealer / and the ignorant pedlar / are all one / and we are nobody (. . .)]

or the title of a story by the Syrian Yousef Wakkas, *Io marocchino con due kappa* [*I'm a Moroccan with Two Ks*], in which the writer provocatively renounces his own nationality and adopts the one most commonly assigned by unthinking or uneducated speakers (Wakkas 105–52).

Diffidence and sometimes hostility on the part of the host society have been the most frequent reactions to the immigration phenomenon, even if later the actual capacity to interact with it has often proved greater than expected. Indeed it only remains to ackowledge that multiracialism and multiculturalism are permanent structures in contemporary societies, including Italy (Bonifazi 241–42). Whereas in the early stages of the process, and in the wake of French experience, assimilation was seen as a desirable measure of success, it has been superseded by the principle of integration, according to which "immigrant groups accept certain values of their new society and maintain certain others from their original culture."[7]

---

[6]Quoted sentences are of Moroccan immigrants.
[7]G. Rosoli, ed., *Integrazione*, in G. Tassello, ed., *Lessico migratorio* (Rome: Cser, 1987) 119. The quotation is drawn from Bonifazi 242.

Coloro che non hanno altra
ricchezza che la loro differenza
etnica e culturale sono votati
all'umiliazione e ad ogni forma di
razzismo. Danno anche fastidio.
La loro presenza è di troppo.
Il viaggio, per loro, non sarà mai
una villeggiatura. Per loro
il viaggio è la valigia legata con
lo spago, pacchetti di roba
da mangiare e un pugno di terra
o di menta del paese, nel fazzoletto.
Con la terra si cospargono il viso
quando tutto va male
e la nostalgia diventa il solo
rifugio, l'unica consolazione. (vii)

[Those who have no other / wealth but their own ethnic and / cultural difference are consigned / to humiliation and every form of / racism. / They are also a nuisance. / Their presence is unwanted. / For them the / journey will never be / a holiday trip. For them / the journey is a bag tied up with / string, bundles of stuff / to eat and a handful of earth / or of mint from home, wrapped in a handkerchief. / They spread the earth on their faces / when everything goes wrong / and nostalgia becomes the sole / refuge, the only consolation.]

These lines from the preface to the Italian edition of *La réclusion solitaire* [*Solitaire*] by Tahar Ben Jelloun are our introduction to a heart-rending work of literature, possibly the finest of the narratives of emigration. The immigrant who shelters in a trunk, where he is greeted by the figure of a woman cut out of a magazine, has survived memory and loneliness thanks to his victory over reality through dream. Only three years later the theme of both body and memory being dispossessed occurs again in the poetry of the Albanian immigrant Gezim Hajdari:

Piove sempre
in questo

paese
forse perché sono
straniero.
Il mio corpo
nato in un paese povero
è un vaso cieco
senza memoria. (21)

[It's always raining / in this / country / perhaps because I am / an
alien. / My body / born in a poor country / is a blind vessel / without
memory.]

Tahar Ben Jelloun, known to Italians as a sensitive political commen-
tator writing for the daily newspaper *La Repubblica,* must be acknowledged as the leading figure in the cultural mediation between his own
country, Morocco, and France where he is resident; and also between
Morocco and Italy. In fact all his works have been translated into Italian;
Giorno di silenzio a Tangeri [*Day of Silence in Tangiers*] was premiered in
Italy; his novel *Les raisins de la galère* (*Nadia* in Italian) — winner of the
1996 International Prize Flaiano — which focuses on the liberation of a
woman from the subordination imposed by her sex, race, and immigrant
status, is also set in Italy. His collection of stories *Dove lo Stato non c'è,* is a
complete anomaly in the panorama of immigrant literature. It arose from
an initiative promoted by the Neapolitan daily *Il Mattino,* for an investigation into Southern Italy within a literary rather than journalistic
framework. The investigation was also transformed by the presence of
elements acknowledged as belonging to the cultural tradition of the
Southern Mediterranean shore.

From the early nineties comes an example of civil and social commitment, an initiative that brought into focus the real-life experiences of intellectual African immigrants in Italy: namely, the literary magazine
Caffè, per una letteratura multiculturale [*Café for Multicultural Literature*],
which published texts written in Italian or in translation. It was published by "Sensibili alle foglie" [Sensitive to the Leaves], the publishing
cooperative founded by Renato Curcio; the originator and director was
Massimo Ghirelli, a keen observer of the immigration phenomenon in
Italy, and scriptwriter of a famous television program called *Nonsolonero*

[*Not Just Black*]. Unfortunately, after only five editions the experiment failed, which was perhaps predictable; it resumed publication in February 1998 under another publisher.

The same commitment that had earlier inspired Ghirelli was shared by the journalists and writers who put their pens at the disposal of immigrants recounting their experiences in Italy: I am thinking here of Mario Fortunato, co-author of *Immigrato*, by the Tunisian Salah Methnani; of P. A. Micheletti, co-author of *La promessa di Hamadi* [*The Promise of Hamadi*] and of *La Memoria di A.* [*The Memory of A.*], by the Senegalese Saidou Moussa Ba; of Oreste Pivetta, editor of *Io, venditore di elefanti* [*I, Seller of Elephants*] by the Senegalese Pap Khouma, a "street" author, whose first work had reached its sixth edition in 1996; and of Carla De Girolamo and Daniele Miccione, editors of *Chiamatemi Ali*, by the Moroccan Mohamed Bouchane. The duo of Saidou Moussa Ba and P. Alessandro Micheletti merits greater attention than the other writers since, unusually in the panorama of the new emigrant narrative, they have sought the approval of public and critics with a second novel, in which autobiographical ideas overlap with historical references and material gathered from newspaper items (the story takes place in August, 1993, and puts great emphasis on the new German legislation governing the right of asylum, which became a symbol of the closure of "fortress Europe" to the waves of immigrants from the East and South).

For his second literary venture, but not for that alone, the Tunisian Mohsen Melliti can be considered a special case: in view of his narrative fiction, an essential ingredient in his first work, *Pantanella, canto lungo la strada* [*Pantanella, Song Along the Road*]; in view of his choice of language, Arabic; in view of the presentation by Rachid Boudjedra that sounds like a consacration. The story unfolds around the Pantanella, a former pasta factory, lying derelict on the outskirts of Rome, having undergone a period of worker-management by immigrants until February 1991, when it was evacuated by the police. The characters are not drawn individually but as elements in a fresco and their stories are narrated but never commented on or interpreted. The writing is naïve, rather childishly lyrical. *I bambini delle rose* [*Children of Roses*], with the same publisher, is written directly in Italian and is also aimed at young readers: the main characters are children — Nico, a gypsy of Serbian origin, and Ly, a Chinese girl.

Both sell roses, and from their initial confrontation over territorial partition the story evolves over a period of seven days, which witness the
transformation of their hostility into complicity and, possibly, love, all
set against the background of a sometimes hostile Rome by night.

Nadia, the heroine in Tahar Ben Jelloun's novel of the same name in
the Italian edition, is a girl who "frightens men." When they meet her
they "lower their eyes." Nadia is "a woman who embraces the challenge
of the whole family" of Algerian immigrants in France.[8] Her long journey takes her from the immigrant quarters of Naples to Milan and *radical
chic* Turin. She has gone in search of Naïma, a Moroccan girl who has
fled in pursuit of a man she loves, and lands up in the glossy world of
Benetton advertisements. This journey is nothing but the inner journey
of her own "ambition," her own "anger," her own "passion" and her
own "rebellion" (91).

Naci is inspired by the same feelings, although less intensely. Born in
Marseille of Saharawi parents resident in Algeria, she is the heroine of
Volevo diventare bianca [*I Wanted to Become White*] by Nassera Chohra. The
irony and humor in its events make this novel/autobiography by a
woman about a woman stand out from the other texts, in which pre-
literary experiences whose value is mainly sociological prevail. *Lontano
da Mogadiscio* [*Far from Mogadisho*], by the Somalian authoress Shirin
Ramzanali Fazel, is entirely in keeping with the *naïveté* of this literature.[9]
For her "my country was once the land of fables" (13), where the memory of the sweetness of life dissolves into a somewhat mannered lament.
Here too the prose is simple and descriptive, perhaps at the expense of
development of themes and emotions.[10]

Behind every literary work by an immigrant there is the passion and
intellectual courage of a publisher, often a small one, who decides to in-
vest energy and financial resources in a project that has never yet proved

---

[8]Pp. 48 and 53 of the Italian translation.
[9]An elegiac content has also *Aulò. Canto-poesia dall'Eritrea* by Ribka Sibhatu (Rome:
Sinnos, 1993).
[10]For a survey of immigrant literary works in Italian, see Armando Gnisci, *La letteratura
italiana della migrazione*; see also Ghezzi, "Da Driss Chraïbi a Tahar Ben Jelloun."
Armando Gnisci also published a collection of essays entitled *Creoli meticci migranti
clandestini e ribelli*. Roman publisher Lilith also published in 1998 a long poem by
Ndjock Ngana Yogo, *Il segreto della capanna*.

to be profitable in commercial terms. Nevertheless, Costa & Nolan, Datanews, Edizioni Lavoro, e/o, Lilith, Meltemi, Sensibili alle foglie, Sinnos, Theoria soldier on despite the inevitable frustrations. On the other side of the coin, two giants of Italian publishing, Bompiani and Einaudi, who publish Tahar Ben Jelloun in Italy, are content to follow a conservative wait-and-see policy that has so far borne good fruit, that is to say has found a profitable market.

The presence of foreign pupils in our schools is constantly increasing and is an important sign that immigration has become established and immigrants are being progressively integrated into our society. For this reason the whole of school textbook publishing is a sector to be conquered, because it is precisely in schools that the reality of multiculturalism is becoming most pressingly felt.

As soon as you mention small publishers of immigrant literature, you think of Alessandro and Francesco Ramberti, who have been running Fara Publishing since 1993. The name, of Longobard origin, means "the clan to which you belong" but is also the acronym of the two brothers from Santarcangelo di Romagna (in the province of Forli). Their desire to experiment with new areas of activity led them in 1997 to publish *Il Segreto di Barhume* [*The Secret of Barhume*] and in 1998 *La foglia di fico e altri racconti* [*The Fig Leaf and Other Stories*], both by the Egyptian Mohamed Ghonim, who for several years has resided in Lombardy. He is a scholar of philosophy and psychology who has also earned a good reputation in his own country as a writer of poetry and theatrical works. Among the noteworthy initiatives undertaken by Fara, mention must be made of the literary competition Eks&Tra, which enjoyed its fourth run in 1998. It is promoted in agreement with the multicultural association of the same name, the municipal museums of Rimini, the Municipality and Province of Rimini and the Emilia-Romagna Regional Council. The aim of the promoters is "to make known to the Italian public the cultural values that immigrants have to offer and to encourage the integration of differing traditions and forms of expression."[11] These are the themes from the four competitions held so far: "Confrontation between different cultures:

---

[11]See the posters of the various editions of the competition and Giovanni Razzani, "Editrice 'Fara,' libri appassionati," *Corriere di Rimini* 25 gennaio 1997: 15.

a challenge and its obstacles"; "The meeting of different cultures: what possible identity?"; "A place for memory: my tradition in a suitcase"; "Equilibrists in hired homelands? The new horizons of the multicultural society." The competition is limited to non-EU immigrants from Eastern Europe, Africa, Asia, and Latin America and is also open to their children. It is organized in two sections, poetry and prose. The works presented may be written in Italian or in the immigrant's native language with an Italian translation. Fara has collected all the winners and finalists in four volumes, one for each year of the competition: *Le voci dell'arcobaleno* (1995; *Voices of the Rainbow*) edited by Alessandro Ramberti and Roberta Sangiorgi; *Mosaici d'inchiostro* (1996; *Ink Mosaics*); *Memorie in valigia* (1997; *Memories in a Suitcase*); *Destini sospesi di volti in cammino* (1998; *Suspended Destinies of Faces on the Move*). The multicultural juries for each year of the competition are made up of university teachers and immigrant writers: Armando Gnisci; Graziella Parati; Saidou Moussa Ba; Tahar Lamri, the Algerian winner of the prose section in the first competition; also Erminia Dell'Oro and Shirin Ramzanali Fazel. The reading of these texts is an adventure of awareness, even for someone who by training and occupation is accustomed to considering literature not only as aesthetic pleasure but also as an instrument for the communication and understanding of an emerging hybrid literature.

"Non ho scelta devo raccontare" [I have no choice I must tell my story], say the lines by the Nigerian Samuel Ayotunde Kalejaiye, published in the third volume, *Memorie in valigia* (25). A literary prize actually means the chance to emerge from the anonymity, loneliness, and marginalization which mark the life of an immigrant. And then: "Voglio urlare, ma ho paura! / Mi zittiranno per sempre. / Allora lavoro in nero e basta . . ." (*Voci* 15; I want to scream, but I'm afraid! / They'll silence me forever / So I work on the black market and that's that . . .). These are the words of Vincent Depaul from the Ivory Coast in his "Lavoro nero," winner of the first prize for poetry in the first competition. And then Clementina Sandra Ammendola from Argentina writes in "Per fare teoria": ". . . emigrare. . . . / E' come far passare un'anima / da un corpo all'altro . . ." (*Mosaici* 20; . . . emigrating. . . . / Is like transferring a soul / from one body to another . . .).

In the second half of the last century Quintino Sella, Minister of Finance in several governments of the newly created Kingdom of Italy, formulated the principle that "where there is work, there is my homeland." But in this century, which will go down in history as the century of migration, Ismail Kadaré's aphorism is more fitting: "My country is Albania, but my homeland is literature." So these poets and writers in exile genuinely deserve the title "citizens of poetry," to quote the evocative title of an anthology of poetry by writers from Nigeria, the Cameroons, and Eritrea, because for them literature is the only homeland possible.[12] The force of poetry and the violence of reality are combined in an oxymoron of levity and pain in the lines written by Tahar Ben Jelloun for Driss Moussafir, an immigrant from Casablanca who died in Milan in a car-bomb explosion on the 27th of July 1993:

> Io sono quell'altro
> che ha attraversato
> un paese
> su una passerella
> sospesa
> tra due sogni.

[I am that other man / who crossed / a country / on a catwalk / suspended / between two dreams.]

Works Cited

Ben Jelloun, Tahar, with Egi Volterrani. *Dove lo Stato non c'è. Racconti italiani.* Torino: Einaudi, 1991.

___. *Giorno di silenzio a Tangeri.* Ed. Egi Volterrani. Torino: Einaudi, 1989.

___. *Nadia.* Milano: Bompiani, 1996.

___. *La Récluson solitaire.* Paris: Denoël, 1976.

Bonifazi, Corrado. *L'immigrazione straniera in Italia.* Bologna: Il Mulino, 1998.

Bouzidy, Aziz. "Nostalgia." Ramberti and Sangiorgi 27–28.

Carlini, Giuliano, ed. *La terra in faccia. Gli immigrati raccontano.* Roma: Ediesse, 1991.

Chohra, Nassera. *Volevo diventare bianca.* Roma: Edizioni e/o, 1993.

De Amicis, Edmondo. *Sull'Oceano.* Ed. Giorgio Bertone. Genova: Herodote, 1983.

---

[12]*Cittadini della poesia. Quaderni africani I* (Nigeria, Camerun, Eritrea, Firenze: Loggia de' Lanzi, 1998).

Ghezzi, Carla. "Da Driss Chraïbi a Tahar Ben Jelloun: il tema dell'emigrazione nella letteratura maghrebina di espressione francese e italiana." *Africa* 5.4 (1995): 533–43.

___. "Una politica dell'immigrazione: clandestini, pericolosi, anzi necessari." *Il Ponte* 8.5 (maggio 1997): 61–74.

Gnisci, Armando. *Creoli meticci migranti clandestini e ribelli.* Roma: Meltemi, 1998.

___. *La letteratura italiana della migrazione.* Roma: Lilith, 1998.

Hajdari, Gezim. "From *Ombre di cane.*" Ramberti and Sangiorgi.

___. *Immigrato.* Roma: Theoria, 1990.

Melliti, Mohson. *Pantanella: canto lungo la strada.* Roma: Ediziioni Lavoro, 1992.

Methnani, Salah. "Una frase gonfiata." *Caffè* 4 ottobre 1995: 6–7.

Micheletti, Alessandro, and Saidou Moussa Ba. *La promessa di Hamadi.* Novara: Istituto Geografico De Agostini, 1991.

Polveroni, Adriana. "L'immigrato racconta in italiano." *L'Unità* 26 aprile 1995.

Ramberti, Alessandro and Roberta Sangiorgi, eds. *Memorie in valigia.* Santarcangelo di Romagna: Fara, 1997.

Ramzanali Fazel, Shirin. *Lontano da Mogadiscio.* Rome: Datanews, 1994.

Sangiorgi, Roberta, and Alessandro Ramberti, eds. *Mosaici d'inchiostro.* Santarcangelo di Romagna: Fara, 1996.

___. *Le voci dell'arcobaleno.* Santarcangelo di Romagna: Fara Editore, 1995.

___. *Destini sospesi di volti in cammino.* Santarcangelo di Romagna: Fara, 1998.

Valgimigli, Nadia. "La letteratura dell'immigrazione." *Africa e Mediterraneo* 1 (settembre 1997): 26–27.

Wakkas, Yousef. "Io marocchino con due kappa." *Le voci dell'arcobaleno.* Ed. Alessandro Ramberti and Roberta Sangiorgi. Santarcangelo di Romagna: Fara Editore, 1995. 105–52.

ITALIAN IDENTITY AND IMMIGRANT WRITING
The Shaping of a New Discourse

Gabriella Romani
University of Pennsylvania

In a recent publication on postcolonial studies, the editors, Alec Hargreaves and Mark McKinney, begin their introduction by saying "Postcolonial studies have recently become one of the most dynamic fields of scholarly inquiry and debate in the English speaking world" (*Postcolonial Cultures in France* 3). Then, they proceed to lament the lack of such dynamism in the realm of French scholarly inquiry. Furthermore, Hargreaves and McKinney argue in their book that while the postcolonial discourse is ignored by the main institutions, French society shows the presence of such discourse at different levels of cultural production.

Anyone who has worked on the literature of immigration in Italy is well aware that the lack of scholarly interest in postcolonial studies is not exclusively a French problem, as on Italian soil very little attention has been paid by the Italian academy to this branch of scholarly investigation. In Italy, as well as in France, there seems to be a dichotomous representation and visibility of the immigrant presence. While, in fact, the Italian literary academy does not acknowledge the immigrant text production of the last ten years, different cultural venues such as small publishers, scholars from departments other than Italian Literature, scholars from the United States, and various literary and cultural organizations provide space and visibility to those immigrant writers who would otherwise be unable to make themselves heard, seen, and noticed by the Italian public. Far from being a mere marginal phenomenon, immigrant literature is today relevant to anyone who is interested in the current Italian cultural panorama, and to those who are eager to look forward in time and imagine what Italy will be racially and culturally in twenty years. The literature of immigration provides today a great potential for creating new and innovative spaces in the Italian cultural discourse.

The discussion on postcolonial issues in Italy cannot evidently be totally compared to that taking place in France, given the latter country's longer history of colonialism and larger presence of immigrants than Italy. The French experience is nevertheless illuminating. Despite the more recent phenomenon of foreign immigration to Italy, it is important to keep in mind some of the questions raised by Hargreaves and McKinney within the French context in order to investigate the effects that immigration is having on Italian society at large, that is not only at the level of economic and social changes but also at the level of cultural representation. With this objective in mind, we need first of all to explore the reasons for which the study of immigrants' cultural influence can no longer be ignored. In this regard, Ezio Raimondi reminds us that:

> La letteratura non può realizzare sino in fondo la propria forza, la propria disposizione, la propria invenzione, se non si fonda su un'intensa vita interiore della coscienza. Questa deve essere l'eco della vita contemporanea, deve avere il segno dell'attualità, deve essere in rapporto col proprio tempo presentandone i conflitti. (*Letteratura e identità nazionale* 22)

> [Literature cannot realize its own potentiality, its own disposition and invention, unless it relies purposefully on the interior life of our own conscience. It should be the echo of our contemporary life, it should carry the sign of actuality, it should be in rapport with, and address the conflicts of, its own time.]

If it is true, as Raimondi suggests, that literature is significantly intertwined with the interior and exterior reality of those who live on its national territory, then the literary critic who approaches today's Italian cultural panorama has to take into account also the social transformation of Italy and, in particular, he or she has to be able to recognize the existence of an 'area,' a domain within the Italian cultural society and production that is inhabited by immigrants. By the term 'area,' I do not mean the ghettoes, the *banlieues* that surely exist anywhere, in the outskirts of Paris as well as those of Turin, but rather the space of the social and cultural world of today's Italy that is characterized by what Francoise Lionnet defines as "hybrid identities," that is by the co-presence of diverse cultural values and identities. While coming from different ethnic, religious, and cultural plains, these elements tend to occupy "interrelated, if not overlapping, spaces" (Lionnet 101). The encounter between foreign and national identities in Italy, therefore, should be envisioned in terms of its interrelating effects, rather than in terms of its conflictual and problematic outcomes, of which the national press does not fail to remind us on a daily basis. Today in Italy there are more than a million immigrants who are not only engaged in manual work, but who participate in the cultural and literary life of the country. As a result of this participation, Italian cultural production is becoming significantly more varied and heterogeneous in its composition, introducing a scenario of multiculturalism and multiracialism that is already a reality in Italian classrooms, and that points to a much more extended development of the phenomenon.

In recent years, the study of literature has been under great scrutiny, with scholars questioning old and new directions that the discipline has been and should be taking. It has become a common theme to talk about the crisis of literary criticism in Italian literary studies, as elsewhere. Alberto Asor Rosa in his recent publication *Genus italicum* finds one of the causes of such a crisis in the rising "provincialism" of Italian critical studies (xiv), and Armando Gnisci reinforces this notion by advocating the dismissal of the "decayed and insignificant national literature" in favor of the "many and good traditions of literatures from around the world. So at least it [the Italian literary public] participates in a planet-wide colloquium"[1] (*Creoli, meticci migranti clandestini e ribelli* 100). In a similar polemical vein, Raimondi reminds us that the literary tradition "non è solo qualcosa da conservare: è anche qualcosa da far crescere e, forse, da trasformare, quasi si trattasse di una radice su cui dovrà crescere il nuovo" (21; is not only something to preserve, it is also something to let grow and, perhaps, to transform, as if it were a root from which something new would grow). Asor Rosa's and Gnisci's statements are provocative and well taken, as I believe the time has come for the field of Italian Literature to pay serious attention to the literature of im-

---

[1]All translations are mine, unless otherwise stated.

migration and to its potential for opening new venues for cultural production and critical inquiry.

A theoretical formulation of the notion of planet-wide colloquium, evoked by Gnisci, has been proposed by Edouard Glissant. Glissant uses the term "creolization" to define the cultural life of several parts of the American continent, particularly the Caribbean area and Louisiana, and expands that definition to other parts of the world that today present the irreversible process of social, racial, and cultural intermixing. "Creolization" explains Glissant, is a process that presupposes assigning 'equal value' to all the different elements pertaining to a given cultural discourse. Edouard Glissant writes:

> Les phénomènes de créolisation sont des phénomènes importants, parce qu'ils permettent de pratiquer une nouvelle approche de la dimension spirituelle des humanités. Une approche qui passe par une recomposition du paysage mental de ces humanités d'aujourd'hui. Car la créolisation suppose que les éléments culturels mis en présence doivent obligatoirement être "équivalents en valeur" pour que cette créolisation s'effectue réellement. (*Introduction* 17)

> [The phenomena of creolization are very important, because they permit the practice of a new approach to the spiritual dimension of humanity. An approach which implies a recomposition of the mental landscape of contemporary humanity. In this way, for the process of creolization to actually take place it is necessary that the cultural elements that comprise it will be "equal in value."]

The premise for a renewal of the spiritual, cultural, and, therefore, literary dimension of our national life lies, according to Glissant,[2] in the promotion of a discourse that presents all elements as comparable, that is worthy of comparison, because equal in their essence and value. Moreo-

---

[2]I realize that Glissant's theorization does not refer specifically to a discourse circumscribed by national boundaries, but on the contrary considers any such discourse outside of geographical as well as national constrains. In this regard, see his notion of "une pensée archipélique" (43). For the sake of my argument, however, I do find it useful to look at Glissant's description of the mechanisms that govern the interrelations between different racial and cultural values regardless of the location.

ver, Glissant emphasizes the factor of unpredictability (*l'imprévisibilité;* 19), which is fundamental for the process of creolization and interrelation. When different cultural elements meet, they interrelate in a fashion that is unpredictable but that results in the inevitable intermixing of the various elements engaged in the discourse. Glissant's theorization of the interrelation between different cultural forces calls to mind the work of another scholar, Francoise Lionnet, who formulated the concept of "métissage."[3] In *Logiques métisses,* Lionnet underlined two fundamental points of postcolonial discourse: first of all, the so-called 'inferior' or subaltern elements "contribute to the evolution and transformation of the hegemonic system by producing resistances and counter-discourses" (102). Secondly, the patterns of influence "are never unidirectional. Since the influence is usually mutual and reciprocal" (103). Both Lionnet and Glissant emphasize the "inter"relation and inevitable mutual influence of different cultural forces that, regardless of their "status," play a significant role in the cultural production of the country. While Glissant's theory of creolization might seem utopian to some, or seem like an overly optimistic interpretation of cultural and social conflicts in modern society, it provides a valuable theoretical framework for my study of immigrant literature in Italy insofar as it explains the unavoidable linguistic and cultural interrelation of multicultural societies.

Immigrant texts, therefore, although still marginalized in Italian national literary and cultural discourse, have the potential to contribute to, and to reinvigorate the Italian national literary discourse. This potential relies on the disclosure of new cultural and linguistic elements and their unpredictable intermingling with the Italian cultural background. The academic shortsightedness with respect to immigrant writing prevents critics from recognizing how immigrant writing is already and inevitably part of the new Italian reality and identity. As Glissant points out, the

---

[3]It must be noted that Glissant explicitly differentiates his work from that of Lionnet. His theory of creolization, according to him, differs from the notion of *métissage,* specifically for its capacity to be unpredictable. Glissants writes: "La créolisation exige que les éléments hétérogènes mis en relation "s'intervalorisent," c'est-à-dire qu'il n'y ait pas de dégradation ou de diminution de l'etre, soit de l'intérieur, soit de l'extérieur, dans ce contact et dans ce mélange. Et pourquoi la créolisation et pas le métissage? Parce que la créolisation est imprévisible alors que l'on pourrait calculer les effets d'un métissage" (19).

world today is formed by micro and macro worlds of cultural and linguistic 'compenetration' (*interpénétration*; 19). The texts of immigrants to Italy represent, perhaps, the best and most promising example in Italian literature today for the interpretation and representation of a more modern and perspicacious vision of society. Far from speaking solely about the immigrant experience, immigrant literature has much to say about Italian society at large.

In the last few years a plethora of publications thematically focused on the notion of Italian identity have appeared in Italian bookstores. A few examples are: *Genus italicum* (1997), by Alberto Asor Rosa; *L'italiano: il carattere nazionale come storia e come invenzione* (1996), by Giulio Bollati; *Letteratura e identità nazionale* (1998), by Ezio Raimondi. All these texts provide a thorough scholarly investigation of the past Italian literary and historical tradition and attempt to define the notion of Italian identity and Italian literariness. What I find most interesting about them is the way in which they point out the urgency and pertinence of a discourse on identity within the realm of Italian studies. They do not, however, include in their critical investigation an analysis or even a mention of how current Italian literary identity is or will be affected by the appearance of immigrants both in everyday experience and in the broad cultural realm of Italian life.

The question of identity undoubtedly constitutes a central aspect of immigrant writing. It is possible to identify two different, and yet interrelated, directions of narrative development of this topic. The first one is represented by the author's implicit or explicit attempt to portray the immigrant's search for a new identity in Italy. The protagonist of the story, often the author himself or herself, recounts the events that accompany the experience of immigration to Italy. The narration of this experience, far from being limited to factual observations, also provides reflections on the condition of the immigrant in a foreign land. An example of this type of narration can be found in *Immigrato* by Salah Methnani, who talks about "viaggio nel Sud di me stesso"[4] [voyage in the

---

[4]Salah Methnani writes: "Alla fine, con lucidità, ho pensato che risalire l'Italia corrispondeva, nella mia personale geografia, a una discesa nel Sud di me stesso" (Fortunato and Methnani 42).

South within me] when he is traveling from Sicily toward the North of Italy in a desperate attempt to find work. The protagonist of *Immigrato* realizes that the further he moves away from his homeland (Tunisia) the more he feels the necessity to search inward and analyze the changes that his moving to Italy implied, not only in relation to the exterior aspects of his life, but also and especially to those more deeply connected to his personal identity.

Along the lines of this search for identity, immigrant writers also strive to represent the relationship between the immigrant and the Italian. The portrayal of this relationship is characterized by a double interpretative act. On the one hand these writers look at Italian identity from the point of view of the immigrant and, on the other, they try to interpret their reflected image into the 'eyes' of the Italian and thus deal with their own foreign identity as seen from the point of view of the Italian. In short, what the immigrant writer relates is not only what he/she perceives around him/herself, but also how the writer perceives being seen by the Italian. Graziella Parati, in an essay significantly entitled "Lo sguardo dell'altro" [The Gaze of the Other], examines the mechanism of reciprocal observation and underlines that: "lo straniero diventa una costruzione culturale separata dall'identità fisica dell'altro e si carica ideologicamente di significati che riflettono le tensioni all'interno della società ospitante" (Sangiorgi and Romberti, eds., *Destini sospesi di volti in cammino* 17). With their narratives, immigrant writers destabilize established and preconceived cultural models.

Such a narrative, developed on the disclosure and interpretation of identity, is often based on a process that I would like to call of 'familiarization.' This is a strategy that aims at presenting something alien or strange in a manner that makes it seem familiar. Both the Italian words, *straniero* and *strano* derive from the Latin *extraneum*, which means coming from outside, that which is unfamiliar. The literature of immigration strives to make familiar what the Italian perceives as *strano/straniero* in order to open a space for itself within Italian cultural discourse. This process develops through two distinct segments of narrative discourse that usually occur in sequence. On one hand the writer tends to introduce the reader to the writer's cultural origins and customs, relating his or her past life still in the country of origin, and on the other the writer projects him/herself into the future, by envisioning a reader who will have learned about and will be made familiar with the different customs. Familiarization is therefore the opposite of what is generally referred to as the process of "estrangement." Historically the terms "estrangement" or "alienation" have been used respectively by Victor Shklovslky and Walter Benjamin to define a narrative strategy that introduces certain cultural or linguistic elements that would be "foreign" to the context in which they appear. The result of this process is one of poetic creation built on the hiatus between the expectations of the audience and the estrangement caused by the insertion of uncontextualized elements. Walter Benjamin, in his description of Brecht's epic theatre, underlines how Brecht's method is "counterposed to the identification of the viewer with the work (and its characters) in traditional theatre" (Wolin 149). While the familiarization strategy proceeds in a direction opposite to that of estrangement because it poses strangeness as its premise and not its end, it does not necessarily imply or welcome the reader's or the viewer's identification. The immigrant text that adopts a strategy of familiarization aims at the recognition of its existence and the affirmation of its cultural, social, and human value. Ultimately it aims at creating a dialogue with the Italian audience.

The strategy of familiarization often implies the correction of an ill-perceived image of the foreigner. It establishes a creative process of legitimization. Talking about one's past life and one's cultural habits presents not only a narration of events in the immigrants' life, but also and foremost serves as an affirmation of the speaking subject, who is trying to correct a stereotyped and prejudiced vision of the immigrant and thus to open new spaces for dialogue between Italian and non Italian cultural forces. Immigrant writers, with the writing and publication of their texts, seek to affirm their subjectivity by resisting Western notions of immigrant victimization and subordination.

The need to correct a distorted image of the immigrant is often the catalyst for the literary production of, specifically, female immigrants. Anty Grah, a woman from the Ivory Coast now living in Italy, while receiving a prize in 1996 for her story "Cronaca di un'amicizia," made a short speech in which she denounced the spreading popularization, supported by the media, of a negative image of African women living in

Italy. She said: "African women are not all prostitutes." I will not embark here upon a discussion of mass media representation of the female immigrant (a topic that would require in itself a separate study). The point, for present purposes, is that Anty Grah's speech and short story are emblematic of a writing that, again, purports to correct a negative image by introducing the reader to the author's life and country of origin. Alessandro Portelli has noted that female immigrant writers tend to write more of what he defines as "autobiography proper," that is texts devoted to the narrator's pre-emigration experience and native environment (11). Describing one's past allows the writer to affirm her past and cultural identity and thus engage the reader in a dialogical interaction about immigrants and their identity. Furthermore, it introduces the Italian reader to new cultural and linguistic information as these texts often present a lexicon and customs that are unfamiliar to the reader. Anty Grah opens her "Cronaca di un'amicizia" explaining to an Italian the use and connotations of the words brother and sister within an African context:

> Eravamo cresciuti tutti nello stesso quartiere, loro erano le sorelle maggiori. In Africa, le sorelle maggiori non sono sempre quelle di sangue, ma sono chiamate così per rispetto della persona più grande di te. Ma a forza di vivere insieme finiamo per chiamarci tutti fratelli grandi o piccoli. (60)

> [we all grew up in the same village, they were the older sisters. In Africa, older sisters are not always related by blood, but are called this as a sign of respect for a woman older than you. But living together we all end up calling each other brothers, regardless of age.]

Anty Grah's text also introduces the reader to some expressions in the original language, which are part of the narrative but cannot be translated into Italian. This choice of leaving the untranslatable vocabulary in the original language, rather than paraphrasing or approximating its meaning, is commonly found in immigrant texts and reflects the author's determination to maintain a direct and vivid connection with one's cultural and linguistic roots.[5] It also enhances the mediating role of the text

---

[5]An example of this type of untranslatable vocabulary is provided by the word "ghurba"

between the culture and language of origin and the Italian reader and context, thus producing a narrative of hybridization.[6]

The dialogue opened by immigrant writing is also one between present and future. The narrative of immigrant literature projects itself into the future, toward future generations by implicitly or explicitly envisioning a society with better relations between immigrants and the country at large; it is not a coincidence, in fact, that many books written by immigrants are today printed by publishers that target a young market of schoolchildren and teenagers. Much can be said about the problems and difficulties connected to the Italian publishing world in regard to immigrant texts. Here, however, I limit my inquiry to those texts that specifically address a young readership.

In particular I would like to focus on two female writers whose books target children: Maria de Lourdes Jesus who wrote *Racordai* (1996), and Ribhka Sibhatu with her *Aulò: canto-poesia dall'Eritrea* (1993); both books were published by Sinnos Editrice. Tullio De Mauro states in the introduction to Maria de Lourdes Jesus's book that he hopes that Sinnos "faccia scuola," that is that the publisher's decision to publish books written by immigrants becomes not only a model for other publishers but also an instrument for teachers who help form the minds of future generations. De Mauro projects his vision to the future where he sees the possibility of a plurilinguistic and multicultural society in Italy. The authors themselves include this vision in their narrative. Maria de Lourdes Jesus explains that "Racordai" :

> È un augurio di Buon Anno, ma è soprattutto un canto di speranza per tutte le persone che aprono la porta della loro casa, e che quindi, partecipano all'attesa di un tempo migliore. A capodanno come in qualunque altro giorno della nostra vita. Allo stesso modo anch'io pretendo di entrare con il mio *racordai* nelle vostre case, sia capoverdiane che non capoverdiane. Non è un progetto ambizioso, è solo un'oc-

---

(approximately meaning homesickness, nostalgia) used by Mohsen Melliti in *Pantanella: canto lungo la strada* (Roma: Edizioni lavoro, 1992).

[6]Two very good example of the above mentioned narrative of hybridization can be found in Paul Bakolo Ngoi's "L'immigrata" and Cristina De Caldas Brito's "Ana de Jesus" in Sangiorgi and Romberti, eds., *Le voci dell'arcobaleno*, respectively, 73–80, 59–61.

casione per parlare tra noi, un modo per stare insieme, al suono semplice, ma ricco di auguri e promesse. (8)

[It is a New Year wish, but above all it is a song of hope for all the people who open the door of their home and who, therefore, participate in the coming of a better future. On New Year's day as on any other day of our life. In a similar fashion, I try also to enter with my *racordai* in your homes, whether you are from Cape Verde or not. It is not an ambitious project, it's only an opportunity to talk to each other, a way to be together, a simple tune but rich with wishes and promises.]

While Ribhka Sibhatu in her attempt to familiarize the reader with new cultural and linguistic terms, writes that:

Nell'altopiano eritreo, la poesia è un'espressione popolare. L'*aulò* è una specie di poesia-canto, così come può essere una poesia-pianto. Non viene né scritta né ripetuta, ma affidata alla memoria degli ascoltatori in varie occasioni, per esempio nei matrimoni, nei funerali, ecc. Si tramanda tramite il racconto. (60)

[On the Eritreian plateau, poetry is the expression of the people. The *aulò* is a sort of poem-song, similar to a crying poem. It does not get either written or repeated, but is entrusted to the memory of its listeners on various occasions, for example at weddings, funerals, and so on. It is transmitted through the telling.]

Both the writing and the publishing of these books clearly display a didactic intention and a desire to participate in the cultural and mental formation of the Italian future generation, a generation, that is, inclusive also of those who, born and raised in Italy, are of different national origins. The figure of the young reader then is charged with symbolic value, as he or she becomes the repository of a future hope, of an image of society in the future, one that recognizes and embraces diversity.

Racordai as well as *Aulò* are published in a double linguistic format: with the writer's language of origin on one page and the Italian equivalent on the other. This choice suggests that the books are not just written for Italian schoolchildren, as they address at the same time an audience of Italian native speakers and one that instead belongs to the writer's language of origin (Portuguese for de Lourdes Jesus and Tigrè for Sibhatu). Both books present at the end a concise "yellow pages" of information that could be useful to both Italian and immigrant readership. The reader of *Racordai* and *Aulò* is potentially, though not exclusively, the child of today who still has to become familiar with the 'other' culture, but is also the adult of tomorrow who will live in a society with Italians not all of Italian origin. The linguistic aspect of these books is very important because the bilingual presentation of the text declares the authors' intention to create a bridge of communication between the host culture and the foreign one, between present and future, through the introduction of new cultural and linguistic elements and the construction of a context that belongs to both the immigrant and the Italian world.

The image of a shared, common ground of national cultural and social development evoked by these texts is very powerful. It suggests the importance of the workings of different cultural trends and systems, both now and in the future.

To return to my initial question (why pay attention to the literature of immigration?), I would like to conclude by again quoting Glissant, who reminds us that:

> l'artiste est celui qui approche l'imaginaire du monde, et sait que les idéologies du monde, les visions du monde, les prévisions, les plans sur la comète commencent à faillir et qu'il faut commencer à lever cet imaginaire. Ce n'est plus là rêver le monde, c'est y entrer. (57)

> [The artist is one who approaches the imaginary and knows that when the ideologies of the world, its visions, its anticipations and plans start falling apart it is necessary to replace this imaginary. It is not a question of dreaming the world but of entering it.]

Immigrant writers are proposing, with their texts, a praxis and a theory of enrichment of the Italian imaginary. Their texts eloquently indicate new directions and perspectives in our national cultural and literary discourse. The task now falls on us, the readers, to respond to the immigrant texts and participate to the debate on multiculturalism that constitutes the reality of not only today's Italy but also, and especially, of the

Italian society of tomorrow. "It is not a matter of dreaming a new world, but of entering it."

Works Cited

Asor Rosa, Alberto. *Genus italicum: saggi sull'identità letteraria italiana nel corso del tempo.* Torino: Einaudi, 1997.

Bollati, Giulio. *L'italiano: il carattere nazionale come storia e come invenzione.* Torino: Einaudi, 1983.

Ceserani, Remo. *Lo straniero.* Roma: Laterza, 1998.

de Lourdes Jesus, Maria. *Racordai: vengo da un'isola di Capo Verde Sou de una ilha de Cabo Verde.* Roma: Sinnos Editrice, 1996.

Fortunato, Mario, and Salah Methnani. *Immigrato.* Roma: Theoria, 1990.

Ginzburg, Carlo. *Occhiacci di legno.* Milano: Feltrinelli, 1998.

Glissant, Edouard. *Introduction à une poétique du diverse.* Paris: Editions Gallimard, 1996.

Gnisci, Armando. *Creoli meticci migranti clandestini e ribelli.* Roma: Meltemi, 1998.

Grah, Anty. "Cronaca di un'amicizia." AA.VV. *Mosaici d'inchiostro.* Santarcangelo di Romagna: Fara Editore, 1996.

Hargreaves, Alec, and mark McKinney, eds. *Postcolonial Cultures in France.* London: Routledge, 1997.

Lionnet, Francoise. "*Logique métisses*: Cultural Appropriation and Postcolonial Representations." *College Literature* 19.3 (Oct 1992): 100–20.

Portelli, Alessandro. "Mediterranean Passage: The Beginning of an African Italian Literature and the African American Example." *Transatlantic Passages.* Oxford: Oxford UP, 1997.

Raimondi, Ezio. *Letteratura e identità nazionale.* Milano: Mondadori, 1998.

Sangiorgi, Roberta, and Alessandro Ramberti, eds. *Le voci dell'arcobaleno.* Santarcangelo di Romagna: Fara Editore, 1995.

___. *Mosaici d'inchiostro.* Santarcangelo di Romagna: Fara Editore, 1996.

___. *Destini sospesi di volti in cammino.* Ramberti. Santarcangelo di Romagna: Fara Editore, 1998.

Sibhatu, Ribka. *Aulò: canto-poesia dall'Eritrea.* Roma: Sinnos Editrice, 1993.

Wolin, Richard. *Walter Benjamin: An Aesthetic of Redemption.* Berkeley: U of California P, 1994.

THE ECONOMY OF OTHERNESS
Modifying and Commodifying Identity

Marie Orton
Brigham Young University

> We are living a globalization of humans. I believe this concept of border as we have had in the past is now a relic of the eighteenth century. . . . In the European community, we have eliminated the border for goods. We eliminate the borders for information. We eliminate the borders for money. The border concept must change completely, and quickly to accommodate the reality of human movement. — Sebastião Salgado

Twentieth-century migrations, specifically those in the second half of the century, distinguish themselves from previous migrations in several significant ways: first, they are far more mobile than earlier migrations; second, they are occurring on a far greater scale than ever before, and third, they cut across all social and economic divisions. In 1979, 20 million people immigrated internationally (Gardezi 2). Preliminary statistics indicate that only two decades later, this number has increased more than five-fold (*World Population Data Sheet 1999*). Theories abound as to the determining factors that govern migration flows, and debates continue for the formulation of models that accurately reflect the interplay of human and economic motivational forces. The point I wish to emphasize is that while global migration is generally viewed economically, it is regulated politically (Rudolph and Morokwasic 19) and, most importantly, informed culturally. As Canadian sociologist Hassan Gardezi has observed, "While interest in determining the magnitudes of migration flows has been widespread . . . related human issues have lagged behind. Much less has been done to address these issues . . ." (1). He further points out that the regulations established to protect property crossing international borders have a long historical precedent and are extensive, elaborate, and enforced when compared to the regulations to protect individuals crossing those same borders that have historically been far less extensive or protective. Gardezi's observations suggest an antithetical relationship between foreign goods and foreign people, at least inasmuch as their value to the importing culture is concerned. It is precisely this relationship between the economy that structures and values material exchange, and the "economy" that structures and values cultural exchange that I wish to explore.

In Italy, the unprecedented waves of immigrants, numbering in the millions of individuals by the early 1980s,[1] have heightened the issues and tensions surrounding the crossing of international borders. As many scholars and journalists have noted, Italy's dramatic and recent transition from being a nation of "emigration" to a nation of "immigration" has made multicultural issues new and pressing in Italy, and the participation of immigrants in Italian society has brought to the fore the possibility of redefining Italian culture. The parallel process of redefining national and personal identity informs the emerging and acclaimed artistic productions by and about immigrants. The early 1990s witnessed the first widely-circulated publications by immigrant authors in Italy about the immigrant experience, several of which have become best-sellers.[2] *Io, venditore di elefanti*, one of the earliest texts by an immigrant author, Pap Khouma from Senegal, is now in its eighth edition and has entered the public school curriculum.[3] His autobiographical account of an African's encounter with the Occident attempts a double project: to construct a hybrid identity negotiated between a Western culture and a non-Western

---

[1]Statistics regarding immigration into Italy are highly approximate; particularly approximative are the statistics from the earlier phases of migrations (late 1970s and early 1980s), and those relative to the large waves of refugees who entered Italy with the outbreak of civil war in Somalia (1991–93) and the war in Bosnia (1991; Bosnias currently represent the largest group of immigrants entering Italy). In broad terms, the official statistics on immigration published annually in *Immigrazione Dossier Statistico* (Rome: Anterem, 1992-present) suggest that in the past two decades, over 4 million people from 180 countries have tried to immigrate into Italy.

[2]Oreste Piavetta highlights the twenty most widely-circulated texts by immigrant authors in Italy. For translations into English of texts by immigrant authors in Italy, see the anthology *Mediterranean Crossroads: Migration Literature in Italy*, ed. and intro. Graziella Parati.

[3]All translations are mine. I cite here from the fourth edition of *Io, venditore di elefanti* (Milan: Garzanti, 1996). Garzanti published the first seven editions of the text; publication rights were bought in 1998 by Petrini Editori of Milan.

culture by dismantling the reductive, essentialized identity imposed upon "the African immigrant" and by so doing, to suggest a re-definition of "Italy" or "Italian." The protagonist, who as the text's title suggests, survives in Europe as a street vendor, and narrates the crossing of multiple borders, both geographic and cultural. In his movement across borders, he continually faces two overlapping economies: the capitalist economy of material exchange, and a second economy, an economy of stereotypes and coterminous restrictions by which nations and cultures relate to the Other. The narrator confronts both economies in every encounter with Europeans, but those encounters make evident that in both economies, the commodity in question is identity.

Khouma's text is clearly informed by the desire to rewrite the dominant stereotype of the uneducated, illegal immigrant (*clandestini* or *extracomunitari*), and restore individual identity to the ever-increasing ocean of faceless African immigrants in Italy. The text relates the multiple migrations of the protagonist, Pap, and his circuitous path to identity construction. Pap trained as a potter in Senegal but could not find work. He leaves his homeland to work as a street vendor on the Ivory Coast, then, still in pursuit of steady employment, goes to Italy, then to Paris, returns to Italy, and then to Senegal before finally settling in Rome where he organizes and becomes the first president of the *Associazione senegalese italiana*.[4] In relating his own story of immigration, Khouma inserts the stories of other immigrants, and casts his own case as representative. In addition, his narration recounts not only Pap's own journey, but the political path of immigration law in Italy as well, entwining the "private" with the "public" story by relating how Pap changes as the environment changes around him. His rewriting of his own identity has wider resonances, however, as Khouma uses the reinvention of Pap's identity to parallel the profound alterations in what it means to be "Italian."

Upon arrival in Italy, the protagonist realizes quickly that survival in Italy is contingent upon his conforming to the cultural expectations of the "immigrant," which include an essentialized view of Africa and Afri-

---

[4]This association, the first cooperative of immigrants in Italy, was organized in 1988 and is still functioning. Khouma resigned as president in 1992. (Interview with the author, October 9, 1998.)

cans. The economic exchange in the selling reflects the larger economy in which Pap finds himself — an economy in which the European conception of his Otherness determines who he is and the possibility of his immediate economic survival. In order to participate in the market economy of the host country, the immigrant must conform to the Western "market" namely, the cultural expectations of what Africa is and can be. Working as a street vendor, Pap survives by selling objects that, according to Italians, represent Africa:

> . . . mi infiltro, allungando le mie belle mani cariche di elefanti, elefanti e maschere dell'India del Kenia, della Costa d'Avorio, del Senegal e del Mali.
> La mia Africa in vendita.
> C'è sempre qualcuno che si mette a esporre le sue idee sull'Africa e racconta di lunghi viaggi, incontri, città. Lasciamolo dire. È un buon modo per incominciare le vendite. (61)

> [I slip in, extending my lovely hands weighted down with elephants, elephants and masks from India, Kenya, the Ivory Coast, Senegal, and Mali.
> My Africa for sale.
> There's always someone who starts to expound his ideas on Africa and relate his stories of long voyages, encounters, cities. Let's let him talk. It's a good way to start selling.]

This exchange typifies the African immigrant's position in the Western world and the Western economy in which "cultural exchange" exists only in the form of one culture "consuming" the (stereotyped) artifacts of another. The "buyer-is-always-right" attitude Pap ironically assumes reveals — and indicts — the non-Western immigrant's situation *vis-à-vis* the Western economy, namely that he must be "knowable" in order to be "marketable." In her article, "Strangers in Paradise," Graziella Parati observes,

> This paradoxical act of selling the symbols of one's culture, as translated into "souvenirs," defines the alienation of the immigrant man isolated in a marginal space defined both by the new Western culture and by the

> symbols, often the stereotypes, of his country of origin ... in this
> movement to Italy, the objects to be sold "become," for Italians, the im-
> migrants' native culture. In this *reductio ad unum*, "difference" is tangi-
> bly objectified and visible on the market. (183)

The objectification of cultural difference ultimately extends to the individual. By identification with the culture for sale ("My Africa for sale"),
the "difference" of the individual is completely objectified, and then
bought and sold. Here, making the culture visible and consumable signals a complete objectification, not only of African culture, but of the individual African. As Homi Bhabha has theorized, "colonial discourse
produces the colonized as a fixed reality which is at once 'other' and yet
entirely knowable and visible" ("The Other Question" 23).

As Bhabha points out, by objectifying the identity of the Other, by
rendering the Other "knowable and visible," the discourse of colonial
power establishes an economy in which power remains with the objecti-
fier, or, in the commercial model, with the buyer. In Khouma's text,
when the protagonist begins selling he becomes readily aware that the
market value of goods is determined exclusively by the desire and actions of his European customers. The buyers' complete control over the
market, and their economic exploitation of the vendors is symptomatic
of the larger discourse that criminalizes the immigrants and protects the
exploiters. One evening, a well-dressed customer threatens the narrator,
"O mi dai la roba al prezzo che dico io, o faccio arrivare i carabinieri"
(65; "Either you give me your goods at the price I say or I'll call the police). The price of the goods is not fixed by supply, demand, or enhanced
by labor. Rather the salesman is forced to sell his goods for whatever the
buyer offers, since the buyer can call the police, and the salesman will be
arrested for selling illegally. The buyer acts as thief, albeit one protected
by the state institution. The unethical business tactics of the elegant customer stand as indictment also for the economy that allows him to take
advantage of the narrator, as well as implicitly condemning the institutions that protect him for his act of theft. The narrator further indicts that
economy by prefacing his account of this theft by extortion with an actual theft:

Un ragazzo si muove furtivo attorno alle nostre collane. Finisce che ne sparisce una. Un furto. Ce ne siamo accorti. Se ne accorge anche l'amico: "Metti giu' la collana." Qui scoppia la rissa. "Adesso chiamo la polizia, se non restituisci la collana." Mamma mia, siamo a posto.

Ci si mette di mezzo il barista: "Dai, muoviti, tira fuori la collana che hai rubato. . . ." A questo punto il venditore senegalese si appiattisce contro il muro, si rifugia dietro l'attaccapanni, cerca insomma di sparire: "Se arriva la polizia, qui a finire dentro sono io." (64)

[A guy moves furtively around our necklaces. In the end, one disappears. A theft. We realize it. A friend recognizes it, too. "Put the necklace back." Now a fight is going to break out. "I'll call the police if you don't put the necklace back." Oh great, this is just what we need.

Now the bartender jumps in. "Come on, move it, pull out the necklace that you stole. . . ." At this point, the Senegalese salesman flattens himself against the wall, hides in the coat rack, basically tries to disappear. "If the police come, the one they will end up putting away will be me."]

In both cases, the victim will be condemned under the law that will protect the victimizer. When someone steals from the street vendor, he cannot report it, knowing that he will be jailed for not having a visa, while the thief will go free. Khouma's account of the two "thefts" act as an indictment not only of the capitalist economy and the institutions that support it, but also of the economy of otherness that protects the "citizen" at the expense of the "other." In both "thefts" the material exchange is actually an encounter of power, power over the market, and how goods are exchanged, but also power over identity, for it is the objectifying discourse of otherness that imposes a disempowered identity on the narrator and allows and protects Westerners who take economic advantage of him.

Khouma's text reveals that the objectified "other" is not only visible and knowable, but marketable and consumable as well. The "knowability" of the other fulfills its sexual connotations in the prostitution of African immigrants. In this way, prostitution becomes the most visible manifestation of the knowability of otherness reduced to souvenir. A Senegalese immigrant woman that the narrator encounters in Italy draws a parallel between this selling of African identity and the selling of African bodies. The narrator describes the nameless woman and her companions:

> Loro, le ragazze, vendevano tutto, tutto. E si giustificavano così: "Dobbiamo vendere per vivere. Come voi con le vostre collane." Si facevano pagare caro ... mi facevano male quelle parole: "Vendiamo tutto." Quella era in realtà la nostra vita. Vendiamo tutto: gli elefanti, le collane, i braccialetti, la nostra dignità il nostro lavoro, la nostra giovinezza, i nostri sogni. Lo capiva bene quella ragazza che si prostituiva. (37)

> [They, the girls, sold everything, everything. And they justified it like this: "We have to sell to live. Just like you with your necklaces." And they charged a lot of money. Those words hurt me: "We sell everything." That in reality was our life. We sell everything: elephants, necklaces, bracelets, our dignity, our work, our youth, our dreams. That girl really understood, the one who was a prostitute.]

The juxtaposition of Pap's selling with that of these Senegalese women clearly indicts the system that reduces the vendor to prostitute. And intertwining other immigrants' stories into his own renders Khouma's text a collective document that testifies of the experience of an entire group. Throughout the text, he continually relates the stories of other immigrants — both male and female, generally tragic, and almost exclusively Senegalese — creating an autobiography of a people. Trinh Minh-ha has said,

> Since marginalised people are always socialized to understand things from more than their own point of view, to see both sides of the matter, and to say *at least* two things at the same time, they can never really afford to speak in the singular. (8)

To assume the role of speaking for the collective Senegalese immigrant experience likens the narrator's position to that of the *griot*, the storyteller/singer in Senegal responsible for preserving oral history. Clark and Phillips explain that *griots*, "Despite an inferior position in society ... supposedly possessed special physical and spiritual powers that earned them a certain respect" (86). In fact, having been trained as a potter in Senegal places Khouma in the same caste as that of the *griot*, the caste of those who "deal with dangerous and unclean materials like fire, metal . . . wood, and in the case of *griots*, words" (86). In singing his own story, he is preserving the story — and thus the identity — of his people; and that very preservation of his own and others' identities acts as a form of resistance to the Western reduction-objectification-consumption of African identity. Moreover, his invoking of the Senegalese *griot* tradition further insulates his text against Western appropriation.

Khouma's strategies of resistance assume two main forms: he turns the objectivizing gaze against those who have objectivized him, and he uses his otherness to remain invisible and unknowable. Trihn Minh-ha has frequently discussed the inherently problematic nature of these forms of resistance to colonizing discourse, for that tactic of appropriating and declaring ownership for a name or space the dominant culture has assigned, even in order to subvert that discourse, runs the risk of buying into the culture of oppression and "endorsing the labels that have been given to us" (15). Khouma however sidesteps and even complicates further the problem of reappropriation by speaking in an ironic key and especially by emphasizing the ironies surrounding immigration legislation. His multiple ironies operate as social critique, and resist discourses of power by revealing their contradictions and absurdities.

In addition to creating a collective story, Khouma's narrative offers a history of immigration law, and then subsumes that history into the text's project of resistance. He tracks the passage from illegality to legality, from the so-called "clandestine" immigrant to acquired legal status, emphasizing that attaining legal status profoundly affects the dignity of the individual immigrant, but not necessarily the attitude or the behavior of the Italian authorities toward the immigrants:

> L'anno nuovo, il 1987, ci regala la famosa legge. Non era un trucco per rispedirci tutti a casa comem sostenevano i miei compagni. I permessi di soggiorno ci vengono davvero concessi. Eccoli, belli e fiammanti. La legge italiana ha riconosciuto la nostra esistenza. Non siamo più ombre. Siamo uomini. . . .

Mi dispiace dirlo, ma dopo l'arrivo dei permessi di soggiorno, non tocchiamo il cielo con un dito. . . . Anzi, grazie ai diritti che abbiamo conquistato, i quai si moltiplicano. . . .

"Caro signor vigile, se vuole sequestare la merce . . . faccia pure, ma non insulti. Non sono un clandestino. Lei mi deve rispettare."

"Come osi, ragazzo, rivolgerti così all'autorità? Stai al tuo posto." (128–29)

[The new year, 1987, gives us a gift, the famous law. It wasn't a trick to send us all back home as my friends had maintained. We actually get legal papers. Here they are, beautiful and flaming. The Italian law has recognized our existence. We are no longer shadows, ghosts, "clandestines." We are people. . . .

I'm sorry to say it, but after getting our papers we don't get to seventh heaven. . . . In fact, thanks to our new rights, we have even more troubles. . . .

"Dear Mr. Policeman, if you have to take away my merchandise . . . go ahead, but don't insult me. . . . I'm not illegal. You have to respect me."

"Do you dare speak that way to an official, boy? Get in your place."]

Khouma is referring to the law passed in 1986 that granted legal status and full civil rights to hitherto illegal immigrants based upon their year of entry in Italy (entry prior to 1984 qualified for legalization); four years later, another "*sanatoria*" law was passed extending date to 1987.[5] Graziella Parati makes a disturbing observation about these laws, "This term, ['sanatoria'] borrowed from the rhetoric of medicine, assumes immigration is a disease and the body of the nation needs to be healed from it" ("Strangers in Paradise" 3). Political scientist James Hollifield has indicated that the Italian "*sanatoria*" laws have parallels in other countries with high immigrant populations: during this same time span, 1986–1990, France, Germany, and the US all introduced similar measures to regularize current illegal immigrants while at the same time restricting new arrivals. Indeed, Hollifield argues that the purpose of the legaliza-

---

[5]When Khouma's text was published in 1990, the immigrant population was approximately 450,000 of whom over 85% were illegal (*Ministero di Lavoro* 87).

tion aspect is to veil the new stringent components of these laws bent on curtailing future immigration (5).[6]

The narrator explains that legalization is a double-edged sword, for the law works in a very ironic way: while on the one hand, it grants them temporary residency, at the same time, it makes them more visible to and findable by the police and points up the economic restrictions that still bind them. The narrator explains, "Anzi, grazie ai diritti che abbiamo conquistato, i guai si moltiplicano" (129; "Thanks to the new rights we have acquired, our troubles increase). He and many others who cannot find other jobs, must still sell to survive; but, as they have no permits, the law still terms them "outlaws." Ironically, their legality makes them more vulnerable, for the narrator notices that the people are now more afraid of them and the police and employers invent new ways to silence them, through fines or intimidation, if they protest illtreatment (139). This social backlash to their new rights includes stricter and harsher police surveillance, more arrests, and more confiscations of merchandise by the police. The narrator further ironizes on the fact that the police are far more harsh with and eager to arrest the license-less souvenir salesmen than they are the drug dealers who frequent the same spaces. The salesmen are paying not for their illegality, but for their visibility:

> Non c'è atto nella vita di . . . un senegalese venditore di elefanti . . . che non possa configurarsi come "resistenza a pubblico ufficiale." Se scappi, è resistenza, se preghi che ti lascino qualcosa da vendere è resistenza, se ti mostri sorridente o se fai la faccia storta è resistenza. Non c'è limite alla resistenza. (129)

---

[6]Since the publication of Khouma's text, the more stringent and specifically "non-sanatoria" Turco-Napolitano immigration law (again, named for the framers of the law) took effect on March 27, 1998, which specifies four requirements in order for immigrants to attain legal status: a job, a residence, a clean police record, and proof of residency in Italy before March 1998. This law also established automatic expulsion for immigrants who committed crimes, and established temporary centers where immigrants are housed up to 30 days until their status is determined. Thousands have been expelled under this law, and the temporary centers have been criticized as "lagers." Complete copies of the entire series of laws relative to immigration is available on the homepage of the *Unione Italiana di Lavoro* [http://www.uil.it].

> [There is no action in the life of a . . . Senegalese elephant . . . salesman that can't be construed as "resisting a public official." If you run away, that's resistance, if you beg them to leave you something to sell, that's resistance, if you smile or frown, that's resistance. There is no limit to resistance.]

Again, irony serves here to critique institutions of power; in fact, the narrator's insistence that he is not resisting authorities becomes in the text an act of resistance to the broader powers of the Orientalist discourse.

Khouma's narrative strategies of resistance include turning the objectifying gaze of the West against his objectivizers, but not as simple reversal. Rather, the narrator hybridizes in an ironic key elements of both his own and Italian culture. Khouma's resistance, manifested in his attempts to remain unknowable, is precisely the resisting of the dominant discourse's attempts to reduce and commodify his identity. He resists the "knowable/consumable" model of the immigrant by appropriating elements of the dominant cultural discourse in order to remain invisible and unknowable, and by embedding cloaked elements of his own culture as comments on his host culture. For example, he refers to Italy as the "land of the *tubab*" and to Europeans as "*tubab*" without ever explaining the Wolof term (which mean "whites"). His substitution of his own unexplained linguistic code reverses the objectifying and essentializing lens by which Europeans have named him as "black" or "African" or "Moroccan" (a generic term applied to immigrants of color in Italy). However, his naming the Europeans "*tubab*" serves to indict the entire economy that privileges the Western discourse of power: the narrator's use of the same tactic of reducing and essentializing identity has no effect whatsoever upon the "*tubab*," because the narrator is marginalized to the point that his naming has no force within the discourse.

Also, his text consistently refers to all police and other officials as "*gli zii*" [the uncles]. On one level, this technique satirizes the Western myth of the benevolent, paternal white official while it echoes and reverses the essentializing Western gaze by rendering the Europeans the nameless, faceless collective; at the same time, referring to the arm of institutional violence as "uncle" underscores the abyss between the immigrant and the Europeans by suggesting a familial relationship. The fact that the maternal uncle has a privileged role in Senegalese culture — in fact, he is referred to as the "king of the family" (Buche 848) — makes the Senegalese nickname for the police a kind of inside joke that requires Western readers to step outside of their own culture (albeit in a very minimal way) in order to understand.

Another of Pap's strategies for remaining unknowable is to never give his real name. Instead, he invents a private history and identity that he names "Pascal," which he uses only with Europeans. The name suggests a double irony — it is at once a clear allusion to the philosopher Blaise Pascal and his theories of freedom through choice and faith; and, at the same time, the obvious French name suggests a connection to that nation's colonial history. That the narrator would only use this invented, colonized identity with Europeans shows that the narrator realized how Europeans are most comfortable with the otherness that they have appropriated (colonization), and at the same time shows his skill at subverting that appropriation with one of his own. When the narrator is arrested and required to give the police his "real" name, his African name, he (and other immigrants) will give any word in their native Wolof, knowing that the language is so unfamiliar, so unknowable, that the police will never be able to verify the real signification. Pap casually explains that when giving his name to police, he will pick any word in Wolof, "shoe" or "turtle" work well (84). Pap's act of self-naming here relies on two images that suggest elements of the immigrant experience: the constant mobility ("shoe"), and isolation and hidden unknowability ("turtle"). Speaking a tongue that is completely unknowable parallels his "unknowable" difference, and using it is a way of subverting that authority that constructs difference as transparent and knowable.

The narrator's appropriation and use of Italian presents parallel cases of resistance to and subversion of dominant discourse. While learning and using a new language represent alterations in identity formation, these can also be forms of empowerment as well. The protagonist "plays dumb" to appropriate elements of the ignorant immigrant stereotype, which he then works to his own and his friends' advantage. For instance, the narrator's ability to speak Italian enables him to negotiate power structures and even to cross a border (physically and legally) closed to him by that structure: upon his return to Italy a third time, the narrator and 22 other Senegalese are denied entry. He waits until the border guards realize he can speak Italian, and then at their request acts as translator:

> Si presentano gli altri senegalesi. Lui interroga, io traduco. . . . Come sempre aggiungo qualcosa di mio. Metto a frutto la mia lunga esperienza e i miei frequenti contatti con la polizia italiana, coreggendo le risposte e fornendo agli amici via via interrogati le spiegazioni piu' opportune. Procedo cosi' con una ventina di compatrioti. Infine il poliziotto si rivolge a me: "E tu? Che cosa sei venuto a fare in Italia?"
> " . . . una breve vacanza."
> "E l'italiano, dove l'hai imparato?"
> "In Senegal. . . ."
> "Sei gia' venuto in Italia?"
> "Mai vista l'Italia. E' la prima volta che ci capito.
> " . . . Ti lascio entrare. Ma non sarai venuto anche tu a vendere?
> "Vendere? Vendere cosa? Non ho mai saputo che la mia gente venisse in Italia per vendere" (112).

[The other Senegalese come forward. He questions them, I translate. . . . As always, I add a little something of my own. I put to use my long experience and my frequent contacts with the Italian police, correcting the [Senegalese's] replies and, little by little during the interrogation, offering my friends more opportune answers. I continue for about twenty of my compatriots. Finally the police officer turns to me: "And you? Why did you come to Italy?"
"Just a short vacation."
"And where did you learn Italian?"
"In Senegal."
"Have you already been to Italy before?"
"Never seen Italy. This is the first time that I happened to land here."
" . . . I'll let you enter. But you didn't come to sell things, did you?
"Sell things? Sell what? I never knew that my people would come to Italy to sell."]

The narrator emphasizes the effectiveness of his subversions by contrasting them with his attempts at direct opposition that consistently fail.

His unmasking his subversion within the space of the text acts as yet another indictment of the institutions of power, for they respond far more readily to manipulations and deceit (as long as the language seems "knowable" and conveys an identity that conforms to the one defined by the dominant discourse) than to conforming to their own standards and regulations.

Hybridity in this text itself functions as a form of resistance, for by preserving and creating his own identity, the protagonist resists the forces that would "name" him. The narrator, by appropriating elements of the dominant discourse, manages to eke out a space for an identity that exists between East and West, Africa and Europe, and defies the latter's objectification while at the same time exposing as false the colonized identity and economies that form it. Homi Bhabha's concept of liminality, that is, the process of identity formation within hybrid spaces and transitions, suggests that crossing borders precipitates both trauma and empowerment. The creation of a liminal identity here is an act of survival in which the tenuousness of Pap's new identity reflects the narrator's tenuous economic survival. The economic concept of "exchange" is the key to the text's resistance. In place of the determining, objectifying "economies," Khouma offers the model of "dialogue," as he states in a 1995 interview regarding the motivation behind his book:

> D: "Il libro . . . è stato scritto per parlare agli Italiani, . . . era importante creare una figura positiva?"
> R: "Sì importante ma non era lo scopo del libro . . . piuttosto volevo prendere la parola perché gli italiani parlavano di noi, ma erano gli stessi italiani che facevano domande e poi si rispondevano. Noi presenti abbiamo preso la parola per interrompere questo monologo tra gli italiani per istaurare un dialogo. Questo era lo scopo del libro" (115–16).

> [Question: "Your book . . . was written to speak with Italians, . . . was it important to create a positive figure [of the immigrant]?"
> Answer: "Yes, it was important, but that wasn't the purpose of the book. . . . Rather, I wanted to take the floor because the Italians talked about us but they were the same Italians who asked questions and then answered their own questions. We took the floor to interrupt this

monologue between Italians to institute a dialogue. This was the purpose of the book."]

Khouma's model suggests that in place of objectifying "economies," another form of exchange can still exist, but only when immigrants' own voices are heard.

The text creates a personal space where the narrator can position his own identity, a hybrid, border-crossing identity that asserts its rights to Otherness that resists Western discourses of essentialization, and that at the same time represents the collective story, space, and identity of all Senegalese immigrants. By then inserting this identity into the capitalist economy in the form of a book — indeed, a best-selling book — the text trumps the economies that purported to make him visible and knowable. Rather, the identity he constructs in his text makes knowable and visible the violence inherent in the attempt to objectify and reduce Otherness to something that can be known and ultimately, consumed. The protagonist's conclusion plays on the term "fortuna," which can mean both luck and material fortune:

> Questa è la vita di un senegalese, la vita che conosco da un tempo che mi pare lunghissimo, ma in fondo fortunato, perchè, come si dice al mio paese, se una cosa la puoi raccontare, vuol dire che ti ha portato fortuna. (143)

> [This is the life of a Senegalese, the life that I've known for a time that seems extremely long to me, but all told, a fortunate time because, as we say in my country, if you can retell something, that means it brought you good luck. A lot of guys rip up their papers and return to Senegal because they've had it with Italy, the police, selling, elephants, necklaces . . . expulsion orders, confiscations, the cold. . . .
> A lot stay, work, sell, become laborers, more exploited than the others.
> A lot stay and meet Italian girls. They fall in love. There are marriages, and then even separations and divorces. And then more marriages. Babies are born.]

This concluding line of the text offers no real conclusion, in fact, the opposite is the case. The text's non-conclusion transposes the problem of identity formation into another key: the questions of identity that Khouma's text raises are not merely for the immigrant, but for Italy as well. The final words of the narrating *griot* of Khouma's text read like a parting shot, reminding the (Italian) reading public that the hybrid identity constructed in the text parallels — and perhaps prefigures — a new and permanently redefined Italian culture.

Works Cited

Adam, Ian, and Helen Tiffin. *Past the Last Post: Theorizing Post-Colonialism and Post-Modernism.* Calgary: U of Calgary P, 1990.

Ahluwalia, D. Pal, and Paul Nursey-Bray. *The Post-Colonial Condition: Contemporary Politics in Africa.* Nova Science, 1997.

Allen, Beverly, and Mary Russo, eds. *Revisioning Italy: National Identity and Global Culture.* U of Minnesota P, 1997.

Ashcroft, Bill, Gareth Griffiths, and Helen Tiffin, eds. *The Empire Writes Back: Theory and Practice in Post-Colonial Literatures.* New York: Routledge, 1989.

Bhabha, Homi. *Nation and Narration.* New York: Routledge, 1990.

___. "The Other Question." *Screen* 24 (December) 1983.

Buche, Frederic. "L'Oncle maternel est roi. La formation d'alliances hiérarchiques chez les Mandingues du Wuli (Senegal)." *Cahiers d'Etudes Africaines* 36.4 (1996): 848–50.

Clark, Andrew F., and Lucie Colvin Phillips. *Historical Dictionary of Senegal.* 2nd ed. *African Historical Dictionaries 65.* Metuchen, NJ: Scarecrow, 1994.

Curry, Renée R., and Terry Allison, eds. *States of Rage: Emotional Eruption, Violence, and Social Change.* New York: New York UP, 1996.

Diop, Abdoulaye-bara. *La société Wolof: Tradition et changement.* Paris: Éditions Karthala, 1981.

Fabre, Geneviève, and Robert O'Meally, eds. *History and Memory in African-American Culture.* Oxford: Oxford UP, 1994.

Gardezi, Hassan N. *The Political Economy of International Labour Migration.* Montreal: Black Rose Books, 1995.

Hammar, Tomas, Grete Brochmann, Kristof Tasa, and Thomas Faist, eds. *International Migration, Immobility and Development: Multidisciplinary Perspectives.* Oxford: Berg, 1997.

Hawley, John C. *Writing the Nation: Self and Country in Post-Colonial Imagination.* Critical Studies 7. Amsterdam: Rodopi, 1996.

Hollifield, James F. *Immigrants, Markets, and States. The Political Economy of Post-War Europe.* Harvard UP, 1992.

Immigrazione Dossier Statistico 1998. Rome: Anterem, 1997.

Kawash, Samira. *Dislocating the Color Line: Identity, Hybridity, and Singularity in African-American Literature.* Stanford: Stanford UP, 1997.

Khouma, Pap. *Io, venditore di elefanti.* Milan: Garzanti, 1994.

Kolar-Panov, Dona. *Video, War, and the Diasporic Imagination.* London: Routledge, 1997.

King, Russell, ed. *Mass Migration in Europe: The Legacy and the Future.* Chichester: John Wiley & Sons, 1995.

Mihailovich-Dickman, Vera. *Return in Post-Colonial Writing.* Cross/Cultures 12. Amsterdam: Rodopi, 1994.

Mihn-ha, Trinh T. "The Undone Interval." *The Post-Colonial Question: Common Skies, Divided Horizons.* Ed. Iain Chambers and Lidia Curti. New York: Routledge, 1996.

Ministero di Lavoro.

Olaniyan, Tejumola. *Scars of Conquest/Masks of Resistance.* Oxford: Oxford UP, 1995.

Parati, Graziella, ed. "Italophone Voices." Special Issue, *Margins at the Centre: African Italian Voices. Studi d'Italianistica nell'Africa Australe* 8.2 (1995).

___. "Looking Through Non-Western Eyes: Immigrant Women's Autobiographical Narratives in Italian." *Writing (New) Identities: Gender, Nationalism, and Immigration in New European Subjects.* Ed. Sidonie Smith and Gisela Brinker-Gabler. Minneapolis: U of Minnesota P, 1997.

___, ed. and intro. *Mediterranean Crossroads: Migration Literature in Italy.* Farleigh Dickenson UP, 1999.

___. "Strangers in Paradise: Foreigners and Shadows in Italian Literature." *Designing Italy: "Italy" in Europe, Africa, Asia, and the Americas.* Ed. Beverly Allen and Mary Russo. Minnesota: Minnesota UP, 1996.

Piavetta, Oreste. "Multiculturalismo, voci di razza." *Effe* 2 (Spring 1996).

Rajan, Gita, and Radhika Mohanran, eds. *Postcolonial Discourse and Changing Cultural Contexts.* Greenwood, CT: Greenwood, 1997.

Rudolph, Hedwig, and Mirjana Morokvasic, eds. *Bridging States and Markets: International Migration in the Early 1990s.* Berlin: Edition Sigma, 1993.

Stewart, William A., et. al. *Introductory Course in Dakar Wolof.* Washington, DC: Center for Applied Linguistics, 1966.

Torres, Sasha, ed. *Living Color: Race and Television in the United States.* Durham, NC: Duke UP, 1998.

Van Hear, Nicholas. *New Diasporas.* Seattle: U of Washington P, 1998.

Young, Robert J. C. *Colonial Desire: Hybridity in Theory, Culture and Race.* New York: Routledge, 1995.

World Population Data Sheet 1999.

INTERVIEW WITH KOSSI KOMLA-EBRI

Peter N. Pedroni
Miami University

Kossi Amekowoya Komla-Ebri, a practicing physician at the Hospital of Erba, Italy and an Italian citizen, was born in Togo in 1954. He won first prize for fiction at the third annual competition of Eks&Tra held in Rimini in 1997 with the short story "Quando attraverserò il fiume" [when I cross the river]. He won fifth prize of the same competition, in 1998, with the short story, "Mal di . . ." [. . . sickness]. He won another prize in 1998 for the short story "Ninna nanna" [lullaby] in a competition held by the magazine *Famiglia cristiana*. He is the author of several articles published in the periodical *L'incrocio* and in the magazine *Progetto Africa*. He collaborated on the book *Afrique, la Santè par Images*. He has written lyric poetry, several short stories, and a novel, entitled *Neyla*. "Quando attraverserò il fiume" was published by the editor Fara in the anthology *Memorie in valigia*. "Mal di . . ." was published by Fara in the anthology *Destini sospesi di volti in cammino*. He has been nominated by the Ulivo coalition to run for a seat in the Chamber of Deputies in the May 13, 2001 elections. The following interview was conducted in Ponte Lambro, Italy at the home of Kossi Komla-Ebri on June 26, 1999.

Pedroni: Why did you decide to emigrate to Italy and then to stay there?

Komla-Ebri: I came to Italy somewhat by chance. My intention was to stay in France. Instead, after I finished my high school degree I had no possibility of continuing my studies.

Pedroni: So you did your preparatory studies in France?

Komla-Ebri: Yes, in France with a scholarship that then ran out. However, I did have the possibility of continuing in Italy thanks to Bishop Lomè who knew Cardinal Lercaro at the University of Bologna who offered a scholarship for students from the Third World in an international residence college. At that time I didn't know any Italian and I said to myself who knows how this will work out. Also because in Togo there was no medical school. So if I wanted to study medicine, the only choice was to expatriate. So I came to Italy, to Bologna, where I had a very interesting experience because in this college there were sixty students from every part of the world — from India, from Sri Lanka, from Zaire, from Poland, from Greece, from Uganda, and from Italy — living together. It caused me to change my way of seeing things. I experienced discussions of intercultural concepts and the universality of certain things. It was important for my prioritization of things, of life, that is of the relationships between individuals and in the search for a common denominator that all people share. Then when I had finished my medical studies in Bologna I thought I would go home to work in the hospital of Afagnan, which is in Togo. It's a hospital administered by the Fatebenefratelli friars. And in fact I had a contract with them and they said that they wanted to find out what my capabilities were. So they proposed an internship at their hospital here in Erba. I lived in the hospital and I enrolled in my specialization, which was general surgery. When I finished the internship they announced that they needed a surgeon in Togo. So during the summer I went down to work with them. Then, since they had set up a project with "Terre des hommes" (a Swiss non governmental organization) to help cure children effected with polio, they assured me that they needed a specialist in orthopedics and traumatology. So, since I was no longer needed as a surgeon, I enrolled in traumatology and accepted a contract to work there for two years. In the meantime at the hospital I had met my wife and when I went down there to work she joined me to see how things were going there. Then I decided to do something serious about our relationship and so we got married. She then came back with me for the remaining time of my contract. The idea was that she would also work there in the laboratory because she is also a laboratory technician. Our son, Davide, was born in Togo. But we were unable to reach an economic agreement because they thought they could get the two of us at the same price because, since she was married to me, she should be paid as a Togolese. But she said that I, since I was married to her, an Italian, should be paid like an Italian. In addition I realized, while I was home, that I come from a family of twelve siblings and that I was the oldest male. At the end of the month we had to distribute money and benefits. The salary that I had did not permit me to maintain my new family and to help my family of origin. For this reason it was necessary to make a decision that was not easy. However, we went back to Italy in spite of knowing that without Italian citizenship I wouldn't be able to work, because I couldn't enroll in the medical register. Without being enrolled in the medical register I couldn't practice my profession. It was a vicious circle. Then I started working at the hospital in Erba without pay. I went on that way for ten years. In the end my mother-in-law was so desperate that she wrote a letter to the President of the Republic asking him how come my citizenship never came through. Perhaps it was chance, but strangely enough, when she wrote, the citizenship came through. However in the orthopedic surgery unit there were no openings. But since my wife was working in the laboratory and I used to always go there too and was already quite familiar with it, the doctor in charge said that if I wanted it there was a job for me in the laboratory. So I had to learn a new specialization and I successfully passed the exams. And so even though I had not been trained as a laboratory technician, I stayed there and my career has gone quite well.

Pedroni: The fact that you went to France for your high school studies means that you had learned French from the time you were little?

Komla-Ebri: Yes, in the schools of Togo, French is the required language. When I got to Italy I was surprised to see that very few people spoke French. Togo was first colonized by the Germans. My maternal grandfather went to the German school. He was a catechism teacher and missed the Germans. One must acknowledge that the things that the Germans did are the things that have remained. That is, the infrastructure, the railroad, and so on. The French brought us a big bureaucracy that we have not been able to get rid of. They did not bring any significant development to the country.

Pedroni: Differently than a colleague of yours, Pap Khouma, you don't dwell very much, in your writings, on the problems of immigrants. Is that because you haven't had these problems?

Komla-Ebri: No, not for that reason. That is, perhaps because I did have them, but in the past. I think of them as the baggage of human experience. In France I tried to work; we used to sleep frozen with ten of us on a couch with our feet on chairs in unheated houses. I had to get up at three to unload kilos of fruit from trucks to refrigerated rooms; I had to pick up cigarette butts off the ground because I didn't have the money to buy them, or I had to go through trash cans behind the supermarkets at night looking for something to eat. I think I have gotten beyond these things, not only in the sense of time, but also psychologically. Sometimes writing has a thaumaturgic value; one unloads oneself, pours it out, and gets cured. Once you get beyond it you don't feel the need to express it. Pap wrote that book right in a moment of intense anger. I have gotten beyond that moment. But not even he would write those things now because he has gotten beyond them. Once you get beyond those things, I think that you need to write about something else.

Pedroni: So, then, in your opinion, is it valid to talk about "immigrant literature"?

Komla-Ebri: For me, no. Because in my opinion you have to get beyond these things. It was in part an idea of the publishing companies because they wanted to expose something. I'm not saying that it's not useful because it does give the possibility to someone to become aware of his or her capabilities. However it's a step beyond which one has to progress. Then, if you want to grow as a writer, you have to come out of that ghetto and allow yourself to be evaluated on an equal basis with Italians. You have to look for a universal language, which does not mean talking about extraordinary things. The universality does not come from the plot, but from the message, from what you want to make felt. If I, with what I write, succeed in making my reader experience an emotion, that is an excellent result because I have succeeded in crossing the threshold of his/her soul and in touching upon those sensations that we have in common. And if it's an immigrant that is writing, it can be useful in as much as it causes others to realize that immigrants experience the same sensations that everybody experiences, and think and dream like everyone else. For example, I started a short story about familial reunification. It's a story about an immigrant in Italy who misses his wife who has stayed behind with their son. He would like to reunite, but encounters a thousand bureaucratic obstacles. But I'm not writing about immigration. I don't start out with that idea. I start out with the idea of personal solitude. It's about an African in Italy, but it could just as well be about an Italian in Switzerland or an Italian that leaves Puglia to come here to the North. But not to express victimization which doesn't do any good for the immigration problem. I don't agree with the idea that you have to write for your own people, because if you write for mankind, you are also writing for your own people. Also in the medical profession they used to tell me, "you have to practice medicine in order to care for your people." But I maintain that for a doctor it makes no difference whether the sick person is white, green, or yellow. In other words, I did not become a doctor only to care for my people. Now it's obvious and inevitable that one talks about one's own life and one's own experiences, but through these experiences one hopes to find something that will be universal.

Pedroni: Then it seems already clear that you are not happy with the label "African-Italian writer" and that you would prefer instead to be considered simply an "Italian writer."

Komla-Ebri: That's more or less a concept for the anthologies since for years they have been talking about African literature in French, African literature in English, but there doesn't exist an African literature in Italian. However I like being simply considered a writer. I don't want to be forced into any attachment to a continent or to a country. The fact that I express myself in Italian is contingent on the situation in which I find myself. I started during my high school years writing some things in French during mathematics classes, because I was good at math and I could allow myself this. But today I wouldn't be able to write in French in the same way. My mother was here the other day and wanted to read what I had written, which however is all in Italian and she doesn't read Italian. So she asked me to translate it into French, something that I could do only with great difficulty, because, even if sometimes a concept comes to me spontaneously in French, I don't use French anymore. I'm aware of dreaming in Italian. I no longer dream in French nor in my language.

Pedroni: I think in fact that, if anything, it is the language in which you write that identifies you as an "Italian" writer, but not an "African-Italian" writer.

Komla-Ebri: No, because I don't start out with the idea that I am an African who is writing. In fact, they often advise me to send my manuscripts to missionary groups, etc., because others identify you as foreign, African. Instead, for me the language I use and what I write have to please me in and of themselves. Then the fact that the writer is African may be of interest to the publishing companies who want to do folklore and present the writers like strange animals. Instead, they should simply be writers whose works deserve to be published. And we do deserve to be published because we are, without intending it that way, a source of enrichment for the Italian language because we bring to it something different filtered through our life experiences.

Pedroni: When you start out writing do the thoughts come to you directly in Italian, or in your African language, or in French?

Komla-Ebri: It depends on the theme. Certain words, certain sensations, sometimes come to me in French. And I look for the equivalent in Italian, that coincides with what I really want to express. And many times I have to look for synonyms until I find what really matches. But I start out in Italian and I write directly in Italian. My African language comes in only when, as in "Quando attraverserò il fiume," I want to express certain particularly African concepts, like proverbs, etc. Then I have to translate the concepts into an Italian that reproduces the sensation that there is in my language. For example there's an African, Togolese, greeting that would translate literally as, "the day has fallen." But I preferred rendering it with "the day has dawned," which seems more effective to me.

Pedroni: In fact, when I read it, it seemed like those Italian words were the actual words that the African characters were saying. But also on a personal level, when you speak with your own children, aren't there some expressions that you recall from when you were a child, that your parents used to say to you, that come to mind? The way we speak to children often reveals the language that is inside us.

Komla-Ebri: Yes, probably, because there are some things that we take with us from childhood. For example, I see the unusual passion that my daughter has for reading. The book that I brought her yesterday, Sarah is already reading this morning. Perhaps because they have always seen the two of us at home reading. Just as I have a passion for writing, so do they. Davide won a poetry contest at the Forum Francescanum. And they hear how I use language, proverbs, etc. Among the first things that Davide learned was the metaphor. And I see in the things that he has written that he understands what is meant by a metaphor. And my language is full of metaphors. He has a command of language that is certainly superior to that of his age group. The teachers themselves say that he uses the precisely correct word when speaking. Sometimes at the dinner table, if I don't use the precise term, he corrects me. He is so precise that I remember, when he was very little in kindergarten and I used to joke and ask him, "when you have to go and do pee pee what do you say to the teacher," he would say, "I have to go and satisfy my physiological needs."

Pedroni: By the way, what is your African language called?

Komla-Ebri: Ewè. It's a language that is spoken in Togo, in Benin, and in Ghana, because the ethnic groups are stratified horizontally. But the countries were cut out vertically. For example, if I encounter someone from the north of Togo we have to speak in French, as the lingua franca, in order to understand each other, because we have no other language in common. On the other hand if I go to the south of Benin or to the south of Ghana and encounter a Beninese or a Ghanian, we understand each other immediately in Ewè.

Pedroni: A literature question: what Italian writers do you know and whom do you consider most important?

Komla-Ebri: As soon as I arrived in Italy I had an Italian language teacher who had me read a lot of Calvino. So he was the first Italian author that I started to read with passion. I liked the world of *The Cloven Viscount* because it was a serious but imaginary world, a world of fables. My background was based on French literature, but as for Italian literature, I've read a little of everything. I've read Moravia. I've read Biagi, too. I read anything that comes my way. Fallaci has a particular way of writing; Dacia Maraini. But if you ask me what Italian writer I like best, I'll say Calvino.

Pedroni: And the classics?

Komla-Ebri: As for the classics, you can see the deficiency of the French schools. We study Moliere and Corneille, but we don't study Dante. Whatever I have been able to learn about classic Italian literature is thanks to my wife who is really into it. It was she who also got me to read Ungaretti and other poets. And it's interesting, for example, to hear someone say that a poem that I had written has some echoes of Leopardi whom I didn't know. As for Italian history, I'm learning that with my children.

Pedroni: Is there some Italian or foreign writer that has had a particular influence on your work?

Komla-Ebri: I like Kafka for his narrative style. And also Edgar Allan Poe.

Pedroni: But your style seems different than that of Kafka or Poe.

Komla-Ebri: But I also like Guy de Maupassant because he is able to express emotions in the limited space of a brief short story. I like short stories more than novels.

Pedroni: It's said that writing is a dialogue between the writer and the reader. When you write, do you have in mind a particular reader, or a type of reader or readers?

Komla-Ebri: When I participated in the Eks&Tra competition I knew that I was writing for Italians. That is, for Italians who are interested in different cultures. So, appropriately, I wrote for particular readers because the purpose was to compare our cultures. And sometimes this leads to exotic writing. But I would like to be able to write what I feel, before thinking about to whom it's addressed. Writing is translating into written form what I think, what I feel.

Pedroni: But is it to make these things known to yourself or to someone else, who could be your wife or your mother, for example?

Komla-Ebri: No, it's never for someone particular. Sometimes it can be a personal unburdening and sometimes it's just because you feel a need to write; but on the other hand nobody writes to keep his/her work in a drawer. You write obviously to communicate with others. Otherwise it wouldn't make sense to write. But I don't think of any particular audience; other than in the case of competitions. But basically I write for everybody. In other words I don't write thinking that an Italian will read this or a French person will read this. I don't write for immigrants; I don't write for my people. Absolutely not. If I talk about Africa it's not just by chance; it's because that's what I know.

Pedroni: But I'll bet that when you write, you at least have a vague idea of a person with whom you are communicating and who perhaps will cry or get angry.

Komla-Ebri: In that sense, yes. There exists a virtual reader. It's essential because that is the most rewarding part about writing. It's the measure of success; whether I can cause emotions to be felt. For example, in *Neyla* you already know ahead of time that things are going to end up badly. When the person gets to the hospital it seems like a calvary in comparison with the hospitals here. Then there is this cold doctor that uses only technical terminolgy. There's no humanity. And in fact there are some doctors that talk that way. Also in "Manif" [demonstration], in the midst of total desperation, the mind latches on to something that is futile but which serves as a safety valve. And I have experienced this. The story of "Manif" is not a real life experience. However, I have often experienced desperation when a happy thought has come to save me, to pick me up. I think that people who don't have this safety valve can get into critical depression. Or you can retreat into an unreal world in order not to have to face up to the real world. Instead, whoever has this safety valve is able to survive. And it's essential. In fact, it's important to laugh. Sometimes I say that this society is no longer capable of laughing. I often say that white men smile, but they don't laugh. Partly because laughing means opening up your soul. It means creating an opening. It means a space through which someone else can enter inside of you. It's a risk. So you laugh only with someone you trust.

Pedroni: In fact, in the short story "Mal di . . ." your African protagonist expresses certain impressions of Italy: "God, the cold! I didn't imagine how biting it could be"; "I think that here, the rhythm of life is such that time washes away feelings, devouring life and people"; "this country, this fog, is not for me, I miss the sun, the village festivals, the weather, the laughter of people, living together with the people";[1] that contradict the usual stereotypical preconceptions of sunny Italy, the Italy of festivals and of collective life in the piazza. Assuming that the protagonist reflects the impressions of the author, could it be a consequence of the fact that you live in Lombardy, in Brianza, in Ponte Lambro and not in some other part of Italy?

Komla-Ebri: Yes and no. Because I'm aware of the fact that for someone who comes to Italy from France, from Germany, from America, Italy is the land of the sun. But for someone who comes from Africa, it's the land of the cold. But above all here in Brianza there is the fog for which an Albanian friend says that it always seems like nighttime. In the winter at five o'clock there's no longer a ray of sunlight. There's constant darkness. But it's also true that in Puglia, which I know well, people are more open; people welcome you into their homes, for example. Even the style of eating there, with several courses, makes a difference, while here the single course is more in use. There's something I noted when I came to work here at the hospital in Erba. I was working with my colleagues and I was sleeping in the hospital. We would finish our shift, but no one would say let's go for coffee. The rapport between individuals was cold. In Bologna, where I studied, the rapport was different. The people of Bologna, when I would ask for directions, would go with me to make sure I got the directions right. Here if they notice that you want to ask something, they cross the street. But there's an evolution in Italy, even in the South, toward cold rapport. In France it's always been that way. The French are withdrawn. They're distrusting. They have no enthusiasm for human rapport like the Italians of the South because they are part of this zone of the North where they give so much importance to work and money and human rapport doesn't exist. Or, if it exists, it's only in con-

---

[1]Kossi Komla-Ebri, "Mal di . . .," *Destini sospesi di volti in cammino*, ed. R. Sangiorgi and A. Ramberti (Santarangelo di Romagna: Fara, 1998) 126, 132, 133.

nection with the kind of work that you do. For example, my white smock makes me become almost white. I see it when I get away from Erba. Where people don't know me the rapport is different. Instead here they know me as a doctor.

Pedroni: It's interesting that the things that the protagonist of "Mal di ..." says correspond almost perfectly to the things that Italian immigrants used to say in America. And they are things that are well documented in Italian-American literature. They always complained about the lack of the big family, of personal contacts, of solidarity. Now here it is Africans that say these things about Italy.

Komla-Ebri: Yes, but there has also been an enormous evolution in the Italian situation. Just look at the increase in the number of nursing homes for the elderly. The patriarchal family of the past no longer exists here. Demographic growth is at zero. So there are no longer any numerous families. Even cars are built for a maximum of two children. And then families, even if they live in the same city don't get together often like they used to — only at Christmas and for funerals. There is no longer that close relationship of the big family like there is where I come from, which can also be burdensome. And someone who comes here for the first time feels lonely. Because you don't know the language and can't communicate with anyone other than to ask directions, but not what you are thinking or feeling. And you end up giving mistaken impressions because people interpret your silence as timidity. In reality you're not timid just because you don't know the language and aren't able to express what you feel. I remember one of the first times I was invited by a family that had made some cauliflower and I don't like cauliflower. But I didn't know how to say so and I forced myself to eat it and the lady offered me some more. And then every time they invited me, they made cauliflower because they thought I liked it.

Pedroni: At this point I'd like to insert a socio-political question. In your opinion, is there something that the Italian state, regarding immigrants, is not doing and should be doing?

Komla-Ebri: Both the state and institutions like the schools need to undertake an enormous educating process to bring about the concept of a new kind of citizenship. In Italy there is no one-world concept. There's a lot of provincialism even among those that think that they are very open minded. They haven't understood that first of all we are human beings on this planet earth. Instead everybody has the train compartment syndrome. In other words, when they come into a train compartment they put their suitcase here and their briefcase there to take up the seats and the compartment becomes theirs. When someone else arrives and knocks on the door it's annoying because they have staked out their territory like animals. Then the new arrival, once accepted, opposes any subsequent arrival. It is not a welcoming culture. But the world is for everybody. It's only chance that makes someone be born in Italy instead of in India or elsewhere. You can't chose where you are born. So how can a child who is born today in Italy say that he/she is more Italian than me who has been in Italy since '74? I think I have contributed more. And yet he has more rights only because he was born in Italy. We need some education in this sense. The mass media are the worst. In my opinion they have no objectivity in reporting and presenting the things that have to do with immigration. If it's true that 4% of immigrants are delinquents, that means that 96% live normally; that is, they pay taxes and pay into pension funds, which is important given the fact that the number of retirees is on the increase. This work force is also important for production. It is important for future generations yet to be born. The second generation of immigrants does not consist of immigrants. Italy will be their country. They will not be content to do the jobs that Italians don't want to do. So we need a process of integration that will lead to a parity of rights and opportunity for immigrants. The mass media underline only the negative side of immigrants and not the positive side. They play a lot on people's fears. In every society people want to have someone who is inferior to them. And it is easy to make this someone a foreigner or anybody who is different, especially if the difference is visible, because of skin color or hair color or whatever. And so it is important to introduce the concept of interculturalism in the schools; not the concept of multiculturalism that many think is right. In my opinion it is wrong because a multicultural society is a ghetto society. It means that someone lives on the first floor, someone on the second, someone on the third, and there is no contact. A transcultural society is an assimilating society. An intercultural society is the image of the piazza where people get together and different cultures interact and contaminate each other. I learn something of your culture; you learn something of mine. To use a simple example: Monday I eat couscous, Tuesday I eat spaghetti, Wednesday I eat Cantonese rice, and so on. In any case the schools have to give the idea of the rainbow. They have to understand that it is not only their culture that exists. The schools are not prepared. We have made some presentations in the schools to introduce African culture. And one of these episodes is in my piece entitled "Imbarazzismi." I call the episode "Etnocentrismo."[2] I asked the children "what is a rascist?" and they answered that it a white who doesn't like blacks. And I said, "then what do you call a black that doesn't like whites?" And they were surprised as if to say, "how could a black permit himself to not like whites?" For me the problem of immigration is a cultural question because it is linked to so many other world problems; for example the lack of democracy in Africa. Democracy would allow economic development so that not so many people would emigrate. With the fall of the Berlin Wall, Africa is no longer the balance point in relations between the great powers. Africa has been left on its own with the puppet presidents that we have. As for international debts, the great powers don't understand that they should be forgiven because as long as Africa is indebted to Europe, the flow of money will always go toward the North and people will continue to follow the flow of money. That's why we have to look for a way to solve the problems at their origins. Today they talk about globalization, but I see that as a globalization of egoisms where the international conglomerates dictate law to the entire world. I don't see how a Senegalese farmer working with a pickax will be able to compete with American threshing machines. It will inevitably lead to a lot of injustices. It shouldn't surprise anyone that ecological trash gets accepted by the poorest countries. I'd like to know where those dioxane poisoned chickens end up. The "mad cow" is still being eaten in Uganda. The capitalist system has the future of a bottomless pit because if we buy five television sets, four cars . . . then after a while we can't buy anything else because there's only so

---

[2]Kossi Komla-Ebri, "Imbarazzismi," *La lingua strappata*, ed. A. Ibba and R. Taddeo (Milan: Leoncavallo, 1999) 34.

much you can buy. An "intelligent egoism" understands that you have to create the power of acquisition in the countries of the South even if only so that those of the North can sell their products. The huge injustices between North and South will inevitably lead to something because the movement of people will be unstoppable. Newspapers exaggerate things. The headline says "Clandestine immigrants kill," without specifying the names of those persons. By contrast, the newspaper does not say, "Pugliese people did something," but rather it says a certain person did a certain thing. Treating immigrants in that way results in penalizing all of them. It ends up where you're afraid to walk on certain streets because people look at you like "one of them." It just creates social tension. The mass media do nothing to help perhaps because they are looking for scoops and scandals. And the schools are not prepared. I see so many teachers filled with good will who ask, "if I have a Moroccan child in class should I concentrate on Italian culture or Moroccan culture?" In my opinion, neither one nor the other. The pupils should be educated in essential values, the values of human rights. Then there will be the peculiarities that distinguish the richness of each person's culture. We, because it is something that we care about, show, for example, the children here, the toys of African children. Here it is a culture in which toys are bought. The children don't make them. We do this for two reasons. One is sociological because it encourages them to use recuperated materials to make the toys. Not to copy those of African children, but to build perhaps a rocket made with tin cans and whatever they are able to find, involving their parents too. And then, most importantly, when they have tried doing it, they see that it's not so easy. Then an admiration is born regarding the African child who is able to do what they are not able to do. Because until now the predominant image of the African child is that of the swollen belly, with the extended hand that asks for money and therefore is in a situation of inferiority. In our presentations the first thing that I ask is, "When you think about Europe what do you think?" "Development, money." If I say, "Africa?" "Disease, war." In other words, only a negative image. But it is an image that has been created, maintained, and nourished. And we think that in order to build positive relations between people, you really have to give to each culture an image that truly corresponds to that culture.

Pedroni: Now getting back to your work, in the short novel *All'incrocio dei sentirieri* [at the crossroads], and in the short story "Mal di . . .," you used a female narrative voice. Why did you make that choice?

Komla-Ebri: One reason, in the case of "Mal di . . .," was, in part, to trick the judges of the Eks&Tra competition, because I noticed that even Eks&Tra has its limitations. They don't judge only the literary value of what one writes. For example I think that they don't want to give a prize two times in a row to the same writer. So I said to myself, "Now I'll write something that makes them think that it is a woman who is writing and that way they won't know that it's me who is writing." I was pleased when my short story won and the funny thing is that when I went up for the prize there was Tahar Lamri who was part of the jury and who didn't know me. When I got up for the prize, he was amazed because he was convinced that I was a woman. But aside of this joke it was also playing with style. That is, an attempt to enter into the female soul and speak in a feminine way and to express sensations that are different in male language.

Pedroni: Another reason for using a female narrative voice could be that sometimes we have certain emotions that perhaps we are embarrassed to express, but are able to do so through the female voice.

Komla-Ebri: Yes, because in my opinion males don't live fully, in the sense that they suffocate many of their emotions because a man isn't supposed to cry, a man has to be tough, a man has to be resistant. Women are more full and complete because they are able to live all their emotions. They don't have to always suffocate things. So, when writing, even a male can allow himself to live these emotions.

Pedroni: In the novel *Neyla* the presumably autobiographical narrator/protagonist says, "Thank you, Neyla, for reconnecting me to myself, to my people and to my childhood."[3] Can you elaborate on the significance of this concept?

Komla-Ebri: Yes. It's normal for an African who comes to Europe to live a kind of inferiority complex. The first thing you try to do is assimi-

---

[3]Kossi Komla-Ebri, *Neyla*, unpublished novel, p. 51.

late as much as possible everything that is European; the manner of dressing, of walking, of eating. Then when you feel a bit of nostalgia, you look for typical foods of your country of origin; foods that you would probably never eat at home; or when the feeling of loneliness gets really strong, many Muslims who never went to the mosque when they were in Africa, start going to the mosques here. Then comes the second phase in which you would like to reevaluate the elements of your own culture because you realize that no matter how much you try to paint yourself white, for them you will always be a foreigner. So you have to try to recuperate your own culture that you had been trying to eliminate. That's why the various associations of Senegalese, of the Ivory Coast, and so on, are starting to pop up here, because everyone is looking for his own identity — linguistic, musical, religious, and so on. Then, in my opinion, there is a third phase in which you realize that humanity is the basis of all cultures. The peculiarities of the various cultures have a relative importance and have to be evaluated in relation to our universal rights. For example, I say to a Muslim, "I can respect the Muslim tradition because it is your religion and you believe in it; however I can not tolerate the fact that you consider women inferior to men, because that is a peculiarity that is contrary to our universal rights." In *Neyla* the protagonist goes back to Africa during his first phase, in the phase in which he was rejecting everything, partly because he was ashamed, partly because, as Cesaire said, we have not invented anything. Still today, my cousins say that whites are superior to us. Yes, we are rich in proverbs, fables, stories, but Africans have not invented anything material. They did not invent writing, they did not invent television, they did not invent the internet. And so, someone who has this in his culture can have an inferiority complex and think that we are not worth anything. During his homecoming the protagonist recuperated some of the elements of his culture and is in the process of reevaluating things when he finds Neyla who becomes his intermediary. When he has to leave her, it is like leaving Africa. And going back to Europe becomes painful.

Pedroni: In the short story, "Sognando una favola" [dreaming a fable], you represent an idyllic scene in the future in which the grandchildren of an African grandfather and an Italian grandmother "were truly happy to belong to worlds at once so different and so similar" and the grandfather can say, "beyond our differences, we are first of all citizens of the earth."[4] Do you really foresee or hope in a future like that?

Komla-Ebri: I hope so. I can only hope. It's a dream. That's why the title is "Sognando una favola." Unfortunately, I know that it won't be that way. At least I don't think we'll see it right away. There will be many changes, unavoidably, partly because Africa and Italy are moving geographically ever closer together. But the displacement of masses of people, the immigration that is going on in our time, is also significant for me. I ask myself how come, in this moment of history, so many people are on the move. Some believe that it is a divine plan. People have to get to know each other. They have to meet each other. Perhaps from this encounter will be born these children of bronze, that is, a new generation. Also out of necessity, because today Europe needs these working hands. Only knowledge can knock down the barriers between people. But it's just a dream that our generation will not see and not my children's generation either. But I hope that our grandchildren's generation will see it. I say that it is only a dream because, as you see with what happened in Kossovo, there is no culture of peace, and yet this is essential. The great powers let ethnic cleansing go on for so long that one might suspect that they acted out of economic interests; perhaps to start up a new Marshall Plan.

Pedroni: Nevertheless, all things considered, you are an optimist and think optimistically.

Komla-Ebri: Yes, for the distant future, yes, because either it will be like that or everything will blow up. There are no real alternatives. Either people learn to live together notwithstanding their cultural and religious differences or there will be chaos.

Pedroni: Do you have some other literary projects that you can talk about?

Komla-Ebri: Yes. I have started a short story that is giving me problems because it has a completely different narrative structure. It's about

---

[4]Kossi Komla-Ebri, "Sognando una favola," *Destini sospesi di volti in cammino* 136, 144.

someone in love who expresses his feelings to a diary. It's the diary itself that speaks and talks about a girl who confides her thoughts with "open heart" to the diary. Some of her thoughts are theological. I think I'll finish it sooner or later. Then there's another one whose theme is the divided life of foreign children. A child arrives and finds himself torn between the beautiful external world, Europe, that he is discovering, and the internal world of his family, where he is repressed according to tradition, even though he is his parents' "passport" to the future. He finds himself playing the role of intermediary between them and the external world because he gets assimilated immediately. In school, when they ask him to talk about his country of origin, he doesn't want to, because he is in the first phase. He refuses because he wants to be assimilated as quickly as possible with the others. There is, for example, an episode in which this little boy goes to the beach and stays under the beach umbrella the whole time because he doesn't want to get any blacker than he already is. And when the teachers ask him to translate so that they can talk with his parents, he tells them only what he wants to. Then there are some other things that I have started but left alone for the moment.

Pedroni: In any case you are more for short stories than novels.

Komla-Ebri: Yes, because novels are more difficult for someone who doesn't have a lot of free time because it's difficult to start up again after having had to leave it for awhile. While on the other hand I can dive into a short story or even lyric poetry and, maybe working until three in the morning, I can finish what I started. In general the things that I write in one spurt are the ones that come out best.

FILIBRARY SERIES PUBLICATIONS

Giacomo Leopardi: Proceedings of the Congress Held at the University of California, Los Angeles, November 10-11, 1988, edited by Giovanni Cecchetti

1. **Interpreting the Italian Renaissance: Literary Perspectives,** edited by Antonio Toscano

2. **Shearsmen Sorts: Italian Poetry 1975-1993,** edited by Luigi Ballerini.

3. **Writings of the Twentieth Century Italian Literature,** by Michael Ricciardelli

4. **Columbus: Meeting of Cultures,** edited by Mario B. Mignone

5. **Homage to Moravia,** edited by Rocco Capozzi and Mario B. Mignone

6. **Etica cristiana nella letteratura contemporanea italiana,** edited by Florinda Iannace

7. **Italian Americans in a Multicultural Society,** edited by Jerome Krase and Judith N. De Sena

8. **Lo studio bolognese,** edited by Leda Giannuzzi Jaworski

9. **Dante: Summa Medievalis,** edited by Charles Franco and Leslie Morgan

10. **The Literary Journal as a Cultural Witness,** edited by Luigi Fontanella and Luca Somigli

11. **Il dialetto di San Leucio del Sannio,** by Gaetano A. Iannace

12. **Italian Americans on Long Island: Presence and Impact,** edited by Kenneth P. LaValle

13. **Studi filologici e letterari in memoria di Danilo Aguzzi-Barbagli,** edited by Daniela Boccassini

14. **The Saints in the Lives of Italian Americans,** edited by Joseph A. Varacalli, Salvatore Primeggia, Salvatore J. Lagumina, Donald J. D'Elia

15. **Paolo Segneri: un classico della tradizione cristiana,** edited by Rocco Paternostro and Andrea Fedi

16. **Adjusting Sites: New Essays in Italian American Studies,** edited by William Boelhower

Most individual volumes may be purchased at a discount price of $18 each. The entire collection may be purchased for $550 USD (includes S/H). Please make checks payable to Forum Italicum, Center for Italian Studies, Stony Brook University, Stony Brook, NY 11794-3358.